The Politics of Environment in Southeast Asia

Resources and Resistance

Edited by
Philip Hirsch and Carol Warren

This book is a project of the Asia Research Centre
on Social, Political and Economic Change,
Murdoch University, Western Australia

London and New York

First published 1998 by Routledge
2 Park Square, Milton Park, Abingdon, Oxon, OX14 4RN

Transferred to Digital Printing 2005

Simultaneously published in the USA and Canada
by Routledge
270 Madison Ave, New York NY 10016

© 1998 Selection and editorial matter Philip Hirsch
and Carol Warren; individual chapters the contributors

Typeset in Times by
J&L Composition Ltd, Filey, North Yorkshire

British Library Cataloguing in Publication Data
A catalogue record for this book is available from the British Library

Library of Congress Cataloguing in Publication Data
A catalogue record for this book has been requested

ISBN 0–415–17298–5 (hbk)
ISBN 0–415–17299–3 (pbk)

The Politics of Environment in Southeast Asia

Southeast Asia has undergone extremely rapid industrialisation and economic growth. This in turn has placed great pressure on the local environment through the increased use of natural resources and higher levels of pollution and urban expansion.

This book is concerned with the growing importance of environmental issues and their relationship to broader processes of social, political and economic change in Southeast Asia. The case studies included document environmental struggles over large dams, forestry, mining, pollution and tourism. The authors draw on new approaches in social and political ecology and relate macro-theoretical frameworks to the case studies.

The growing intensity of the conflict between economic growth, social security and environmental protection in the region make Southeast Asia an especially fertile area for study. The outcome will be of lasting importance to the region. *The Politics of Environment in Southeast Asia* is an original and detailed contribution to this growing debate.

Philip Hirsch is a Senior Lecturer at the Department of Geography, University of Sydney. **Carol Warren** lectures in the Asian Studies and Development Studies Programmes at Murdoch University.

To those in Southeast Asia who have devoted their lives to the struggle for social and environmental justice.

Contents

Figures, tables and maps

x *Figures, tables and maps*

Contributors

George J. Aditjondro is Lecturer in Sociology at the University of Newcastle.

Raymond L. Bryant is Lecturer in Geography at King's College, University of London.

Timothy Forsyth is a research fellow at the Royal Institute for International Affairs in London.

Philip Hirsch is Senior Lecturer in Geography at Sydney University.

Ramanie Kunanayagam is a consultant for the Kelian Equatorial Mining Foundation.

Michael Leigh is Director of the Institute of East Asian Studies at University Malaysia Sarawak.

Anton Lucas is Senior Lecturer in Asian Studies and Languages in the Faculty of Social Sciences, Flinders University of South Australia.

Michael Mitchell works for IUF (the International Union of Food, Agricultural, Hotel, Restaurant, Catering, Tobacco and Allied Workers' Associations) in Sydney.

Chayant Pholpoke has run the Life Tours Alternative Travel Organisation based in Chiang Mai since 1982.

Bach Tan Sinh is Research Fellow at the National Institute for Science and Technology Policy and Strategic Studies, Ministry of Science, Technology and Environment in Hanoi.

Marites Danguilan Vitug works for the Philippine Centre for Investigative Journalism in Manila.

Carol Warren is Senior Lecturer in Asian Studies and Fellow of the Asia Research Centre at Murdoch University, Perth.

Emmanuel Yap has worked with people's organisations and non-governmental organisations in southwestern Negros for more than a decade, and is based at Kabankalan Teachers College.

Ken Young is Professor of Asian Studies at Swinburne University of Technology, Melbourne.

Acknowledgments

The editors and contributors wish to acknowledge the support of the Australian Research Council and the Asia Research Centre for Social and Political Change at Murdoch University for funding the early stages of this project. We also wish to thank Michael Parnwell, Greg Bankoff and Stephen Elliott for comments on early drafts. The invaluable assistance of Penny Claringbull, Rachel Drewry, Catherine Pacey and John McCarthy in tracking down missing items of information and preparing the manuscripts, as well as John Roberts, Peter Johnson and Michael Mickler for map production, are gratefully acknowledged.

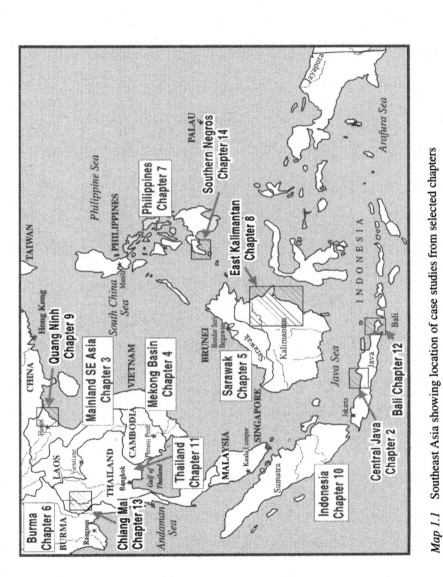

Map 1.1   Southeast Asia showing location of case studies from selected chapters

1 Introduction: through the environmental looking glass

The politics of resources and resistance in Southeast Asia

Philip Hirsch and Carol Warren

Environment has finally risen to the top of the global political agenda. The United Nations Conference on Environment and Development held in Rio de Janeiro in 1992 signified international recognition of the environment as an issue that could not be constrained by the borders of nation states (Robinson 1992). But Rio also revealed deep political divisions on the world environmental stage. Those divisions were represented and articulated primarily as a North–South, rich versus poor country schism (Johnson 1993). Ironically, the ecological internationalism that was to be the breakthrough of the conference gave way to positioning in which negotiations were geared back to the interests of nation states.

Yet the politics of Rio mask a different type of environmental politics, one that is much closer to home for the majority of the world's people. The politics of environment in most countries of the world are played out not only at a different level, but also within a quite different structural framework. Environmental politics within individual nation states reflect, but also increasingly act upon, specific aspects of social relations and power structure within each country, while interests and interdependencies of the main protagonists often transcend national borders. These politics of environment are an important force in their own right as well as a window on broader aspects of political economy. There is thus a reflexive relationship between environmental conditions, discourses and activism on the one hand and changing economic, social and political relations on the other. Nowhere is this more the case than among those countries of the world where environmental and political–economic change is most rapid, notably the dynamic societies and economies of Southeast Asia whose bio-physical environment and resource base have undergone rapid degradation (Brookfield and Byron 1993; Bryant and Parnwell 1996).

In this collection of studies, environment and environmentalism are treated as a looking glass onto broader, perhaps equally fundamental, processes of change – and responses to them. In particular, attention is given to understanding emerging social forces that stem from material changes wrought by rapid economic growth, associated politico-cultural transformation and ecological change. These social forces include the emergence of new interest groups and new means of articulating demands; the disintegration of old social units in some cases and constitution of new coalitions in others (Hewison *et al.* 1993; Rodan 1996; Dirlik 1994).

On the political front, new spaces have been created for putting forward hitherto marginal interests. The decline of traditional radical left politics of opposition in most non-communist Southeast Asian countries has been accompanied by the emergence of new voices and arenas of resistance or response to dominant forces (Rodan 1996). Meanwhile, the transformations associated with market liberalisation in the socialist systems of Indochina are radically changing these societies. Non-governmental organisations have grown in part as a result of this process, particularly as spaces have opened for the development of civil society (Peet and Watts 1993; Princen 1994). While this is not a linear or inevitable process, in most Southeast Asian societies a considerably wider array of voices was heard by the early 1990s than was conceivable a decade earlier. Perhaps nowhere is this more evident than in the politics of the environment.

Environmentalism, particularly since the late 1980s, has become something of a legitimising discourse of opposition. In societies where institutions of political opposition have not been permitted to develop, the environment movement created alternative sites for the expression of contesting positions. At one level, sustainable development, maintenance of biodiversity and inter-generational equity in access to environmental resources are now accepted within the global mainstream as worthy ideals. At another, environment has been used as a basis for articulating claims over resources on the part of marginal groups where previous claims had been ignored or painted as subversive. While there are clearly limits to the conflation of environmental and social issues, environmentalism in its various manifestations in Southeast Asia has taken on the role of a social movement (Touraine 1985; Lyman 1995; Escobar 1995). Environment serves as a legitimised arena of resistance, or as part of accepted discourses on alternative paths to development. Yet the obverse of this is that environmentalism is also subject to forces of cooptation. The window of environmentalism thereby opens onto and reflects many of the subtleties of positioning and cross-cutting interests associated with new social, economic and political forces.

ENVIRONMENT, RESOURCES AND THE POLITICS OF SOCIAL JUSTICE

While the political discourse of environment has many ambiguities, the substance of specific environmental disputes is more concrete and reflects basic questions of allocation of, competition for, and conflict over resources or the uses to which they are put. Disputes that arise over construction of large dams, forest cutting and planting, industrial pollution, mining, tourism and other 'development' activities have a material basis that underlies ideological expression in environmental terms. While this is quite obvious in each case, the extent to which environmental struggles have superseded or served as surrogates for more longstanding questions of control over resources is sometimes less apparent.

Until the 1980s, much of the literature on rural struggle in Southeast Asia dwelt on contexts of agrarian change (Turton 1984; Scott 1985; Hart *et al.* 1989). Essentially this also concerned control over resources, notably land. The debate focused on the degree and means by which processes of social differentiation result in land alienation and concentration, affecting the majority of the population who live in rural areas (White 1989). The political context of this debate took the form of land-to-the-tiller campaigns, ranging from demands for land reform, through opportunistic land seizures, to peasant-based revolutionary movements (Laderjinsky 1977; CIIR 1992; Kerkvliet 1993). This was matched by elite-driven land reform programmes (Feder 1983). The physical and sometimes political inaccessibility of many peripheral parts of the region often precluded wider demands on the rural resource base.

Decline in agrarian unrest and insurgency movements has accompanied fuller incorporation of peripheries into national economies and polities, a process accelerated by the rapid industrialisation of the region over the last decade (Hirsch 1990). This has produced two concomitant tendencies. The first is to intensify competition over the rural resource base, as previously isolated hinterlands have been opened up to loggers, hydropower projects and other resource-dependent activities (Bryant in this volume). The second is to open up spaces for political activity and expression among 'hitherto excluded' (cf. Turton 1987) marginal groups. In the process, the geographical focus of rural unrest has turned from the increasingly commercialised and differentiated core agricultural areas to the periphery in which resource tenure is least well defined (Lim and Valencia 1990). Conflict occurs both in long-settled peripheral areas where the state attempts to enforce its hitherto nominal authority over ownership and management of land and resources, and in frontier areas where the issue of security of tenure lags behind resource competition.

The politics of ethnicity often play an important part in the struggle for control over the natural resource base of peripheries (Rambo *et al.* 1988; Connell and Howitt 1991; Howitt *et al.* 1996). Indigenous minorities such as the Penan in Sarawak find their small populations and customary tenure overridden by 'national interest' claims of the dominant culture (Leigh in this volume). Balinese perceive their religion, cultural identity and economic resources threatened as Javanese and Chinese business interests close to the state appropriate agricultural land and marginalise the locally owned tourism industry for large-scale resort developments (Warren in this volume). On the other hand the voices of minority peoples have growing numbers of listeners through national and international NGO networks including the World Council of Indigenous Peoples, Survival International and Cultural Survival. International advocacy groups have in turn been able to pressure global institutions such as the World Bank which have become big players in the politics of environment. Mounting pressure against the Indonesian transmigration programme on cultural and environmental grounds led the Bank to redirect

funding (Ekins 1992: 146–48) and to some revision of Indonesian government policy (Moniaga n.d.: 135–36; Hardjono 1991: 210). This is but one
example of the countervailing implications of the globalisation process,
where intensified market penetration and appropriation of hitherto peripheral
environments are accompanied by expanding communications networks and
new political possibilities for resistance.

As the nature of resource competition and conflict diversifies, so the range
of actors with resource interests becomes ever more complex. Rural society
in Southeast Asia has become progressively more differentiated as commodity relations have deepened and as access to land, labour and capital has
diverged among the haves and have-nots (Warren 1985; Hart *et al.* 1989;
Hirsch 1989; Dirkse *et al.* 1993). Intensification of capital involvement in
agriculture through agribusiness, and in other forms of rural production such
as small-scale industrialisation, means that vertical linkages between local
and outside players determine resource access more directly than in the past
(Glover and Ghee 1992). This is closely linked to new modes of surplus
extraction, with immediate implications for the range of resources available
for maintaining livelihoods in the local sphere.

The diversification of rural society in Southeast Asia is part of wider
processes producing new social forces across the region, with attendant implications for pre-existing class structures. The middle class has been singled
out as a major emerging force for change in Southeast Asia (Goodman and
Robison 1995; Kahn 1995). Yet the role of the middle class is somewhat
ambivalent in the new politics of environment. On the one hand environmentalism in Southeast Asia, as elsewhere, is commonly associated with urban,
educated middle-class groups, since it is they who dominate environmental
non-governmental organisations and serve as the most prominent public
spokespersons on environmental causes.[1] It is often assumed that environmental concern is a luxury that comes with a certain level of affluence, hence
precluding the active involvement of poorer groups. On the other hand, many
of the key environmental and resource disputes dealt with in this book have
their origins directly or indirectly in the very same processes that have created
the middle class. Energy use, new consumption patterns, new forms of leisure
and other aspects of affluent middle-class lifestyles all make demands on the
rural resource base.

ECONOMY AND ENVIRONMENT IN SOUTHEAST ASIA

The framework developed in this book, using environment as a window on
wider aspects of changing political economy, is one that could in principle
apply to any country or society, whether wealthy or poor, over-developed or
under-developed, temperate or tropical. Nevertheless, the collection adopts a
regional focus on Southeast Asia for a number of interconnected reasons.
This world region is experiencing perhaps more rapid and fundamental environmental and political–economic change than any other, throwing processes

and linkages into particularly sharp relief. Each country is consciously, actively and in certain respects very successfully engaged in the development process, and it is the development arena where economic and environmental contradictions tend to be played out most forcefully. Meanwhile, the ecology of production and livelihood shows parallels from one country to another, providing the basis for a comparative political economy of environment that would be difficult in regions with less consistently patterned human ecological circumstances. Most significant in terms of comparative studies is the set of similarities and differences in country-specific social, economic and political structures and processes in Southeast Asia.

The pace of development and associated environmental and political–economic change in Southeast Asia has been remarked on widely (Hewison *et al.* 1993; World Bank 1994; Rigg 1995). Industrialisation of previously agricultural economies, urbanisation of rural societies, and partial liberalisation of authoritarian states are among trends to be found across the region. Development as a national goal, in the sense of 'catching up', has been applied overtly and often aggressively by national leaders seeking to emulate East Asian patterns of growth and industrialisation. The environmental consequences of such a path are found in widespread deforestation, pollution of waterways, degradation and conversion of agricultural land, poor urban air quality, declining populations of fish and wildlife, and shortages in other areas of traditional abundance as multiple claimants seek to benefit from a declining resource base.

Southeast Asia is problematic as a regional category (Dwyer 1990; Rigg 1991); but one of its cohering features is the ecology of production and livelihood that shows parallels from one country to another. Traditionally, wet rice farming in lowland plains and upland valleys, shifting cultivation in sloping upland areas, along with commercial exploitation of forest resources under colonial and post-colonial concessions together explained a significant part of rural production and resource use (Stott 1978). Extension of cash cropping (Uhlig 1984), rapacious logging and other forces for deforestation (Hurst 1990) have been exacerbated in recent years by new demands placed on natural resources to serve the energy and raw material needs of urban and foreign consumers. Dams, mines, industrial development and tourism have all exploited the regional resource base, with severe local and wider impacts on environment and traditional livelihoods (Lim and Valencia 1990).

A key social question raised in each country in Southeast Asia is the extent to which different groups are benefiting or suffering from the rapid changes affecting each society. Urban versus rural, landed versus non-landed, central versus peripheral distinctions are sharpening, but also becoming more complex. We have already noted that middle classes bring with them both new value systems and new consumption patterns, with mixed implications for the environment. They also portend emerging socio-political alliances that cross traditional divides, opening the way for growth of new social movements, of which environmentalism is one – albeit variegated. Amidst the growing wealth in each country are to be found growing inequality, displacement, alienation, cultural disruption and insecurity. Among aspects of development that exacerbate the marginalisation of particular social groups is destruction or encroachment of the resource base on which livelihoods depend. In the proto-capitalist countries of ASEAN (the Association of Southeast Asian Nations), such processes are quite longstanding, but they are nevertheless intensifying. In the emerging market economies of Indochina and Burma, these processes are more recent and serve as a sobering influence that tempers enthusiasm for economic reforms (Beresford and Fraser 1992).

The over-riding economic process that marks out most of Southeast Asia is rapid growth (World Bank 1993). Indonesia, Thailand and Malaysia have sustained exceptionally high growth rates over a number of years, while Vietnam and Laos are following suit. Even the Philippines and Burma are emerging from long periods of sluggish growth, while Singapore and Brunei have in quite different ways grown to a point where per capita incomes are on a par with those of advanced market economies. Cambodia is also set for rapid economic transformation once security is assured, but even prior to this the financing of the civil war has made major demands on the country's natural resources. The Mekong River Commission brought Cambodia back into the regional economic fold during 1995 in a scheme that involves four countries in potentially massive resource-based development (see Mitchell in this volume). Demands on the resource base entailed by such growth are enormous, and they have been reflected in rapid environmental degradation (Brookfield and Byron 1993; Sluiter 1993). A prominent feature of the 1990s is the convergence of economic strategies around an export-oriented market approach, so that the distinctive patterns of Indochina and Burma's semi-autarkic socialism have given way to outward-looking proto-capitalist economic development based on export-oriented industrialisation and resource exploitation, the latter notably important in Laos and Burma (see Bryant in this volume). Integration of the regional economy through increased trade and cross-investment is particularly significant in the resources sector. Vietnam's accession to ASEAN will doubtless be followed by Southeast Asia's remaining three non-members, further cementing regional economic integration.

Politically, Southeast Asia may seem to remain diverse. Laos and Vietnam continue to maintain nominally communist one-party states, the ASEAN states have various forms of emerging democracy amidst a more or less authoritarian polity, Burma continues its dictatorial rule under SLORC (the State Law and Order Restoration Commission), while Cambodia maintains a fledgling but shaky elected government. In all cases, there are restrictions on expression of resistance and dissent. Yet without exception, there are also increasing spaces for social and political action. One reason for this is the decline of the communist bogey in the non-communist states, and the concomitant gradual opening up of society in Indochina that allows new voices to be heard. All governments are under scrutiny of environment and human rights groups, and the extent and pace of the emergence of civil society is a theme with resonance throughout the region (Peet and Watts 1993; Hewison *et al.* 1993; Berger and Borer 1995). In this context, the politics of environment has emerged as a crucial space in which claims are articulated by or on behalf of a range of social groups.

MODES OF ENVIRONMENTALISM

Responses to objective and perceived links between political–economic change and environmental degradation take a variety of forms. Various modes of environmentalism reflect not only different philosophical approaches (cf. O'Riordan 1981; Pepper 1984), but also the wide range of actors who have adopted the environmental mantle in pursuit of more conventional social, economic and political agendas. While environment surely serves as a legitimising discourse of opposition, it is also a legitimising tool for more powerful vested interests. A disentangling of institutional, political, social and material bases for environmentalism reveals something of its multifarious character and the processes of cooptation that are increasingly apparent.

Institutional bases of environmentalism have multiplied throughout Southeast Asia during the 1990s. NGOs represent the most commonly recognised organisational basis for environmental advocacy and action. In Indonesia, Thailand, the Philippines and Malaysia, environmental NGOs have mushroomed in number and diversified in character. Some environmental NGOs are principally advocacy and campaigning organisations, notably Project for Ecological Recovery in Thailand, Sahabat Alam in Malaysia, Wahana Lingkungan Hidup Indonesia (Indonesian Environmental Forum or WALHI) and Sekretariat Kerjasama Pelestarian Hutan Indonesia (Indonesian Anti-Deforestation NGO Network or SKEPHI) in Indonesia and Green Forum in the Philippines. These groups have secured strong links with one another, and with international environmental organisations. Other groups are involved in more specialised areas such as environmental education, watchdog activities in areas such as chemical pesticide monitoring, or development and application of alternative technologies. Yet others are locally bound, with activities centred around community-based resource management.[2] In many cases, this also involves confronting wider encroachment on the local resource base, for example the fishers associated with the Yad Fon organisation in Trang Province of southern Thailand whose livelihoods have been threatened by large trawlers operating in-shore. Key environmental disputes often bring such groups together, while at other times they pursue separate – and sometimes conflicting – priorities. In Laos, Burma and Vietnam, there are still very limited opportunities for independent NGO action, but foreign NGOs are increasingly staffed locally. The Sustainable Agriculture Forum in Laos, for example, serves as a kind of surrogate indigenous NGO, involving mainly Lao and Lao-speaking expatriates with a constructively critical approach to the country's development strategy similar to that taken by NGOs elsewhere.

Meanwhile, the media plays an increasingly important role in the region's environmental politics. In Thailand and the Philippines, in particular, sections of the press have been influential in lending weight to major campaigns (see Vitug in this volume). In Malaysia and Indonesia, the press has been more tempered in its criticism and subject to political interference, but Aditjondro and Warren show in their studies that even in these circumstances, the media can be central in creating and building strategic alliances around *causes célèbres*. In Vietnam, a country whose press has been quite strictly controlled, the media picks up certain issues such as impacts of the Hoa Binh Dam (see Hirsch in this volume), scandals over the North–South high-voltage power line, or the Daewoo golf course near Hanoi; there is also a great deal of reporting of less controversial environmental issues that both promotes and reflects the high level of environmental awareness in the country. The latter function of routine media coverage, less dramatic and little explored, is undoubtedly also important in the construction and cultivation of an arena of discourse staking out potential new sites of contestation and new frames of reference for pursuing them (see Hansen 1993)

The institutional basis for environmentalism has also grown dramatically within the bureaucracy of most countries, stimulated by and contributing to pressures exerted by the media and NGOs. The Ministries or Offices of Science, Technology and Environment in Malaysia, Thailand, Vietnam and Laos, the Department of Natural Resources and Environment in the Philippines, the National Commission on Environmental Affairs in Burma, the State Ministry of Population and the Environment and the Environmental Impact Management Agency (Bapedal) in Indonesia have expanded, if not in all cases effective, roles. All face tensions within the wider bureaucratic system, particularly with respect to the more powerful instruments of state concerned with promoting investment and growth – notably Boards of Investment, State Planning Committees, Ministries of Industry and Energy. There is also a degree of competition between those government agencies established specifically to deal with environmental protection and those in established departments – notably forestry – which have traditionally taken on what they see as environmental responsibilities as part of a broader resource management and development brief. In Burma there are tensions within the Ministry of Forestry between the Myanmar Timber Enterprise responsible for extraction and the Forest Department charged with conservation. In this context, a key source of contention is the lack of separation of the regulatory and economic roles of such ministries. This issue is most clear-cut in the case of socialist countries moving towards a market economy (see Sinh and Bryant in this volume), but it also applies elsewhere. In Thailand, for example, there have been calls for a Ministry of Environment to be established that would take over conservation duties of Departments such as Forestry and Fisheries (Kasem 1994). Unsurprisingly, there is considerable resistance to such moves, so that a degree of environmental politics is internal to the bureaucracy.

Other institutional bases for the protection of environment include new legislative frameworks and an expanded role for judicial systems. Several countries in the region passed significant new environmental laws preceding, or in the aftermath of, the Rio summit (Bankoff and Elston 1993; Warren and Elston 1994; England 1996). While enforcement still depends on bureaucratic and political power structures and the efficacy of the courts, environmental legislation represents a significant step towards holding various economic and political players accountable for the environmental implications of their actions. Indications of a new role for the judiciary in this sphere can be seen in the 1994 Indonesian court ruling on compensation in the Kedungombo case (Aditjondro in this volume) and the 1993 Malaysian case in which the Ipoh High Court closed a Japanese Malaysian factory accused of illegally dumping radioactive waste at Bukit Merah (*Far Eastern Economic Review* 22 April 1993). Both cases were overturned on appeal, but they are signs that judicial systems are beginning to take a more prominent role as arbiters of public interest in the so far uneven pitting of economic and social forces in the environmental politics of the region. In Indonesia an offshoot of the Legal Aid Foundation (YLBH), the Indonesian Centre for Environmental Law, has been established specifically to encourage the prosecution of environmental cases in the courts.

Several new independent think-tanks and monitoring bodies that give prominent or even primary consideration to environmental issues have been established in recent years. In Thailand, the Thai Development Research Institute has a high-profile Natural Resources and Environment section, while the Thailand Environment Institute was established with business support to investigate key environmental issues and design policy measures to deal with them. The Indonesian Eco-labelling Agency (LEI) was established in 1994 as an independent organisation under the former Environment Minister, Emil Salim. Its task is to establish a system of labelling forest products to comply with the International Tropical Timber Organisation (ITTO) agreement which requires certification of tropical timber traded internationally by the year 2000, indicating that these products have been harvested from sustainably managed forests.[3] Elsewhere, business groups have become directly involved in various environmental causes, and several countries in the region have a Business Council for Sustainable Development.

Governmental agencies and think-tanks, by definition close to the mainstream interests of state and business, tend to adopt and promote technocratic modes of environmentalism (cf. Kong 1994). Initiatives such as polluter-pays legislation, where the emphasis is usually on self-regulation by industry, are favoured policy instruments. Technocratically based environmentalism can be used in socially regressive ways, as in the widespread enlargement of national parks to encompass land settled by established communities, excluding them from their former resource bases. Anti-shifting cultivation measures such as the forced resettlement or outright eviction of minority groups from highland areas have typically been justified as part of the state's environmental agenda, even while other arms of state divert those same forest resources to more destructive uses (Dove 1985, 1993). Environmental justification has also been claimed to rationalise controversial plantation schemes. Thailand's Royal Forestry Department, for example, includes eucalyptus plantations in the national forest area, thus counting commercial pulp and paper operations that have evicted farmers from their land as part of the country's forest rehabilitation programme (Lohmann 1991). In response, NGOs make a point of referring to *'rai euca'* (eucalyptus farms) rather than *'paa euca'* (eucalyptus forests).

An institutional focus on environmental management, however, presents only a partial picture. Just as significant are the various political modes of environmentalism. These range from confrontational advocacy on the part of non-mainstream groups, through non-controversial but often cosmetic campaigning on causes such as litter or tree planting, to technocratic approaches that stress technological and economic solutions to environmental problems. Confrontation usually involves opposition to major projects such as the large dams at Kedungombo and Pak Mun discussed by Aditjondro and Mitchell in this volume. Anti-logging activism has also been widespread (chapters by Vitug and Leigh), while industrial development is creating a new set of rallying points (chapters by Forsyth and Lucas). Tourism projects have also prompted protest movements (chapters by Warren and Pholpoke). Much less controversial are the environmental education programmes undertaken by government and NGO groups alike, and largely aesthetic initiatives such as Thailand's 'Magic Eyes' anti-litter campaign or Indonesia's Clean Cities awards (*Adipura*).

Social bases for environmentalism closely follow material interests, but they also reflect ideological positions associated with particular interest groups. In this collection we heartily reject the notion that environmental concern is a luxury that comes with certain levels of affluence or education. Rather, we see the driving force of environmentalism in Southeast Asia as a response to threats on livelihood, notably those of the poor. Yet these struggles have drawn in many other social actors, in part through the institutional means (notably NGOs and media) outlined above. The ideological underpinning of broadening involvement ranges from notions of social justice to various middle-class-based movements that hark back to the 'roots' of culture perceived as in the process of being lost. In some cases, religious symbols serve as a focal point for environmental movements (for example in the cases of Tanah Lot and Chiang Mai discussed by Warren and Pholpoke), often in conjunction with social justice discourses. While it is difficult to isolate the material from the ideological bases of environmentalism, and the two are clearly mutually reinforcing, there are numerous instances where individuals and groups act beyond narrow self- or group interest. This is one of the important fundamentals on which new alliances and coalitions are built, and it also suggests that the environmental movement is more than a collection of opportunistic or single-issue actions.

The coalescence of varied social forces around particular environmental issues forms a unifying theme linking the studies in this volume. Concrete alliance formations arising initially to confront particular situations have cumulatively built environmentalism into a political–economic force in its own right, representing more than *ad hoc* responses to specific development projects serving powerful interests. Yet such politics of alliance are complex and constantly shifting. To a considerable extent, they are also contingent (Gagnon *et al.* 1993), in the sense that coalitions typically build and dissolve around particular issues, prevailing sentiments and even personalities. In extreme cases, allies in today's struggle may become antagonists in that of tomorrow. In this way, the politics of environment reflect the fluidity of social interest groups as they emerge in response to rapid change, as well as the ambivalent ecological implications of new development processes for all social groups. In such a situation, symbols should not be underestimated as galvanising foci for particular movements, cementing alliances among otherwise disparate social groups. In some cases, notably large dams, the structure itself, represented as a juggernaut of development, presents a ready-made symbol. In others, symbols are created as part of the political process, particularly where religious or ethnic identities are implicated in the appropriation of resources (Leigh and Warren in this volume), matching the traditional significance of natural symbolism in organising cultural life in Southeast Asia (Milner 1978). The aesthetic and affective dimensions of the symbols upon which environmentalism draws are aspects of social movements generally which have not been fully enough treated in conventional political-economy approaches (see Escobar 1995).

Despite the symbolic nature of certain aspects of environmental politics, we have noted that there is in Southeast Asia a very real material basis for most actions. Lying behind environmental struggles are questions of societal control over resources, often intimately connected with social security and collective identity at the local level. As a wider range of resources has become subject to competition, so economic and social processes encompassed in economic development have become embroiled in environmental and resource politics. A moot point then remains the extent to which resource politics and environmental politics can be distinguished. Environmentalism clearly lends strength to those primarily concerned with articulating claims over resources intrinsic to livelihoods. At the same time, the dynamics and the symbolism associated with environmentalism suggest that it is more than a discursive cover for material struggles. Moreover, beyond issues of direct resource access and control is the role of environmentalism as a response to what might be termed the 'politics of externality'.

RESOURCES, INEQUITY AND POLITICS OF EXTERNALITY

The use and abuse of natural resources epitomises many of the inequities and dilemmas thrown up by economic growth. We have shown that at one level, such inequity is represented in processes of encroachment on livelihoods via resource endowments. However, the politics of environment that are generated around resource disputes are not always straightforward issues of competition between different social actors over a singular resource. In many cases, disputes arise over the apparently unintended consequences of resource use and encroachment, the 'side-effects' of extractive or industrial economic activity. Fish migrations upset by dams built across rivers, the downstream river sedimentation, siltation or flooding caused by logging activities and associated land settlement, the effects of tailings from mining, factories' impact on the health of workers and nearby communities, and the cultural impact of tourism are all examples of what may be termed 'externalities'. That is, they are costs external to the project or economic activity in question in the sense that they are borne by individuals and communities other than those reaping the benefits, yet they are not a straightforward issue of alienating resources from one social actor to another. Many environmental disputes, even when not concerned primarily with direct resource competition, are in effect responses to the imposition of such externalities.

The new environmental economics is concerned largely with redressing the social and ecological inequities of externality by internalising costs as well as benefits (Pearce and Turner 1990). The assumption is that markets will then continue to be able to arrive at optimum resource allocation, so long as two tasks are accomplished. First, the range of external impacts needs to be costed. Second, means of imposing the costs on beneficiaries need to be found. In principle, resources thus derived can then be transferred through compensation mechanisms or by other means to offset the losses of those bearing the impact; alternatively, they can be applied to mitigate the impacts.

In practice, such costing and transfers are fraught with difficulty. Many impacts, whether concerned with human health, ecological or cultural disruption, are extremely difficult to cost, notwithstanding various tools such as contingent valuation (Pearce 1993). The valuation process itself becomes contested ground, not only in assessing relativities, but over the commensurability of qualitatively valued costs and benefits in the first place (O'Neill 1993). Even within a modified cost–benefit framework, finding means of then internalising those external costs is also complex, the more so when foreign investors are to be enticed with low-cost production incentives. More problematic still is the practical question of properly compensating or mitigating the effects on people and environments concerned, especially when state organs with conflicting interests serve as intermediaries.

The 'politics of externality' underlie many aspects of environmental politics in Southeast Asia in the sense that internalised and externalised costs and benefits are distributed quite unevenly, both spatially and socially. As a result, questions of what values are placed on impacted cultures and environments, of accountability and responsibility for impacts, and of mitigating and compensating for those impacts, are subjects of intense debate and controversy. The case studies in this book all contain elements of such controversy, taking them beyond the narrow realm of resource politics.

ABOUT THIS BOOK

This book draws on new approaches in social and political ecology, adapting the social-structural concerns of political economy to a yet broader framework which confronts environmental processes and limits. The book attempts to relate macro-theoretical concerns to grounded case studies, and looks to Southeast Asia as the site of analysis for reasons which should make the region a focus of increasing attention from social and environmental analysts.

Because of a combination of political–environmental features perhaps unique to the region, Southeast Asia has retained into the late 20th century arguably the most diverse biotic and cultural landscape in the world. At the same time, the extraordinary pace at which economic development has been taking place in Southeast Asia over the last decade has meant that the contradictions between economic growth and environmental protection, and between winners and losers on both sides of the equation, are exposed to an extraordinary and volatile degree (Bryant and Parnwell 1996: 2).

A region of remarkably low population density in the pre-colonial era, Southeast Asia became a region of very high population growth in the late- and post-colonial periods (Jones 1984; Leete and Alam 1993). From a predominantly forest-covered region which supported a great number of gatherer–hunting and shifting cultivating cultures alongside intensive wet-rice agrarian kingdoms and coastal trading states, Southeast Asia became a natural resource and plantation crop 'mine' for the European colonial economies, fuelling the development of the global market.

Today, in a period of intensive and pervasive global capitalist expansion, the new nation states of the region – heirs to the colonial geo-political project – are rapidly industrialising in the slipstream of the East Asian 'tigers' (Goodman and Robison 1996). In the process, the land, resources and cultures of once peripheral zones of the region have become hotly contested political territory, with levels of environmental stress and degradation showing signs of crisis. News of landslides and flooding, erosion of coastal beaches and previously forested hinterlands, air and water pollution is now commonplace in local and metropolitan newspapers throughout the region.

Where Bryant and Parnwell analyse the implications of environmental policy and management for sustainable development in the political and economic context of changing Southeast Asian societies, this volume specifically addresses the dynamics of the conflicts over resources that are emerging out of that context. The politics of sustainability raise substantive questions about the nature, meaning and conditions of 'sustainable development' agendas; the rhetorical deployment of this and other environmental concepts by nation states and development agencies begs one of the underlying questions which frame the case studies in this book – resources and development for whom?

The class, ethnic–regional and international dimensions of resource and environmental conflicts do not cut along the clear and unambiguous lines once imagined by political economists. The middle class, which always posed problems for class analysis, is now an even more amorphous category, and new actors (NGOs, consumers) and issues (gender, environment and human rights) intersect with the older worker/capitalist, elite/mass, state/local dichotomies. Because much of the stimulus for social change and response is happening outside the sphere of formal political institutions (Rodan 1996), another vocabulary revolving around globalisation, civil society and new social movements (Morris and Mueller 1992; Eder 1993; Lyman 1995) is necessary to speak about the new processes of transformation in which we are enmeshed. But the older political economy and the new political ecology find common ground in so far as capital-intensive forms of resource extraction have become the most politically visible and volatile sites of competing interest between global, state and local actors; and between conceptions of intrinsic value of natural and cultural 'goods' and their instrumental or market value.

The approach of this book is to examine the competing interests at stake and the coalescence of social forces forming around particular sites of resource and environmental conflict in specific national contexts. It follows the line that environmental problems have a social as well as a bio-physical basis (Blaikie 1985; Blaikie and Brookfield 1987), but goes further to examine the politics that emerge as a result. At one level, each chapter is a self-contained case study, but at another level each is part of a more general reflection on the overlap of resource and environmental politics as expressions of local political economy and of cultural or national politics. The studies are organised thematically around disputes that have arisen in particular resource sectors. However, the integrated nature of local livelihoods, the complexities of ecosystems and the overlapping resource economies of particular localities preclude simple investigation on an overly compartmentalised basis. In this respect, overarching questions thread through all the case studies. To what extent is environmental politics a forum for the expression of dissent on broader social and political issues? Can middle-class agents/activists who form the most prominent spokespersons in these contests be regarded as reflecting the needs and interests of the wider public for whom they claim to speak? How does the state apparatus engage with elements of civil society in the politics of environment? How important are formal institutions (the judiciary, the press, environmental protection authorities) in determining the outcome of environmental conflicts? And how do they engage on a broader political plane with informal groupings in promoting the interests of established power, the goals of social movements or the needs of subaltern groups? What competing interests and internal contradictions fracture any preconceived unity of the state or the social movements so often pitted against each other in the rhetorics of power and resistance? Are there new grounds and processes of alliance formation that transcend the class politics of an earlier era? At the same time, the case studies presented here do reveal aspects of environmental conflict specific to particular sectors that warrant separate consideration as part of the larger narrative on environmental politics, resource appropriation and resistance.

The politics of large dams stem primarily from their role as symbols as well as substance of a development path that imposes large-scale, centralised appropriation of natural resources in the name of wider benefits, but at the unequivocal expense of local people and environments. The metaphors of power and resistance are a significant constituent of the discourse on dams (Hirsch 1988), while social and spatial inequities that result from uneven distribution of costs and benefits form the material basis for protest. The environmental politics centred on dams thus dwell on issues of gigantism, local versus national interest and compensation, as well as the details of lost livelihoods and heritage, drowned forests and wildlife, and disrupted river systems. The symbolism of dams as markers of national development has been met by the obverse of dams as Leviathan, in both its material and metaphoric connotations. Campaigns range from opposing dams outright to demands for proper assessment and compensation. The size and influence of individual dam proposals immediately put them at the level of national importance, yet their localisation also affects a limited number of identifiable communities. Hence the contraposition of community and nation in the political discourse surrounding large-scale hydropower and irrigation projects. The discourse of environment is used both by opponents of large dams and by their proponents, the latter notably in the global context of greenhouse gases and the need to generate power by means other than fossil fuels. The link between local politics of dams and anti-dam protest as a social movement is examined in Aditjondro's chapter on Indonesia. Meanwhile, the significance of the political–economic context is treated by Hirsch in a comparative study of large dams in Thailand, Laos and Vietnam. Mitchell's chapter transcends scale by revealing the global significance of local impacts and responses to them in the case of Southeast Asia's grandest dam-building programme, the Mekong scheme. Together these case studies illustrate the political symbolic importance and legitimating function of massive dam projects as monumental achievements. The scale and visibility of these engineering feats magnify their priority on the nation-building agenda and simultaneously increase the difficulty of defending local claims against these materialised constructions of the 'national interest', or of addressing externalised environmental, social and even economic costs in the face of their semiotic value as symbols of power, 'progress' and the capacity to make nature conform to human will.

Where dams bear the symbol of modernity, forests tap into an inherently more ancient resonance. The case studies of forest struggles contain a strong historical dimension. The colonial and post-colonial history of state formation and of struggle between state, peasantry and tribal peoples in Southeast Asia includes much that has to do with control over forest, whether it be the territory occupied, land covered, timber contained or people resident therein (Peluso 1992). Within this history, sovereignty emerges as a perennial issue. National sovereignty asserts itself over forest regions and timber resources against claims of local inhabitants whose traditional management practices have maintained the forest as a viable habitat and resource into the present; it also threatens the cultural sovereignty of these previously independent cultural minorities whose identity is governed by longstanding and complex relationships with the forest and the land on which it stands. The political economy of logging closely reflects wider issues of ethnicity and state, capital and local people. Thus, in Sarawak the combination of provincial patronage politics, state government dependence on timber revenues and the ethnic politics of logging help Leigh explain the interests that lie on either side of the issue. In Bryant's chapter on Burma, timber concessions and opposition to them reflect the territorial and fiscal interests of colonial and post-colonial regimes, on the one hand, and the sovereign and material interests of marginal ethnic groups on the other. In the Philippines, meanwhile, Vitug shows that as the impacts of over-exploitation are felt, and political economies are reconfigured, environmental protection itself offers an alternative political support base to the historically dominant association of patronage politics with the timber industry. She suggests that the environment and other social movements in the Philippines have brought about a major shift in the agenda and workings of the Philippine political system. (On this subject, however, Yap, in a later chapter, is somewhat less sanguine.) Forest politics enter the international environmentalist arena in a more immediate and tangible way than does dam development, since timber products are directly exported to overseas consumers. Like industrial and mining development, the transformation of the natural landscape through forest clearing presents a visually dramatic negative image to a global, increasingly urban, public whose primary source of information is through television and for whom wildlife documentaries are more accessible than any direct experience of pristine environments. The sheer speed and expanse of global forest clearing and mounting evidence on climate change have made the exploitation of the world's forests among the most urgent and emotive environmental issues. It is therefore the sector in which the international dimensions of environmental politics have most stridently asserted themselves, if not yet to great effect (Leigh in this volume; Eccleston and Potter 1996; Bryant and Parnwell 1996; Arentz 1996).

While forest politics reveal the historical relations between state and local people, with international capital and consumers becoming important intermediary players, the politics of mining development place corporate interest more squarely at centre stage (Connell and Howitt 1991; Howitt *et al.* 1996). The transnational nature of most large-scale mining operations, and the role of the state as facilitator rather than operator or manager of resource exploitation, gives the transnational corporations involved in mining and its downstream operations a more prominent place in the associated environmental politics. Commercial interests in forest resource exploitation are backgrounded somewhat by complex and parcelled licensing arrangements linked to higher-profile local and regional political patronage systems. The high technology, centralisation and capital intensity of mining operations typically overwhelm local infrastructure and governance regimes. In this sense, mining companies can even supersede the state, especially in localities where large corporations monopolise employment and resource use. Recent conflicts surrounding environment and land tenure issues at the Freeport gold and copper mine in Irian Jaya, and at Ok Tedi mine in Papua New Guinea belonging to the Broken Hill Proprietary Company (BHP), are indicative of the ambiguity of state and corporate identities, and of national and international agents and interests in such cases. Freeport was accused of causing serious environmental degradation and complicity in human rights abuses by the Indonesian military and its own security forces in dealing with local protests. Indonesian and US NGOs pressured for cancellation of the giant company's political risk insurance (FEER 1996; Dames and Moore 1996). BHP was taken to court in Australia in a class action pursued by local communities in Papua New Guinea for environmental damage caused by tailings from the Ok Tedi mine site. It was found to have been involved in drafting legislation for the Papua New Guinea government intended to prevent court action in foreign countries. Corporate interests and 'national interest' predictably become conflated in the discourse and practice of mining operations (Connell and Howitt 1991). In this book, case studies from Vietnam and Indonesia trace the impacts of transnational capital pursuing resource extraction in remote, small-scale communities. Bach Tan Sinh shows how international, national and provincial interests play themselves out in the environmental politics of coal mining and ancillary operations in northeastern Vietnam. Kunanayagam and Young describe the situation of unplanned and unserviced settlements which appeared in the wake of a mining development artificially grafted onto the Kalimantan landscape. In this context, the surrogate role of governance taken on by the mining corporation is of particular interest. The potential for NGO activist disruption and public relations damage, which accompanies multinational involvement in all capital-intensive global industries, forms the backdrop to social and environmental image-making efforts of companies like Conzinc Rio Tinto of Australia (CRA), KPC, BHP and Freeport. Their very size and global exposure offer broadside targets for consumer-oriented strategies of response, a theme explored further in case studies on industrial pollution (Lucas in this volume).

Industrialisation is a less direct but more pervasive process generating impacts on the resource base as well as environmental quality, impacts which affect different social groups unequally. The politics of industrialisation again reveal the centrality of the state–corporate nexus in the political economy of Southeast Asian development, and the politics of environment surrounding disputes over industrial pollution underscore the differential distribution of costs and benefits. The over-riding pressure for Southeast Asian nations to industrialise tends to prioritise one set of bureaucratic interests (economic) and responsibilities over another (environmental), and this is reflected in intra-bureaucratic politics. The politics of environmental health and safety in Thailand are a case in point, as Forsyth shows from the perspective of workers inside electronics factories at the leading edge of the country's industrial boom. The externalised impacts of industry on the health and livelihoods of rural dwellers, and their responses, are addressed in Lucas' case study of river pollution in Java. Industrial pollution of the Tapak River destroyed the resource base of hundreds of rice and shrimp farmers and damaged the health

of local residents. In both cases, economic interests (not only of factory owners, but of workers threatened by unemployment) pervade and complicate
responses on both sides of the politics of environment generated by industrialisation processes. The degradation of the most fundamental forms of
common property – air and water – illustrates the complexity of the internal
conflicts generated by industrialisation. To the extent that certain kinds of
environmental degradation affect everyone and present political subjects with
conflicting interests (economic advantage vs. quality of life), the grounds for
breaking down old political alignments and building new ones transcending
class distinctions expand and lead us to consider the importance of discursive
as well as material factors in the positioning of political subjects in the contest
zones of environmental politics.

   The tourism sector offers perhaps the most direct window into the complex
relationship between symbols and environmental ideologies and politics. In
the Thai and Balinese case studies, where both nature and culture are
resources upon which the industry relies, it is not surprising that the appropriation and deployment of symbols should come to the foreground in the
promotion of competing interests, or that environmental and cultural
metaphors should become conflated in the discourses of resistance. But the
potency of religious and natural symbols as catalysts to action and in the production of a common ground for resistance is not merely a consequence of
contingent connections between culture and nature as contested 'assets' in the
cultural- and eco-tourist models of local development in Bali and Chiang
Mai. The deeper relationship that surfaces in these cases between symbolic
and natural resources in the construction of collective identity and social
security is relevant to environmental and other social movements generally. It
was aesthetic, ethical and religious sentiments associated with environmental
and socio-economic impacts that brought important sections of the community who did not have immediate material interests in the outcome of these
development projects into the contested domain of environmental politics. If
the appropriation of the symbolic domain to private interests represents the
ultimate form of 'enclosure of the commons', as when the tourist industry
attempts to make capital out of the mystical–exotic imagery surrounding Thai
and Balinese sacred sites, then that domain is also a critically important site
of reclamation struggles. These studies suggest that attention to the symbolic
associations within environmental discourses is also a critical aspect of the
process of developing strategic frameworks for engaging public support and
negotiating political agendas. Perhaps the greatest struggle facing the environment movement in general is the struggle to construct shared meanings
from a largely alienated natural and cultural landscape. The process of reclamation will critically revolve around the capacity of the mediators of public
discourse to understand these symbolic processes and to construct a sense of
shared interests in the face of common environmental limits.

   Processes of alliance construction and fragmentation are closely analysed
in the contribution by Yap on local initiatives, militarisation and the environ-

ment on the island of Negros in the Philippines. As part of the politics of response within a broader framework of political and economic oppression under the Marcos regime, coalitions emerged linking the Catholic Church, the media, local communities and non-government organisations. The Church and NGOs, which shared at least the rhetoric of social justice, despite significantly divergent environmental and political agendas, were particularly important because they could channel external resources (funds and access to international pressure group networks) to support social action at the local level. What is especially interesting about Yap's argument is the importance of the stability and security of those linkages to sustained grass-roots activism beyond the phase of oppositional coalescence during the martial law era. Where this base had not been secured, alliances dissolved and environmental activism dissipated.

THE POLITICS OF RESPONSE

Yap's study raises the important question of the extent to which the institutional grounding of social movements is necessary to sustain political momentum – to 'routinise' the responses that alliances of resistance are able to mount during perceived crisis situations. In most of the studies presented here, the capture of institutional ground became a critical step in securing political space which previously did not exist for contesting these issues. The relative strength or weakness of the institutions through which alliances are forged may be pivotal to outcomes. Effects are compounded when the degree of public pressure or institutional involvement is such as to make the case take on 'watershed' proportions. The susceptibility of the press, environmental protection authorities and the regional parliament to political pressure from central government or cooptation by business interests in the Tanah Lot case, Warren argues, not only enabled the resort project at Tanah Lot to proceed despite exceptionally vocal and almost universal opposition to it in Bali, but paved the way for a flood of similar luxury tourism development projects in its wake. And, as the mooted revival of the Chiang Mai cable-car project illustrates, even apparently successful resistance cannot be regarded as more than provisional.

Privileged access to the institutional bases of civil society has granted the middle class disproportionate attention and strategic importance on both sides of the struggles surrounding the politics of resources and environment. It is middle-class journalists, judges, university lecturers, consultants and bureaucrats whose control of information channels and decision-making processes gives them such importance in the development of social movements. Yet their privileges are in varying degrees contingent on prevailing power structures, and their social location tends to compromise them in advance. Apart from the temptations of bribery and other forms of cooptation, institutional functionaries may face considerable personal risks if they overtly confront dominant interests. Indicative of competing pressures which make the middle classes a focus of particular interest are the occasional departures from the mould that suggest real possibilities of institutional reform and change in political culture. The courageous finding by a retiring Supreme Court judge in favour of the plaintiffs (later reversed) in the Kedungombo compensation case was the first of a number of decisions in the 1990s pointing to the possibility of a return to judiciary independence. For many non-government organisations and political dissidents the courts now offered a potential institutional ally in the defence of local people and environments in an Indonesia of different political configuration (Bourchier 1998; Pompe 1996).

The politics of funding, linking local groups with national and international advocates, is also a double-edged sword. Financial resources facilitate alliances and produce shifting orientations across emerging movements. Yap shows that when international donors weighed in to provide assistance in Negros, they had the effect of conservatising the agenda for social action there. Yet external funding and institutional support often provide political legitimacy to groups otherwise vulnerable and voiceless on the national or international stage. Local efforts of peasant groups in Negros to establish self-help farming systems have been protected from harassment by threatened economic interests and the military through formalisation of ties with church support groups and a university-based association of scientists. More generally, the very global acceptance of environmentalism as a positive value, despite its underlying complexity, means that environmental rhetoric itself becomes an ambivalent tool. As often as the term may be wielded in defence of subaltern interests, it can be used to legitimate the exclusion of local people from their traditional sources of livelihood. 'Resource protection' will be found among the arguments to justify stakes claimed by large over small industry, central over local authority, and private over public access.

Perhaps more than any of the other cases in this book, Lucas' study of responses to Tapak River pollution illustrates how uneven the playing-field of environmental politics remains. In this 'watershed' case, even the combined weight of scientific evidence and local knowledge, environmental legislation, legal aid assistance and the open sympathy of the Indonesian environment minister could not produce a successful court prosecution. The threat of a boycott and media exposure eventually brought the offending industries to a settlement. But that settlement, after 14 years of struggle, by no measure adequately compensated for the damages incurred by local people and has not to date brought about significant reduction in the levels of river pollution at the heart of the struggle. The showcase Clean Rivers Programme has been given top priority in Indonesian environmental management policy, but the practical difficulty of achieving its objectives because of the weakness of the legal and political institutions meant to protect the public are revealed in this poignant study of the human costs of pollution.

Yet in all these instances, discursive frames and their institutional expressions have shifted considerably. Indeed, the terms 'resistance' and 'response' perhaps understate the growing strength of environmentalism. The cumulative effects produced by local collective actions participating in a globally significant movement have enhanced the bargaining power of activist groups. There is powerful potential in the synergism between the social and symbolic dimensions of environmental politics. Environmentalism cultivates a sphere of overlapping interests and discourses capable of sensitising a broad spectrum of the population to common cause. Often an initially apolitical group founded on a passionate shared interest in some aspect of nature is taken by its initially narrow agenda into the political arena on a broader front. Vitug notes that the Haribon bird-watching society in the Philippines took up a more scientific approach and activist role as one of the core founders of the Green Forum coalition because of members' direct experience of dismissed concerns. Organised political forces are sometimes caught off guard by the unexpected pervasiveness of a new culture of environmental sensitivity fostered by their own halting efforts, as the global popular reaction to French nuclear testing in the Pacific, despite declining membership in anti-nuclear organisations, illustrated.

The transformation of environmental politics from a fringe set of discrete interest and advocacy groups into a broadly based social movement with political import depended everywhere on alliances between informal groupings and institutional practices, between local, national and international agents, between material interests and powerful symbols and values. These have taken environmentalism into the mainstream and normalised many of its claims. It may well be that the effects of these still largely inchoate new social movements and forces, combined with economic and environmental constraints or crises, will produce a radically different politics in the 21st century (see Brulle 1995). Certainly, environmental politics in Southeast Asia will be one of the global focal points of change in the coming decades.

The looking glass of environmentalism both expands the framework for analysing contemporary processes of transformation and reintroduces important cultural and social dimensions to the still-strident narratives of a more narrowly framed political economy. The politics of environment surrounding these case studies offer revealing perspectives on the dynamics of change in the Southeast Asian region as well as on the global systems and movements whose common future they will help to construct.

NOTES

1 Papadakis' (1993: 139–172) very interesting work on the politics of environment in Australia, however, contradicts the assumption that environmental concern is a predominantly middle-class issue. His data show very small variations (in both directions) between middle and working classes in perceptions of the relative urgency of particular environmental issues, and in the policy options favoured. But he found no significant relationship between class, income and attitudes towards environment groups or environmental protection generally. Ethnographic evidence (Warren, Aditjondro, Leigh in this volume) is suggestive of a similar exaggeration of emphasis on the middle class in the emergence of environmentalism in Southeast Asia.

2 For detailed discussions of the activities of some of these groups see: Pfirrman and
   Kron 1992, Hirsch 1994 on Thailand; Broad and Cavanaugh 1993, Vitug 1993 on
   the Philippines; Eldridge 1995, Moniaga n.d. on Indonesia.
3 But NGOs are already on record criticising the likely effects of industry involvement in the process (*Republika* 19 August 1995; Reving 1995).

REFERENCES

ACFOA (1995) 'Trouble at Freeport: Eyewitness accounts of West Papuan resistance
   to the Freeport–McMoran mine in Irian Jaya, Indonesia and Indonesian military
   repression: June 1994–February 1995'. Australian Capital Territory: Australian
   Council for Overseas Aid.
Arentz, F. (1996) 'Forestry and Politics in Sarawak: The experience of the Penan', in
   Richard Howitt, John Connell and Philip Hirsch, eds, *Resources, Nations and
   Indigenous Peoples*. Melbourne, Oxford University Press.
Bankoff, G. and K. Elston (1993) *Environmental Regulation in Malaysia and Singa-
   pore*. Perth, University of Western Australia Press, and Murdoch University, Asia
   Research Centre.
Beresford, Melanie and Lyn Fraser (1992) 'Political Economy of Environment in
   Vietnam', *Journal of Contemporary Asia* 22(1): 3–19.
Berger, M.T. and D.A. Borer, eds (1995) *Pacific Visions: The rise of the East and the
   end of the Cold War in the Asia–Pacific*.
Blaikie, Piers (1985) *The Political Economy of Soil Erosion in Developing Countries*.
   London, Longman.
Blaikie, P. and H. Brookfield (1987) *Land Degradation and Society*. London,
   Methuen.
Bourchier, D. (1998) 'Magic Memos, Collusion and Judges with Attitude: Notes on
   the politics of law in contemporary Indonesia', in K. Jayasuriya, ed., *The Rule of
   Law and Legal Institutions in East Asia*. London: Routledge.
Broad, Robin and John Cavanaugh (1993) *Plundering Paradise: The struggle for the
   environment in the Philippines*. Berkeley, University of California.
Brookfield, Harold and Yvonne Byron (1993) *Southeast Asia's Environmental Future:
   The search for sustainability*. Tokyo, United Nations University Press.
Brulle, Robert J. (1995) 'Environmentalism and Human Emancipation', in Stanford
   Lyman, ed., *Social Movements: Critiques, concepts, case-studies*. London,
   Macmillan.
Bryant, R. (1992) 'Political Ecology: An emerging research agenda in Third-World
   studies', *Political Geography* 11(1): 12–36.
Bryant, R. and M. Parnwell, eds (1996) *Environmental Politics in Southeast Asia*.
   London, Routledge.
CIIR (1992) *Land Reform and the Environment in the Philippines and Southeast Asia*.
   London, Catholic Institute for International Relations.
Connell, John and Richard Howitt, eds (1991) *Mining and Indigenous Peoples in
   Australasia*. Sydney, Sydney University Press.
Dames and Moore (1996) *PTFI Environmental Audit Report* 25 March 1996.
Dirkse, Jan-Paul, Frans Hüsken and Mario Rutten (1993) *Development and Social
   Welfare: Indonesia's experiences under the new order*. Leiden, KITLV Press.
Dirlik, Arif (1994) *After the Revolution: Waking to global capitalism*. Middletown,
   CT: Wesleyan University Press.
Dove, Michael (1985) 'The Agro-ecological Mythology of the Javanese and the
   Political Economy of Indonesia', *Indonesia* 39: 1–36.
—— (1993) 'A Revisionist View of Tropical Deforestation and Development', *Envi-
   ronmental Conservation* 20(1): 17–24.

Dwyer, Denis (1990) *Southeast Asian Development: Geographical perspectives*. Harlow, Longman.
Eccleston, B. and D. Potter (1996) 'Environmental NGOs and Different Political Contexts in South-east Asia: Malaysia, Indonesia and Vietnam', in R. Bryant and M. Parnwell, eds, *Environmental Politics in Southeast Asia*. London, Routledge.
Eder, Klaus (1993) *The New Politics of Class: Social movements and cultural dynamics in advanced societies*. London, Sage.
Ekins, Paul (1992) *A New World Order: Grassroots movements for global change*. London, Routledge.
Eldridge, Philip (1995) *Non-Government Organizations and Democratic Participation in Indonesia*. Kuala Lumpur, Oxford University Press.
England, Philippa (1996) 'UNCED and the implementation of forest policy in Thailand', in Philip Hirsch, ed., *Seeing Forests for Trees: Environment and environmentalism in Thailand*. Chiang Mai, Silkworm Books.
Escobar, Arturo (1995) *Encountering Development: The making and unmaking of the Third World*. Princeton, Princeton University Press.
Feder, E. (1983) *Perverse Development*. Quezon City, Foundation of Nationalist Studies.
FEER (1996) 'Company under Siege: Mining firm Freeport Indonesia hits back at critics', *Far Eastern Economic Review*, 25 January: 26–27.
Gagnon, Christiane, Philip Hirsch and Richard Howitt (1993) 'Can SIA Empower Communities?', *Environmental Impact Assessment Review*, 13: 229–53.
Glover, David and Lim Teck Ghee (1992) *Contract Farming in Southeast Asia: Three country studies*. Kuala Lumpur, Institute for Advanced Studies, University of Malaya.
Goodman, David and Robison, Richard, eds (1996) *The New Rich in Asia: Mobilephones, McDonalds and the Middle Class Revolution*. London, Routledge.
Hansen, Anders, ed. (1993) *The Mass Media and Environmental Issues*. Leicester, Leicester University Press.
Hardjono, Joan (1991) *Indonesia: Resources, ecology, and environment*. Singapore, Oxford University Press.
Hart, Gillian, Andrew Turton and Benjamin White, eds (1989) *Agrarian Transformations: Local processes and the state in Southeast Asia*. Berkeley, University of California Press.
Hewison, Kevin (1993) 'Of Regimes, State and Pluralities: Thai politics enters the 1990s', in Kevin Hewison, Richard Robison and Gary Rodan, eds, *Southeast Asia in the 1990s: Authoritarianism, democracy and capitalism*. St Leonards, Allen and Unwin.
Hewison, Kevin, Richard Robison and Gary Rodan, eds (1993) *Southeast Asia in the 1990s: Authoritarianism, democracy and capitalism*. St Leonards, Allen and Unwin.
Hirsch, Philip (1988) 'Dammed or Damned? Hydro-power versus people's power'. *Bulletin of Concerned Asian Scholars* 20(1): 2–10.
—— (1989) 'Local Contexts of Differentiation and Inequality on the Thai Periphery'. *Journal of Contemporary Asia* 19(3): 308–23.
—— (1990) *Development Dilemmas in Rural Thailand*. Singapore, Oxford University Press.
—— (1994) 'Where Are the Roots of Thai Environmentalism?', *TEI Quarterly Environmental Journal* 2(2): 5–15.
Howitt, Richard, John Connell and Philip Hirsch (1996) *Resources, Nations and Indigenous Peoples*. Melbourne, Oxford University Press.
Hurst, Philip (1990) *Rainforest Politics: Ecological destruction in Southeast Asia*. London, Zed Books.
Johnson, Stanley (1993) *The Earth Summit: The United Nations Conference on Environment and Development (UNCED)*. London, Graham and Trotman/Martinus Nijhoff.

Johnston, Hank and Bert Klandermans, eds (1995) *Social Movements and Culture*. London, University College London.

Jones, G. (1984) *Demographic Transition in Asia*. Singapore, Maruzen.

Kahn, Joel (1995) 'The Middle Class as an Object of Ethnological Study', in M. Said, ed., *Festschrift for Syed Husin Ali*. Kuala Lumpur.

Kasem Snidvongs (1994) interview recorded in *TEI Quarterly Environmental Journal*, 2(1): 67.

Kerkvliet, Benedict (1993) 'Claiming the Land: Takeovers by villagers in the Philippines', *Journal of Peasant Studies* 20(3): 459–93.

Kong, Lily (1994) 'Environment' as a Social Concern: Democratizing public arenas in Singapore?', *Sojourn* 9(2): 277–87.

Laderjinsky, Wolf, ed. (1977) *Agrarian Reform as Unfinished Business*. New York, Oxford University Press.

Leete, R. and I. Alam, eds. (1993) *The Revolution in Asian Fertility*. Singapore, Oxford University Press.

Lim Teck Ghee and Mark Valencia (1990) *Conflict over Natural Resources in Southeast Asia and the Pacific*. Singapore, Oxford University Press.

Lohmann, Larry (1991) 'Peasants, Plantations and Pulp: The politics of eucalyptus in Thailand', *Bulletin of Concerned Asian Scholars*, 23(4): 3–17.

Lyman, Stanford, ed. (1995) *Social Movements: Critiques, concepts and case studies*. Basingstoke, Macmillan.

Milner, G.B., ed. (1978) *Natural Symbols in Southeast Asia*. London, School of Oriental and African Studies monograph.

Moniaga, Sandra (n.d.) 'Catalyzing International and National NGO Linkages: WALHIs experiences', in Environmental Liaison Centre International, *People's Participation and Environmentally Sustainable Development*. Manila, ANGOC.

Morris, A. and C. Mueller (1992) *Frontiers in Social Movement Theory*. New Haven, Yale University Press.

O'Neill, John (1993) *Ecology, Policy and Politics: Human well-being and the natural world*. London, Routledge.

O'Riordan, Timothy (1981) *Environmentalism*. London, Pion.

Papadakis, Elim (1993) *Politics and the Environment: The Australian experience*. St Leonards, Allen and Unwin.

Pearce, David (1993) *Economic Values and the Natural World*. London, Earthscan.

Pearce, David and R. Kerry Turner (1990) *Economics of Natural Resources and the Environment*. New York, Harvester Wheatsheaf.

Peet, Richard and Michael Watts (1993) 'Development Theory and Environment in an Age of Market Triumphalism', *Economic Geography*, 69: 227–53.

Peluso, Nancy (1992) *Rich Forests, Poor People: Resource control and resistance in Java*. Berkeley, University of California Press.

Pepper, David (1984) *The Roots of Modern Environmentalism*. London, Routledge.

Pfirrman, Claudia and Dirk Kron (1992) *Environment and NGOs in Thailand*. Bangkok, Thai NGO Support Project and Friedrich-Naumann-Stiftung.

Pompe, S. (1996) 'The Indonesian Supreme Court: Fifty Years of Judicial Development'. Unpublished doctoral dissertation, Law Faculty, Leiden University.

Princen, Thomas (1994) *Environmental NGO in World Politics: Linking the local and the global*. London, Routledge.

Rambo, A. Terry, Kathleen Gillogly and Karl Hutterer, eds (1988) *Ethnic Diversity and the Control of Natural Resources in Southeast Asia*. Ann Arbor, Centre for South and Southeast Asian Studies, University of Michigan.

Reving, John, ed. (1995) *World Rainforest Report* no. 31, Lismore, Rainforest Information Centre (Australia).

Rigg, Jonathan (1991) *Southeast Asia: A region in transition*. London, Unwin Hyman.

Rigg, Jonathan ed. (1995) *Counting the Costs: Economic growth and environmental change in Thailand*. Singapore, Institute of Southeast Asian Studies.

Robinson, Nicholas (1992) *Agenda 21 and the UNCED Proceedings*. New York, Oceana.

Rodan, Garry, ed. (1996) *Political Oppositions in Industrialising Asia*. London, Routledge.

Scott, James (1985) *Weapons of the Weak: Everyday forms of peasant resistance*. New Haven, Yale University Press.

Sluiter, Lisbeth (1993) *Mekong Currency: The lives and times of a river*. Bangkok, Project for Ecological Recovery – TERRA.

Stott, Philip, ed. (1978) *Nature and Man in Southeast Asia*. London, School of Oriental and African Studies monograph.

Touraine, Alain (1985) 'Social Movements and Social Change', in Orlando Fals Borda, ed., *The Challenge of Social Change*. London, Sage, pp. 77–92.

Turton, Andrew (1984) 'Limits of Ideological Domination and the Formation of Social Consciousness', in Andrew Turton and Shigeharu Tanabe, eds, *History and Peasant Consciousness in Southeast Asia*, pp. 19–73. Osaka, National Museum of Ethnology (Senri Ethnological Studies 13).

—— (1987) *Production, Power, and Participation in Rural Thailand: Experiences of poor farmers' groups*. Geneva, UNRISD [United Nations Research Institute for Social Development].

Uhlig, Harald, ed. (1984) *Spontaneous and Planned Settlement in Southeast Asia*. Hamburg, Institute of Asian Affairs.

Vitug, M. (1993) *Power from the Forest: The politics of logging*. Manila, Philippines Centre for Investigative Journalism.

Warren, Carol (1985) 'Class and Change in Rural Southeast Asia', in Richard Higgott and Richard Robison, eds, *Southeast Asia: Essays in the political economy of structural change*. London, Routledge and Kegan Paul.

—— (1994) *Centre and Periphery in Indonesia: Politics, environment and human rights in the regional press (Bali)*. Working Paper No. 42, Asia Research Centre, Murdoch University.

Warren, Carol and Kylie Elston (1994) *Environmental Regulation in Indonesia*. Perth, University of Western Australia Press and Asia Research Centre, Murdoch University.

White, Benjamin (1989) 'Problems in the Empirical Analysis of Agrarian Differentiation', in Gillian Hart, Andrew Turton and Benjamin White, eds, *Agrarian Transformations: Local processes and the state in Southeast Asia*. Berkeley, University of California Press.

World Bank (1993) *Sustaining Rapid Development in East Asia and the Pacific*. Washington, D.C., World Bank.

—— (1994), *The East Asian Miracle: Economic growth and public policy*. New York, Oxford University Press.

Part I

Large dams, community and nation

2 Large dam victims and their defenders

The emergence of an anti-dam movement in Indonesia

George J. Aditjondro

Anti-large dam struggles have been among the important arenas of environmental politics and environmentalism in capitalist as well as socialist nation-states.[1] The aim of this study is to explore the dynamics and the systemic effects of large dam struggles in Indonesia, in particular, to consider whether they have empowered the immediate victims of these projects. Although this analysis of Indonesia's contemporary large dam struggles will focus on the highly publicized Kedungombo case, an overall picture of other cases of resistance to dam development during the New Order will also be provided as background to analyzing the shared features of these struggles.

THE POLITICAL CULTURE OF INDONESIAN LARGE DAM CONSTRUCTION

Indonesia's large dam building history began in 1914 during the Dutch era, and entered a boom period during the New Order (see Table 2.1). For half a century, the colonial government and its successor, the newly independent Indonesian state, focused on building irrigation dams. The major, and only, dam-building agency in the early period was the Irrigation Directorate General of the Department of Public Works (DPW). Indonesia began to build more hydropower dams in the 1960s and 1970s when a second dam-building agency, the National Electric Power Company (PLN), rose to prominence. This state corporation was initially positioned under DPW, but for the last two decades has been under the Department of Mining and Energy.

The monumental growth of the Indonesian dam-building industry took off under Suharto's presidency, after Indonesia's first president, Sukarno, was deposed in the 1965 military-backed *coup d'état*. Initially, the New Order inherited five major projects from the Sukarno era: the French-financed Jatiluhur dam on the Ci (River) Tarum in West Java; the Selorejo and Karangkates dams on the Brantas river system in East Java, and the Riam Kanan dam in South Kalimantan (Nishihara 1993: 142), financed from the Japanese war reparation fund; and the large hydropower plant on the Asahan river in North Sumatra, comprising the Siguragura and Tangga dams, also financed with loans from Japan (see Seda 1989).

Table 2.1 List of Indonesian large dams in operation in 1990

Year began operation	Name of dam	Name of river and/or lake	Province	Height (m)	Function
1914	Ngelangon	Ngelangon	C. Java	15	I
1916	Tempuran	Kedung Padas	C. Java	18	I
	Prinjetan	Prinjetan	E. Java	21	I
1923	Delingan	Tempuran	C. Java	23	I
1924	Cileunca	Cileunca	W. Java	16	E
1925	Gunung Rowo	Rowo	C. Java	19	I
1927	Situpatok	Mundu	W. Java	18	I
1928	Plumbon	Baron	C. Java	23	I
1930	Cipanunjang	Cipanunjang	W. Java	34	E
	Ngebel	Simenok	E. Java	19	I
1933	Gembong	Sani	C. Java	36	I
	Pacal	Pacal	C. Java	35	I
1940	Malahayu	Kabuyatan	C. Java	30	I
1946	Ngancar	Jarak	C. Java	19	I
1958	Cacaban	Cacaban	C. Java	37	I
1962	Darma	Cisanggarung	W. Java	36	I
	Ir. Juanda (Jatiluhur)	Citarum	W. Java	96	I, E, F
	Pasir	Gombong Citarum	W. Java	34	I, E, F
	Ubrug	Citarum	W. Java	46	I, E, F
1972	Selorejo	Konto	E. Java	46	I, E, F
	Ir. Sutami (Karangkates I)	Brantas	E. Java	98	I, E, F
1973	Ir. Pangeran Mohammad Noor	Riam Kanan	S. Kalimantan	57	I, E, F
1976	Nawangan	Kedung Nangka	C. Java	25	I
	Way Jepara	Jepara	Lampung	18	I
	Klampis	Klampis	E. Java	20	I

Year	Dam	River	Location	Height (m)	Purpose
1977	Lahor (Karangkates II)	Lahor	E. Java	60	I, E
	Wlingi	Brantas	E. Java	28	I, E
	Batubesi	Larona	S. Sulawesi	32	E
1978	Sempor	Cingcingguling	C. Java	61	I, E, F
1980	Parangjoho	Tempuran	C. Java	20	I
1981	Bening	Bening	E. Java	35	I, E
	Wonogiri (Gajah Mungkur)	Solo	C. Java	32	I, E, F
	Siruar (Asahan Project)	Asahan	N. Sumatra	39	E
	Ketro	Ketro	C. Java	17	I
1982	Sampean Baru	Sampean	E. Java	42	I, E
	Siguragura (Asahan Project)	Asahan	N. Sumatra	46	E
	Way Rarem	Rarem	Lampung	31	
	Garung	Menjer	C. Java	36	E
1983	Tangga (Asahan Project)	Asahan	N. Sumatra	73	E
	Batujai	Penunjak	W. Nusa Tenggara	16	I
1984	Saguling	Citarum	W. Java	98	E
1985	Song Putri	Melati	W. Sumatra	26	I
	Maninjau	Maninjau Lake	W. Sumatra	—	E
1987	Wadaslintang	Badegolan	C. Java	121	I, E
1989	Gen. Sudirman (Mrica)	Serayu	C. Java	109	E
	Kedungombo	Serang	C. Java	66	I, E, F
	Sengguruh	Brantas	E. Java	34	E
	Cirata	Citarum	W. Java	125	E
	Tes	Tes Lake	Bengkulu	—	E
1990	Bakaru	Mamasa	S. Sulawesi	16.5	E
	Palasari	Sangiang Gede	Bali	39.5	I

(Ir = Engineer; I = irrigation; E = electric-power generation; F = flood control)

Note: All dams higher than 15 m are classified as 'large dams' by the International Commission of Large Dams (ICOLD), the Paris-based organization of civil engineers and other professionals in this field. Other dams with heights between 10 and 15 m can also be classified as 'large dams' if they fulfill one of the following criteria: the dam's length is not less than 500 m; the capacity of the dam's reservoir is not less than one million m³; the dam's maximum flood discharge capacity is not less than 2,000 m³/second; the dam had particularly difficult foundation problems and an unusual design.

Sources: Soedibyo, 1993: 3, 371–372; Abdul Kadir, 1990: 151–183.

The construction of large dams outside Java all took place under the New Order, beginning with the Riam Kanan in South Kalimantan and the Asahan project in North Sumatra. These large dams are not so numerous, and mainly function for hydroelectric power generation. Meanwhile, the greatest number of Indonesia's large dams were built on Java for irrigation purposes, and more recently for hydropower.

During the New Order a certain political culture was constructed which supported the continuous building of large dams. A review of Indonesian engineering journals published since Indonesia's independence shows that the foundation of this political culture was laid during the tenure of the New Order's first Public Works Minister, Sutami (see Aditjondro, 1993a: 37–54).[2] As the first and longest-serving Public Works Minister under Suharto (1966–1980), the late Sutami – who joined the DPW under Sukarno – left a strong ideological imprint on the DPW and PLN. He had educated an entire generation of Indonesian engineers through his position at the University of Indonesia, where he initially taught engineering subjects, especially the mechanics of reinforced concrete. But after years of experience as Minister of Public Works, which allowed him to travel around Indonesia and see the poverty in the countryside, he added more social science and ecology into the engineering subjects he taught and broadened his horizons by reading and discussions with lecturers at his *alma mater*, the Bandung Institute of Technology (ITB). Eventually, in late 1976, Sutami was granted a new chair in regional science at the University of Indonesia and developed his own textbook on this subject. Hence, in the DPW community Sutami is regarded as the first minister to develop official environmental awareness in Indonesia, not Emil Salim, the Berkeley graduate who held the first Environment Minister portfolio during the New Order.

Sutami's identification of engineering feats with patriotism seemed to be his most powerful legacy. As a member of the generation that had fought for freedom, Sutami often emphasized that Indonesian engineers were facing a new form of *perjuangan* (struggle) to prove their technical expertise, which had often been ridiculed by colonial engineers. Sutami's success in framing engineering feats as 'patriotic acts' was reinforced by his sober and hardworking lifestyle, his clean reputation in a corrupt bureaucracy, and his closeness to the press. He challenged his younger colleagues to put the *perjuangan* (struggle) spirit to work by building as many dams as possible, even with very limited equipment.[3]

Sutami believed in the political neutrality and objectivity of engineers. In an interview with a student news weekly in Bandung in 1976, he stated that 'politicians can lie, [but] for technicians it is impossible to manipulate the facts.' Somewhat at odds with his social commitments and the proclaimed impartiality of his profession is Sutami's appropriation of the old Javanese slogan, *jer basuki mawa bea* (literally: 'every benefit must carry a price'). After he passed away in 1980, this slogan was immortalized by successive Public Works ministers.[4]

Sutami was obsessed with saving the 'overloaded' island of Java from a prospective ecological disaster. He repeatedly expressed this theme, using various colorful metaphors, comparing Java, for example, with a hen which laid golden eggs but which was not well fed and whose feathers were constantly plucked until it was nearly bald, and with an overloaded boat which was going to sink or capsize because of its excessive cargo. Regardless of the metaphors used, his solution to the problem was always consistent. Java had to be rescued – in the short run, by building more reservoirs on the island and resettling Java's excessive population on the outer islands where irrigation could be provided for them. In the long run, Java should be reforested and regreened.

Reinforced by Sutami's legacy, dam-builders have continued to portray large dams as monuments of the New Order. This first required sanitizing them from association with Sukarno. The construction of the Brantas River Project, for instance, was initiated not by Suharto but by the last Public Works Minister under Sukarno. Based on a 1959–1961 feasibility study by a Japanese firm, Nippon Koei, the construction of the first Brantas dam, Karangkates, began in 1962. Two older dams planned under Sukarno have also disappeared from the New Order's large dam discourse. Jatiluhur, Indonesia's first nearly 100 m high dam, was not treated as *the* milestone in Indonesia's modern large dam construction history out of nationalist pride, since it was designed and constructed by French engineers. Sempor, designed entirely by a young Indonesian engineer in 1958, had tarnished the industry's reputation when its cofferdam broke during a flash flood in 1967 killing 127 people. It was one of two Indonesian dam disasters recorded in the dam engineering literature.[5]

In line with their roles as monuments of the New Order, large dams have also been framed as symbols of the just inter-regional distribution of development benefits. In response to the inauguration of the Riam Kanan hydropower dam in South Kalimantan in 1973, a local ethnic writer stated that the South Kalimantan people felt 'proud and glad' to have a large dam like the ones in Java; and in 1981, a journalist from Riau criticized PLN for building eight hydropower dams in the neighboring province of West Sumatra but none in Riau.

In Java, where the largest number of large dams have been built, rivalry between provinces has also been expressed in the number and size of their dams. In 1972, the then Central Java Governor, Munadi, stated that 'West Java has Jatiluhur and East Java has Karangkates and Selorejo, [but] Central Java has no multipurpose dam yet. This discourages foreign and domestic investment in Central Java.'[6]

This habit of framing large dams as symbols of regional equality was reflected in the media after the construction of the Asahan hydropower dams in North Sumatra. Indeed, Suharto's personal attention through frequent visits to this project in 1980, 1982, and 1984 raised the political importance of the Asahan dams. Nevertheless, not the magnificent Asahan dams, nor the 9,200 ha Riam Kanan reservoir in South Kalimantan, which was larger than all dam reservoirs in Java, but Java-based dams and reservoirs instead became the barometers of progress for outer-island provinces that wanted to 'catch up with Java.'

The Indonesian media have actively supported the Indonesian dam-builders' 'appetite' for large dams by portraying Indonesia as the number-one dam-building nation in Southeast Asia. Many Indonesian dams have been wrongly presented as superior in some of their features to all other dams previously built in Southeast Asia.[7] Such aggrandizing claims apparently increased public tolerance for the price that had to be paid to build so many large dams.

ECONOMIC INTERESTS BEHIND THE DAM-BUILDING DRIVE

It was not only national pride, the effort to glorify Suharto's New Order, or the intent to distribute development benefits equally among the provinces that fueled the drive toward building more large dams in Indonesia. Three strong economic interests also motivated the large dam construction spree in Indonesia: the cement industry, DPW-related companies, and Japanese financial interests (see Aditjondro, 1993a: 54–57). The thriving cement industry acted as a major impetus for building large dams. Suharto's extended family dominate the industry (*Prospek*, February 13, 1993: 26), controlling nearly 75 per cent of the industry's production capacity from Bohorok in North Sumatra to Baucau in East Timor (see Table 2.2). Apart from the cement factories, the construction and consultant firms owned by the DPW also profited from the large dam-building drive. As well as increasing the Department's income, these companies constituted 'revolving doors' to accommodate DPW retirees. With the exception of two companies involved in the asphalt and heavy equipment businesses, all other DPW-owned companies enjoyed high profits in 1991–1992.

Besides those domestic interests, Japanese interests played a decisive role in boosting Indonesia's large dam-building drive. Beginning with the financing of three large dams inherited from the Sukarno era, Japanese loans have ever since provided the majority of funds to build Indonesia's large dams. These loans subsidized the Japanese economy through fully-owned Japanese companies as well as Japanese joint ventures with Indonesian companies. The first four dams funded by Japan – Asahan, Karangkates, Selorejo, and Riam Kanan dams – became the bases of the emergence of one of Japan's largest consultancy firms. Nippon Koei, supported by its 'friends in high places' in both countries, obtained a near monopoly over most of Indonesia's dam and other infrastructure projects for more than 30 years. In Indonesia, this company, which was founded by a Japanese engineer who served in the occupation forces in Sumatra, Yutaka Kubota, has been religiously supported by the two main large dam-builders, the DPW and PLN. In Japan, Nippon Koei enjoyed tremendous support from Japan's main overseas development finance agencies, the Overseas Economic Cooperation Fund (OECF) and Japan's Export Import Bank (see Seda, 1989).

Table 2.2 Production capacity of Indonesian cement producers (in 1,000 tonnes)

Groups members		Production capacity	Percentage of total capacity
Indocement Group		10,600	26.53%
PT Indocement Tungall Perkasa	(8,200)		
PT Tridaya Manunggal Perkasa	(1,200)		
New Cirebon West Java plant	(1,200)		
Semen Cibinong Group		9,600	24.03%
PT Semen Cibinong	(4,500)		
PT Semen Nusantara	(5,100)		
Maharani Group		1,500	3.75%
Pabrik Semen Bahorok, N. Sumatra	(1,500)		
Poleko Group		1,500	3.75%
PT Osmo Semen Indonesia, Kupang	(1,500)		
Djajanti Group		4,000	10.01%
PT Maluku Dinamika Semen, Seram	(4,000)		
Citra Lamtorogung Persada Group		2,300	5.75%
Bacau East Timor cement plant	(2,300)		
State corporations		9,450	23.65%
PT Semen Padang	(4,230)		
PT Semen Gresik	(2,300)		
PT Semen Tonasa	(2,300)		
PT Semen Baturaja	(500)		
PT Semen Kupang	(120)		
Foreign companies		1,000	2.50%
PT Semen Andalas	(1,000)		
Total capacity		39,950	100 %

Notes:
The Indocement Group is part of the largest Indonesian conglomerate, the Salim Group, where the Suharto family's interest is represented by Sudwikatmono, Suharto's cousin, Siti Hardiyanti Rukmana ('Tutut'), Suharto's eldest daughter, and Sigit Harjojudanto, Suharto's eldest son. In Hashim Djojohadikusumo's Semen Cibinong Group, Hashim's sister-in-law, Siti Hediati Hariyadi ('Titiek Prabowo'), the second daughter of Suharto and wife of rising Army star Major General Prabowo Subianto, is a co-shareholder. This group is planning to build a 1 million ton per annum cement factory in Burma, through a joint venture with a Burmese state-owned company. The Maharani Group is another joint venture between Titiek Prabowo and the Djojohadikusumo family. The Djajanti Group is owned by a Sino-Indonesian businessman, Burhan Uray, but with Sudwikatmono, Suharto's cousin, as its President Commissioner, controlling 10 per cent of its shares. Vice President Tri Sutrisno's son, Isfan Fajar Satryo, is the President Commissioner of Djajanti's cement factory. Citra Lamtorogung Persada's cement factory is planned to be a joint venture with former East Timorese resistance leader Abilio Araujo.

Sources: *Asia Wall Street Journal*, February 2, 1993: 19–20, May 20, 1995; *Asia Times*, December 10, 1996; *Economic & Business Review Indonesia*, June 19, 1996, February 12, 1997: 12, 38; *Indonesian Business Weekly*, June 18, 1993, December 2, 1994, December 16, 1994: 38; *Prospek*, December 19, 1992: 24, February 13, 1993: 26, August 1994: 22; *Swasembada*, May 1994: 56; *Warta Ekonomi*, April 19, 1993: 25, October 24, 1994: 17

PROTEST CAMPAIGNS AGAINST LARGE DAMS IN INDONESIA

Despite the propaganda of the dam-building industry and its supporters in the media, collective resistance against the construction of large dams did occur periodically. These protest campaigns have been increasing steadily over the last two decades. The most publicized case is certainly the struggle against land eviction and compensation practices during the construction of the Kedungombo dam in Central Java (see e.g. Pakpahan, 1990; de Adelhart Toorop, 1990; Aditjondro, 1993a; Stanley, 1994). Contrary to popular belief, however, Kedungombo was only one of many anti-large dam struggles which occurred in Indonesia during the last 25 years, some with strong similarities to the Kedungombo struggle.

To obtain a broader picture of the interaction between the dam-building industry and its host communities from September 1971 until July 1992, I carried out extensive library research in Indonesian general news, criminal, and engineering media at Cornell University. With the assistance of David Kowalewski, 93 reported cases of protest campaigns against water projects which occurred between 1971 and 1992 were computer analyzed (see Aditjondro and Kowalewski, 1994, 1995). From that broader picture, several observations can be made. First of all, the frequency as well as intensity of these protest campaigns grew dramatically during the 1980s, in accordance with the increasing number of dams built during that period. Secondly, the grievances which most often characterized those protest campaigns were poor compensation and poor resettlement conditions. Thirdly, the protesting groups were dominated by farmers who used peaceful tactics; and most of them had no support from third parties. Fourthly, in response to those protest campaigns, New Order officials have mainly concentrated their efforts in addressing religio-cultural grievances. Fifthly, from the four major militant strategies employed by the protestors – sending petitions, organizing lawsuits, refusing to cooperate with the dam-building agency, and obstructing or attempting to damage the projects' properties – the last strategy seemed to have had the highest chance of obtaining concessions from the authorities, followed by lawsuits. To illustrate the extent and intensity of popular resistance against large dams prior to the Kedungombo case, several cases deserve to be highlighted.

● In the early 1970s a dam project on the Tandui River in West Java, financed by the US Agency for International Development, was opposed by Sundanese villagers. They claimed that the dam would impound a cultural reserve believed to be the habitat of Ciung Wanara, the Sundanese holy monkey. Strong protests from the people and even the Ciamis district head forced the DPW and USAID to shelve this project.

● In 1973, villagers in South Kalimantan initiated a campaign against the Riam Kanan hydroelectric dam. They protested at the poor compensation for their property and the lack of economic support for removing their ancestors' graves from lands to be flooded. Some of the Banjarese villagers took local authorities to court and won their case. On the other hand, a thousand other villagers appointed a private lawyer to demand Rp 14 billion compensation, but the lawyer disappeared, and two villagers were taken to court instead, accused of forging signatures. A couple of the villagers collected money from relatives and fellow villagers to appeal for justice at the Supreme Court in Jakarta – an ultimately unsuccessful legal attempt.

• In July 1976, villagers in East Java killed their village head, who was involved in attempts to force them to transmigrate to make way for a large dam. It was estimated that the Jipang Dam would impound 16 villages, displacing 6,000 households with 30,000 members. Fifteen months later, the 14 defendants received jail sentences of 20 months to 13 years. Ironically, in 1990 the project – which was never started – was officially cancelled by the DPW owing to its potential social impact. As a substitute, a movable weir was built near the provincial capital to halt sea-water intrusion.

• From 1979 to 1984, Batak highland villagers waged a protest campaign against the Asahan Project dams in North Sumatra. First, eight village heads petitioned the governor, objecting to the sale of their land and suggesting that the project rent the land for a rate equal to their annual rice harvest. The authorities insisted on a compensation rate of Rp 130 per m^2, which was only enough to buy a pack of cheap cigarettes. So the farmers continued to plant their rice, although the regulating dam was about to be closed and their fields flooded. At the suggestion of the late August Marpaung, a retired army general who hailed from the region, the project operator and the local government held a traditional ceremony to show their respect for the local people's customs, just before the regulating dam was closed, and raised the compensation to Rp 700 per m^2. In addition, a resettlement site was provided for the displaced farmers.

After the resistance of the first group was subdued, two other groups of villagers complained that their rice fields were compensated at a lower rate than that provided for the first group, that they were not allowed to salvage their rice harvest from their fields, which were damaged by mud, gravel and rocks dredged from the river, and that the soil in the resettlement site was worse than in their original villages. Hence, they returned to their old village on the banks of the Asahan River, to cultivate a nearby hill as their common farmland. The villagers' resistance was supported by lawyers, students, and journalists in the provincial capital (Medan) and Jakarta. With the support of the lawyers, Idris Siahaan, a local villager, took the project operator and the local government to court in November 1984, demanding compensation for the losses from his rice fields, which he could not harvest for five years. After losing the case in the lower court, he appealed to the High Court and eventually to the Supreme Court in Jakarta. But, at least as of 1989, the Supreme Court had still neglected to address the farmer's appeal (Pakpahan, 1990: 3; Aditjondro, 1993a: 205, 338–339).

• While the Batak villagers were fighting the Asahan project in North Sumatra, in 1980 ninety-five households who lived on the bank of the Towuti Lake in South Sulawesi took PT Inco Indonesia to court for flooding their mosque, houses, rice fields, and coconut gardens. This human-made disaster took place after the engineering firm contracted by the subsidiary of the Canadian nickel mine company dammed the Larona River, which flows out of the Towuti Lake. The Buginese villagers, who were defended by two private lawyers, demanded Rp 750 million compensation for their inundated properties. The case was settled out of court, after Inco agreed to pay substantial compensation, which included the costs of moving the mosque to high ground.

● In 1983, Riau villagers petitioned authorities against the proposed Kotopanjang hydroelectric dam funded by the Japanese OECF. They demanded that the process of decision-making be made more democratic; that flooded land remain under community control; that three honored graves be saved from inundation; that compensation rates be raised; and that the resettlement process be reviewed. After 17 years' campaigning by themselves, the villagers finally received support from students, human rights activists, and environmentalists in Sumatra, Jakarta, and Japan. Two representatives of the protesting villagers flew to Japan to petition OECF officials and meet Diet members. After minor revisions of the project, some of the protesting villagers eventually accepted the new conditions, while others remained unsatisfied.

● In March 1984, seventy-five villagers from Pinrang district in South Sulawesi travelled 250 km to the provincial capital, Ujungpandang, to complain about the social problems caused by the PLN Bakaru hydropower dam. A year earlier, the same group of villagers had taken the dam's contractor to court, demanding Rp 4.9 billion compensation for their land, crops, and property. After nearly two years' deliberation, the court ruled in favor of the contractor. The villagers' struggle did persuade the government to investigate the land-appropriation process, which led to a second trial case in the same court. Between 1985 and 1987, three cadastral officials were given sentences of from two to six years in jail for swindling between Rp 136 million and Rp 730 million of the project's budget. The provincial high court, however, reduced their sentences drastically and eventually released one of them from jail for health reasons. However, before the second case was completed, the Pinrang court was used by the local government to launch a legal vendetta against the protestors. In late 1985, seven persons – mostly student activists – were tried, accused of inciting villagers to reject the government's resettlement scheme. Two of them had led the March 1985 rally in Ujungpandang. In March 1986, six of the seven defendants received four-year sentences, while the seventh person was freed of any charges and was able to finish his law degree. After serving their sentences, the leader of the villagers who had taken the contractor to court and the village religious leader emigrated to Malaysia. Most of the villagers, however, kept opposing the government's resettlement program. When the dam was inaugurated in September 1990, PLN took security precautions to prevent the villagers from disturbing the ceremony.

● In October 1986, a 28-year-old villager in West Java, Mahfuddin Hermanto, was killed by local security officials. The law student from the

Parahyangan Catholic University in Bandung had used his legal knowledge to investigate and expose compensation frauds in land alienation for the Cirata hydropower dam. His death triggered reactions from fellow students, who staged a vigil on campus and marched to Cirata. As a result of pressure from Parahyangan law students and lecturers, a police assistant was taken to court and sentenced to 13 years in jail. Two other civilians were sentenced to six years, while two village heads were dismissed. After two years, two police officers who ordered the murder were tried by a military court and sentenced to 15 and 17 years in jail. The dam's construction went on, without a thorough investigation into the compensation frauds. Nevertheless, the displaced villagers were allowed to settle on the reservoir banks and were even assisted to develop lucrative aquaculture farms on the artificial lake (Aditjondro, 1993a: 205, 327–345).

THE KEDUNGOMBO CASE

With that picture of earlier struggles in mind, we turn our attention to the most publicized Indonesian dam dispute, the Kedungombo case (see Map 2.1), which will be presented from the perspective of the displaced villagers and their urban-based supporters. We will then consider the responses to these campaigns from two important state actors: the army and the State Minister for Environment, Emil Salim.

Resistance originated from former inhabitants of five villages in the Sragen district, which between 1984 and 1986 were officially deleted from the Central Java map by decrees of Governor Ismail, since these villages were to be inundated by the Kedungombo reservoir. All inhabitants were encouraged to transmigrate. The initial response was passive resistance. Most of the former inhabitants of three villages – Pilangrembes, Porongan, and Nglorog – moved to nearby Gilirejo, causing the population of that village to triple from 496 to 1,252 households between 1977 and 1989. Residents of the two remaining villages, Boyolayar and Ngargomulyo, only moved to higher ground.[8]

After moving to Gilirejo, some former residents from Pilangrembes, Porangan, and Nglorog, supported by some of the original villagers of Gilirejo, began to resist the state openly in 1986. They demanded that the Sragen district head correct the mismeasurement and under-valuation of their land. Initially they requested legal assistance from the Yogyakarta Legal Aid Institute, but later shifted their patronage to another legal aid institute based in Solo, Yayasan Pengabdi Hukum Indonesia (Indonesian Legal Service Foundation), which they found to be more openly supportive. Apart from that, some of those Sragen villagers also joined Central Java and Yogyakarta student activists in rallies at the national parliament, demanding improvement of living conditions in the overcrowded village of Gilirejo, and probes into the mismanagement of land and property compensation. While many of their grievances concerning physical conditions were addressed by the government, demands for the investigation of compensation frauds were constantly turned down.

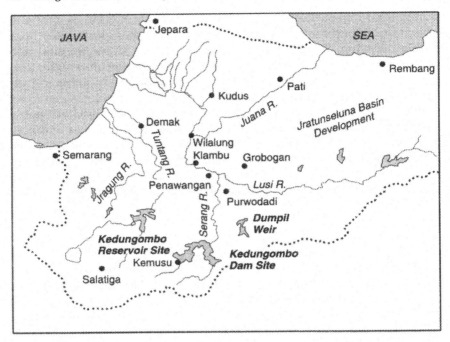

Map 2.1   Location of Kedungombo Reservoir, Jratunseluna River Basin, Central Java, Indonesia

Joining in quite a bit later than the grass-roots resistance in Sragen were the protest campaigns by villagers in the next district to be inundated, Boyolali. The Boyolali villagers' resistance attracted more media attention because during the late 1980s the student movement in Java had become more consolidated. Likewise, Indonesian non-governmental organizations had also become linked to international NGO networks based in the West, which wanted to amplify local resistance against World Bank-funded projects. Hence, in early 1989, the resistance of the Boyolali villagers led by Jaswadi, who refused to be transmigrated in the midst of the rising water, was broadcast world-wide by the press. The government finally yielded, and two new resettlement sites were built near the reservoir, in addition to another one which had previously been built.

Grass-roots resistance, however, had not yet ended. At one of the reservoir tails in Boyolali, there were still other hamlets, which completely refused to accept the very low compensation rates forced upon them, or to settle in the government-built resettlement sites. They demanded instead the right to farm their original farmland, which had been included in the reservoir's green belt and drawdown area. Farming activities in these areas were prohibited by the Jratunseluna Project, the dam-building and operating agency, which claimed that farming in the drawdown and green-belt areas would reduce the reservoir's life-span. In 1990, supported by lawyers from the Semarang Legal Aid Institute, 54 households from Kedung Pring, a hamlet in the district of Boyolali, took the Central Java governor and the Jratunseluna project officer to court, demanding that they increase the ridiculously low compensation rates of Rp 250 per m² of house lot land and Rp 300 per m² of dry farmland decided by the governor in 1984 to Rp 10,000 per m².

After six months of deliberations, when the number of plaintiffs had dwindled from 54 to 34 households, the lower court in Semarang turned down the people's claim. The farmers and their lawyers immediately appealed to the Central Java High Court, which in a very brief time reaffirmed the lower court's decision. They then appealed to the Supreme Court. Finally, in a pathbreaking decision, on July 28, 1993, a Supreme Court panel of judges under the leadership of Justice Asikin Kusumah Atmaja granted the people's request. It even raised the compensation rate which the governor and the Jratunseluna Project had to pay to the people to Rp 50,000 per m² for their house lot and Rp 30,000 per m² for their garden land. In consequence, the government was ordered to pay total compensation of more than Rp 9 billion (about US$ 4.5 million) to the 34 families. For unexplained 'administrative' reasons, the decision was not announced until a year after it was made, at first to the Kedungombo lawyers, who then passed it on to the media. The chair of the Supreme Court panel, Kusumah Atmaja, retired two days after the 1994 ruling was belatedly released.

President Suharto promptly intervened to overturn the Supreme Court's decision. He met with the Chief Justice of the Supreme Court, Poerwoto S. Gandasoebrata, insisting that the July 1993 decision be reviewed. While a Supreme Court decision normally takes up to four years, four months after the initial ruling was made public, on October 29, 1994, this new panel annulled the earlier decision and relieved the government from the obligation to pay the high compensation funds (*Indonesia Business Weekly*, November 18, 1994: 9; *Forum Keadilan*, November 24, 1994: 26). Justice Gandasoebrata said the reversal was made because the Supreme Court had failed to take into account the 1993 Presidential decree, which superseded that of 1975 and which allowed for land appropriation to proceed even if a compensation agreement had not been reached. In May 1995, after Justice Gandasoebrata's retirement, in remarks to the Jakarta Lawyers' Club about another land compensation case, he was reported as saying: 'We [the Supreme Court] often receive requests from the government to cancel or delay the execution of a Supreme Court ruling in the name of development' (Lawyers' Committee for Human Rights 1995: 93).

The Kedung Pring villagers were not the only group from Kedungombo to persist in fighting the government. Two months prior to the announcement of the first Supreme Court decision, the Yogyakarta Legal Aid Institute appeared with another surprise for the Central Java government. Jaswadi's group had suddenly risen from its apparent compliance, accusing the government of appropriating the compensation funds deposited at the Boyolali lower court.

A year later, in late September 1995, representatives of 500 households from the Sragen villages which were the first to be inundated by the Kedungombo reservoir came to complain to the Human Rights Commission in Jakarta about compensation irregularities. Members of this new agency, which had been set up by Suharto to address international concerns about human rights violations in Indonesia, promised to speak to the proper governmental bodies (*Kompas*, September 30, 1995; *Republika*, October 27, 1995).

In a nutshell, the majority of the inhabitants of the 22 villages inundated by the reservoir were relatively successful in resisting the government's involuntary resettlement policy: their presence around the reservoir, and even the cultivation of the reservoir's green belt and drawdown area, was silently tolerated by the project management.

Kedungombo had a different meaning for the student activists. While for the farmers, the campaign was a matter of survival as farmers near their home villages, for the students Kedungombo became a new stage in their relation with the state:

In the early period of the Kedungombo campaign, KSKPKO[9] activists advocated dialogue, organised delegations and looked to sympathetic New Order officials to assist the residents of the dam site. According to Stanley [a former KSKPKO coordinator], Interior Minister Rudini in particular was viewed with hope because he was known to 'make many statements which defended the poor'. At an amicable meeting in February 1989, Rudini promised to set up a 'hot line' with KSKPKO. With the failure of the authorities, including Rudini, to respond satisfactorily to their criticisms, and as the flooding of the reservoir area proceeded, the tactics of KSKPKO became rapidly more radical. In late March 1989, protestors attempted to enter the reservoir area in Boyolali without asking for government permission, and shouted slogans against the President, Vice President, and Governor of Central Java. At a Jakarta demonstration, also in March, it was stated that KSKPKO did not have faith 'in Minister Rudini as a symbol and representative of the whole executive' or indeed in 'any living officials'. Eleven students were arrested. At the next KSKPKO demonstration in April 1990 outside the parliament building in Jakarta, protestors refused an offer to have a delegation received by the parliament and insisted that they be addressed as a group. Thus, in a period of little over one year an important transformation of KSKPKO took place. Its mode of action evolved from dialogue to radical and confrontational demonstration. There was also an evolution of attitudes toward the state: from a level of faith in government officials to complete rejection of them.

(Aspinell, 1993: 47)

In fact, although preceded by other student demonstrations, the 1989–90 Kedungombo demonstrations became an 'opening salvo' for a series of other student–farmer public protests against land evictions all over Java (Lucas, 1992), which eventually spilled over into mass protests against luxury tourism projects in West Java, Lombok, and Bali (SKEPHI and KAAPLAG, 1994; Warren, this volume), against other dam projects in Sumatra, Sulawesi, and Madura (Sangaji, 1994; *Jawa Post*, June 9, 1995), and against the American Freeport mining company in Irian Jaya during the 1995 Easter period (*Republika*, August 29, 1995).

In addition, the students' mass actions *for* and *with* the Kedungombo farmers became the point of departure between the younger and more radical activists and the older and more professional ones, who preferred less militant tactics by confronting the state through lawsuits and international advocacy campaigns (see Aditjondro, 1990, 1991, 1993a; Budiman, 1990a and b, 1994; Tirtosudarmo, 1991). The non-student NGO movement had chosen not only to 'go public,' but also to 'go international.' In April 1989, Indonesian activists attending an international NGO conference in Belgium signed a petition to the World Bank, protesting against the human rights violations in the Bank-financed dam area. The controversy caused by President Suharto's order to retaliate against these 'unpatriotic' NGOs created the media label 'the Brussels incident.'

Realizing that 'the Brussels incident' did not solve the immediate problems faced by displaced villagers while creating problems for the petition's signatories, who became targets of intensified military scrutiny, the Indonesian Legal Aid Foundation (YLBHI) retreated to the courtroom. As noted earlier, the Foundation's branches in Semarang and Yogyakarta assisted the farmers in taking the dam management and the local government to court. This tactical shift was encouraged by a Javanese priest, J.B. Mangunwijaya, who initially joined the Kedungombo campaign by assisting children in the inundated villages with emergency schools and other services, but who, in response to the political circumstances, extended his tactics from charity to challenging the state's policy.

The involvement of Mangunwijaya, who was seen as representing the small yet powerful Christian minority in Indonesia, raised some Muslim eyebrows. Consequently, accusations of a hidden 'Christianization' agenda were hurled at him. To counter those accusations, Mangunwijaya recommended that the newly established government-sponsored association of Islamic intellectuals, ICMI (*Ikatan Cendekiawan Muslim Indonesia*), become involved in the campaign. This suggestion was eventually carried out, through the involvement of a Muslim poet and good friend of Mangunwijaya, Emha Ainun Najib.

However, despite the high profile of ICMI, which was chaired by the Minister of Research and Technology, B.J. Habibie, an overall solution for the farmers who rejected transmigration and unilaterally-determined compensation had still not been found by the end of 1995. INFID, the international NGO coalition which was formerly called INGI, tried to raise the issue again on March 28, 1995 in a letter to the World Bank's Operations Evaluation Department. But the majority of the former supporters of the Kedungombo people were already absorbed in various other campaigns, so the INFID letter did not receive the public and media support it deserved.

In this dispute, the response of the army and the Minister of Environment, Emil Salim, to the demands of the villagers and their intellectual supporters was crucial.[10] The continued media focus on Governor Ismail appeared to serve the interests of a group of active and retired army officers who had not been so happy with Ismail's reappointment by President Suharto for a second term as Central Java's governor.

There are a number of indications that the Kedungombo protests served the interests of politically dissatisfied army officers. The army made no serious efforts to prevent the demonstrations or ban media coverage, although mass demonstrations were actually prohibited by law. A retired general who claimed to be sent by the then Defense Minister, Benny Murdani, even offered funds to the student leaders in Salatiga during the 1989 demonstrations, which they had rejected. This retired general also visited Father Mangunwijaya in his parish home in Yogyakarta and recorded the priest's criticism of the government's handling of the Kedungombo case. Meanwhile, the Kedungombo demonstrations in Jakarta were tacitly supported by the Jakarta army commander, who kept a hot-line with one of the NGO leaders who was a strong supporter of the student demonstrations.

In 1990 and 1991, the army continued to act favorably toward the student–farmer demonstrations. Only once, before the second public rally of Sragen villagers in Jakarta, did the local army commander intervene to order the 200 villagers to return to their villages. The army's tacit support for the student protestors was also observed by *Far Eastern Economic Review* correspondent Michael Vatikiotis, who had closely covered the Kedungombo demonstrations in 1989. Between 1989 and 1991, none of the student media had their license revoked by the Department of Information, which often bans newspapers at the request of other powerful political lobbies – especially the army. So, there is reason to believe that a larger degree of political space was permitted to the students by the military, who were happy to see someone else discrediting the aging president and his protégé, Governor Ismail.

The limits on the political space allowed to the student movement, however, are illustrated by the response to their circulation of the 1990 *Land-for-the-People* calendar. This one-page calendar, published by nine student organizations, listed all major land eviction cases during that year. When this calendar started to circulate among student activists at the Diponegoro and Satya Wacana university campuses in Central Java, the regional military and police immediately seized stocks of the calendar and interrogated its distributors. Two Satya Wacana student activists were threatened with court action, although no legal action was taken against the nine non-governmental organizations that produced the calendar. The calendar itself was banned by the Attorney General two months after the interrogations began. However, the controversy caused by the threat of legal action against the Satya Wacana distributors increased the calendar's publicity value, even without any licensed media in Indonesia reproducing the cartoon, which has a caricature of President and Mrs Suharto in the center.

The final observation has to do with the inauguration of the Mrica dam – also in Central Java – by President Suharto on March 23, 1989. Suharto named the dam after the founding father of the Indonesian army, General Sudirman. Superficially, the choice of this name seemed logical enough. Sudirman was born in the Banyumas region where the Mrica dam was located. A state university dedicated to General Sudirman was also located in this region, in the town of Purwokerto. It is important, however, to look at the timing of the dam's naming. Suharto inaugurated this dam after massive student demonstrations in solidarity with the Kedungombo people had taken place. On that occasion also, Suharto publicly denounced the Kedungombo protestors as 'communists,' and claimed that 'in God's name, the government had no ill intentions against the people.' So, by naming the Mrica dam after the legendary army general, while branding the Kedungombo dam protestors as 'communists,' and emphasizing the government's goodwill with a Muslim vow, Suharto might have been attempting to consolidate the support of army as well as Muslim politicians, as he had in 1965–6, when he commanded the army-led 'cleansing' of Indonesian leftists. And conveniently enough, the Kedungombo reservoir site was formerly covered by dense teak forests where underground communist factions, brutally hunted down by the army in the late 1960s, had hidden.

The student movement had felt the brunt of the army's power during the 1978 occupation of the campuses of the Bandung Institute of Technology (ITB) and the Gadjah Mada University in Yogyakarta. This brutal behavior of their former ally in overthrowing Indonesia's first president might have left deep animosity among the young activists toward Suharto, had the position of Ministry of Environment not been created in 1978, with Emil Salim – a Berkeley-trained economist and former student activist – at the helm. By constructing Indonesian official environmentalism as 'a new covenant' between the young activists and the Suharto regime, Emil Salim became the 'political buffer' between the activists and Suharto's hard-core military supporters.

As Suharto's hand-picked Environment Minister, Salim tried to 'domesticate' Indonesian environmentalists by repeatedly warning them not to copy the activist style of the German Green Party and Greenpeace. In the short run, Emil Salim managed to woo the former student activists away from power politics. However, in the long run this strategy failed to take into account two parallel radicalizing processes that occurred among students and young university graduates and drop-outs who worked in various NGOs. As students became radicalized by repression on campus, where student government was dominated by lecturers, the young off-campus activists became radicalized by the emasculation of the political parties, which alienated villagers and urban slum-dwellers marginalized by the development process. In many of the land and development conflicts of the late 1980s and 1990s disadvantaged groups approached – and were approached by – students and former student activists to fight the state bureaucracy and its security apparatus. A convergence between campus- and non-campus-based activists emerged in the late 1980s, creating a radical strand of environmentalism which became a new form of political opposition. So, ironically, while Suharto had created the Environment Minister's portfolio in 1978 to divert the student opposition away from his presidency, among other reasons, environmentalism became the focus of dissent over a broad range of issues.[11]

Facing such a drastic reinterpretation of Indonesian environmentalism, Emil Salim adopted a quite conservative environmental tack to defend the regime's authority. This environmental backsliding can be observed most clearly by contrasting the Minister's attitude to Father Mangunwijaya's campaign against the eviction of the Code River bank inhabitants in Yogyakarta in 1986 (see also Eldridge, 1994: 225) and the later campaign waged by the priest in 1990 to defend the rights of the Kedungombo farmers to inhabit and cultivate the reservoir banks. In both instances, the point of dispute was the same, namely whether the conservation of these water bodies would be better guaranteed with, or without, poor villagers living on the banks. In 1986 Emil Salim accepted Mangunwijaya's arguments that the inhabited Code River banks were much better maintained by the slum dwellers, who took care of the riverbanks for the sake of their own survival. However, in 1991, although the priest, a German-trained architect, applied the same logic to the Kedungombo case, Emil Salim categorically opposed the use of the reservoir 'green belt' by the farmers, arguing that it might destroy the green belt's function to protect the reservoir's water.

What caused the reversal of Emil Salim's environmental rhetoric? Certainly protecting the reservoir was not the real issue. It was Indonesia's political climate that had changed drastically in the previous five years. In April 1986, Emil Salim's support for Mangunwijaya, which boosted the priest's popularity among student activists, was still tolerable to Suharto, since the Code River protest was mainly aimed at a municipal government agency. But in 1991, support for the priest's position on the reservoir's green belt could be interpreted as supporting the dissenting villagers whom Suharto himself had branded as communists. This would certainly not be tolerated by the aging president, since it could exacerbate tensions within the ruling elite.

ANTI-DAM STRUGGLES AND ENVIRONMENTAL POLITICS IN INDONESIA

What do these protest campaigns against Kedungombo and other large dam projects tell us about environmental politics in Indonesia?

First of all, in most cases the initial and the most enduring protests came from villagers who were to be directly affected by the construction of the dams and their associated facilities (e.g. reservoirs, waterways, and corridor roads). For instance, in the case of Kedungombo we see that after ten years (1985–95), the Sragen villagers marginalized by the dam's reservoir had not given up their struggle, which outlived the support they had received from the Central Java activists, national and international NGOs, and an association of

Islamic intellectuals. They eventually turned to another government-sponsored body, the National Human Rights Commission (Komnas HAM), but with little more likelihood of a positive outcome. In the case of Kotopanjang, only after 17 years' campaigning by themselves did the villagers finally receive support from students, human rights activists, and environmentalists in Indonesia and Japan. In only half of the cases recorded did urban-based university-trained activists support the protest campaigns of the local people affected by the large dam projects. The Kedungombo case was an exception rather than the rule, however, in that outsiders have consistently pushed the plight of the displaced villagers into national and international decision-making arenas; in most cases, nevertheless, the victims' grievances were never fully addressed by the relevant government agencies, even when the villagers were supported by outside groups.

The fact that the majority of cases where victims of large dam projects carried out their campaigns without support from members of the urban middle class were not successful in having their grievances addressed, is indicative of the class bias in the Indonesian political system. This is exacerbated by the 'floating mass' system, which prohibits non-ruling parties such as Partai Demokrasi Indonesia (PDI) and Partai Persatuan Pembangunan (PPP) from setting up branches below the district or municipality level. Apart from its class bias, Indonesian anti-dam struggles have brought the extra-parliamentary, patron-mediated, *ad hoc* and Java-centric nature of Indonesian politics to the fore. *Extra-parliamentary*, in the sense that the political forces outside the parliament, e.g. the students and the World Bank, seem to be given more serious consideration by the regime than factions within the parliament; *mediated*, because only extra-parliamentary struggles which have received wide publicity in the media seem to be taken seriously by the government; *ad hoc*, in that current national and international political constellations and considerations seem to be more important – for the government as well as the dissidents – than long-term considerations. In the case of Kedungombo, various *ad hoc* factors worked to the advantage of the displaced villagers, such as the apparent rift between Suharto and factions within the army, the consolidation of the student movement, and the international NGO campaign to make the World Bank more accountable. *Java-centrism* is evident when comparing Kedungombo with similar cases that occurred outside Java, where extra-parliamentary forces, especially the student movement and the media, are less powerful. The opposition against the Asahan dams in North Sumatra and the Bakaru dam in South Sulawesi (see Aditjondro, 1994c) did not receive as much attention as did analogous cases in Java.

By moving the decision-making battleground from the parliament to the streets and the media, and eventually to the bilateral and multilateral development finance agencies, such as the World Bank and Japan's Overseas Economic Cooperation Fund (OECF), the Kedungombo and other anti-large dam struggles may have inadvertently reinforced the New Order's unconstitutional practice of eroding parliamentary power.[12] The dependence of dam development victims on urban-based university-trained intellectuals has undoubtedly also exacerbated the *ad hoc* nature of the outcome of large dam controversies. For the outside activists involved, the victims' struggle is only one item on the agenda. Often, when other social problems are felt to be more urgent or strategic, such as the 1994 press bans, dam victims are again left to wage their campaigns alone – as they have had to do most of the time, without much success. [13]

The middle-class bias of the political system in Indonesia has also reinforced a dependency on specialists – in media campaigns, in lobbying governmental agencies, in environmental and social impact assessment, in hydraulic engineering and electric power generation. Whenever vested interests or cooption tactics tie them too closely to government agencies or corporate interests, or where their attention is committed elsewhere, the bargaining power of resistant groups is drastically reduced.

Dependency on the global expertocracy has become more visible in the anti-Kedungombo dam struggle, where the World Bank's headquarters in Washington, DC, became one of the major arenas for putting pressure on the Indonesian government. Likewise in the anti-Kotopanjang dam struggle, Indonesian and Japanese activists have cooperated to change the policy of the OECF in assessing the social impacts of the project and the compensation to be paid to displaced villagers. Without this assistance of specialists based in the global power centers, the large dam victims seemed to be powerless to change the policies of dam-building agencies. [14]

In other words, the history of anti-dam struggles in Indonesia is a history of reinforcing a global expertocracy instead of strengthening institutions of participatory and direct democracy. This dependency is characterized by a profound irony: the more Indonesia borrows from overseas development assistance agencies to finance its own economic development needs, the more Indonesians have to 'borrow' the services from democratic institutions in the host countries of those overseas financial agencies to obtain their rights to be consulted in this development process.

The over-dependency on development aid from Japan and the West carries with it another side effect: it postpones the urgency for Indonesia as the borrowing nation to democratize its own political system – to develop its own institutions of representative democracy, such as multiple political parties, free elections, and an independent press, as well as the institutions of direct democracy, such as referendums, public hearings, and public approval by local people to the establishing of large development projects in their backyards, all of which will eventually lead towards a government which is more accountable to its own people, not only to the citizens of the borrowing states. [15]

Owing to the *ad hoc* nature of the involvement of urban-based and university-trained activists in most of the anti-large dam struggles, the major dam-building agencies in Indonesia have been saved from the pressure to change fundamentally their own ways of dealing with the potential victims of their projects. Likewise, beyond some minor reforms within the World Bank, it and the main

Japanese financial underwriters of Indonesian large dams have also been saved from the need to reform their ways of carrying out business in a more fundamental manner, owing to the lack of a consistent and concerted opposition.

Finally, the Kedungombo case clearly indicates the inability of Indonesia's legal system to do much to help displaced victims of development projects. As we have seen, government intervention reconstituted the Supreme Court panel to ensure a favorable revision of its decision. This weakness of the legal system has also been observed in previous anti-dam struggles (Aditjondro and Kowalewski, 1994).[16] The lack of judicial independence is a systemic weakness affecting all contemporary struggles in Indonesia to obtain justice for people displaced by large development projects and other anti-democratic practices. Walhi, a major environmental umbrella organization, has tried to take up the concerns of the Amungme people in Irian Jaya whose river and alpine ecosystems have been degraded by the mining activities of the US Freeport McMoran subsidiary. Walhi took the Secretary General of the Mining Department to court for approving the environmental management and monitoring plans of Freeport,[17] in spite of proof that the US mining company had not seriously addressed its environmental problems. After nearly half a year of sitting in the Jakarta Administrative Court, the presiding judge turned down Walhi's request (*Forum Keadilan*, June 22, 1995: 64; *Sinar*, June 24, 1995: 26; *Republika*, October 31, 1995). Another instance is the case of the Sentani people in Irian Jaya versus the Indonesian state, which has taken over their land without any compensation. In this case, the Supreme Court canceled an earlier decision of an Irian Jayan court which ordered the governor to pay them Rp 18.6 billion (about US$9 million) compensation (*Jawa Pos*, April 26, 1995; *Forum Keadilan*, April 27, 1995; *Tiras*, May 11, 1995: 52).

It is quite rare for judges to favor local victims of development,[18] as happened when farmers from the district of Gorontalo, North Sulawesi, won their case against PT Naga Manis sugar cane plantation, and were eligible for Rp 1.6 billion (about US$0.8 million) compensation from the company (*Republika*, September 6, 1995). It remains to be seen whether the farmers will win their case after the well-connected plantation company has appealed to higher courts. All these cases show the systemic difficulties faced by displaced villagers when they attempt to force the government to address their grievances. Within the political system their problems are compounded by a class bias. Since the two existing non-ruling political parties – PDI and PPP – are not free to set up branches at the grass-roots level, villagers displaced by dams and other large development projects have to depend on urban-based intellectuals working as volunteers or in poorly funded NGOs to act as their intermediaries in the national and international arenas.

CONCLUSION

We have seen that large dams came to symbolize conflicting perceptions of social justice between the state and the anti-dam activists. Agents of the state

see large dams as symbols of justice in distributing the benefits of development among the provinces. On the other hand, dam victims and their defend-
ers point to the inequities involved in this redistribution of resources, namely
that some people's welfare had to be sacrificed – by unfair compensation,
removal from their homeland, and resettlement in a new and strange place –
for the benefit of others.

This contemporary history of anti-large dam struggles in Indonesia sheds
some light on the modes of environmentalism operating in a nation-state desperately trying to 'catch up' with the more industrialized world by alienating
the majority of the populace from the decision-making process while depending heavily on bilateral and multilateral sources of development finance. In
response to this socio-political configuration, a mode of activist environmentalism has emerged in Indonesia during recent decades, which has become
an alternative form of political opposition, closely linked with global environmental movements in the industrial world which in turn underwrites
Indonesia's economic development. In other words, the environmental
movement which has emerged in Indonesia is not ultimately embedded in
the immediate material interests of the people who were most directly – and
often most adversely – affected by large development projects, but is dependent instead on the abstracted ideal interests of the urban-based, middle-class
university-trained activists.

The representation of the dam victims' interests has been entrusted to a
small group of urban-based activists, whose commitment to anti-dam struggles is inevitably *ad hoc*, and to a global environmental lobby based in aid-
providing countries. The global environmentalists also necessarily have
shifting priorities, one day defending large dam victims, the next directing
their attention elsewhere. Therefore, it cannot be concluded from the high
national and international profile achieved by Indonesia's anti-large dam
struggles, especially the recent anti-Kedungombo case, that the movements
supporting the environment or the human rights of local people affected by
development projects have made great strides. Unfortunately, to date,
response to these popular struggles has been characterized by adhocracy and
expertocracy rather than democracy.[19]

NOTES

1 See Goldsmith and Hildyard, 1984.
2 The engineering journals studied were *Energi & Listrik, Indonesia Membangun,
Berita PU, Berita Dep. P.U. & T.*, and *Pekerjaan Umum*, published by the Indonesian Ministry (Department) of Public Works, which at a certain stage was also
the 'home' of the State Electric Power Company (PL); *Insinyur Indonesia*, the
journal of the Indonesian Engineers' Association (PII – Persatuan Insinyur
Indonesia), *Konstruksi*, an Indonesian civil engineering journal, and three international civil engineering journals, namely *Engineering News-Record, International Water Power & Dam Construction*, and *Asian Building & Construction*.
These journals, available in Cornell University's main and engineering libraries in
Ithaca, New York, were useful to understand the dam-builders' 'language' and

way of thinking, and provided background for my doctoral thesis research on the Kedungombo dam dispute. Since they are too numerous to refer to individually, in this chapter I refer only to pages from the thesis (Aditjondro, 1993a) instead of individual citations.

3 Once Sutami carried a young engineer on his shoulders after the young man finished building a hydropower dam on a river in West Sumatra without sophisticated heavy equipment.

4 In 1981, for instance, a monument was erected near the Gajah Mungkur dam in Central Java to commemorate the 13,000 families which had to move. Inscribed on the monument is a map with the names of the 51 inundated villages and the six workers who died during the construction of the dam. Inserted between the map and the lists was a brief text entitled '*Jer Basuki Mawa Beyo*,' signed by President Suharto on November 17. In that text, Suharto expressed hope that 'this sacrifice would not be in vain, and would instead bring blessings to those who had transmigrated, the people around the Wonogiri reservoir, and all the people of Indonesia.'

5 The 1967 Sempor dam disaster killed 127 people, destroyed 1,100 houses and a mosque in six villages as well as 800 m of railway and killed thousands of farm animals; six villagers who lived along the Serayu River banks drowned in 1986 when a high flood of 4,486 m^3 caused the Mrica's tailrace cofferdam owing to collapse due to overtopping and erosion of the rockfill. Besides the human victims, 15 bridges were washed away, 300 houses were submerged and among them seven were washed away (Aditjondro, 1993a: 48).

6 This perceived correlation between private capital investment and multipurpose dams is questionable. There were certainly other factors which attracted investors to West and East Java, such as the quality of the Tanjung Priok (Jakarta) and Tanjung Perak (Surabaya) harbours.

7 For instance, after Jatiluhur's inauguration in 1967, two French engineers are reported as claiming it to be 'the largest dam yet built in Southeast Asia,' while actually in 1964, before the 103 m high rockfilled Jatiluhur dam was completed, the Philippines was already operating its 129 m high Ambuklao and 128 m high Angat dams, and Thailand its 154 m high Bhumphol dam. In 1979, the 120 m high Wadaslintang dam in Central Java was portrayed as 'the highest dam in Southeast Asia,' while by that time Thailand was constructing its 140 m high Srinagarind dam. In 1987, the 125 m high concrete-surface Cirata dam in West Java was cast as 'the highest dam in Southeast Asia,' although at that time the 210 m high San Roque dam in the Philippines was also finished (see Aditjondro, 1993a: 52).

8 After the reservoir land was impounded, some former Boyolayar inhabitants took visitors for boat trips around the reservoir from the dam site in the neighboring district of Grobogan.

9 Committee for Solidarity with Victims of Development at Kedungombo.

10 See Aditjondro, 1993a: 34–36, 56–63; Stanley, 1994: 338 fn 80.

11 Yenny Damayanti, a former biology student and Kedungombo activist, once stated that her 'environmentalism' was a cover for her opposition to Suharto. Although the daughter of a retired military officer, she has remained consistent in her political stance. On December 14, 1991, she became one of the 21 members of the Indonesian Student Action Front (FAMI) who were detained and eventually tried for their part in the demonstration in front of the national parliament building, protesting against Suharto's reappointment as President and against human rights violations by the military. After release from jail, in April 1995 she allegedly took part in anti-Suharto demonstrations in Dresden, Germany (*Tiras* April 27, 1995: 13). Advised to delay returning to Indonesia, she obtained a scholarship to study at the Institute for Social Studies (ISS) in The Hague, Netherlands. She remained active in the pro-East Timor solidarity movement in Europe, and has recently had her passport revoked by the Indonesian Embassy in The Hague.

12 According to Article 23 of the Indonesian 1945 Constitution, for example, the power to make decisions on financial matters lies with the people, represented by the parliament, and not with the executive arm of government. This budgetary power has consistently been usurped by the executive under the New Order (see Aditjondro, 1993b, 1995; Pamungkas, 1995: viii–ix).

13 Through INFID (Indonesian NGO Forum on Indonesian Development), some Kedungombo activists have continued to lobby the World Bank on behalf of the dam victims. They have published their criticism of the Kedungombo dam in a joint report of the New York-based Lawyers' Committee for Human Rights and the Institute for Policy Research and Advocacy (Elsam), published simultaneously in English and in Indonesian in New York and Jakarta in 1995.

14 In the case of the campaign against the Sardar Sarvodar dam – or more popularly, the Narmada dam – in India, local resistance similarly depended on the intervention of international specialists which resulted in the Japanese government halting funding for the project. However, in 1993 the Indian government decided to go ahead, using its own public finances, to the detriment of tens of thousands of displaced villagers (personal communication from Ramachandra Guha, Indian scholar, journalist, and historian of the Indian environmental movement, in Berkeley, March 2, 1997).

15 I have elaborated this process in greater detail in Aditjondro, 1994a.

16 See, for instance, how unsuccessful lawsuits were in relation to the Riam Kanan dam (South Kalimantan), the Asahan project (North Sumatra), and the Bakaru dam (South Sulawesi), where the displaced villagers tried to use the court to demand fair compensation (see also Aditjondro, 1993a: 336–339, 343–345).

17 For more information on the Indonesian environmental impact regulations, see Warren and Elston, 1994.

18 In various other instances, local villagers also lost their cases on the legal battle-field. For instance, the case of the Batak women from Sugapa village in North Sumatra, who sued the large pulp and paper company PT Inti Indorayon Utama, was also rejected by the Supreme Court. Likewise, three Balinese farmers who sued the luxurious Bali Nirwana Resort in Bali lost their case in the Tabanan court (see Warren in this volume). Recently, an attempt by poor citizens of Kedoya Utara in West Jakarta to oppose eviction by their municipal government was turned down by the Jakarta administrative court (*Suara Pembaruan*, January 9, 1996).

19 I mean the term democracy in the Habermasian sense, where all affected parties participate equally in the decision-making process. In this regard, not only political impediments to full participation within authoritarian regimes like Indonesia, but also the disproportionate impact of vested economic interests in Western 'democracies' must be contested. According to Jürgen Habermas, as rephrased by social impact analysis specialist Thomas Dietz, 'A society is democratic if and only if all members of the society can participate equally in unconstrained discussions of political and policy issues. It is through this discussion that values come to bear on political and policy issues' (see Dietz, 1987: 58).

BIBLIOGRAPHY

Abdul Kadir (1990) *Energi: sumber daya, inovasi, tenaga listrik, potensi ekonomi.* Jakarta: Universitas Indonesia.

Aditjondro, G.J. (1990) 'Dampak sistemik dan kritik kultural yang terlupakan: suatu refleksi terhadap kampanye Kedung Ombo yang lalu,' *Kritis*, 4 (3), January, Salatiga: LPU-UKSW, pp. 44–52.

—— (1991) 'Aksi massa dan pendidikan masyarakat hanyalah dua aspek gerakan kaum terpelajar di Indonesia (Suatu tanggapan balik buat Arief Budiman),' *Kritis*, 5 (3), January, pp. 87–104.

—— (1993a) 'The media as development 'textbook': a case study on information distortion in the debate about the social impact of an Indonesian dam.' Unpublished Ph.D. thesis at Cornell University in Ithaca, USA.

—— (1993b) 'Lima dampak politis penting akibat pembangunan PLTN di semenanjung Muria,' *Gita Dharma*, 10 (34), April–June, Salatiga: Yayasan Motivator Indonesia, pp. 5–19.

—— (1994a) 'The democratization process as two "double-edged swords": rethinking the political agenda of the pro-democracy movement in Indonesia'. Paper presented at the regional seminar on 'Democratizing development in Asia: implications for theory construction,' organized by the Faculty of Political Science, Chulalongkorn University, and the International Political Science Association (IPSA)'s Research Committee on Rethinking Political Development at Chulalongkorn University, Bangkok, Thailand, August 17–19.

—— (1994b) 'Suatu kritik terhadap teori dan praktek analisa dampak lingkungan (ADL) bendungan-bendungan besar,' in Sangadji, Arianto (ed.), *Bendungan, rakyat, dan lingkungan: catatan kritis rencana pembangunan PLTA Danau Lindu*. Jakarta/Palu: Wahana Lingkungan Hidup Indonesia (Walhi) dan Yayasan Tanah Merdeka, pp. 25–58.

—— (1994c) 'Balada bendungan-bendungan raksasa di Indonesia.' Foreword to Stanley, *Seputar Kedungombo*. Jakarta: Elsam, pp. 17–37.

Aditjondro, G. and David Kowalewski (1994) 'Damning the dams in Indonesia: a test of competing perspectives,' *Asian Survey*, 34 (4), April, pp. 381–395.

—— (1995) *Indonesian protests against water projects: why some succeed and others fail*. Report No. 30. Social Sciences Research Working Paper Series. Alfred, NY: Division of Social Sciences, Alfred University. Paper prepared for annual meeting of the New York Conference on Asian Studies, SUNY-Buffalo, September.

Budiman, Arief (1990a) 'Gerakan mahasiswa dan LSM: ke arah sebuah reunifikasi (Catatan untuk GJA),' *Kritis*, 4 (3), January, pp. 53–59.

—— (1990b) 'Crisis of the state: globalization of civil societies in the making.' Paper presented at the Seventh Annual Conference of the Nordic Association for Southeast Asian Studies on Asian Societies in Comparative Perspective in Danland, Klintholm Hava, Mon, Denmark, September 30–October 3.

—— (1994) 'Kasus Kedung Ombo: sebuah catatan akhir.' Foreword to Stanley, *Seputar Kedungombo*. Jakarta: Elsam, pp. 3–8.

de Adelhart Toorop, Yvette (1990) 'Kedung Ombo door de Bank genomen: een verklarend onderzoek naar de gevolgen van het door de Wereldbank medegefinancierde Kedung Ombo dam en irrigatie project in Indonesia.' MA thesis at the University of Amsterdam, Amsterdam, the Netherlands.

Dietz, Thomas (1987) 'Theory and method in social impact assessment,' *Sociological Inquiry*, 57 (1), Winter, pp. 54–65.

Eldridge, Philip (1994) 'NGOs and the state in Indonesia,' in Arief Budiman (ed.), *State and Civil Society in Indonesia*. Monash Papers on Southeast Asia No. 22. Clayton, Victoria: Centre for Southeast Asian Studies, Monash University, pp. 503–536.

Goldsmith, Edward and Nicholas Hildyard (1984) *The Social and Environmental Effects of Large Dams*. San Francisco: Sierra Books.

Lawyers' Committee for Human Rights (1995) *In the Name of Development: Human Rights and the World Bank in Indonesia*. A Joint Report of the Lawyers' Committee for Human Rights and the Institute for Policy Research and Advocacy, New York and Jakarta.

Lucas, Anton (1992) 'Land disputes in Indonesia: some current perspectives,' *Indonesia*, No. 53, April, pp. 79–92.

Mehmet, Ozay (1994) 'Rent-seeking and gate-keeping in Indonesia: a cultural and economic analysis,' *Labour, Capital & Society*, 27 (1), April.

Muhaimin, Yahya (1995) 'Hubungan penguasa-pengusaha: dimensi politik ekonomi pengusaha klien di Indonesia,' *Kelola*, Gadjah Mada University Business Review, No. 10/IV, pp. 18–28.

Nishihara, Masashi (1993) *Sukarno, Rat Sari Dewi & Pampasan Perang: Hubungen Indonesia-Jepang, 1951–1966*. Jakarta: Grafiti.

Pakpahan, Mochtar (1990) *Menarik Pelajaran dari Kedungombo*. Jakarta: Forum Adil Sejahtera (FAS).

Pamungkas, Sri Bintang (1995) 'Menggugat absolutisme lembaga kepresidenan.' Foreword to Subhan, S.D., *Suksesi Presiden: rekaman aspirasi pinggiran*. Jakarta: Puspa Swara, pp. vii–xxv.

Pangaribuan, Robinson (1995) *The Indonesian State Secretariat 1945–1993*. Murdoch: Asia Research Centre on Social, Political and Economic Change, Murdoch University.

Sangaji, Arianto (ed.) (1994) *Bendungan, rakyat, dan lingkungan: catatan kritis rencana pembangunan PLTA Danau Lindu*. Jakarta/Palu: Walhi/Yayasan Tanah Merdeka.

Schmid, Thomas and Ernst Hoplitschek (1985) 'Auf dem Weg zur Volkspartei: Ökolibertäre Thesen zur Entwicklung der Demokratie,' in Wolfram Bickerich (ed.), *SPD und Grüne: Das neue Bündnis?*, Spiegel-Buch, pp. 78–79.

Seda, Francisia S.S.E. (1989) 'The politics of development: a case study of the Asahan project in North Sumatra (Indonesia).' Unpublished MA thesis at Cornell University, Ithaca, USA.

Sekretariat Kerjasama Pelestarian Hutan Indonesia [Joint Secretariat for Forest Protection in Indonesia] and Kesutuan Aksi Anti Pembangunan Lapangan Golf [Joint Action against Construction of Golf Courses] (1994) *Golf: anti people and ecologically unfriendly sport*. Jakarta: SKEPHI and KAAPLAG.

Soedibyo (1993) *Teknik Bendungan*. Jakarta: PT Pradnya Paramita.

Stanley (1994) *Seputar Kedungombo*. Jakarta: Elsam.

Sutadi, Graita (1982) 'Operation plan of the Wonogiri reservoir, Central Java, Indonesia.' Unpublished MSc thesis at the University of Arizona, USA.

Tirtosudarmo, Riwanto (1991) 'Mampukah LSM menjadi *counter-hegemonic movement*. Komentar atas tulisan George J. Aditjondro (GJA) dan Arief Budiman (AB) dalam *Kritis*, No. 3, Tahun V, 1990,' *Kritis*, 5 (3), January, pp. 105–108.

Warren, Carol and Kylie Elston (1994) *Environmental Regulation in Indonesia*. Asia Papers No. 3, Perth: University of Western Australia Press and the Asia Research Centre on Social, Political and Economic Change, Murdoch University.

Wirodono, Sunardian (1994) *Gerakan politik Indonesia: catatan 1993*. Jakarta: Puspa Swara.

3 Dams, resources and the politics of environment in mainland Southeast Asia[1]

Philip Hirsch

INTRODUCTION

Politicisation of the environment in Southeast Asia can be interpreted in a number of ways. Environmental politics are sometimes seen as part of the 'globalisation' that has drawn worldwide environmental concern, along with other ideological, social, political, and economic currents, into Southeast Asia. Thus, at one level, protest over large dams may be dismissed as imitative of the Franklin, James Bay, or Danube disputes. A parallel analysis has environmentalism in the Southeast Asian context, and the politics that go with it, as a natural outcome of the growing influence of the middle classes and their concerns over quality-of-life issues. Both these approaches, one externally oriented and one domestically driven, tend to be elite-focused.

An alternative approach is that of political ecology, which addresses environmental questions through a political–economic lens of state, capital, and social formation, which determines patterns of control over natural resources. Closely associated with this approach is environmentalism based on unequal distribution of costs and benefits associated with particular paths of development. Within the framework of environmentalism, focused on struggle over control of resources and social or spatial inequities in development, the politics of environment have crystallised most clearly around large-scale resource projects, particularly those that involve appropriation of the local resource base by interests of state, capital, and dominant social groups in the name of national development.

LARGE DAMS IN MAINLAND SOUTHEAST ASIA

Large dams are a case in point of appropriation of locally based resources (land, water, forests) in the name of national development. Materially, this is typically evident in the inundation of large areas of land and forest on national peripheries to provide power, irrigation benefits, and flood control to more or less distant cities and lowlands. Discursively, the justification of dams in the name of national development is an example of the prioritising of 'national' over local interest. In principle, compensation mechanisms alleviate the inequities involved. In practice, aspects of resource tenure and resettlement practice mitigate against effective reconstruction of livelihoods by or for those affected. Latterly, the concept of 'environmental compensation' has been mooted, whereby an area of natural forest, for example, is protected to 'replace' natural forest that is inundated. Typically this would be in the watershed area feeding into the dam, serving the additional purpose of protecting the project. Unfortunately, this may only serve to place additional pressure on people displaced who have little option but to relocate to areas surrounding or above the reservoir.

There is a litany of experience with large dams that points towards environmental degradation and marginalisation of affected people as general, if not universal, experience (Green 1981; Goldsmith and Hildyard 1984; Alvares and Billorey 1988; Cummings 1990). In response, the World Bank, which has financed many of the larger dams in Southeast Asia and elsewhere around the world, has developed new guidelines for compensation (Cernea 1988) and environmental 'mitigation' (Dixon *et al.* 1989), and, in a unique recent case, funded a study that ultimately led to the institution's withdrawal from the giant Narmada River scheme in India (Morse and Berger 1992; see also World Bank 1994). For some time, it appeared that the era of large dam construction was drawing to a close, as a combined result of the best sites having already been taken, the realisation that more comprehensive cost–benefit accounting would show dams in a less favourable light than hitherto, and the growing opposition to dam projects in numerous countries. However, recent proposals suggest that hydroelectric dams are back on the national development agendas of many countries, including those of Southeast Asia, notably in Indochina. The untapped potential of the Mekong and its tributaries provides a point of focus (cf. Sluiter 1992), but potential hydropower developments exist even further afield within mainland Southeast Asia.

In discussing dams, and indeed most large-scale resource projects, it is often difficult to separate environmental from social impacts. This is particularly the case in Southeast Asian societies whose people, despite rapid moves towards industrialisation, continue to live mainly in rural areas and depend in greater or lesser degree for their livelihood on their immediate physical environment. In this sense, any encroachment on forest, land, and water resources on which people depend is also a claim on their sustenance, hence the inseparability of social impact and environmental degradation. Social dislocation also has its own environmental consequences. Concomitantly, local material interests that are threatened are often most conveniently represented on a wider political stage through environmentalist discourse, which creates spaces not always available (or seen as legitimate) in straightforward claims over resources, tenure of which is often ambiguous, and over which challenges may be represented as subversive to the state itself.

THREE CASE STUDIES

This chapter examines resource competition and conflicts associated with dams in Thailand, Laos, and Vietnam. In each case, national and local issues of dam construction are considered, as is the interface between national and local politics of environment and resources. There are commonalities in the cases treated below, but also differences arising from specific local conditions and political–economic context. The political economy of environment is simultaneously a national and a local question, but it is also integral to the relationship between localities and their place in the national system of which they are a part. The question of what constitutes national interest versus local interest is itself an issue of contention, one that emerges clearly from the study of controversies associated with dams at community, watershed, national, and even international levels.[2]

National contexts

The question of what constitutes national interest is inherently complex, and it is further complicated by the political economy of control over resources in specific national contexts. Discourse on large resource projects commonly privileges national over 'parochial' local or sectoral interest, but a number of questions are hidden in this discourse of power. Does national equal state interest? Whose interests does the state in fact represent? In what sense is the national interest more than a sum of multiple local interests? These and other issues lie behind the conflict associated with dams and other large resource projects implemented in the name of 'national development'.

Thailand

Thailand has had an extensive programme of dam construction since the 1960s, when the 535 MW Bhumiphol Dam, still the country's largest, was completed with World Bank funding. In 1986 there were 25 dams exceeding 30 m in height and more than 80 over 15 m. Excluding international projects, the country's hydroelectric potential is estimated at 10,600 MW (Thailand Development Research Institute [TDRI] 1987). While the Royal Irrigation Department took early responsibility for dam construction and operation, more recently the Electricity Generating Authority of Thailand (EGAT) has assumed control over the larger structures. Dams became increasingly controversial during the 1970s and 1980s, culminating in the seminal dispute over, and ultimate cancellation of, the Nam Choan Dam in 1988 (Hirsch 1993: Chapter 10).

Dam construction in Thailand has largely been in response to the rapidly growing demand for energy that is part and parcel of the country's capitalist growth and industrialisation strategy. Irrigation has been an important but secondary consideration, particularly for the larger dams; most of Thailand's agriculture remains rain-fed. In several years of drought during the early 1990s, competing interests in the limited reserves of water in the country's dams have highlighted the low priority given to farmers' interests. A number of dam projects have aroused particular controversy in recent years, notably Nam Choan in western Thailand, Kaeng Seua Ten in the north, Kaeng Krung in the south, and the Pak Mul Dam in the northeast. Conflict associated with others, including the Tab Salao Dam (see Map 3.1 and pp. 60–62), has

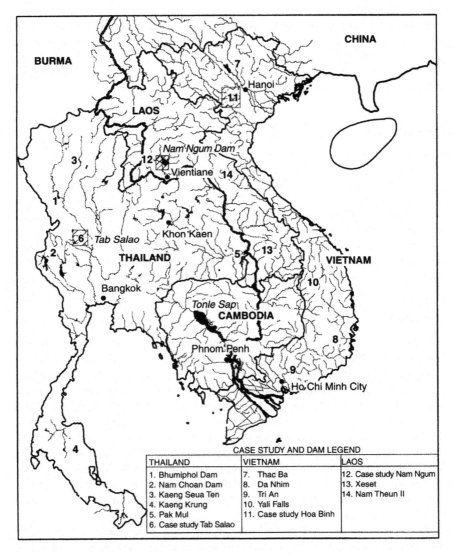

CASE STUDY AND DAM LEGEND		
THAILAND	VIETNAM	LAOS
1. Bhumiphol Dam	7. Thac Ba	12. Case study Nam Ngum
2. Nam Choan Dam	8. Da Nhim	13. Xeset
3. Kaeng Seua Ten	9. Tri An	14. Nam Theun II
4. Kaeng Krung	10. Yali Falls	
5. Pak Mul	11. Case study Hoa Binh	
6. Case study Tab Salao		

Map 3.1   Mainland Southeast Asia: three reservoirs of Tab Salao, Nam Ngum, Hoa Binh and dams mentioned in text

remained localised. In all cases, it is important to see dam issues in the wider context of competition for land, water, and forest resources, and as part of related conflicts such as those over forest reserve land.

Laos

Laos has only two dams of significance, the 150 MW Nam Ngum Dam (see Map 3.1) completed in 1971, and the more recently completed 40 MW Xeset Dam. Despite its modest capacity, the Nam Ngum Dam is highly significant in the national context of Laos as it provides a quarter of the country's foreign exchange earnings, through electricity exports to Thailand, and most of the country's own electrical energy. Moreover, there is currently an ambitious dam construction programme to make use of the estimated 17,000 MW hydroelectric potential of the country. Among imminent new projects is the Nam Theun II Dam, in which Australia's Transfield corporation has a major stake: this project has already become a significant environmental issue in Laos and further afield owing to its impact on the Nakay Plateau (Hirsch 1991). While there are many environmental concerns over dam projects in Laos, the politics of environment in the country remain more hidden within the bureaucracy. Local people have little direct input into national-level decision-making, so the conflicts and contradictions involved in dam projects remain somewhat latent. This makes the case of Nam Ngum Dam of special significance, since it is the only benchmark against which future impacts, and the politics they generate, might be measured.

The major force promoting dam construction in Laos is the opportunity to earn export income from its energy-hungry southern neighbour. With the collapse of the socialist bloc and the domestic economic reforms that have moved Lao PDR rapidly towards an externally oriented market economy, the need for foreign exchange and the opportunities for foreign investors to participate in large-scale resource development have multiplied. A significant aspect of this restructuring process is the promotion of large-scale private sector investment in build–operate–transfer schemes.

Vietnam

Vietnam is dependent for 45 per cent of its electricity on the 1920 MW Hoa Binh Dam (Map 3.1), situated 75 km west of Hanoi (see Hirsch *et al.* 1992). Three other dams also contribute to the grid, two of which were completed during the 1960s (Thac Ba in the north, now almost defunct, and Da Nhim in the south), while the more recently built 440 MW Tri An Dam, north of Ho Chi Minh City, is supposed to be a major source of power for the increasingly energy-deficient south. However, Tri An suffers chronic water shortages, and only with the completion of the controversial high-voltage north–south transmission line has the surplus currently generated at Hoa Binh, whose eighth and final 240 MW turbine was installed in early 1994, been made available to alleviate power shortages in the south. Ironically, this has contributed to renewed brownouts in Hanoi. As in the case of Laos, Vietnam has an ambitious programme of dam construction, including some highly contentious projects such as the Son La Dam upstream of Hoa Binh on the Black River (*Song Da*). Work commenced on the Yali Falls Dam in November 1993. The estimated hydropower potential in Vietnam is 18,000 MW. Considerable debate has been generated by dams in Vietnam, most notably Hoa Binh. While concern over dams tends to be expressed in non-confrontational ways when compared with Thailand, polarisation of stances is greater than in Laos.

Unlike in Laos, the main force for expansion of hydropower in Vietnam is domestic. Nevertheless, international considerations need to be taken into account, both in financing of dam construction and in providing the foreign investment and finance elsewhere in the economy to provide the economic growth that will create the continued expansion in demand for new sources of power. It is estimated that power demands will grow at between 10 and 18 per cent per annum for the rest of this decade. Vietnam's problems in dam construction are exacerbated by high population densities, which make resettlement a major issue in the larger projects. This is illustrated in the case of Hoa Binh, described below.

Local contexts

While dams have become an item of consideration and debate in the national political arena of all three countries, many of the real issues are most clearly evident locally and can be illustrated with reference to specific cases. The politics of environment as expressed in competition over resources is galvanised first and foremost within and between affected communities, and between local communities and wider claimants on resources. However, the ways in which resource competition and disputes are played out locally depends on aspects of local political ecology, ranging from land tenure arrangements, through structures of leadership, to specific features of natural and human ecology. The case of one dam in each of the three countries under consideration is outlined below. Each has been the subject of fieldwork by the author; in each case, the dam and its social and environmental impacts are described in brief, local responses are summarised, and key features of local ecology and political economy are identified.

Tab Salao

The Tab Salao Dam is a medium-sized irrigation dam in Uthaithani Province, western Thailand (see Hirsch 1989 for further detail). The dam was designed to irrigate a command area of up to 5000 hectares. Completed in 1988, the 18 sq. km reservoir (see Map 3.2) flooded several square kilometres of dry dipterocarp and mixed deciduous lowland forest, and it also inundated the

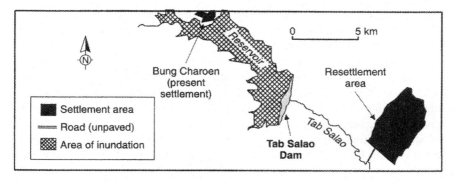

Map 3.2   Tab Salao Dam, Thailand

homes and agricultural lands of about 1500 people in five villages. None of these farmers had land title, since they were situated within a national forest reserve. Of those displaced, about one-third received compensation in the form of some removal costs and two hectares per family of agricultural land allocated in Phet Nam Pheung, a village 10 km downstream from the dam that was provided with an irrigation system to be supplied by the dam with the assistance of electric pumps. The remainder were ineligible for compensation, as they had arrived since the dam was first planned, or they had been missed by the 1981 survey in what was then a quite inaccessible area.

During the period 1985 to 1988, while the dam was being constructed, there was vehement resistance to resettlement. Although Phet Nam Pheung was *de jure* forest reserve land, it was *de facto* agricultural land, whose occupants regarded themselves as owners, the more so as they had been paying agricultural land taxes on the land for some years. Few were willing to give up land to newcomers from villages inundated by the reservoir. Moreover, those who had no right to compensation refused to move according to the timetable stipulated by the Royal Irrigation Department (RID) authorities and the District Office. Exhortations and threats were made by officials both at public meetings and to individual families. They were based, first, on the legal premise that villagers were illegally settled on forest reserve land, and second, on the moral assertion by officials that local people were selfishly obstructing a project with widespread benefits in order to pursue their own narrow interests. Petitions were drawn up by villagers, first to the District Office and later to the Prime Minister. Phet Nam Pheung villagers threatened RID machinery operators with violence, and confrontations resulted in a number of arrests for obstruction, including the Phet Nam Pheung village head. Villagers threatened with inundation without compensation took their grievance to Bangkok, with a demonstration outside the Prime Minister's official residence. Despite this, the issue was not taken up by the national press in a major way, perhaps because attention was diverted by many similar disputes occurring over forest reserve land elsewhere in the country, for example over eucalyptus planting in the northeast (Sanitsuda

1990). Since Thailand's regional press is limited to a few centres such as Chiang Mai (see Pholpoke in this volume), there was no other publicity outlet (cf. Warren in this volume).

Ultimately, once the dam was completed, most of the displaced villagers moved to areas on the reservoir edge and took up fishing in several communities, the largest being Bung Charoen. However, the fishery has proven unsustainable, particularly with the arrival of professional fisherfolk from elsewhere. Livelihood opportunities have been further constrained as a result of strictly enforced prohibitions on cropping by the Royal Forestry Department (RFD). Bung Charoen is due to be included in the buffer zone for Huai Kha Khaeng Wildlife Sanctuary (Hirsch 1995). A majority of those with rights to land in Phet Nam Pheung eventually negotiated with the previous owners to gain access to land, but for few families have the two hectares of infertile soil proven adequate, particularly as the irrigation system has failed to deliver water as promised.

The Tab Salao dispute was marked most prominently by the issue of land, and particularly forest reserve land. Although the dam inundated a type of forest environment that is now quite rare in Thailand, it was the ambiguous tenure of cleared and cultivated forest reserve land that underlay the acrimony between bureaucracy and villagers and between the different groups of villagers thrown together by the resettlement scheme. The issue was complicated further by competition and ambiguity *within* the bureaucracy, as several departments operated at cross-purposes: RID, RFD, the Lands Department, and the Agricultural Land Reform Office, which eventually took over administration of the Phet Nam Pheung lands and used the Chuan government's land reform programme to attempt land allocation in Bung Charoen among the remainder of those ousted.

The prominence of Huai Kha Khaeng following the widely publicised suicide of Sanctuary head Seub Nakhasathien in 1990 further encouraged RFD to clamp down on those trying to work agricultural land in the area. Seub's death prompted a national outcry over poaching by senior officials and villagers alike, which was thought to have contributed to the despondency of this committed environmentalist and government official. Diverse interests came together in a campaign on behalf of the sanctuary, establishing the Seub Nakhasathien Foundation (Hirsch 1993: Chapter 1). Together with the adjacent Thung Yai Naresuan Wildlife Sanctuary, Huai Kha Khaeng was shortly thereafter assigned World Heritage status based on a submission co-authored by Seub before his death. The result has been an official environmentalism that further legitimises imposition of restrictions on livelihood opportunities for those settled above Tab Salao Dam.

Nam Ngum

The 150 MW Nam Ngum Dam in Vientiane Province, Laos, was completed in 1971. The reservoir inundated about 450 sq. km of forested and agricultural land (see Map 3.3). Some 800 families lost their homes and land. The environmental and human impact of inundation was complicated by the fact that it took place during the wartime conflict, which meant that villagers had in many cases fled their homes before they were flooded, and in addition it was not possible to clear timber from the flooded area. Some of those displaced resettled at a designated site downstream of the dam, but many have settled on the reservoir edge and in valleys above the reservoir (Hirsch *et al.* 1994).

Namon village is a case in point. After fleeing into the forest in 1969, when their village was strafed and crops were sprayed with herbicides by US aircraft, lowland Lao from the village of Naasangha returned in 1974 and 1975 to settle, close to their inundated homes and rice-fields at Namon, on the limited area of land between the reservoir edge and steep slopes of surrounding mountains. No compensation has ever been received for the lost homes, livestock, fruit trees, and land. During the 1980s, an adjacent settle-

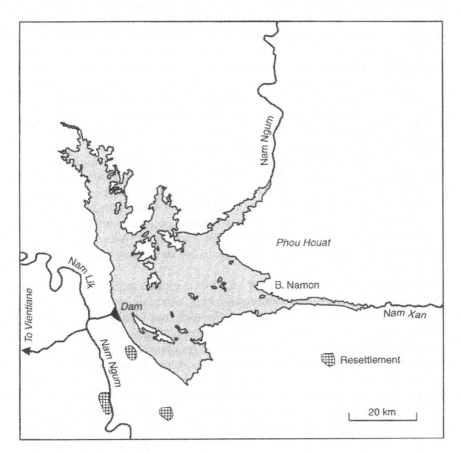

Map 3.3   Nam Ngum Reservoir, Laos

ment of Hmong farmers has been established at Huai Nhyaang, and this has created further problems with competition over limited areas of irrigable wet rice land and, more seriously, clearance of upper slopes for swiddens that has resulted in drying up of streams watering Namon rice-fields. The most recent threatened further encroachment of the resource base comes with an Asian Development Bank (ADB) funded project to divert the Nam Song and Nam Leuk Rivers into the Nam Ngum Reservoir. This will raise average water levels and inundate land currently used for wet rice cultivation and seasonal grazing.

For a number of reasons the local response to the dam has been quite muted, even though its impact was devastating for affected communities. The fact that it occurred more than two decades ago, at a time when there was little organised opposition to dams anywhere, not to speak of isolated communities in an isolated country facing much wider devastation under wartime conditions, means that there has been little opportunity for galvanised opposition or negotiation of compensation. The response of most has been to go quietly about rebuilding their livelihoods, just as have the approximately one-quarter of the Lao population whose homes and lands were devastated during the war between 1964 and 1973. Nevertheless, the impacts of the dam remain poignantly with those affected, in particular in the form of a much constrained resource base that is now facing new forms of competition and encroachment. Tension between Namon and surrounding Hmong communities is one expression of this, although it is a simmering rather than open conflict.

On occasion, more direct links are made between current hardship and the dam that contributes so much to the national purse. In 1991, villagers at the resettled village of Dan Sawan organised a written petition to the National Assembly asking that those who had sacrificed their livelihoods for the national interest receive some sort of compensation. The petition was returned several months later with a reprimand for those who had submitted it. In 1993 at a workshop in Vientiane, to discuss watershed issues among a range of 'stakeholders' in resource management in Nam Ngum Watershed, a Namon village leader expressed similar sentiments, but met with a stern rebuke from government officials present.

The politics of environment and resource competition in the case of Nam Ngum are thus governed by certain overriding extraneous conditions, notably the complications of the war and its aftermath, not least of which involved the change of regime in 1975. This at once removed the authorities from immediate responsibility for what had occurred previously, and brought in a socialist system of production and land tenure that militated further against attention to individual cases of dispossession. Other aspects of government policy have come to bear on the situation of Namon farmers, notably the resettlement policy that has brought upland cultivators into close proximity and direct competition for lowlanders' land, water, and forest resources. Recently, policy on land and forest allocation that is part of the government's partial decentralisation of resource management, including devolution of certain rights and responsibilities over land and forest, has opened up new challenges (Government of Lao PDR 1993). The open door policy has had a direct potential impact with the Nam Song/Nam Leuk scheme referred to above. Namon and other communities on the reservoir edge have not been considered in the impact assessments for these projects (Electricité de Laos 1992).

Hoa Binh

Constructed with Soviet assistance between 1979 and 1991, the 1920 MW Hoa Binh Dam in Vietnam is the largest dam in Southeast Asia. The 200 sq. km reservoir extends 230 km up the narrow Black River Valley through Hoa Binh Province and into Son La Province (see Map 3.4). The reservoir inundated the homes and rice-fields of between fifty and sixty thousand people, mainly from Muong and Thai ethnic minorities. Many others were affected indirectly, as were forests in areas surrounding the reservoir, as those displaced encroached on agricultural lands and forest resources in order to seek alternative livelihoods. Most of the steep slopes close to the reservoir edge have been cleared for cultivation, which is unsustainable in its present form. An example is the commune of Hien Luong in the heavily affected District of Da Bac in Hoa Binh Province. Two communities, Mai and Ngu, were too high to be directly affected, but the new resettlement community of Luong Phong and the displaced villages of Ke, Gioi, and Mo have all placed heavy pressure on surrounding forests in their struggle to make ends meet. Additional problems have been created, for example, as newcomers' livestock have strayed onto the fields of established villagers. Problems have been exacerbated somewhat with the shift to individualised family production whereas resettlement planning, to the extent it took place, assumed the cooperative model. This has created ambiguities over resource tenure. Impacts ultimately feed back to the reservoir itself, whose useful lifespan is estimated to have been reduced from 300 years to between 50 and 100 years as a result of soil erosion and consequently increased siltation.

As in the case of Laos, response by local people has been quiet adaptation to new conditions. To the extent that resistance has occurred it has ultimately been to the detriment of local people, for it took place mainly in the form of refusal to move to the levels stipulated by the authorities. In some cases, this simply resulted from refusal to believe that water levels would rise as high as they eventually did between 1983 and 1991, and it caused greater losses and heavier expenses for those who had to move several times. The response by others, for example the majority of families who initially resettled at Luong Phong, has been to move to New Economic Zones in the Central Highlands and the south, which for Muong people is quite a dramatic step. There is a great deal of latent anger, not so much at the dam itself, as at the way in which funds allocated for resettlement were wasted or corruptly used. However, on a day-to-day basis, villagers have mainly tried to protect their interests *vis-à-vis* neighbouring villages, for example by designating boundaries of forests

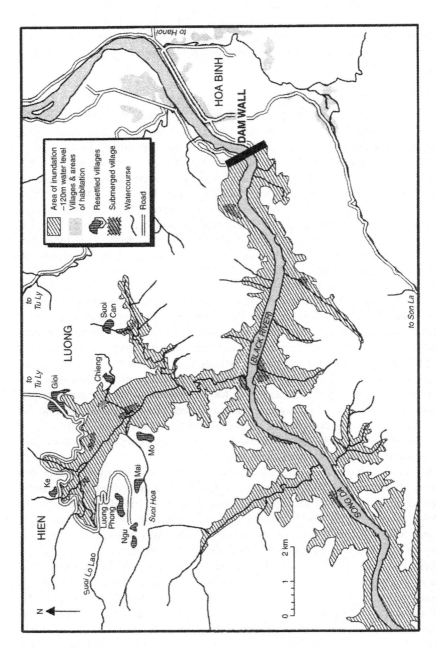

Map 3.4 Hoa Binh Reservoir, Vietnam

belonging to each community and, in more extreme cases, by the shooting of encroaching livestock from neighbouring villages.

The case of Hoa Binh is marked above all by its massive scale and the particular topography and ecology of the Black River Valley, but there are also specific aspects of Vietnam's changing rural political economy that need to be considered. Decollectivisation has complicated the adaptation process, but it has also provided new production opportunities in tandem with the emergence of markets. However, this case differs significantly from Nam Ngum in Laos in that there has been open criticism of the dam and its impacts in the print and television media, while there is a body of Vietnamese scientists who are quite critical or sceptical about the prospects for future large dams in light of the Hoa Binh experience. Another feature of the Hoa Binh experience that reflects on the political–economic context is the centralised, non-participatory form of resettlement administration that was part of the socialist planning framework.

DAMS, RESOURCES AND POLITICS OF ENVIRONMENT

The purpose of the comparative approach taken in this paper has been to examine the relevance of political–economic context in shaping resource competition and associated environmental disputes, and concomitantly to investigate the wider role of environment, environmentalism, and associated claims over resources in the respective emerging political economies. A few concluding comments attempt to bring together some of the lessons of dams in the three countries.

First, it is difficult and probably misleading to conceive of large dams as simply a question of trading off national versus local interests. The politics of environment surrounding dams are commonly played out in the national arena *as* politics between different interest groups and locally as competition and conflict over resources that have been constrained as a direct or indirect result of the dam. In neither case is there a clear or straightforward alignment of interests along the axis of local versus national interest. Those affected by Hoa Binh and Nam Ngum are morally aggrieved not so much at the loss of their resource, in the name of national development, as at the perceived one-sided nature of their sacrifice. The politics of damming played out at the national level in all three countries still tends to involve local people only to a minor degree, although in the case of Thailand it does involve NGOs acting on behalf of those who would be or have been affected.

A second set of implications from the three cases centres on the need to take account of background contexts of impact on the resource base and livelihoods. These issues are wider than straightforward inundation of villagers' lands considered by the state to be the eminent domain. In other words, the politics of damming involves more than a trade-off of resources between local people and national authorities. In Thailand, the forest reserve status of most marginal lands that are flooded effectively disenfranchises those affected, and state authorities are left to their own 'magnanimity', as they often see it, to compensate people for what the state considers is not rightfully theirs in the first place. In Laos and Vietnam, the status of all land and forest as state property, and the fluid situation of decollectivisation and land allocation, greatly complicate questions of compensation and resource tenure at individual and community levels. In the case of Laos, this has been further complicated by the war and its revolutionary aftermath, so that the regime representing the state that was responsible for construction of Nam Ngum Dam is deemed no longer to exist.

A third and notable aspect of environmental politics, interpreted in its broadest sense as exertion of moral or legal claim over resources by those whose livelihoods have been encroached by large-scale projects, is that conflict tends to emerge most forcefully at the local level between villages or villagers who have been brought into proximity and competition as a result of a constrained resource base resulting from the project. This is not to suggest that blame is myopically laid only at the doorstep of proximate rather than ultimate causes or culprits, but rather needs to be interpreted as a means of getting at the most accessible perceived threat to livelihood.[3] This is evident in the way in which resource competition between villagers from Tab Salao and Phet Nam Pheung, Namon and Huai Nhyaang, and Luong Phong, Mai and Ngu emerged as the most overt form of conflict associated with the three cases presented in this chapter.

Turning more directly to the way in which political–economic context shapes disputes, we need to consider aspects of political economy at the local as well as national level, and also the structures of political and economic power that determines relations *between* village and state. One of the more pertinent variables influencing environmental politics and large dams revolves around the political space open to local people and others to question or challenge decisions made 'in the national interest'. Clearly this is much further advanced in Thailand than in Laos or Vietnam, and there are concerns that this fact underlies EGAT's interest in pursuing hydropower development in neighbouring countries rather than within Thailand's borders. Integration of economies within the region and beyond is a powerful force in support of dam construction, and helps explain why Thailand, with experience of nearly three decades of export-oriented industrialisation, is further advanced in this respect; similarly, it also indicates why Laos and Vietnam only now find dams to be a major issue on their national economic and environmental agendas. More locally, individualisation of production in Laos and Vietnam, and increasingly capital-intensive production in Thailand, tend to complicate resettlement, while ambiguous resource tenure is a major issue in each case described in this chapter and one whose resolution depends on the playing out of local and wider political–economic interests in control and management of land, water, and forest resources.

Finally, the role of environment and environmentalism itself in shaping emerging political economies needs to be considered. In Thailand, interest in promoting regional integration within mainland Southeast Asia, an important part of the country's internationalisation, is closely associated with interests in neighbouring countries' energy, forest, water, and mineral resources. In some cases this has arisen owing to depletion within Thailand's borders, but in the case of dams, political limits to further construction set by the growth of environmentalism are also significant. In Laos, environmental concern is closely linked to historical suspicion and conservatism in dealing with Thailand, but also arises from awareness among policy-makers that the country is dependent on natural resources whose degradation would have severe economic and social implications. This concern has served as something of a brake on full-scale hydropower development, and it is also leading to substantive debate (mainly behind closed doors) on the merits of different development paths. In Vietnam, environment is high on the national policy agenda, but economic growth and industrialisation appear to be higher priorities, pointing toward an increasingly polarised situation with regard to projects such as large dams. In coming years, decision-making processes and outcomes of large dam projects in Vietnam will be an interesting indicator of the extent to which the plurality of interests, inherent in the country's move toward a diversified market economy, is reflected in open political discourse.

NOTES

1 This chapter draws on research carried out with funding from the Australian Research Council and the Asia Research Centre at Murdoch University.
2 This chapter pays relatively little attention to international questions; see Michael Mitchell's chapter 4 on Mekong Basin development.
3 Cf. Scott's (1985) account of Sungai Bujur in Malaysia, where Malay landlords were the target of peasant disquiet over impacts of the green revolution, not because the landlords were seen as the greater evil when compared, for example, with the ethnic Chinese syndicates of combine harvesters that were the real threat to livelihoods, but rather because it was these landlords over whom some social sanction was still available.

BIBLIOGRAPHY

Alvares, Claude and Ramesh Billorey (1988) *Damming the Narmada: India's Greatest Planned Environmental Disaster*, Penang, Third World Network/APPEN.
Cernea, Michael (1988) *Involuntary Resettlement in Development Projects: Policy Guidelines in World Bank Financed Projects*, Washington, DC, World Bank Technical Paper No. 80.
Cummings, Barbara (1990) *Dam the Rivers, Damn the People: Development and Resistance in Amazonian Brazil*, London, Earthscan.
Dixon, John, Lee M. Talbot, and Guy J.-M. Le Moigne (1989) *Dams and the Environment: Considerations in World Bank Projects*, Washington, DC, World Bank Technical Paper No. 110.
Electricité de Laos (1992) *Nam Song Diversion Project Feasibility Study: Environmental Impact Assessment*, prepared by Beca Worley International in association with Lahmeyer International.

Goldsmith, Edward and Nicholas Hildyard (1984) *Social and Environmental Effects of Large Dams*, San Francisco, Sierra Books.

Government of Lao PDR (1993) *Decree on Management and Use of Forest and Forest Land*, Prime Ministerial Decree 169, Vientiane, November 1993.

Green, Roger (1981) *Battle for the Franklin*, Sydney, Fontana.

Hirsch, Philip (1989) 'Settlement and Resettlement on Marginal Land: A Case Study from Thailand', *Australian Geographer*, 20(1) pp. 80–7.

Hirsch, Philip (1991) *Environmental and Social Implications of Nam Theun Dam, Laos*, Working Paper No. 5, Economic and Regional Restructuring Research Unit, Departments of Economics and Geography, University of Sydney.

Hirsch, Philip (1993) *Political Economy of Environment in Thailand*, Manila, Journal of Contemporary Asia Publishers.

Hirsch, Philip (1995) 'A State of Uncertainty: Political Economy of Community Resource Management at Tab Salao, Thailand', *Sojourn*, 10(2) pp. 172–97.

Hirsch, Philip with Bach Tan Sinh, Nguyen Nu Hoai Van, Do Thanh Huong, Nguyen Quoc Hung, Tran Ngoc Ngoan, Nguyen Viet Thinh and Vu Quyet Thanh (1992) *Social and Environmental Implications of Resource Development in Vietnam: The Case of Hoa Binh Reservoir*, Occasional Paper, Research Institute for Asia and the Pacific, University of Sydney.

Hirsch, Philip, Khamla Phanvilay and Kaneungnit Tubtim (1994) *Resource Management in Nam Ngum Watershed*, Report of Phase I study supported by International Development Research Centre, Department of Forestry and Environment, Ministry of Agriculture and Forestry, Vientiane, Lao PDR.

Morse, Bradford and Thomas Berger (1992) *Sardar Sarovar: The Report of the Independent Review*, Ottawa, Resource Futures International.

Sanitsuda Ekachai (1990) *Behind the Smile: Voices of the People of Thailand*, Bangkok, Thailand Development Support Committee.

Scott, James (1985) 'History According to Winners and Losers', in Andrew Turton and Shigeharu Tanabe, eds, *History and Peasant Consciousness in Southeast Asia*, Osaka, National Museum of Ethnography (Senri Ethnological Studies No. 13)

Sluiter, Liesbeth (1992) *The Mekong Currency*, Bangkok, Project for Ecological Recovery/TERRA.

TDRI [Thailand Development Research Institute] (1987) *Thailand Natural Resources Profile: Is the Resource Base for Thailand's Development Sustainable?* Bangkok, TDRI.

World Bank (1994) *Evaluation Results: A World Bank Operations and Evaluation Study*, Washington, DC, World Bank.

4 The political economy of Mekong Basin development

Michael Mitchell

INTRODUCTION

Since the late 1980s, there has been a revived interest in plans to develop the resources of the lower Mekong Basin. This renewed interest in the Mekong Scheme is evolving together with new geopolitical and economic dynamics operating between the nations of mainland Southeast Asia. The long-range vision of the scheme is a legacy of the 1960s, a period in which grandiose dam projects were in vogue. However, the scheme's revival follows an intervening increase in awareness about social and environmental consequences of building large dams. Meanwhile, sensitivity to greenhouse issues has encouraged a recent push by electrical generating authorities towards non-carbon dioxide emitting energy alternatives, such as hydropower. Conflicting social, environmental, economic, and political issues are therefore at play in discussing the implications of the Mekong Scheme development.

There are multiple scales at which influence on Mekong Basin development is brought to bear. Environmental consequences of development are manifest at local, regional, and global scales, and are rarely contained within national boundaries. Social effects also need to be analysed in terms of scale to avoid the simplistic and misleading rhetoric of 'local' versus 'national' interests. Contemporary social and political reality demonstrates the complexity of competing societal influences on development. For example, the commonality of local experiences of dam construction and development worldwide has become a major factor affecting international funding agencies considering loan requests from national development authorities. This has stimulated awareness of the need to promote local participation in the decision-making process regarding projects within the wider Mekong Scheme development. However, the desire to avoid confrontation over development proposals still on the drawing-board has hitherto led to inadequate local consultation, let alone local participation in the decision-making process. Consequently, the Mekong Scheme decision-making process remains 'top-down' in approach, and is centred on national and international bureaucracies well removed from the social bases and needs of the people living in the Mekong Basin.

This chapter interprets the political economy of lower Mekong Basin development with reference to interacting geographical scales of impact and influence. The chapter proceeds by introducing the Mekong Scheme and its key decision-makers. It then outlines key issues in the political economy of basin development and how they relate to scale. Finally, these issues are discussed in terms of major areas of conflict in the development of the lower Mekong Basin, exemplified by reference to key projects.

THE MEKONG SCHEME

The Mekong Scheme denotes a plan to develop the water and related resources of the lower Mekong Basin of mainland Southeast Asia (see Map 4.1). It is a plan first conceived in the late 1950s. The long-term goal of the basic plan centres on the Mekong Cascade, a series of dams to be constructed along the full length of the lower Mekong River (see Figure 4.1).

As yet, no dams have been built on the lower Mekong River mainstem itself, although the Man Wong Dam has been constructed by China on the upper Mekong. Many dams have, however, been completed along major tributaries of the lower Mekong, especially in Thailand. Nam Ngum Dam in Laos is the most internationally significant of the dams to have been constructed to date (see Map 4.2). Its international significance is primarily due to the fact that the bulk of the electricity generated is exported to Thailand.

As a geographical and ecological entity, the lower Mekong Basin area is quite distinct from the narrow valley which forms the Mekong River's upper reaches. The river in its upper reaches is fast-flowing and is predominantly snow-fed, whereas in its lower reaches, it changes to become more slow-moving and is predominantly fed by a highly seasonal tropical rainfall regime. Even so, about 18 per cent of the Mekong's annual flow originates from the upper river, and this contribution is still significant enough for concerns to be raised by Mekong Scheme planners about the effect of dams being constructed by China across the upper Mekong.

The concept of the lower Mekong Basin as a single geographical entity is also complicated by the fact that its area traverses several international boundaries. The lower Mekong Basin area covers most of Laos and Cambodia, as well as significant parts of Thailand and Vietnam. In the past, the importance of the lower basin area to these four riparian nations helped define the Mekong Scheme as an international project to be coordinated among them. However, the same area has since been subject to dramatic geopolitical change. Cold War conflict and divisions within the basin area severely interrupted the original programme of Mekong Scheme development as defined during the 1960s.

The issues of power and control in the comprehensive development of the resources of the lower Mekong Basin are thus not limited to nation states and local communities. Also integral to the politics of developing the Mekong are the international relations operating between the nation states which share the

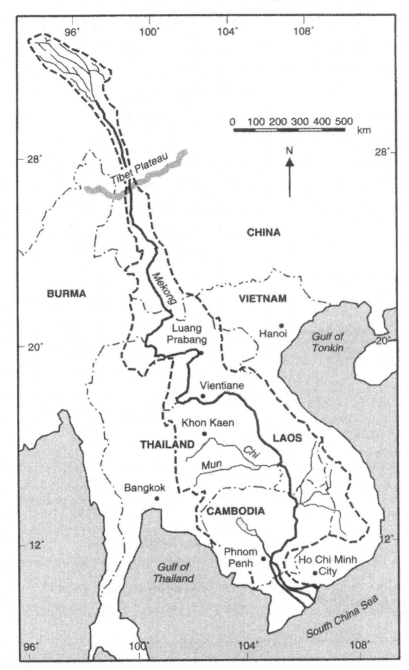

Map 4.1 Location of the Mekong Basin
Source: Pantulu, 1986, p. 697

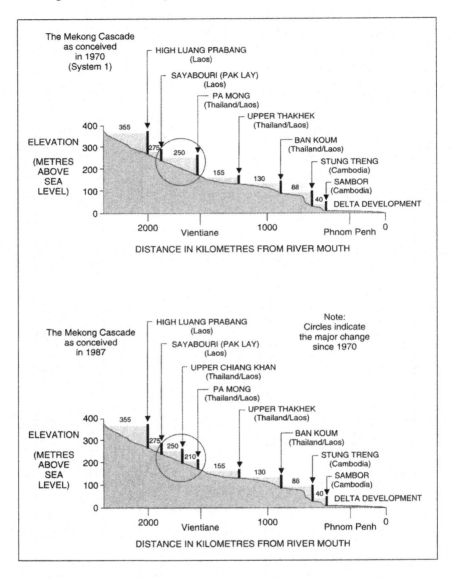

Figure 4.1   Lower Mekong River profile showing the Mekong Cascade as conceived in 1970 and 1987
Source: Interim Mekong Committee, 1988, p. 47 and Mekong Committee, 1970, Fig. V-12

resources of the basin. The Scheme's current development comes at a time when national development strategies are increasingly reliant on regional cooperation, especially when it comes to the use and development of mainland Southeast Asia's natural resources. Yet, at the same time, and because of the increased probability that major resource development projects in the

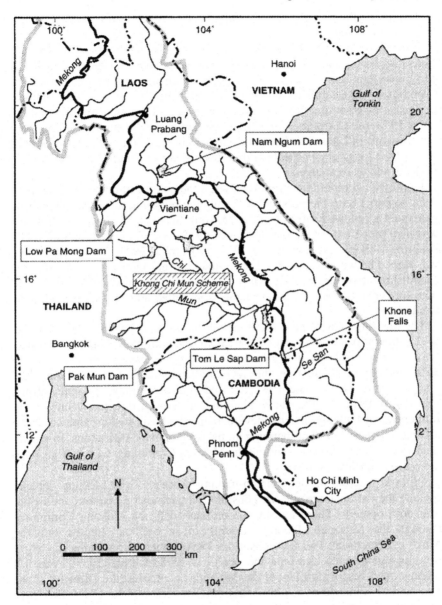

Map 4.2 Location of dams (proposed) in the Mekong Basin
Source: Interim Mekong Committee, 1988, p. 53

basin will proceed, negotiations between nations over how best to manage, use, and share the resources of the basin are fraught with potential diplomatic disasters. In particular, the issue of development in upstream nations and its effects in downstream nations has meant that the environmental consequences of developing the Mekong have become a major issue for discussion between the riparian nations.

The Mekong Committee has been responsible for making most major decisions concerning the Mekong Scheme, and especially the elements involving early investigations of basin-wide projects which are part of the Scheme. The Committee was established in 1957 under the auspices of the United Nations, to consist of government representatives from each member riparian nation. After 1978, the Committee functioned under an interim status, with only the governments of Laos, Thailand, and Vietnam participating. During the 1980s, most of the long-range aspects of the Mekong Scheme and its key basin-wide projects had to be shelved.

Increased economic integration between the nations of mainland Southeast Asia, together with the prospect of Cambodia rejoining the Committee, have generated a renewed interest in the Mekong Scheme. This renewed interest was also propelled by the production of the Revised Indicative Plan in 1987 (Interim Mekong Committee, 1988). In November 1994, a draft agreement was signed between Cambodia, Laos, Thailand, and Vietnam which led to the establishment of the Mekong River Commission in April 1995. This Commission replaces the original Mekong Committee and the Interim Mekong Committee.

The Mekong Secretariat is the Bangkok-based agency which manages day-to-day operations arising out of the Mekong Committee's decisions. It also plays a major role in developing the long-range aspects of the Mekong Scheme. As part of this role, the Secretariat provided most of the input and analysis which led to the 1987 Revised Indicative Plan. Its main efforts recently, in terms of long-range planning, have been directed at integrating influences on Mekong Scheme development at a basin-wide scale with those arising out of each of the riparian nations' development aspirations. In a practical sense, this involves providing the Mekong Committee with various project options for it to consider.

Other key actors in the decision-making process of the Mekong Scheme include the national agencies responsible for electrical generation and irrigation development. These agencies coordinate with the Mekong Committee through the National Mekong Committees as well as directly with the Mekong Secretariat. The United Nations Development Programme is a major funding agency and appoints the positions of Executive Agent, who has management responsibilities at the Mekong Secretariat, the Director of the Secretariat's Finance and Administration Division, and the Chief Executive Officer of the Mekong River Commission.

From a historical perspective, the current revival of the Mekong Scheme raises many important questions. During the 1960s, United States support for the Scheme was a vital element in its diplomatic efforts to induce acquiescence to United States hegemony across the region. While such diplomatic efforts necessarily focus on nation states, the promotion of a cooperative basin-wide development strategy between the riparian nation states over independent sovereign strategies also helped to engender regional cooperation as an integral element of Mekong Scheme development. The cultivation of a regional programme of resource development was also a feature of efforts by the United Nations, which are upheld to this day. However, the prospect of major infrastructural development on the Mekong and its tributaries will at the same time severely strain relations between riparian nations if this development is not carefully coordinated and managed.

A major factor in the current revival of the Mekong Scheme is the new regional integration being led by Thailand. It is also a factor which has a profound effect on the manner in which Mekong Basin development will proceed in future. After years of conflict and strained diplomatic relations between Thailand and its Indochinese neighbours, the nations are finding that it is in their mutual interests to integrate their development agendas. This has been particularly noticeable in the dependence by Laos on foreign exchange from Thailand through export of hydroelectricity and, more recently, in the construction of a bridge between Thailand and Laos which spans the Mekong near Vientiane.

The current revival of the Mekong Scheme has also come about at a time of major change in the influences on resource development generally. Since the Scheme's last period of major financial investment and development, led by the United States during the 1960s, environmental and social issues have received much greater attention by the media, the public, governments, non-governmental organisations (NGOs), financial institutions, as well as resource-planners and policy-makers themselves. The stresses from development on the environment, and on communities which depend on the environment, are fast becoming a major security concern. Arguments are being put forward that security provision based on nation states needs revision better to take into account the transnational character of ecosystems and ecological impact (Colby, 1990; Dalby, 1992).

Part and parcel of these changes is the growing forcefulness of local opposition to proposed Mekong Dam projects, which has penetrated into the national and international political arenas. In terms of power and control, the appropriation of the local resource base in the name of national as well as basin-wide development is occurring with limited consultation, and with no meaningful local participation in the resource development decisions being made. Consequently, a major issue which Mekong Scheme decision-makers will need to address is the current dearth of mechanisms to guarantee local participation in the decision-making process.

POLITICAL ECONOMY, SCALE, AND MEKONG ENVIRONMENTAL POLITICS

The current discussion of the politics of environment relating to the Mekong Scheme is founded on two intersecting interpretive frameworks. Firstly, it is necessary to view the issues of resource development and the environment from a political–economic perspective. That is, developing resources entails a decision-making process that is inherently political, and the institutional context within which this process is managed helps to determine the extent to which specific social, economic, and political interests have greater or lesser control, or influence, over the decisions made. A concomitant aspect of the political–economic approach is to assess the consequences of these decisions in terms of how certain sectors of society and economy benefit over others, by identifying uneven distributions of benefit and impact.

Secondly, these same political–economic issues need to be interpreted in relation to geographical scale. There is a set of geographical scales that form the basis upon which the issues of resource competition, conflict, and co-operation surrounding the Mekong Scheme need to be analysed. A simple scale framework is as follows:

1   global international scale;
2   regional or basin-wide international scale;
3   each riparian national scale; and
4   myriad local scales.

It is clear that developing such a major international river basin as the lower Mekong will have an impact not only on those people who live in the wake of the projects proposed, but on the social and economic development of all four riparian nations, and the way they relate to each other both economically and politically. It involves relationships with various external funding agencies which have their own impacts.

These are all issues which beg interpretation in terms of geographical scale affecting those who live in the wake of projects. 'Local' issues are then set against 'national' issues derivative of state-formulated development strategies, and those 'basin-wide' issues which derive from the compulsion of riparian nation states to cooperate in the development of the Mekong's resources. Finally, there are 'global' influences on development, being those which are imposed by international funding agencies, both multilateral and bilateral. Recent geopolitical changes in the Mekong Basin have brought about a shift from global to regional primacy.

Given the importance of scale in interpreting issues and influences of Mekong Basin development, it is vital that all the key political–economic issues, such as a just distribution of resources resulting from Mekong development, control over the decision-making process, and management of the development programme, as well as its social and environmental impact, are analysed in terms of how they are manifest at local, national, regional, and global scales, as well as the manner in which they are connected between each of these scales. It is also important to note that scale is already inherent in the discourse of political economy as applied to resource questions, for example when national interest is pitted against local resistance.

A practical agenda for research within this paradigm is to ensure that the process of marginalisation of local groups from decisions which are made about them be more fully understood (Mitchell, 1994). To achieve this, it is necessary to identify local influences on, and impacts of, development within a much broader and more complex structure of social and political influences at various other geographical scales (Howitt, 1993: 33).

When resource development issues are defined in terms of the influences on development in the context of a political debate over Mekong Scheme project proposals, it is too easy to perceive the debate in overly simplistic terms based on misconceptions with respect to scale. For example, it is misleading to view the politics of water resource development as a conflict between influences conventionally defined as (more important) 'national' interests and (less important) 'local' interests. Those resource development issues conventionally deemed as being 'local' concerns cannot be viewed any longer as far removed from the influences of 'global' concerns. The environmental politics of Mekong Basin development need to be interpreted in terms of an understanding of scale that more accurately reflects the contemporary social and political context in which they are situated.

To facilitate this reinterpretation of the political economy of Mekong Basin development through the lens of environmental and resource politics, the rest of this chapter is structured according to the major areas of conflict within the decision-making process related to scale. The first and most obvious area of conflict, which is under constant review and examination by those who plan the Mekong Scheme, is that between the Mekong Scheme as a basin-wide project, and as a scheme defined more by the sovereign interests of each individual nation. The second area of conflict is that between the regional and national interests just mentioned, and those emanating from the myriad local communities affected by the proposed resource development projects which are part of the Scheme. With a more accurate understanding of these two areas of conflict, and the relations between them, the final section reinterprets the influences on Mekong Basin development with respect to all four scales. It concludes that incorporating 'local' scale concerns into the decision-making process is imperative for the long-term interests of the Mekong Scheme.

BASIN-WIDE AND NATIONAL INFLUENCES ON MEKONG BASIN DEVELOPMENT

> Ideas for [projects that require basin-wide cooperation] usually come from the Mekong Secretariat as it has better knowledge [than individual nations] of the basin as a whole. Individual nations are more focused on their own needs, and may not look beyond these. The Mekong Secretariat has a special role in this regard, as there is no other organisation that could effectively initiate basin-wide projects.
>
> (Nguyen Duc Lien, Senior Project Officer in Water Resources and Hydropower Unit, Mekong Secretariat, interview, 30 April 1992)

The role of the Mekong Secretariat as an institution able to guide the long-term agenda of the Mekong Scheme is constrained by the political environment within which it functions. This has been especially felt by the Secretariat as a consequence of its efforts to integrate the Basin plan as a single unit with each nation's particular development strategy. Basin-wide influences on development are not necessarily in conflict with national influences, but there is still a great potential for conflicts to arise. The Secretariat emphasises its special role in promoting projects which are based on the need for basin-wide cooperation between riparian nations. By extension, the Secretariat must concern itself with projects being planned by national governments which would undermine the cooperative approach to basin development.

However, events in 1992 suggest the limits of regional priority, particularly in Thailand. Chuck Lankester, the Executive Agent at the time, suddenly found himself being forced to leave Thailand at short notice after being too assertive in his dealings with the Thai government over its controversial Khong-Chi-Mun River Basin diversion proposal. The proposed project, which had already been approved by the Thai government, involves the diversion of water from the Mekong River near Nong Khai for irrigation use along the Chi and Mun river system in northeast Thailand, from which the water would be allowed back into the Mekong River at its confluence with the Mun River. There is understandable concern about the project's effects on water quality and quantity downstream in Cambodia and Vietnam, and the Secretariat had for some time sought more information about the proposal from the Thai agency involved.

In March 1992, Lankester approached the Thai government to seek clarification about whether any funding had been committed to the project. Shortly after Lankester was assured that no funding had been allocated, unnamed Thai government officials were reported in the *Bangkok Post* newspaper (8 March 1992) as believing that the Mekong executive agent not only was 'too powerful', but was 'inciting Vietnam to object to the project'. Lankester responded by sending a strongly worded fax to correct what he believed were misconceptions. The Foreign Ministry of Thailand responded to this by telling him that he was no longer welcome to work in the country, effectively forcing him to resign from his position with the Secretariat.

Lankester's forced resignation came at a time of considerable uncertainty about the future direction of the Mekong Committee and its Secretariat, a period which had also been spearheaded by the actions of the Thai government. In February that year, Thailand had, at the last minute, postponed indefinitely a meeting in which the reinstatement of the full Mekong Committee had been planned. Thailand's concern was that this may also lead to the reinstatement of the 1975 *Joint Declaration of Principles for Utilisation of the Waters of the Lower Mekong Basin* (Mekong Committee, 1975), which incorporates the right of veto over any proposed project by any member nation. This has remained a delicate issue throughout the process leading to the signing of the joint statement in 1994 that laid the basis for future cooperation for Mekong Basin development and the establishment of the Mekong River Commission.

These events need to be observed in the context of the changing geopolitical and economic relations between Thailand and its neighbours, which have brought about an improvement in trade and diplomatic relations. The strongest proponent for improving regional relations has been the Thai government. As an industrialising nation in the throes of rapid economic growth, Thailand is well placed to take advantage of the opening up of the Indochinese nations to foreign investment. Moreover, Thailand is increasingly looking to its neighbours for natural resources, including timber, gas, gems, and hydropower (Hirsch, 1992).

Against this background of internationalisation in the resource economy of the basin area there is also an internationalisation of the environmental agenda (Hirsch, 1993). That is, in the face of growing opposition to dams within Thailand, it is becoming politically easier for its government to pursue dam construction beyond the country's borders, couched in the rhetoric of helping to create a regional marketplace. Differences between the nations of mainland Southeast Asia, in the freedom with which their civil societies and non-governmental organisations can oppose state-sanctioned development programmes, exacerbate this tendency by Thailand to export to its neighbours those elements of its development programme that are socially and environmentally disruptive to local communities. While Thailand has the most to gain from improved relations and from an increased development of the basin's resources, as an upstream nation its water resource projects are more likely to create international dispute.

Even if basin development can be built on a cooperative approach between these riparian nations, there are major difficulties in the actual process of integrating national requirements for water resource development within a coordinated basin-wide plan. One of the most complex issues is that of how upstream projects might alternatively exacerbate or assist in the alleviation of problems in the Mekong Delta of Vietnam. For the people in the delta, water quantity and quality are of paramount concern. If any upstream development proposal has the potential to reduce dry-season water quantities downstream, then it has been suggested that water levels would need to be maintained from some other source, such as from a major tributary dam like those proposed for construction in Laos. This implies multilateral cooperation and coordination not only in project development, but also in the day-to-day management of water releases.

The Mekong Scheme is built on the concept of multi-purpose development. A fundamental element of this is to be able to use the water stored behind dams for different purposes, including hydropower generation, irrigation supply, navigation, and fisheries improvement, as well as to reduce damage from salinity intrusion in the delta area and from floods. However, the concept of servicing several different needs through one dam project is not as promising as it may appear, as indicated by the experience of dam developments across the Asian region:

> The perceived multi-purpose nature of dams, which are seen as supporting hydroelectric and irrigation projects, is largely illusory, since these two functions are competitive rather than complementary. Timing of release of irrigation water is as important as volume, and the demands of electricity consumers are not the same as those of farmers. Since large dams are generally controlled by electricity-generation authorities rather than by irrigation departments, it is the needs of the largely urban, industrial-energy consumers rather than those of rural agriculturalists that take precedence.
>
> (Hirsch, 1988, p. 3)

In discussing these issues during an interview with the author, the Director of the Resources Division at the Mekong Secretariat, Do Hong Phan, expressed the belief that 'all conflicts could be solved with integrated planning'. How this integration would be achieved in the future was still 'under consideration'. Staff at the Planning and Policy Division suggest that the role of the Mekong Secretariat is potentially very important in the operation of the system of Mekong reservoirs for different purposes. However, both the Mekong Committee and the Mekong Secretariat only deal with decisions in the early investigative stages of proposed projects, and it is unlikely that the Secretariat would be given any responsibility in coordinating and managing the shared use of water in the basin. More importantly, it indicates that the problem of how to manage the coordination of planned multi-purpose development in the Mekong Basin is far from resolved, and it has not kept pace with the planning of individual projects.

These conflicts, both over proposed projects, and over how water use would be managed in a multi-purpose river basin scheme, have clearly become a delicate international relations concern within the basin. Of course, in many other parts of the world, conflicts have arisen over the shared use of water resources between nations; for example, between India and Pakistan (Mehta, 1988), the United States and Mexico (Worster, 1986, p. 22), Slovakia and Hungary (*Sydney Morning Herald*, 9 November 1992, p. 12), and potentially between Turkey and Iraq (Roberts, 1991), as well as a host of other neighbouring countries which share a common river. Transnational environmental effects of river basin development have also become a security issue between nations (cf. Linnerooth, 1990).

Indeed, because environmental politics are transnational, the issue has also contributed to a recognition that the concept of security *per se* needs to be rethought. Dalby (1992) argues that the dominant Cold War approach to security, which focused on nation states as the sole agents in security provision, downplays internal political factors, notably elements of civil society, as well as complicating transboundary environmental management. He notes that 'the predominant geopolitical understanding of security focused on the spatial limitations of Soviet political control'. In this regard, he makes the observation that 'what was being rendered "secure" by the spatial exclusion of Soviet influence was an energy and resource consuming industrial capitalist model of "development" and a political system based on territorial states' (Dalby, 1992, p. 505).

The contemporary world of politics undermines many of the assumptions upon which these Cold War approaches to security are based. Aside from the demise of the Cold War, and the fact that environmental effects are not contained within national boundaries, there is also the growing political reality that non-governmental organisations are playing a much more influential role in international discussions, particularly in relation to environmental issues, where the most important political factors are often 'local citizens' groups, social movements, international environmental organisations, global corporations or the social arrangements of land tenure' (Dalby, 1992, p. 517). These new geopolitical and eco-political contexts help explain the importance of 'local' influences on Mekong Basin development, and lead to questions of how these influences are viewed by different actors as being distinct from and in conflict with 'national' and 'basin-wide' influences on development.

LOCAL INFLUENCES ON MEKONG BASIN DEVELOPMENT

The nature of the Mekong Scheme decision-making process, which now centres on the Mekong River Commission, leads to a focus on basin-wide integration versus individual national development aspirations in the debate over development issues. In the process, it downgrades concern for issues emanating from local community interests, which are perceived as parochial. This placement of 'national' above 'local' interests is evident in the way some Mekong Scheme planners approach the question of resettlement:

> [The local people] will accept having to move if compensation is reasonably defined, while clear explanations are given to them concerning the water resources development at the basin-wide and/or national levels.
>
> (Do Hong Phan, Director of Resources Development Division,
> Mekong Secretariat, interview, 27 April 1992)

Such a statement suggests that resettlement is viewed as an issue of local interest that is intrinsically less significant in the face of more important 'national' or 'basin-wide' interests, and that its mere explanation would somehow rationalise away the grievances of the local community. However, 'local' opposition by those facing resettlement is not peripheral to the development of the Mekong Scheme. Indeed, such concerns have penetrated the national and international political agendas concerning Mekong Basin development.

Local influences have unequivocally affected wider environmental politics in Thailand. Part of the vocal and politicised response to resettlement in Thailand is clearly due to the fact that the government has built many more dams than have neighbouring countries. However, there are also different opportunities in Thailand, and its neighbours, for local communities to oppose state-sanctioned development programmes. These opportunities include greater freedom to criticise and demonstrate, less state control of the press, and some support from Thailand's growing and increasingly environmentally conscious middle class, as well as frequent interaction with international environmental NGOs. Combined with a strong grass-roots livelihood basis for environmental activism (Hirsch, 1994), these influences have greatly strengthened the environmental movement in Thailand.

Not only have local influences affected national and international environmental politics, but, most noticeably with the example of resettlement, these influences have also profoundly affected the development of the Mekong Scheme as a whole. A comparison of the core elements of the 1970 Indicative Basin Plan (Mekong Committee, 1970) and the 1987 Revised Indicative Plan (Interim Mekong Committee, 1988) illustrates this point. The core element in each of these plans, the Mekong Cascade concept, remains substantially unchanged (see Figure 4.1). The only significant alteration is the lowering of the original Pa Mong Dam, at 250 m above sea level, to a reduced Low Pa Mong option at 210 m above sea level. It had 'become clear that the Pa Mong Scheme as proposed [in the 1970 plan was] no longer tenable because of the need to resettle upwards of 250,000 people' (Interim Mekong Committee, 1988: XV). That is, the political consequences of such massive resettlement would not only far outweigh the benefits of the project, but also make it an unacceptable liability for funding agencies concerned with their international public image.

Because large reservoirs so often give rise to a massive upheaval of the population from the area to be inundated, they can create fierce opposition and significant national insurrection. For example, in the case of the Kariba Dam, dispossession of the local people in the 1960s was a major contributing factor in the civil opposition to the colonial administration of Northern Rhodesia, thereby bringing about its downfall, and the breakup of the Federation of Rhodesia and Nyasaland (Scudder and Colson, 1972, p. 45). This kind of pressure against unwelcome, socially disruptive development programmes is still very real, despite there being more money now allocated to improving resettlement programmes. It is likely that, in mainland Southeast Asia, this pressure will increase through the continued resilient efforts of affected communities, non-governmental organisations, and supportive journalists, the more so as civil society strengthens throughout the region. In part, as a result, there has been a clear movement recently by Mekong Secretariat planners towards investigating projects which are smaller and less ambitious than those conceived in the 1960s.

Another issue which could be thought of as 'local' is the effect of dams on forest cover. This may easily be seen in isolation as a marginal issue about a few trees. However, the cumulative effect of environmental destruction in a number of localities, particularly when multiplied by flow-on effects that lead to forest destruction well beyond reservoir edges, ultimately becomes significant at much larger scales, in terms of the effect of deforestation on regional hydrological cycles and on global warming (Brookfield, 1992). Thus, it was partly a growing concern for global biodiversity protection, as well as the strength of local opposition, that led to a decision to abandon the proposed Nam Choan Dam in western Thailand in 1988 (Hirsch and Lohmann, 1989).

Frequently, when debate focuses on particular dams, there is clearly a tendency to view all these issues as local and therefore parochial. Moreover, it is normally the case that proponents of dams have a near-monopoly of information relating to the dam, and a major element of local dissatisfaction centres on there being inadequate consultation, let alone participation, in decisions made about the dam. However, the local experiences of affected community groups can no longer be seen in isolation. The commonality of these kinds of experiences is finally being recognised the world over, and is becoming a major factor affecting international funding agencies in their approval of loans requested by national development agencies. It is also affecting development of the Mekong Scheme. These so-called 'local' issues have become 'global' issues which can no longer be easily ignored.

SCALE, INFLUENCE, AND THE POLITICS OF ENVIRONMENT

A political–economic approach to decision-making is to view it as rooted in, and controlled by, socio-economic structures which 'deprive the poor of both effective demand and political influence' (Emel and Peet, 1989, p. 53). It is easy, when reformulating this idea in terms of geographical scale, to treat local influences on development policy as subordinate and opposed to influences derived at a national or international scale. However, such a formulation is misleading. In the contemporary social and political context of Southeast Asia, each time a dam is proposed, the 'local' issue of resettlement becomes a crucial factor in discussions at the national and international level. Bilateral and multilateral aid and lending institutions are bearing down upon national development agencies to stipulate that they attend more closely to the social and environmental consequences of resource development projects, such as dams. It is also increasingly the case that local community groups, through non-governmental organisations seeking to serve as the advocates of 'local' interests, or even by the efforts of local groups alone, have been able more readily to reach the national and international audience. The case of the controversy surrounding the Pak Mun Dam in northeast Thailand is a case in point.

The investigations for Pak Mun Dam, located near the point where the Mun River reaches the Mekong River in eastern Thailand (Map 4.2), were initiated by the Mekong Committee during the 1960s, but were then taken over by the Electrical Generating Authority of Thailand. Local opposition to the project, including local dissatisfaction over the consultation process generally, received substantial media coverage in Thailand prior to the meeting of the World Bank in Bangkok in 1991. At the time of the meeting, the World Bank was delaying a decision over whether to provide funds for the project's implementation. At a forum for international non-governmental organisations running parallel to the World Bank meeting, Pak Mun Dam received considerable attention. The local people were able to highlight their case as part of the international debate between non-governmental organisations and the World Bank over the latter's development policies. Indeed, they were able to demonstrate that their 'local' concerns were actually part of an international experience whereby local communities are denied participation in the decision-making processes which so profoundly affect their livelihoods. While the World Bank later decided to approve the loan (though with opposition from three of the Bank's executive directors), part of the rationale for that decision, as stated by the Bank's Japanese director, was that 'blocking this project would give non-governmental organisations momentum to prevent much needed dam projects in the Mekong Basin' (*The Nation*, 19 January 1992, p. B3).

The examples above illustrate not only the incorporation of the 'local', and perceivably marginalised, agenda into the wider agenda of those who actually make the decisions, but also an inherent problem associated with the so-called 'rational' approach to decision-making. Such an approach assumes the certainty of expert opinion as a basis for decisions, whereas real-world options more often reflect political interests. In addition, decisions are made in the 'public interest', without acknowledging a diversity of public opinion or, in many cases, without even consulting the public at all (Abs, 1988). The latter point can be further illustrated with reference to the Low Pa Mong proposal.

The Mekong Secretariat's preferred option is to build Low Pa Mong Dam at its originally proposed location, but with a crest height revised downwards from 250 m to 207.5 m above sea level, as detailed in a publicly available briefing report (Mekong Secretariat, 1991). However, the Mekong Secretariat has chosen not to make public the existence of an alternative option suggested by the consultants to locate the dam further upstream, 'if the number of persons to be displaced [by the dam] is a paramount issue' (ACRES International, 1992, pp. 108 and 110; see Map 4.3). As discussed above, resettlement *is* seen as a paramount issue, not only internal to Thai politics (it was Thailand's proposal that the consultants look into relocating the dam upstream [Nguyen Duc Lien, Senior Project Officer in Water Resources and Hydropower Unit and Project Officer for Pa Mong, Mekong Secretariat, interview, 30 April 1992]), but for potential funding agencies as well: Erik Skoglund, former Chief of the Mekong Secretariat's Environment Unit, is quoted as suggesting that 'no donor in the world will allocate funds for Pa Mong with this [resettlement] problem' (Hiebert, 1991, p. 25).

The political influences surrounding Mekong Scheme development paint a complex picture, especially when they are depicted with relation to geographical scale. If the politics of environment relating to Mekong Scheme development are viewed as a trade-off between issues at different scales, then

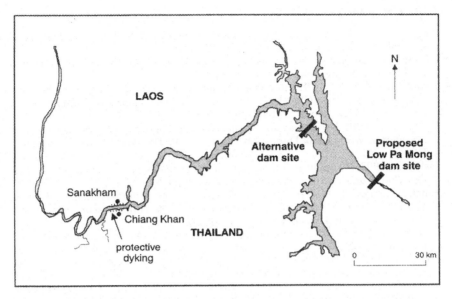

Map 4.3 Low Pa Mong Reservoir at 207.5 m above sea level, showing two
alternative dam sites
Source: ACRES International Ltd, 1992, Plate 6

national and/or basin-wide issues are given greater weight by those who actually make the decisions. In the minds of the decision-makers, 'local' issues
are frequently given less weight in the trade-off equation. However, 'local'
people in the basin area, mainly small farmers, actually constitute a majority
of the basin's population. As a consequence of 'local' issues being seen as
less important in the overall scheme of things, it is also the case that the
'local' people suffer disproportionately from the many environmental and
social problems that outweigh benefits they might acquire from the scheme.
In comparison, the benefits from hydropower generation, which flow disproportionately to Bangkok-based consumers and industrialists, are mainly
reaped by those who live at considerable distance from the immediate social
and environmental impacts. Taking this perspective, one could argue that the
basin-wide interests (of much of its population) are being superseded by the
'local' interests of a few rich individuals.

In conclusion, when clarifying social and political influences in terms of
geographical scale, there is a danger of over-simplification and conflation of
terms. 'Local' issues are not necessarily subordinate to 'national' or 'international' issues in the politics of decision-making. Rather, the discourse of what
is 'local interest' (by implication parochial) and what is 'national interest' (by
implication public good) is itself part of the politics of legitimation that reflect
dominant power structures. In the interest of more rational and equitable
decision-making, it behoves policy-makers to pay more attention to involving
affected people at all levels in the decision-making process.

BIBLIOGRAPHY

Abs, S.L. (1988) 'The Limits of "Rational" Planning: A Study of the Politics of Coastal Extraction' in *Geoforum*, 19, pp. 227–244.

ACRES International (1992) *Report on Low Pa Mong Optimisation Study*, prepared for Interim Mekong Committee, February 1992.

Brookfield, H. (1992) '"Environmental Colonialism", Tropical Deforestation, and Concerns Other Than Global Warming' in *Global Environmental Change: Human and Policy Dimensions*, 2: 2, June, pp. 93–96.

Colby, M. (1990) *Environmental Management in Development: The Evolution of Paradigms*, World Bank Discussion Paper No. 80, The World Bank, Washington, DC.

Dalby, S. (1992) 'Ecopolitical discourse: "environmental security" and political geography' in *Progress in Human Geography*, 16: 4, pp. 503–522.

Emel, J. and Peet, R. (1989) 'Resource Management and Natural Hazards' in Peet, R. and Thrift, N. (eds.) *New Models in Geography: The Political-economy Perspective*, vol. 1, Unwin Hyman, London, pp. 49–76.

Hiebert, M. (1991) 'The Common Stream' in *Far Eastern Economic Review*, 21 February, pp. 24–26.

Hirsch, P. (1988) 'Dammed or Damned? Hydropower versus People's Power' in *Bulletin of Concerned Asian Scholars*, 20: 1, pp. 2–10.

—— (1992) *Resource Development in Mainland Southeast Asia: Political and Environmental Considerations*, Research Institute for Asia and the Pacific, University of Sydney.

—— (1993) 'Epilogue: Internationalisation of Environment in Mainland Southeast Asia' in Hirsch, P., *Political Economy of Environment in Thailand*, Journal of Contemporary Asia Publishers, Manila, pp. 148–168.

—— (1994) 'Where Are the Roots of Thai Environmentalism?' in *TEI Quarterly Environmental Journal*, 2: 2, pp. 5–15.

Hirsch, P. and Lohmann, L. (1989) 'Contemporary Politics of Environment in Thailand' in *Asian Survey*, 29: 4, April, pp. 439–451.

Howitt, R. (1993) '"A World in a Grain of Sand": Towards a Reconceptualisation of Scale' in *Australian Geographer*, 24: 1, May, pp. 33–44.

Interim Mekong Committee (1988) *Perspectives for Mekong Development: Revised Indicative Basin Plan (1987) for the Lower Mekong Basin*, Committee Report, Bangkok, April.

Linnerooth, J. (1990) 'The Danube River Basin: Negotiating Settlements to Transboundary Environmental Issues' in *Natural Resources Journal*, 30: 3, Summer, pp. 629–660.

Mehta, J.S. (1988) 'The Indus Water Treaty: A Case Study in the Resolution of an International River Basin Conflict' in *Natural Resources Forum*, 12: 1, February, pp. 69–77.

Mekong Committee (1970) *Indicative Basin Plan*, Bangkok.

—— (1975) *Joint Declaration of Principles for Utilisation of the Waters of the Lower Mekong Basin*, Committee for Coordination of Investigations of the Lower Mekong Basin (Khmer Republic, Laos, Thailand and the Republic of Vietnam).

Mekong Secretariat (1991) *Low Pa Mong Project Studies: Briefing Note on Findings*, Mekong Secretariat, Bangkok, October.

Mitchell, M. (1994) 'Scale and Influence in Mekong Basin Development: Analysing the Effects of Changing Social and Environmental Awareness on the Mekong Scheme Decision Making Process', unpublished MPhil thesis, University of Sydney.

The Nation, various editions, Bangkok.

Pantulu, V.R. (1986) 'The Mekong River System' in Davies, B.R. and Walker, K.F. (eds) *The Ecology of River Systems*, Dr W. Junk Publishers, Dordrecht, The Netherlands, pp. 695–719.

Roberts, Neil (1991) 'Geopolitics and the Euphrates' water resources' in *Geography*, 76: 2, April, pp. 157–159.

Scudder, T. and Colson, E.F. (1972) 'The Kariba Dam Project: Resettlement and Local Initiative' in Bernard, H.R. and Pelto, P.J. (eds) *Technology and Social Change*, Macmillan, New York, pp. 40–69.

Sydney Morning Herald, various editions, Sydney.

Worster, D. (1986) 'The Hoover Dam: A Study in Domination', Ch. 1 in Goldsmith, E. and Hildyard, N. (eds) *The Social and Environmental Effects of Large Dams*, volume 2: *Case Studies*, Wadebridge Ecological Centre, Cornwall.

Interview sources

Do Hang Phan, Director of Resources Development Division, Mekong Secretariat, interview, 27 April 1992.

Le Huu Ti, former Acting Director of Policy and Planning Division, Mekong Secretariat, interview, 29 April 1992.

Nguyen Duc Lien, Senior Project Officer in Water Resources and Hydropower Unit, Mekong Secretariat, interview, 30 April 1992.

Part II
Political economy of forestry

5 POLITICAL ECONOMY OF LOGGING IN SARAWAK, MALAYSIA

Michael Leigh

INTRODUCTION: AN OVERVIEW OF FOREST PRACTICE IN SOUTHEAST ASIA

It is axiomatic that political office holders should seek to control the allocation of resources. Those resources include not only natural endowments such as land, forest and mineral resources, but also government contracts and divestment of public equity to private individuals.

This chapter will focus upon the forest as a political and economic resource. A wide range of extractive activities has been initiated in Southeast Asia throughout the colonial period, and since. In recent years one of the most destructive has been the logging of tropical hill forests. In ecological terms, the process has been destructive both locally and globally. In human terms rapid clearance has withdrawn traditional forms of sustenance from those whose livelihood is dependent upon the living forest.

Treatment of forests as wasting assets has been apparent in Thailand, where significant incursions have even been made into nature reserves, and into the neighbouring nation states of Burma and Laos. In Burma teak extraction has been centralized in state hands, and extraction accelerated since 1988 with the urgent need to gain revenue and foreign exchange. Sales have been made in advance of extraction, by up to two years, to gain quick revenue. Twenty concessions went to Thai firms within three months of the SLORC *coup d'état*. In 1989–90 timber made up to 40 per cent of all export earnings (see Bryant in this volume). In 1994 the annual return from the export of 300,000 m^3 of teak exceeded US$200 million (*New Straits Times* 19 July 1995). Teak remained Burma's second most important legal source of foreign exchange, according to Myanmar Government figures. SLORC has been selling Burma's natural resources like fast food.

In the Philippines there has been rampant damage throughout the national territory, the peak phase of extraction being under Marcos during the two decades between 1965 and 1985. President Marcos, his family and cronies profited from his power to grant and revoke logging licences. One result was massive deforestation, to the extent that by 1991 only 6.46 million hectares of the 27.5 million hectares of original forest cover remained. In 1973 a record value of timber was exported.[1] However, after years of excessive logging activities, where maximum profits were reaped in the shortest time possible with no real concern for a sustainable forest industry, logging in the Philippines declined sharply (Bowring and Tasker 1977; Broad 1995). Since the Marcos years, forest policy and regulation has been largely overhauled.

Most of the valuable timber has gone from the Malayan Peninsula, often cleared for plantations; and Sabah has been virtually logged out. Indonesian round log exports, banned since 1987, have been replaced by a rapacious domestic plywood industry. The termination of log exports presented a golden opportunity for the ten largest timber tycoons to take over the holdings of the smaller companies, as the latter did not have immediate access to sufficient capital to meet the downstream costs of establishing plywood factories and facilities (*Asiaweek* 1 September 1993; Schwarz and Friedland 1992). Indonesia now has the cartel Apkindo led by 'Bob' Hasan, whose own production increased sevenfold over the decade 1981–1991.[2]

Papua New Guinea and the Pacific Islands are presently the focus of the economically dynamic Sarawak timber tycoons, and publicizing of their activities internationally has offended the sensibilities of certain Malaysian business and political leaders.[3] More recently there have been highly publicized equity linkages between Indonesian and Malaysian timber conglomerates.[4] Opportunities have been seized wherever they arose, by the Samling group in Cambodia and Guyana and by its competitors in Belize.[5]

LOGGING IN SARAWAK

This chapter draws on a long-term study of the area that has experienced the most rapid log clearance in the whole Southeast Asian region, an export volume that rivalled the rate of extraction for the whole Amazon basin. In 1993 more than 17 million m³ of sawlogs were exported from this one Malaysian state. In the late 1970s about 76 per cent of Sarawak was under forest cover; 90 per cent of this was under logging concessions, and one-third of this concession area had been logged (Chala 1995: 114). Hong estimates that between 1963 and 1986 over 30 per cent of the total forest area was logged (Hong 1987). This chapter spells out the political process through which half of the globe's exports of tropical sawlogs have been extracted, and then shipped to overseas markets.

While the discussion focuses on logging, this chapter is primarily a study of political economy. The political significance of the forest is that it contains a highly marketable commodity, a commodity that is unambiguously under the control of state- or regional-level political authority and is not in the hands of the central government of Malaysia. In Malaysia the Federal Government holds jurisdiction over matters that relate to defence, national security, income tax and petroleum resources. The jurisdiction of the State Government includes land ownership and title, alienation and land use as well as forest resources (Boniface 1990: 2). Thus the royalties from the timber industry form a very important source of income for state governments, particularly the state of Sarawak. Though some aspects of what I am describing are unique to the timber industry, the processes employed are transferable and have been used in other domains, especially when institutional constraints have not applied.

The rural hinterland of Sarawak has been transformed over the past twenty years for closely intertwined economic, political and technological reasons. The *economic* motivation was principally the opportunity to appropriate community resources for private purposes. The *political* rationale is the dramatic increase of political power for those who have control over allocating these resources *vis-à-vis* those who do not. The *technological* breakthrough came when machinery was available to extract hill timber at a cost that changed the economic calculus for the entrepreneur. It was not until 1975 that there were substantial exports of hill sawlogs from that part of Borneo.

The process of licence granting and renewal is the political–economic dynamic that drives, indeed determines, the rate at which deforestation has taken place. In critical respects the views of the forest-dwellers are irrelevant, or at worst of minor nuisance value, and have remained so except when the articulation of those views threatened to affect the market for tropical timber. Those championing the interest of the Penan, for example, often forget the overwhelming influence of the economic and political interests powering the rapid exploitation of sawlogs.[6] This study focuses on the coalition of social forces leading the political and business sector, which has near-untrammelled influence. That influence has been achieved more through cooption than through coercion, though both methods have been employed by the state and its agencies. It is quite evident that there is a close connection between Sarawak's forest policy and the demands of the timber industry (see Kaur 1994). For example, in 1987 an amendment to the Forest Ordinance for Sarawak made it a criminal offence to barricade logging roads.[7]

Prior to the start of logging the flow of funds is upwards, with the greatest risk being taken at the lower levels, by the contractors and the sub-contractors (Lian 1988: 122–123). The contractors are the most visible component of the whole timber industry. They are the ones who are often referred to as the 'timber tycoons'; many of them have become very rich. It is they who provide the managerial skills and expertise to extract, transport and market the sawlogs. The contractors in the field are the butt of almost all criticism because they are highly visible, whereas the licence granter and licensees are only rarely held responsible by the local people.

For hill padi farmers the initial benefits of logging were apparent. Firstly, the logging roads provided access to areas of jungle that were hitherto inaccessible, areas that then lend themselves to slash and burn agriculture. The fact that the tall timber had already been removed from those areas made them even more attractive, for there was much less to clear and burn before planting the rice. Various statements have been made to the effect that the Penan of Sarawak were largely to blame for destroying the forests as a result of shifting cultivation. 'The Europeans should blame the Penans instead of the Government for destroying the forests but of course, they would rather blame the Government and logging concessionaires.' The Penan 'should stop moving place to place for shifting cultivation but instead stay in one area and manage the land properly' (Dr Mahathir, *New Straits Times* November 17, 1987).[8] The benefits of the cutting of logging tracks for shifting cultivators were clearly not there for the nomadic Penan, who do not cultivate hill padi. It was these nomadic Penan who mounted highly publicised blockades to stop the loggers felling their jungle (see Sesser 1991: 42–67). They of all Sarawakians could see no gain from this kind of 'development'.

What is unambiguous to those concerned with the actual exploitation is a clear financial imperative to market the greatest volume of sawlogs as rapidly as possible, in order to recoup their quite substantial capital outlay before timber prices might slump below the figure calculated by the contractor. Thus, the requirement that licensees establish sawmills and other processing facilities to enhance local value added was ignored, as quick money could be more easily gained through extensive logging activities (Eaton 1990). It is only quite recently that groups such as Rimbunan Hijau have invested heavily in downstream processing facilities, in anticipation of the prospect of Government-decreed limits to the sheer volume of sawlog exports that will be permitted in the future.

Furthermore, care to extract only trees above a certain girth, and particularly not to harm the smaller species in the process of extraction, was regarded as a largely theoretical constraint, as was the need to prevent erosion from logging roads cut roughly into the hillsides. The local ecology was the first casualty of the process, though the significance of the damage only became apparent as the scale of logging and the resultant heavy silting and pollution of the major rivers came to affect a high proportion of the rural dwellers. The impact upon the supply of protein (fish and wild boar) is documented in a rising incidence of infant malnutrition in the Rejang and Baram river basins (*Borneo Bulletin*, October 1, 1988).[9]

USE OF IDEOLOGY

There are five themes on which this study has a clear bearing: the use of ideology, political and economic leadership, regime legitimacy, privatization and rationality.

The 1969 race riots in Kuala Lumpur, sparked by a growing ethnic divide, a perceived growth of inter-ethnic income differences, and rising dissatisfaction with government social and economic policies, precipitated a dramatic alteration of national policy. Institutional boundaries were breached by use of an affirmative action programme, somewhat a-historically named the New Economic Policy (NEP). The NEP envisaged a deliberate shift of productive resources from the immigrant to the indigenous segment of the Malaysian population.[10]

The avowed intention was to eradicate poverty and to eliminate the identification of economic function with ethnicity. In practice it was the latter of these two functions which was emphasized. To this end much of the NEP focus was placed on positive discrimination to advance the *bumiputra* section of society, and in particular increasing the role and power of Malays in the economic sphere. Quite fundamental changes could then be legitimized by the NEP ideology. The Sarawak coalition government came into power at the time of the NEP's introduction, and the new state leader consciously employed the ideology of the NEP to legitimate the process of reallocating wealth and power. He set out quickly to create a group of rich Muslim businessmen, who would then be in a position to play the role hitherto exercised by his immediate rivals, the rich Chinese 'towkays'. He especially wanted Muslims with sufficient economic means to underwrite political leaders, factions and parties. It was now justifiable to discriminate in favour of *bumiputra,* and to select who should benefit 'on behalf of' their community.

The Chief Minister frankly acknowledged his strategy:

I have selected those *bumiputra* who are able to make a success of the economic opportunities afforded them ... It sometimes appears that the implementation of a policy benefits only a few. But where this is so, it is simply because we must start step by step. Then the circle of development will gradually widen.

(*Sarawak Tribune* 30 October 1977)

The overall effect of this use of political prerogative was to shift decisively the concentration of wealth and power into the hands of those businessmen and politicians close to, and dependent upon, the Chief Minister of the State. Fortunes were made by many of those who placed themselves in an appropriate political position, and the reciprocal relationship between the economic and the political was never more clearly apparent.[11] This was appropriation of the state for private gain by individual businessmen, rather than business following broad class interests. The key was a relationship between the state apparatus and particular groups, not classes.

Political articulation remained focused upon the issues of race and religion, ideological constructs that acted as effective camouflage. It was effective because the issues of race and religion were seen as salient by a good proportion of voters. Real political *discourse* shifted to the question of who was to control the allocation of resources. The links established at the elite level clearly transcended ethnicity, while at the popular level ethnic differences were emphasized in order to hold the loyalty of the constituents.[12] Peninsular Malaysians had the greatest input in the drafting of the NEP, while scant attention was given to the specific problems that existed in Sabah and Sarawak (Jomo 1990: 4). Further, in the implementation of the NEP in these states it has been argued that the indigenous people have been treated like 'second class bumiputras, suffering losses of rights to communal land for the benefit of the timber giants' (Boniface 1990: 9).[13]

The institutional barriers that had previously inhibited widespread corruption were broken down, once it was deemed legitimate to allocate community resources for private benefit. The justification for doing so was on the highly questionable grounds that private gains would eventually trickle down to other members of the relatively disadvantaged communities. The fact that it was the urban newly-rich who were presiding over the process of expropriating the wealth of the rural majority made it even less likely that the latter would benefit from this version of 'development'.[14]

Much the same practice occurs at the national level with the processes involved in privatization. In this case it is those individuals or groups with UMNO (United Malay National Organization) links who are the beneficiaries, and the government's actions in awarding these groups with lucrative contracts are justified as fulfilling the goals of the NDP.[15]

LEADERSHIP AND REGIME LEGITIMACY

Key Muslim Melanaus and Foochow Chinese[16] seized the opportunities opened up by the NEP and linked together for their mutual advantage. Leaders of each of those groups were considered 'upstarts' by the old-established scions of Malay and Chinese communities, the aristocratic *perabangan* and the older wealth of the Hokkien and Teochew communities. There was a reciprocal relationship between these two somewhat marginal new leadership groups, both sides of the equation becoming quite dependent upon the other.

The significance of this new pattern of alliance did not fully blossom until the timber boom of 1979. From then on, all other groups, whether they were local aristocratic Malays or the old Hokkien Chinese, were clearly left behind. Those without either economic or political clout were entirely marginalized. The opportunity was *not* grasped by joint ventures with foreign capital (from the USA or Japan) as happened by the early 1970s over the border in Indonesian Kalimantan. Tight local control was maintained over the process, even successfully excluding until quite recently a company associated with the then powerful Malaysian Finance Minister, Tun Daim Zainuddin.

Foochow energy and entrepreneurship spearheaded logging extraction in Sarawak, and certainly also made its mark in Kalimantan, Sumatra and in Papua New Guinea and other Pacific Island nations. Their expertise in this domain has displaced many established groups who had previously controlled the timber industry – as far away as in New Zealand and Western Australia.[17]

How autonomous is the leadership in such a society? The relationship between structural determinism and leadership autonomy has been explored in the context of the Latin American experience of the transition to authoritarianism, and the subsequent re-establishment of democratic structures. The accepted explanation shifted from a focus upon structural determinism to an acknowledgment of the discretion exercised by those in positions of political control. Crucial was the manner in which changes were handled, and that assigned a key role to the political leadership.

Legitimacy in Malaysia is derived from a functioning parliamentary system that has become institutionalized through three changes of Prime Minister, and numerous Chief Ministers of its constituent states. Legitimacy is thus maintained through the electoral system. Three aspects need to be emphasized when discussing Malaysian elections, none of which is in any sense unique to Malaysia. First, vast resources are deployed in order to gain voter support. Second, the media has either been coopted or is controlled, and constantly reinforces the world view that the governing regime is the nation, and that electing parties not part of the government will bring instability, or worse. Third, political opposition is caricatured as communal and therefore dangerous. The ghost of the 13 May 1969 race riots is brought out of the cupboard to stalk the opposition whenever necessary.

Racial sentiments are exacerbated in the process of ethnic labelling and name-calling, undermining the stake of major groups in society. In the process, the Barisan (National Front) parties serve as institutions of societal control, sometimes rather more than as articulators of popular views. Indeed, the whole electoral system can be viewed as furthering both functions. In many quite tangible ways the populace has become complicit in the system of power, in its political and economic dimensions. There have been real and tangible short-term employment opportunities and realizable wealth distribution to a large number of people associated with the timber industry.[18] Cooption rather than coercion has been the norm.

The whole process of being granted a timber licence and being named as contractor is dependent upon one's links with the top state-level political leadership. That is not institutionalized, hence unpredictability reigns. Uncertainty is exacerbated by the existence of regular contested elections. Enormous financial resources are deployed to fight those contests. In the key 1987 election, fought over the right to allocate the spoils of office, some US$40 was spent per voter. In a constituency of one Deputy Minister, he acknowledged spending more than RM 2 million for his campaign. A reciprocal relationship exists between the timber tycoons and the top party leadership at those times, for each needs the other's help. At election time, one might add, the leadership spares no effort to gain the votes of the population at large, and constituents in vulnerable electorates are often wooed with a range of incentives (Bowie 1994: 182). So 'reciprocation' takes place at a popular level at least once every five years. In addition to this, state political patronage is extended to influential headmen to ensure longhouse votes. The logging companies play their role by paying monthly salaries to headmen, to keep them 'onside', and to allow for the smooth continuation of their activities, and those of the government in office (Chala 1995: 112).

Another element of uncertainty results from the operation of a federal system, with the central leadership having the power to intervene, using security powers and information garnered by the anti-corruption agency. Ironically, contested elections plus the federal structure add an important element of unpredictability and uncertainty, viewed from the perspective of the holders of the timber concessions and operating contractors.

PRIVATIZATION OF COMMUNITY RESOURCES

Shifting resources from the public to private domains is legitimized by a pro-market privatization ideological trend or fashion. Dr Mahathir has stressed a view of development that involves appropriating all available natural resources, and their conversion into investible capital. Others having done that, historically through the processes of colonialism and post-colonialism, and throughout the globe, he sees no reason why Malaysia should constrain its own processes of economic growth. The only major flaw in that economic argument is if the capital so derived is not invested locally, but is simply transferred overseas for individual gain.[19]

The state leadership enhanced its own clout by extending the practice of annual renewal of licences, and removing access to the courts by those who might seek to contest any change of award. Under the Forest Amendment Ordinance 1987 (Sarawak) the Government increased its power to suspend or cancel logging licences and to control their transfer. Naturally this further undermined their security of tenure over contracted areas of timber and gave licensees and contractors even less reason to nurture or protect uncut reserves in their allocated concession area.

Precisely because contracts, licences and approvals had been gained principally through political connections, the holders were highly vulnerable to any significant change of political alignment. This created a climate of uncertainty, a situation where contractors had constantly to nourish the source of the permits and also keep open lines to potential successors and challengers.

The logic of such a situation was that the gains should be made as quickly as possible, and the 'booty' placed in safe havens overseas, beyond reach in the event that someone from 'the other camp' might wish to stake a claim. The substantial flight of that capital from Malaysia imposes a heavy opportunity cost upon the nation and its people. There is significant anecdotal evidence that much of that resource-based wealth has contributed to the vast fund of mobile international capital sloshing around this region. Given the high level of economic growth in Malaysia since 1987, there is every likelihood that much of that free capital has been reinvested into Malaysia from Hong Kong, Europe and elsewhere. However, if the return is higher elsewhere, it can just as quickly move away.

> These timber men have properties all over the world. Instead of redeploying the capital in the state, they prefer to either invest or spend it abroad and cause the outflow of capital.[20]

Timber tycoons who wish to move to contracting in other, now more lucrative domains have sought to capitalize their logging assets through reverse buyouts. Their private owners have the problem of controlling companies that have been hugely profitable for the owners while having registered only very modest profits. There is now a problem in establishing their true worth, before the owners can attract new capital, and diversify their activities to protect themselves against being locked into exploitation of a declining asset.

RATIONALITY: INSTRUMENTAL VERSUS SUBSTANTIVE

The huge financial stake involved, the absence of institutionalized procedures and the political unpredictability together give an instrumental rationality to current logging practices where contractors are often seen to extract the timber as quickly, as cheaply and as destructively as they can. Appeals to follow substantive rationality, to maintain the forest reserve as a sustainable resource (whether measured in the somewhat narrower silvicultural terms or taking into account the full range of uses of the forest), inevitably fall on deaf ears because of the driving short-term political and economic determinants. Pledges to reduce output and modify current practices are often not much more than camouflage until those determinants are addressed. Response to the International Timber Trade Organisation Report, once shorn of the rhetoric, demonstrated the overriding importance of the huge economic stake held by those who control the process of extraction and marketing of sawlogs.

In one respect, to emphasize the autonomy of elite decision-making means de-emphasizing international political economy. However, what is most important to stress is that individual decision-makers have exercised a crucial element of discretion, and done so effectively within the context of a set of internationally validated norms of behaviour, norms that have been legitimated by and within the international business community. Those individuals have followed an instrumental rationality that can be contrasted to concerns about the substantive consequences for the broader society – of which not only are they part, but for which they are also responsible.

There is a clear and overriding rationality to the process of timber extraction, driven by the huge financial rewards derived from this most valuable and readily available natural resource. The benefits have accrued primarily to those who have the power to allocate, to harvest and to market timber, and the gains have been on behalf of their companies, their parties or themselves. What has made the whole process politically sustainable is the extent to which broad sectors of the rural population have gained some reward, meagre and short-term though it may be, and the closure of avenues to articulate effectively the long-term costs of such rapid exploitation. A normatively positive ideology of development has been actively employed to marginalize those who raise questions about the need to preserve customary rights to land and to the forest. Those who point to future difficulties for the rural dwellers are publicly tainted for their association with those foreigners who are supposedly jealous of Malaysia's rapid economic development during the past decade. Rapid extraction continues, while the absence of long-term employment opportunities is temporarily ameliorated by increased investment in downstream plywood factories.

NOTES

1 Marites Danguilan Vitug in this volume discusses aspects of forestry and political connections in the Philippines. According to her chapter, the value of timber exported in 1973 rose to $472 million. A *Far Eastern Economic Review* report (22 December 1977) gave a somewhat lower figure.
2 For a more detailed account of the Indonesian logging industry see Cullen 1994 and Broad 1995. Schwarz 1994: 139–141 states that Hasan wields considerably more influence over the forestry sector than the Ministry of Forestry. See also Dauvergne 1993–94: 497–518.
3 The Australian Broadcasting Corporation Four Corners team produced a programme on that subject, telecast on 16 May 1994 under the title *Malaysian Invasion*. That programme provoked quite a defensive Malaysian reaction. The Primary Industries Minister, Datuk Seri Dr Lim Keng Yaik, said that the documentary 'is a conspiracy against East Asia and Malaysia by those who are jealous and can't stand to see us developing' (*New Straits Times* 8 and 9 November 1994).
4 Barito Pacific, led by an Indonesian Hakka, Prajogo Pangestu, joined with a Sibu Foochow, Tang Sing Kang, and injected assets into the formerly ailing Construction and Supplies House Bhd (CASH). Already possessing extraction rights to a 40,000 hectare concession in Kapit through Hutrama s.b., they both went on to form a plywood concern, Rindaya Wood Processing s.b. Rindaya plus two other ventures owned by Prajogo (Golden Pacific in China and Lombda Holdings in Papua New Guinea) were injected into CASH Bhd as part of a RM 2.59 billion cross-border deal with the Barito Pacific group (*Star* 11 July 1994).
5 In August 1994, the Samling group signed a US$100 million timber agreement with the Cambodian Government, under which it obtained two concessions totalling 787,000 hectares and contracted to build and operate a sawmill and establish two plywood factories. Samling already had a 1.6 million hectare timber concession in Guyana (*Star* 19 August 1994).
6 Works of interest in the areas of environmental protection and the struggle of the indigenous peoples of Sarawak include Hong 1987; Brosius 1995; Khor Kok Peng 1988; INSAN, 1989; Colchester 1989.
7 Much has been written on this subject and that of claims for customary rights to land including Sawing 1993; Lian 1993; Khor Kok Peng 1988.
8 See also 'Stumble in the Jungle', a series of articles written by Datuk James Wong, the Minister of Environment and Tourism. In those articles he lambasts shifting cultivation as causing enormous losses to the timber industry and in consequence to society (*People's Mirror* 11–15 April 1988). By contrast Cramb carefully sifts the evidence and finds that the conventional dogma on the subject is largely unsupported by fact. See Cramb 1988: 115–149.
9 'In general indigenous groups in Sarawak are reported to experience chronic malnutrition comparable to the poorest groups of indigenous peoples in Latin America' (*Malaysian Forester* 42: 4).

10 For a general discussion of the NEP and its impact on business government relations see Bowie 1991 and 1994; for a review of the aims and the outcomes of the NEP see Jomo 1990. See also Jesudason 1989.

11 This well-known situation was confirmed by the players themselves in 1987, after a bitter fight between uncle and nephew for the election of Chief Minister. Details of the involvement of each in allocating logging licence concessions to family members and business associates were leaked to the press by these men in order to discredit the other. After Chief Minister Datuk Patinggi Abdul Taib Mahmud told the press that timber concessions belonging to family and friends of the former chief minister, Tun Abdul Rahman Yakub, totalling 1.25 million hectares had been frozen, Tun Abdul Rahman Yakub gave evidence that 1.6 million hectares of timber concessions were in the hands of associates and family members of Datuk Patinggi Abdul Taib Mahmud (*The People's Mirror* 12 April 1987, *Sarawak Tribune* 11 April 1987, and *New Straits Times* 10 April 1987. See also INSAN 1989, especially 73–74).

12 Wyzan 1990: 77 gives the example of Chinese business people going out of their way to create indignation in ordinary Chinese voters over policies such as restructuring that really do not affect Chinese workers very much.

13 See also James Clad, 'Dayaks Want their Share of Land Riches Now', *Far Eastern Economic Review* 30 May 1985.

14 Wyznan 1990: 62 describes the process as a 'top down bureaucratic approach to poverty reduction', which enriched larger landowners and politicians and often did nothing for the intended beneficiaries.

15 For more discussion on this issue see Bowie 1994.

16 For more information on the background and rise of the Foochow Chinese see Leigh 1988.

17 For instance, in New Zealand the family of Datuk Tiong Hiew King has among its interests Ernslaw 1 Limited, which currently holds rights to 25,000 hectaresa of forests and owns a further 20,000 hectares on Matakana Island near Auckland. The Tiong family's flagship company in Malaysia is Rimbunan Hijau s.b., which has the largest timber concession in the nation: *New Straits Times* 15 November 1995. Oregon Forestry, one of the NZ companies owned by the Tiong family, until March 1996 had a stake in the Port of Tauranga, specializing in the export of timber to Asian countries: *ibid.* and *Australian* 18 March 1996.

18 Sarawak Study Group (1986) notes that 9% of the total labour force in 1984 was employed in the timber sector: Repetto 1988. See also Sesser 1991.

19 Brosius 1995: 20 points out that in response to pressure from environmentalists and governments from the North, the Malaysian Government links forest destruction in the South to Northern consumption. The Government has likened Northern environmental activism to the legacy of colonialism, identifying it as a latter-day form of colonialism.

20 Lau Kah King, Chairman of the Sarawak Building and Civil Engineering Contractors Association. He went on to state that some timber organizations have benefited enormously from the exploitation of forest resources in the state. He added that all development projects 'should be put up for tender so that members of the association . . . could stand a fair chance of participating': *Sarawak Tribune* 22 July 1986.

BIBLIOGRAPHY

Boniface, Dorne (1990), *The Human Cost of Sarawak's Timber Revenue*, Observer Mission Report, Lawasia.

Bowie, Alasdair (1991), *Crossing the Industrial Divide: State, Society, and the Politics of Economic Transformation in Malaysia*, Political Economy of International Change series. New York: Columbia University Press.
—— (1994), 'Business–Government Relations in Industrialising Malaysia', in Andrew MacIntyre (ed.) *Business–Government Relations in Industrialising Asia*, Ithaca: Cornell University Press.
Bowring, Phillip and Tasker, Robert (1977), 'Philippines in Decline', *Far Eastern Economic Review*, 2 December 1977.
Broad, Robin (1995), 'The Political Economy of Natural Resources: Case Studies of the Indonesian and Philippine Forest Sectors', *Journal of Developing Areas*, 29: 3, April: 317–339.
Brosius, J. Peter (1995), 'Voices for the Borneo Rainforest: Writing the Biography of an Environmental Campaign', paper presented to the *Conference on Environmental Discourses and Human Welfare in South and Southeast Asia, Social Science Research Council, Volcanos, Hawaii, December 28–30 1995*.
Cant, Garth (ed.) (1993), *Indigenous Land Rights in Commonwealth Countries: Dispossession, Negotiation and Community Action*: University of Canterbury Department of Geography.
Chala, Theresa (1995), 'Separating the Trees from the Forest: The Material Basis of the Dayak Struggle in Sarawak, Malaysia', *Kajian Malaysia*, xiii: 2 December: 100–126.
Colchester, Marcus (1989), *Pirates, Squatters and Poachers: The Political Ecology of Dispossession of the Native Peoples of Sarawak*, Kuala Lumpur: Survival International and INSAN 1989.
Cramb, R.A. (1988), 'Shifting Cultivation and Resource Degradation in Sarawak: Perceptions and Policies', *Review of Indonesian and Malaysian Affairs*, 22: 1, Winter: 115–149.
—— (1993), 'The Evolution of Property Rights to Land in Sarawak: An Institutionalist Perspective', *Review of Marketing and Agricultural Economics*, 61: 2, pt 2, Aug.: 289–300.
Cramb, R.A. and Willis, Ian R. (1990), 'The Role of Traditional Institutions in Rural Development: Community-Based Land Tenure and Government Land Policy in Sarawak, Malaysia', *World-Development*, 18: 3, March: 347–360.
Cullen, Anne (1994), 'Forest Policy in Indonesia: Protected in the Hands of Tycoons?', paper for the *ASAA Biennial Conference, Murdoch University, Perth WA, 13–16 July 1994*.
Dauvergne, Peter (1993–94), 'The Politics of Deforestation in Indonesia', *Pacific Affairs* 66(4): 497–518.
Eaton, Peter (1990), 'Forest Policy and Legislation in Borneo', *Environmental and Planning Law Journal* 7: 1, Mar.: 49–54.
Gillis, Malcolm (1988), 'Malaysia: Public Policies and the Tropical Forest', in Robert Repetto and Malcolm Gillis (eds) *Public Policies and the Misuse of Forest Resources*, Cambridge, Cambridge University Press.
Hong, Evelyne (1987), *Natives of Sarawak: Survival in Borneo's Vanishing Forests*, Malaysia: Institut Masyarakat, 1987.
INSAN (1989), *Logging against the Natives of Sarawak*, Petaling Jaya: Institute for Social Analysis.
Jesudason, James V. (1989), *Ethnicity and the Economy: The State, Chinese Business, and Multinationals in Malaysia*, Oxford, New York, Singapore and Toronto: Oxford University Press.
Jomo Kwame Sundaram (1990), 'Beyond the New Economic Policy? Malaysia in the Nineties', *The Sixth James C. Jackson Memorial Lecture*, Asian Studies Association of Australia.

Kaur, Amarjit (1994), 'The Fate of the Forest: Forestry and Deforestation in East Malaysia', paper presented to the *Asian Studies Association of Australia Biennial Conference, Murdoch University, Perth, WA, 13–16 July 1994.*

Khor Kok Peng (1988), 'Rural Poverty in Malaysia and the Sarawak Natives' Defence of the Forests', unpublished paper.

King, Victor T. and Parnwell, Michael J.G. (eds) (1990), *Margins and Minorities: The Peripheral Areas and Peoples of Malaysia*, Hull University Press.

Leigh, Michael (1988), 'The Spread of Foochow Commercial Power before the New Economic Policy', in R.A. Cramb and Reece (eds) *Development in Sarawak: Historical and Contemporary Perspectives*, Monash Paper on Southeast Asia No. 17, Centre for Southeast Asian Studies, Monash University.

Lian, Francis (1988), 'The Timber Industry and Economic Development in Sarawak: Some Contemporary Trends and Proposals for 1990 and Beyond', *A Working Paper Presented at the Seminar on Development in Sarawak, Kuching, October 10–12 1988.*

—— (1993), 'Blockades of Timber Roads in Sarawak: Assertion of Land Rights', in Garth Cant (ed.) *Indigenous Land Rights in Commonwealth Countries: Dispossession, Negotiation and Community Action*, University of Canterbury Geography Department.

MacIntyre, Andrew (ed.) (1994) *Business and Government in Industrialising Asia*, Ithaca: Cornell University Press.

Masing, James (1989), 'Logging Industries in Sarawak: The Clash of Cultures', seminar paper for the *Sixth Malaysia Colloquium of the Malaysia Society, University of Sydney.*

Osborne, P. (1990), 'Environmentalists Seek Ban on Sarawak's Rich Timber Exports', *The Financial Review*, 28 August.

Repetto, Robert (1988), 'Overview', in Robert Repetto and Malcolm Gillis (eds) *Public Policies and the Misuse of Forest Resources*, Cambridge, Cambridge University Press.

Repetto, Robert and Malcolm Gillis (eds) (1988), *Public Policies and the Misuse of Forest Resources*, Cambridge, Cambridge University Press.

Sawing, Antalai (1993), 'The Protection of Native Customary Lands under the Sarawak Laws', in Cant Garth (ed.) *Indigenous Land Rights in Commonwealth Countries: Dispossession, negotiation and community action*, University of Canterbury Geography Department.

Schwarz, Adam (1994), *A Nation in Waiting: Indonesia in the 1990s*, Sydney, Allen and Unwin.

Schwarz, Adam and Jonathon Friedland (1992), 'Green Fingers', *Far Eastern Economic Review*, 12 March.

Sesser, Stan (1991), 'A Reporter at Large: Logging in the Rainforest', *The New Yorker*, 27 May: 42–67.

Vincent, Jeffrey (1990), 'Rent Capture and the Feasibility of Tropical Forest Management', *Land Economics*, 66: 2, May: 212–223.

Wyzan, Michael L. (1990), 'Ethnic Relations and the New Economic Policy in Malaysia', in Michael Wyzan (ed.) *The Political Economy of Ethnic Discrimination and Affirmative Action: A Comparative Perspective*, Westport, Conn. and London: Greenwood, Praeger: 49–80.

Journals and newspapers

Asiaweek
Australian
Borneo Bulletin

Far Eastern Economic Review
New Straits Times
People's Mirror
Star
Straits Times

6   The politics of forestry in Burma

Raymond L. Bryant

The link between environmental degradation and the political process in Southeast Asia has received considerable attention in recent years. The politics of forestry management has been a theme of particular prominence. In addition to region-wide surveys (e.g. Hurst 1990; Bryant *et al.* 1993), there have been studies on Indonesia (Potter 1991; Peluso 1992; Dauvergne 1993/94), Malaysia (Hong 1987; Colchester 1989; King 1993; Leigh in this volume), Thailand (Mekvichai 1988; Leungaramsri and Rajesh 1992; Lohmann 1993), and the Philippines (Kummerer 1992; Remigio 1993; Vitug in this volume). In contrast, little has been written on the forest politics of socialist Southeast Asia: Vietnam, Cambodia, Laos, and Burma (now officially known as Myanmar). What difference, if any, does it make that these countries pursued a socialist as opposed to a capitalist development path (cf. Beresford and Fraser 1992)? A central goal therefore must be to investigate Southeast Asian forest politics in the context of non-capitalist political economies to examine what they reflect of the relationship between states, ideology, and forestry. This objective assumes even greater significance at a time when these countries are undergoing rapid political and economic changes (on Vietnam, see Bach Tan Sinh in this volume). The significance of these changes in terms of national forest management strategies and politics awaits detailed examination.

The case of Burma is illustrative in this regard. For much of the post-colonial era, the Burmese state has pursued a socialist development strategy. Recently it has adopted a new strategy premised on a greater role for private capital and a partial opening to the international economy in a context of continued state economic intervention. This chapter explores in a preliminary manner how the changing political economy of Burma has affected forest politics in the country. It first provides an overview of forest politics during the colonial era, before discussing the politicised and socialist nature of forestry since independence in 1948. Particular attention is paid to recent trends in forestry politics during the State Law and Order Restoration Council (SLORC) era (i.e. since 1988), and possible explanations for SLORC forestry policy are considered. The chapter is based partly on fieldwork undertaken in Burma in July and August 1994. However, references to individuals and organisations have been kept to a minimum to ensure confidentiality. Historical material is derived from archival work undertaken at the India Office Library and Records, London.

COLONIAL FORESTRY POLITICS

To understand forestry in Burma is to appreciate how contemporary developments are shaped by a colonial legacy of attempted state control as well as popular resistance to such control. This dynamic of state control and popular resistance is in turn central to an understanding of colonial forestry as a political process.

During the early years of colonial rule of Lower Burma (1826–56), the British failed to regulate forest use. In the teak forests of Tenasserim, a system of *laissez-faire* forestry was introduced in which traders extracted teak in accordance with market demand. As teak was much desired, the depletion of these forests was achieved in only 30 years. Influenced by the doctrine of economic liberalism (i.e. Smith, Ricardo) and subject to business pressure in India, the colonial state pursued a non-interventionist strategy with disastrous results both for the teak forests and for the imperial exchequer. The failure of *laissez-faire* forestry led the colonial state to adopt an interventionist approach in the 1850s. At the behest of Indian Governor-General Lord Dalhousie, the German botanist-turned-forester Dietrich Brandis was sent to Burma in January 1856 to establish a forest department. This event marked a shift from *laissez-faire* to 'scientific' forestry management (Bryant 1994d).

Attempted control of Burma's teak forests by superior authority was not new. Indeed, the monarchical state sought to regulate key forests from the seventeenth century (Lieberman 1984). What was new, however, was the ability of the colonial state actually to enforce its claims. Whereas the monarchical state claimed much, but controlled little in practice, the colonial state was able, through a combination of military force and organisational skill, to assert its jurisdiction (however tenuously) in all but the most remote teak forests.

There were various elements to the assertion of state control over forests in colonial Burma. Here, two elements will suffice to illustrate the process. First, the forest department began in 1870 to create reserved forests: state owned and managed forests dedicated to commercial timber exploitation. From only a few hundred square miles in the 1870s, the area under reserved forest grew to more than 30,000 square miles (78,000 sq. km) in the 1930s. In these reserves, foresters aimed to exclude all natural and human 'hazards' to the teak tree. In the latter category were most forms of indigenous forest use: shifting (*taungya*) cultivation, cattle grazing, tree tapping, timber extraction, and honey collection. An integral part of forest management was thus the imposition of access restrictions on Burmese peasants, timber traders, and shifting cultivators. In this way, the colonial state's claim to Burma's teak forests was often asserted at the expense of other forest users.

A second element of the assertion of forest control concerned the relationship between the state and Karen shifting cultivators who inhabited Burma's southern teak forests. Imperial foresters initially considered these cultivators to be a menace to the teak forests, and thus to forestry itself. However, this view was challenged after 1856 as it was realised that the detailed forest knowledge of the Karen might be of assistance to the state after all. Specifically, forest officials sought the participation of these cultivators under a reforestation scheme known as *taungya* forestry (Bryant 1994b). Under this system, Karen planted teak alongside crops in their *taungya*; when it was time to clear new fields after several years the process was repeated. Shifting cultivators thereby created teak plantations that in 100 to 150 years would reach commercial maturity. As increasing numbers of Karen participated in this system, the realisation that the area available for cultivation was declining in the measure that teak plantations were being created was a source of tension between cultivators and foresters.

Popular resistance to the assertion of state forest control was fierce, but it varied depending on the actors and interests involved as well as the political context. Two examples illustrate the point. During the colonial era, the mainstay of peasant resistance was what Scott (1985) has termed 'everyday forms' of resistance. As in Dutch Java (Peluso 1992) and British India (Guha 1989), peasants in British Burma reacted to access restrictions through a covert resistance campaign: timber was extracted, cattle were grazed, and *taungya* were cleared in defiance of the forest rules. Further, sporadic arson attacks on reserved forests and teak plantations were an even more forthright challenge to state control (Bryant 1994a).

Only covert resistance was possible in a context of severe political repression that characterised most of the colonial era in Burma. Yet, as the second example illustrates, during the 1920s and 1930s, Burmese opposition to colonial forestry was also expressed openly in so far as altered political conditions permitted. Everyday resistance persisted, but opposition also took the form of political protest through the legal political process (Bryant 1994c). Under the dyarchy system of limited self-rule introduced in 1923, Burmese elected to the Legislative Council mounted a vociferous campaign against both the denial of peasant forest access and the inequitable distribution of teak leases which worked against the Burmese timber trading community. As developed by such politicians as U Ba Pe and U Thin Maung, the argument that Burma's forests were not being managed in the 'best' interests of the Burmese was elaborated. This argument contradicted the official view, which held that 'progress' in forestry was being achieved.

Even before British rule in Burma came to an abrupt end in early 1942, it was apparent that state forest control was tenuous. Challenged on various fronts, such control was difficult precisely because state power was generally weakest in the forests. Yet the colonial experience has not prevented a similar attempt by the state in an independent, and for a long-time socialist, Burma to control and exploit the forests; as we shall see, the results have been equally ambiguous.

POST-COLONIAL FORESTRY POLITICS

Following independence in 1948, the Burmese state embarked on a socialist development strategy that culminated in the Burmese Way to Socialism programme of the 1960s and 1970s. Inevitably, forest practices were shaped by this programme. The shift from colonial capitalism to socialism also highlighted the dominance of a centralised system of forest control. As during the colonial era, such control has been the watchword of forestry in modern Burma.

Four themes characterise Burmese forest politics since 1948. First, the Burmese state has centralised teak extraction in state hands in response to nationalist and socialist considerations. Among the first acts of the U Nu government on taking power at independence was to nationalise the leases of the European firms that dominated Burma's teak industry in colonial times (Diokno 1983). A Forest Nationalisation Committee composed of representatives from government and business oversaw this process, but the outbreak of civil war in mid-1948 hastened the departure of these firms (MAF 1952). This move satisfied a long-standing nationalist grievance concerning the power and influence of imperial companies (Tun Kyaw 1956; Bryant 1994c). Further, nationalisation ensured that control of the lucrative teak trade rested with the Burmese state, an important element in the broader quest to establish a socialist economy in Burma. A few Burmese traders were allowed to extract teak during the 1950s and early 1960s, but their role was a minor one (Thein Han 1951; MAF 1953); in 1961–62, for example, the private sector accounted for only 12,176 tons out of a total output of 262,361 tons (UB 1985: 115). Following the military coup of March 1962, the operations of even these firms were nationalised as part of an intensification of the socialist experiment under the Burmese Way to Socialism (UM 1989).

Teak extraction thereby became the responsibility solely of the State Timber Board (STB), an agency established in 1948 under the control of the Ministry of Agriculture and Forests. The power of the STB derived from its control over all aspects of the teak trade: extraction, milling, and marketing (MAF 1952). In contrast, the forest department, which had once played a major role in teak extraction, found itself largely confined to conservation work, and the girdling (killing) of teak trees in preparation for extraction by the STB. This division remains today, and is the source of intra-bureaucratic tensions. As a result of its control over the teak trade, the STB (in 1972 renamed the Timber Corporation and after 1988 the Myanmar Timber Enterprise) has been the key agency in the forestry sector, with its activities given priority by senior political leaders over those of the forest department. In so far as teak exports have been a crucial source of foreign exchange, the pre-eminence of the STB has been assured.

A second theme of post-colonial forest politics centres on the Burmese state's campaign to assert territorial control in the face of a series of prolonged insurgency movements that began in 1948 and persist in a number of areas even today (M. Smith 1991). As forests are a haven for anti-government forces, the multiple insurgencies that have characterised modern Burmese politics have impeded state efforts to exploit the teak forests. Thus, in comparison with a production level of 447,000 tons in 1939–40, teak output since independence has never reached that figure, although in various years (i.e. 1981–82, 1990–91) extraction has approached that symbolically important target (UB 1985; UM 1993).

The spectre of insurgency has cast a heavy shadow over the forestry sector. In order to work in teak forests subject to insurgent activity, STB and forest department employees have required a military escort (Aung Tin 1956; MAF 1962; Shwe Bo 1963). Even today in certain districts (e.g. Tenasserim), forest officials are unable to visit the forests formally under their charge. Yet the general trend has nevertheless been one of growing state control over an ever larger proportion of the national territory. From a situation in 1949 when most of the country was in insurgent hands, the Burmese state has today forced insurgent troops back into remote border regions. Indeed, its military success has been such that various insurgent groups have been forced to strike deals with the government, most notably the Kachin Independence Army in February 1994 (Lintner 1994b). Negotiations with the Karen National Union (KNU) and the New Mon State Party, two groups fighting the SLORC along the Thai–Burmese border, have taken place as well against a backdrop of continuing Burmese military victories such as the capture of the KNU headquarters at Mannerplaw in January 1995.

As military control has been achieved, teak extraction has accelerated in many parts of the country. In this regard, the ending of the communist insurgency in the Pegu Yoma in the mid-1970s as a result of the army's 'Four Cuts' programme (M. Smith 1991) was particularly significant. This victory meant that government control was fully restored for the first time since 1942 in the country's most valuable teak forests. Ironically, this has resulted in a situation whereby these valuable forests, long protected as a result of the fighting, are now being seriously over-cut (C.F. Smith 1991). One consequence of the 'normalisation' of state power in hitherto 'no-go' forested areas, therefore, has been the degradation of the teak forests.

A third theme in post-colonial forest politics in Burma concerns the state's ongoing efforts to deter forest use that is not compatible with large-scale commercial forestry. As with their colonial predecessors, Burmese foresters persist in the view that Karen and other ethnic minority shifting cultivators are destroying prime forest land (Tin Htut 1955; Long 1957; UM 1989). The response of forest officials has been predictably similar to that of colonial foresters. On the one hand, efforts have been made to perpetuate the *taungya* forestry system. In the late 1970s, for example, the rapid expansion in the planted area (by at least 1,600 hectares per year) owed much to the participation of shifting cultivators under this system; each participating family was allocated three to five acres of land on which to inter-crop commercial tree species and various agricultural crops (FAO 1978: 8). On the other hand, an attempt has also been made to persuade cultivators to halt their 'destructive' activities and adopt a sedentary lifestyle. Thus, as part of a programme to protect ecologically vulnerable watersheds, the Kinda Dam watershed management project was initiated in 1987, an important aim of which was to 'stabilize shifting cultivators through incentives, demonstration, and technical assistance' (UM 1990: 5). Ecological concerns had prompted the British to follow a similar course of action in the early twentieth century. Yet, just as in the colonial era, shifting cultivators have resisted these attempts to alter their lifestyle.

A fourth theme of Burmese forest politics for most of the period since 1948 has been the attempt to organise the forestry sector according to state socialist principles. As noted, this was reflected in the progressive nationalisation of the teak industry. Yet, notwithstanding this sweeping measure, teak production has failed to attain pre-war levels, an official goal throughout the period since 1948. The reasons for this failure are associated with the specific form that socialism took in Burma, especially between 1962 and 1988 under General Ne Win's leadership. In effect, the socialism adopted at this time in Burma was a distinctive blend of Marxist doctrine and traditional Burmese Buddhism encapsulated in the Burmese Way to Socialism (BWS) programme (Steinberg 1981; Taylor 1987).

Two aspects of this programme merit attention here. First, the BWS was associated with the dramatic curtailment of trading links with the outside world such that between 1962 and 1972 Burma became a 'hermit' nation with very few external political, economic, or cultural links. In a general context of virtual economic autarky, forestry along with other economic sectors suffered; sawmilling equipment was not replaced, and became increasingly obsolete and inefficient. Paradoxically, the general economic decline enhanced the export profile of the teak trade *vis-à-vis* rice and other primary exports, in 1970/71, for example, forest exports (mostly teak) constituted 25 per cent of total exports, and this figure climbed to as much as 50 per cent in later years (Steinberg 1981). Thus, while all natural resource sectors suffered from policies introduced under the BWS, the forestry sector suffered relatively less than did others. Second, the BWS was predicated on rapid industrialisation such that capital investment was allocated disproportionately to this sector at the expense of the natural resources sector. Here again, the possibility of expanding teak production to pre-war levels was quashed as a result of the Burmese state's socialist policies.

However, at a special conference of the ruling Burma Socialist Party Programme in mid-1971, it was decided to promote natural resource extraction as part of a belated recognition of the importance of that sector. Under this revised official strategy, the forestry sector enjoyed greater access to funds in the 1970s and early 1980s, including grants and loans from the Asian Development Bank, the World Bank, and official donor countries (Steinberg 1981). Yet this recognition of the importance of the forestry sector was at best half-hearted, and did not result in a systematic programme of economic liberalisation and investment. The sector remained under the strict control of the STB, and the BWS continued to operate. As a result, the activities typically associated with the development of a forest industry under a capitalist system, including notably the systematic development of new foreign markets as well as the generation of a powerful set of vested private interests keen to expand production levels, did not develop in Burma at this time as it did in such other Southeast Asian countries as Thailand, the Philippines, and Malaysia. Paradoxically, the economic ineptitude of the Burmese state, as manifested in its BWS programme, helped (along with the insurgency which also limited production in contested areas) to maintain Burma's forest cover for a longer time period than in neighbouring countries. It is only relatively recently that Burma has begun to 'catch up' with the deforestation records of other states in the region, as outlined below.

The common thread running through the four themes of post-colonial forest politics noted above is that of attempted state control according to state socialist principles. The Burmese state has moved to increase its control over the forests through the consolidation of extraction activity in the hands of the STB, the seizure of an ever-wider area of national territory from the insurgents, and attempts to regulate non-state forest uses deemed detrimental to commercial forestry; all in the context of an official commitment to the Burmese Way to Socialism.

Following the military 'coup' of 18 September 1988, the State Law and Order Restoration Council (SLORC) was set up to stabilise the political and economic situation. A widely reported aspect of SLORC rule was the decision to grant logging concessions along the Thai–Burmese border to Thai firms (Birsel 1989; Harbinson 1992; Geary 1994; Smith 1994). In the words of the Burma Action Group, the SLORC 'began to sell Burma's natural resources like fast food' (cited in Howard 1993: 3). However, if this issue is an important one, it has tended to obscure the wider significance of SLORC rule to Burmese forest politics.

The Thai logging deals are reviewed by Geary (1994) and thus need only brief consideration here. Within three months of the military coup in September 1988, Thailand's General Chaovalit Yongchaiyuth flew to Rangoon to meet the SLORC leader General Saw Maung. This was one month before Thailand's logging ban was imposed. In early 1989, the Burmese government announced that 20 logging concessions along the Thai–Burmese border had been allocated to Thai firms, and further concessions were granted thereafter. In total as much as 18,800 sq. km may have been alienated in this manner, divided among 47 companies (Geary 1994). The resulting social and ecological impact has been severe. Cultivators were displaced to make way for logging; in turn; they moved to upland areas, exacerbating land degradation there. The combination of careless and extensive logging, poor road construction, and upland agricultural clearance has resulted in extensive deforestation, soil erosion, and flooding. If, in 1993, the link between the Thai loggers and the Karen and Mon insurgents led an angry SLORC to cancel the logging concessions (but see Lintner 1993), the history of this region as a natural resource frontier is far from over. Plans detailed below to develop the Salween River and its tributaries along the border as a huge hydroelectric project and a major natural gas pipeline in Tenasserim are indicative of some of the SLORC's ambitions in the region.

If the SLORC era has been marked by extensive logging along the Thai–Burmese border, it has also been characterised by unsustainable logging elsewhere in the country, notably in central and northern Burma. Two factors in particular have contributed to this process. First, the Myanmar Timber Enterprise (MTE) has sold teak exports in advance to improve cash flows; in 1991 the discrepancy between advance sale and delivery was two years. This practice not only is financially risky, but also 'creates undue pressure to over-harvest accessible teak' (C. Smith 1991: 8). Moreover, the way in which calculations of the annual allowable cut are applied exacerbates the pressure on accessible forests. Thus, an annual allowable cut is calculated on the basis of the entire national teak forest, including forests as yet off-limits owing to insurgent activity, but is applied without modification to the accessible (non-insurrection) areas. Inevitably, this has resulted in a serious teak over-cut in accessible forests. Indeed, as a result of the fact that 'the forests have been systematically mined for years', a national teak shortage is predicted for early in the next century (Smith 1990: 9).

The practices that have contributed to this situation have been instituted despite the opposition of many forest officials. The urgent quest for higher production after 1988 has thus led the SLORC to over-ride its own advisers in the forest department. The relative powerlessness of the department that has been a characteristic of the post-colonial period as a whole has increased under the SLORC. Notwithstanding the enhanced public profile of the forest department as a result of the SLORC's greening campaign in central Burma, it remains an institution beholden to the dictates of the MTE as well as to the SLORC itself. This has contributed to a culture of cynicism in the forest department that is compounded by salary scales that leave many staff below the official poverty line (Smith 1990). Even senior forest officials earn salaries which amount to as little as US$20–25 per month, as a result of which they need to find supplementary sources of income in order to survive. As in other Southeast Asian countries, forest officials in Burma have been reduced to the role of poorly paid 'validators' of often highly destructive state policies (Bryant *et al.* 1993).

A further change introduced by the SLORC has intensified both the marginalisation of forest officials and the degradation of the teak forests. Specifically, the Burmese state has begun to encourage private enterprise in the natural resource sector as part of an 'open-door' and 'market-based' approach to economic management (Taylor 1991). This has been most notable in the oil and natural gas sector where trans-national corporations have been actively involved in exploration and extraction work (Wellner 1994). In terms of teak extraction, the role of the private sector has been confined to Thai logging firms operating in the border areas; in central Burma the MTE retains control over teak extraction. In contrast, the extraction of other commercial hardwoods was opened up to private firms under the SLORC, but despite strict guidelines (MF 1993) overcutting resulted in the re-imposition of a total ban on private logging in January 1994; it has been subsequently relaxed. However, recent years have witnessed a proliferation of small private timber mills that has increased pressure to raise production levels to address the problem of milling over-capacity. One result has been the growth of illegal logging, which an under-staffed and demoralised forest department is unable to check (Smith 1990). The 1994 decision of the SLORC to ban all log exports by land is unlikely to stem the tide of illegal extraction. Notwithstanding these recent throwbacks to a more interventionist past, the regime seems committed to allowing the private sector a role in future forestry operations, thereby abandoning a central feature of the long-standing post-colonial quest for a socialist forestry policy under the BWS. Whether the new 'market' approach will also lead to a reversal of the post-colonial Burmese state's quest to retain direct control over teak extraction remains to be seen, however.

SLORC, OPPOSITION, AND FOREST POLITICS

The preceding discussion has highlighted general themes in post-colonial forestry politics. The remainder of the chapter considers potential explanations for SLORC forestry strategies. Why has this regime acted in the way that it has?

Four possible explanations spring to mind. First, current forest policies need to be situated in the broader context of the Burmese state's ongoing struggle with ethnic insurgents, especially the Karen along the Thai–Burmese border (Bryant 1996). Thus, the Burmese may have encouraged destructive forestry in this area so as to deprive Karen forces of strategic forest cover. The creation of a network of logging roads may also be seen to be of assistance to the Burmese military. The point here is not to exaggerate the importance of logging as an aid to military strategy but merely to suggest that one benefit may be the facilitation of military control in the area. Perhaps more significantly, the logging was an attempt by the SLORC to undermine a key source of revenue available to Karen forces. The KNU (and other ethnic resistance groups such as the New Mon State Party) have long partly funded their military struggle through the extraction of teak (Falla 1991; Smith 1994). With the disruption of smuggling routes for other commodities between Burma and Thailand as a result of Burmese military action, this dependency on timber sales has grown in recent years such that it may represent virtually the only remaining source of revenue. The logging concessions were designed to attack this weak spot of the insurgents by cutting out the Karen and Mon 'middlemen' through direct links between the Thai loggers and the Burmese state. Karen and Mon groups still earn 'protection money' from Thai loggers, with which they have purchased military equipment in Thailand (Lintner 1993; Geary 1994). However, in so far as the ethnic minorities have been forced into unsustainable logging practices, they will find it increasingly difficult to extract timber from a degraded resource base – a process rendered even more difficult in early 1995 with the military victories of the Burmese army in and around Mannerplaw. For the same reason, they will find it more difficult to counter long-standing SLORC claims that insurgents, and not the Burmese state, are despoiling the environment in the border areas (e.g. WPD 1990).

A second explanation for SLORC forestry practice centres on the question of regime survival. The domestic political unrest that culminated in 1988's 'summer of discontent' underscored the political vulnerability of the Burmese state (Lintner 1989). The response, a massive and bloody crackdown on all dissent and an accelerated build-up of military capabilities, was predictable. Yet, if the need for funds to purchase military equipment was great, Burma's financial position in the late 1980s was dire. In 1987, for example, Burma suffered the humiliation of having to plead for 'least developed nation' status before the United Nations in order to obtain debt relief (Morello 1987). Following the September 1988 coup, the situation became even worse. As the country was ostracised by the international community, foreign trade came to a virtual halt, foreign exchange reserves declined to US$12 million, and the government faced the prospect of being unable to service its debt of nearly US$6 billion (Lintner 1993).

In this situation, the need to sell the country's natural resources 'like fast food' becomes readily apparent. The significance of teak in this great resource sell-off was considerable; in 1989–90 timber exports (mostly teak) worth US$135,790,000 accounted for 42 per cent of all export earnings (C. Smith 1991: 5–6). The centrality of teak to SLORC's political survival subsequently remained great, even if non-teak timber assumed a greater role as a result of a flourishing trade with Yunnan (Lintner 1993; UM 1993). This trade has hardly been dented by the formal ban on log exports by land. The result has been that forestry management has been 'out of control' (Smith 1990), with widespread over-harvesting in border areas matched by over-cutting in central areas. The growing political and economic stability of the SLORC may lead to the restriction of unsustainable logging practices, a possible reason for the 1993 suspension of border logging (Lintner 1993). Yet the integration of Burma into the booming Chinese economy may have the opposite effect in so far as the temptation to cash in the country's forest heritage proves too great.

A third possible explanation for current forestry practices relates to the question of corruption. If present moves towards a 'market-based' economy continue, the opportunities and incentives for official corruption may grow.

The implications for the forestry sector are immense. As the experiences of other Southeast Asian countries illustrate, the potential for corruption to shape all aspects of forest management is great. Evidence from the late colonial era (Bryant 1994c), as well as the early years of independence (Anon. 1959), illustrates the ways in which forestry in Burma can become caught up in the political economy of corruption under a market economy. If evidence of corruption on the scale witnessed elsewhere in the region is as yet largely anecdotal, incidents have nevertheless been reported of official involvement in illegal logging (Smith 1990; Smith 1994). The low pay and demoralisation of the forest department today is as strong an inducement for corruption within the department as it was during the colonial era. Further, factionalism within the military is increasing as the demise of Ne Win draws nearer (Lintner 1994a, 1994b). The possibility that timber extraction will become a source of patronage to be fought over in any subsequent power struggle raises the prospect of high-level military profiteering in the forestry sector.

A fourth factor explaining contemporary forestry practices encompasses the issue of 'modernisation'. Following independence, most countries in the Third World embarked on national development strategies predicated on the idea that they were economically 'backward' and thus needed to follow the Western (or in some cases Soviet) model of industrialisation if they were ever to achieve 'modernity'. Concurrently, Third World countries maximised the exploitation of their natural resources as a means to generate the revenue necessary to pay for industrialisation. As during an earlier period in the West, Third World countries have rapidly depleted their forests in the quest to modernise (cf. Mather 1990 and the 'forest transition').

As the SLORC begins to open up the national economy to the outside world, the role of the forests in Burma's modernisation programme is increasing. The push to adopt 'more efficient' mechanical logging techniques in Burma's forests, for example, represents an early official goal (e.g. Von Monroy 1952) that was stymied during the Burmese Way to Socialism era, but which is now promoted by the SLORC (C.F. Smith 1991; Blower *et al.* 1991). Yet, as 'modern' mechanical forestry techniques replace 'vintage' methods, associated with the use of timber elephants, the ability to clear-fell large areas increases. With intense pressure on Burma to 'catch up' developmentally with its neighbours, the likelihood that the country will follow in the footsteps of such countries as Malaysia and Indonesia and clear large areas of national forest in the quest for development is great. In the process, the country's already high deforestation rate (6,000 sq. km per year) will accelerate (Blower *et al.* 1991).

As the role of the forests in Burma's modernisation grows, the plight of the ethnic minorities living in the border area forests can only worsen. As noted, groups such as the Karen and Mon have already been adversely affected by SLORC-sanctioned border logging. Notwithstanding the formal end of those deals in 1993, timber extraction by conscripted villagers for use (including sale) by army units is common, and is associated with the perpetuation of massive human rights abuses in these areas (Smith 1994; Wellner 1994; Karen Human Rights Group 1994). Beyond logging, deforestation in aid of modernisation (and foreign exchange for the SLORC) is taking place as part of the construction of a pipeline to transport natural gas from two offshore fields in the Gulf of Martaban, overland through the Tenasserim forests, and into Thailand. The pipeline will lead to the degradation of some of the last remaining pristine forests in the region, rich in wildlife and biodiversity (Hill 1993; Wellner 1994). This threatens to impoverish even further the lives of ethnic minorities along the Burma–Thailand border. Plans for a series of hydroelectric dams in eastern Burma (i.e. the proposed Upper Salween Dam) will only add to the woes of Burma's ethnic minorities (on the impact of dams in other countries in the region, see Mitchell, Hirsch, and Aditjondro in this volume). As is so often the case with modernisation (cf. Hong 1987; Hurst 1990; Leigh in this volume), the primary victims are the ethnic minorities whose livelihoods depend on the natural resources within their territories but who are forcefully pushed aside by more powerful states and peoples. In Burma, as elsewhere in Southeast Asia, deforestation is simultaneously an ecological and an ethnic crisis (Bryant 1996).

CONCLUSION

This chapter has examined the politics of forestry in colonial and post-colonial Burma. It has suggested that, while the general political and economic context may have changed over this period, notably during the Ne Win years when socialism was the official policy, the central preoccupation of the state with the control of the country's forests has remained unwavering. This conclusion is hardly surprising. The forests have long been an important source of revenue and foreign exchange. Moreover, they have been a traditional base for insurgent activity, which has rendered them politically sensitive as well. Control over the forests has thus formed part of a broader attempt to assert the primacy of the state in Burma (Taylor 1987).

In this respect, the SLORC is no different from its predecessors. Nevertheless, the present regime is pursuing policies associated with the rejection of socialism that will have a major impact on the future of Burma's forests. The precise nature of that impact remains in doubt, and will depend notably on the extent to which state control is surrendered in favour of the private sector. Yet what is certain is that the use of the forests will continue to be the subject of intense conflict among forest users, especially between the state and non-state groups (i.e. ethnic minorities, business organisations). It is likely too, however, that bureaucratic conflict will intensify as the quest for modernisation and development leads to proposals for incompatible land uses. Plans to flood large sections of forest in eastern Burma as part of the construction of a series of hydroelectric dams is a case in point, with forest officials less than enamoured at the prospect of permanent forest losses on a grand scale. Yet whether conflict occurs between different state institutions or between the state and non-state actors, the need to see Burmese forestry as a political process is inescapable. The guiding political ideology may have changed, but the central link between politics and forestry remains the same.

BIBLIOGRAPHY

Anonymous (1959) 'Wholesale illicit felling of teak trees discovered', *Guardian* (Rangoon) 26 November.
Aung Tin (1956) 'Girdling in abnormal times: Zigon forest division 1955–56', *Burmese Forester* 6, 104–107.
Beresford, M. and Fraser, L. (1992) 'Political economy of the environment in Vietnam', *Journal of Contemporary Asia* 22, 3–19.
Birsel, R. (1989) 'Few winners in Burma's teak war', *Cultural Survival Quarterly* 13 (4).
Blower, J. *et al.* (1991) 'Burma (Myanmar)', in N.M. Collins, J.A. Sayer and T.C. Whitmore (eds), *The conservation atlas of tropical forests: Asia and the Pacific*, Macmillan, London, 103–110.
Bryant, R.L. (1994a) 'The rise and fall of taungya forestry: social forestry in defence of the Empire', *Ecologist* 24, 1–26.
—— (1994b) 'Shifting the cultivator: the politics of teak regeneration in colonial Burma', *Modern Asian Studies* 28, 225–250.
—— (1994c) 'Fighting over the forests: political reform, peasant resistance and the transformation of forest management in late colonial Burma', *Journal of Commonwealth and Comparative Politics* 32, 244–260.
—— (1994d) 'From laissez-faire to scientific forestry: forest management in early colonial Burma 1826–85', *Forest and Conservation History* 38, 160–170.
—— (1996) 'Asserting sovereignty through natural resource use: Karen forest management on the Thai–Burmese border', in Richard Howitt, Philip Hirsch and John Connell (eds), *Resources, nations and indigenous peoples in Australia, Southeast Asia and the Pacific*, Melbourne, Oxford University Press.
Bryant, R.L., Rigg, J. and Stott, P. (eds.) (1993) *The political ecology of Southeast Asia's forests: trans-disciplinary discourses*, Global Ecology and Biogeography Letters Special Issue, Basil Blackwell, Oxford.
Colchester, M. (1989) *Pirates, squatters and poachers: the political ecology of dispossession of the native peoples of Sarawak*, Survival International and INSAN, Kuala Lumpur.
Dauvergne, P. (1993/94) 'The politics of deforestation in Indonesia', *Pacific Affairs* 66, 497–518.
Diokno, M.S.I. (1983) 'British firms and the economy of Burma, with special reference to the rice and teak industries, 1917–1937', PhD thesis, University of London.
Falla, J. (1991) *True Love and Bartholomew: rebels on the Burmese border*, Cambridge University Press, Cambridge.
FAO [Food and Agriculture Organization] (1978) 'Burma', *Forest News for Asia and the Pacific* 2 (1), 5–8.
Geary, K. (1994) *The role of Thailand in forest destruction along the Thai–Burma border 1988–1993*, Project for Ecological Recovery, Bangkok.
Guha, R. (1989) *The unquiet woods: ecological change and peasant resistance in the Himalaya*, Oxford University Press, Delhi.
Harbinson, R. (1992) 'Burma's forests fall victim to war', *Ecologist* 22, 72–73.
Hill, G. (1993) 'Wildlife trade in Mergui Tavoy District (Kawthoolei), December 1991–April 1993', *TRAFFIC Southeast Asia* field report no.2 (Thailand).
Hong, E. (1987) *Natives of Sarawak: survival in Borneo's vanishing forests*, Institut Masyarakat, Penang.

Howard, M.C. (1993) Introduction, in M.C. Howard (ed.), *Asia's environmental crisis*, Westview Press, Boulder, 1–35.

Hurst, P. (1990) *Rainforest politics: ecological destruction in South-East Asia*, Zed Books, London.

Karen Human Rights Group (1994) 'Continuing SLORC actions in Karen State', mimeo, Mannerplaw, 26 May.

King, V.T. (1993) '"Politik pembangunan": the political economy of rainforest exploitation and development in Sarawak, East Malaysia', in R.L. Bryant, J. Rigg and P. Stott (eds) *The political ecology of Southeast Asian forests: transdisciplinary discourses*, Global Ecology and Biogeography Letters Special Issue, Basil Blackwell, Oxford, 235–244.

Kummerer, D.M. (1992) *Deforestation in the postwar Philippines*, Ateneo de Manila University Press, Manila.

Leungaramsri, P. and Rajesh, N. (eds) (1992) *The future of people and forests in Thailand after the logging ban*, Project for Ecological Recovery, Bangkok.

Lieberman, V.B. (1984) *Burma's administrative cycles: anarchy and conquest c.1580–1760*, Princeton University Press, Princeton.

Lintner, B. (1989) *Outrage: Burma's struggle for democracy*, White Lotus, London.

—— (1993) 'Soft option on hardwood: Rangoon to scrap Thai logging deals on border', *Far Eastern Economic Review* 22 July, 25.

—— (1994a) 'City of nerves: a sick Ne Win gives the Rangoon regime the jitters', *Far Eastern Economic Review*, 10 February, 30.

—— (1994b) 'Conflict of interests: army chief's promotion tilts factional balance', *Far Eastern Economic Review*, 19 May, 28.

Lohmann, L. (1993) 'Land, power and forest colonization in Thailand', in R.L. Bryant, J. Rigg and P. Stott (eds), *The political ecology of Southeast Asian forests: transdisciplinary discourses*, Global Ecology and Biogeography Letters Special Issue, Basil Blackwell, Oxford, 180–191.

Long, A. (1957) 'Some aspects of shifting or taungya cultivation in Burma', *Burmese Forester* 7, 115–121.

MAF [Ministry of Agriculture and Forests] (1952) 'The State Timber Board', *Burma* 2 (2), 36–38.

—— (1953) 'The Forest Department', *Burma* 3 (3), 71–73.

—— (1962) 'Forest Department', *Burma* 11, 233–237.

Mather, A.S. (1990) *Global forest resources*, Belhaven, London.

Mekvichai, B. (1988) 'The teak industry in north Thailand: the role of a natural-resource-based export economy in regional development', PhD thesis, Cornell University.

MF [Ministry of Forestry] (1993) *An outline of the forest situation and investment opportunities in Myanmar*, Yangon.

Morello, T. (1987) 'Forlorn conclusion: Burma nears the expected U.N. approval for LDC status', *Far Eastern Economic Review* 22 October, 101.

Peluso, N.L. (1992) *Rich forests, poor people: resource control and resistance in Java*, University of California Press, Berkeley.

Potter, L. (1991) 'Environmental and social aspects of timber exploitation in Kalimantan 1967–1989', in J. Hardjono (ed.) *Indonesia: resources, ecology, and environment*, Oxford University Press, Singapore, 177–211.

Remigio, A.A. (1993) 'Philippine forest resource policy in the Marcos and Aquino governments: a comparative assessment', in R.L. Bryant, J. Rigg and P. Stott (eds) *The political ecology of Southeast Asian forests: trans-disciplinary discourses*, Global Ecology and Biogeography Letters Special Issue, Basil Blackwell, Oxford, 192–214.

Scott, J.C. (1985) *Weapons of the weak: everyday forms of peasant resistance*, Yale University Press, New Haven.

Shwe Bo (1963) 'Burma's teak', *Forward* 1 (15), 15–18.

Smith, C.F. (1990) Memo to FAO resident representative, 6 November.

—— (1991) *Report on the Myanmar forestry sector*, field document no. 11. Union of Myanmar for the FAO, Yangon.

Smith, M. (1991) *Burma: insurgency and the politics of ethnicity*, Zed Books, London.

—— (1994) *Paradise lost? The suppression of environmental rights and freedom of expression in Burma*, Article 19, London.

Steinberg, D.I. (1981) *Burma's road toward development: growth and ideology under military rule*, Westview Press, Boulder.

Taylor, R.H. (1987) *The state in Burma*, C. Hurst, London.

—— (1991) 'Myanmar 1990: new era or old?', in *Southeast Asian Affairs 1991*, Institute of Southeast Asian Studies, Singapore, 199–219.

Thein Han (1951) 'Forestry in the Union of Burma', *Burmese Forester* 1, 5–7.

Tin Htut (1955) 'A note on "shifting cultivation"', *Burmese Forester* 5, 108–109.

Tun Kyaw (1956) 'A short note on the working of the State Timber Board', *Burmese Forester* 6, 71.

UB [Union of Burma], Ministry of Planning and Finance (1985) *Report to the Pyithu Hluttaw on the financial, economic and social conditions of the Socialist Republic of the Union of Burma for 1985/86*, Rangoon.

UM [Union of Myanmar], Ministry of Agriculture and Forests (1989) *Forestry situation in Myanmar*, Yangon.

—— (1990) *Watershed management in Myanmar*, Yangon.

UM [Union of Myanmar], Ministry of National Planning and Economic Development (1993) *Review of the financial, economic and social conditions for 1993/94*, Yangon.

Von Monroy, J.A. (1952) *Report to the Government of Burma on integration of forests and industries*, FAO Report no. 16, Food and Agriculture Organization, Rome.

Wellner, P. (1994) 'A pipeline killing field: exploitation of Burma's natural gas', *Ecologist* 24, 189–193.

WPD [*Working People's Daily*] (1990), 'Sound forest management', 29 June, 6.

7 The politics of logging in the Philippines

Marites Danguilan Vitug

INTRODUCTION

The Philippine forests have been the most coveted among the country's natural resources, and the few who have been granted the privilege of 'taming' portions of them have reaped power and wealth. Deforestation in the Philippines, as in other parts of Southeast Asia, has been intimately connected with power politics. The dangerous intertwine of forests and politics was most glaring under Ferdinand Marcos (1969–1985). In bestowing upon himself the power to grant and revoke logging licenses – formerly held by the Department of Environment and Natural Resources – the Marcos government used the Timber License Agreement or TLA as a tool of political patronage.[1] Law enforcement was weak; violation of forestry laws went unpunished. Politicians, because of their direct or indirect stakes in logging (as lawyers for timber concessionaires, for example), pursued the interests of the industry over public and community rights to these resources.

FORESTS AND POLITICS: THE PLUNDER

> If necessary, I will cancel all [logging] licenses in order to protect the forest . . . This is not said in anger; nor in pettiness or impatience . . . I have seen fortunes made overnight from the forest, and the wastage, and it makes my skin crawl to realize that there are many Filipinos who just don't care about the future generations' legacy in the way of forest resources.
>
> (*Philippine Lumberman* 1978, cited in Vitug 1993: 25)

The above statement came not from some unyielding environmentalist, but from former President Ferdinand Marcos, the man who presided over massive deforestation in the Philippines and who, together with friends and relatives, plundered much of the country's forests for 20 years. He said this in 1978 before a congress of logging concessionaires, threatening the industry with reduced incentives and restricted license tenure. Why? That was his way of reminding the timber concessionaires that he was still in charge and that if they wanted to continue in the business, they had to put up with, among other things, sharing the largesse with him.

In public, Marcos cleverly distanced himself from the ravage of forest resources which took place under his regime. He could conveniently lay the blame on the concessionaires – but did nothing to prosecute those who violated the law and overexploited the forests which had become a source of income for himself, other politicians and business cronies. The dangerous connection between forests and politics was most glaring during the Marcos era and demonstrates how politics became a driving force in the ravenous and short-sighted exploitation of the country's forest heritage. The deforestation rate peaked in the late 1960s at 300,000 hectares a year as the number of logging concessions grew, the export market for logs thrived and population increased. As a result, in 1991, only 6.46 million hectares of the original 27.5 million hectares was left. Of this, 1.79 million hectares is non-productive, meaning they are mossy forests unable to grow trees, while 1.8 million hectares is old-growth or virgin forests (DENR 1992).

The explanation for this rapid process of deforestation lies partly in the political and economic structure of the Philippines. The elite – some four hundred families – dominate big business, in both industry and agriculture. They own tracts of the best land, have access to the forests, have the capital to diversify into manufacturing and exports. Their wealth in turn secures political offices, influence and favors.

Since the Spanish period, the Philippines had been dominated by a strong land-owning oligarchy. When Marcos perpetuated himself in power – imposing martial law at the end of his second four-year term in 1972[2] – he dismantled the old oligarchy, blaming it for the backwardness and inequality of Philippine society. But Marcos fashioned his own 'oligarchy' – this time made up of cronies whose businesses he helped expand. Some took over old wealth while others were given new opportunities in construction and logging.

HISTORICAL ROOTS

The reputation of Philippine wood was already well-established by the turn of the century. So enamored were the Spanish colonizers of the Philippines' lush, tropical forests that Fajaro wrote to Philip III, 'At least 10 ships can be built every year in these islands, and by taking care of their many forests, even if a hundred ships were built now, there would be enough timber left to construct every year the 10 [I have] mentioned' (Corpuz 1989: 91).

When the Spaniards began their 300-year colonization of the Philippines, they were seduced by, among other things, mountains blanketed by unending forests. In 1575, the forest cover was estimated to have been 27.5 million hectares, almost 92 per cent of the total land area of the Philippines. The population then was only 750,000 (Roque 1990). During the Spanish regime, trees were cut mainly for building ships which serviced Spain's galleon trade with Mexico and other countries. Shipyards were established in various parts of the country. With the setting up of the 'Inspección General de Montes' and the Forest Service in 1863, all timber on public lands was required to be cut under license. Certificates for forest exploitation began to be issued to private companies.

It was American colonial forestry in the Philippines, however, which pursued the systematic denuding of the forests. The Bureau of Forestry, headed by an American, had power to issue timber concessions on whatever scale and duration it deemed a lumberman's resources could match. Nearly 20 million hectares of forest lands was under the Bureau's control.

One of the reasons the US continued to be involved in the Philippines was that the colony offered a rich supply of wood. Speaking before the US Senate in January 1900, Senator Alfred J. Beveridge argued: 'The wood of the Philippines can supply the furniture of the world for a century to come . . . And the wood . . . and other products of the Philippines supply what we need and cannot ourselves produce' (Congressional record 1900 in Schirmer and Shalom 1987: 23).

LICENSING THE PLUNDER

The Timber License Agreement (TLA) was the main instrument used to exploit the forests. The state issued this license to corporations to cut trees in a forest area of not more than 100,000 hectares for a period of 25 years, as provided by the Constitution. It was the powerful and well-connected who had access to these licenses. For politicians, retired generals, relatives and friends of Marcos, the TLA was a reward for loyalty. Among those who benefited were Fortuna Marcos-Barba, Marcos's sister, who operated five timber concessions; Herminio Disini, a Marcos business associate; and Alfonso Lim, a political supporter of Marcos. TLAs were distributed as a political and diplomatic tool. To attract Muslim rebels back to the fold, Marcos offered short-term licenses to fell trees in the forests of Mindanao, southern Philippines. When Marcos needed to buy electoral support in the 1970s the TLA was one currency. In return, money from logging supported a number of candidates during election campaigns. The timber industry determined the outcome of elections in areas wherever logging was dominant, as it was in Mindanao and northern Luzon.

To obtain a license to a forest concession entailed an appallingly low cost. In the 1970s the application fee for a timber concession was P 1 per hectare (US$0.38). With an average selling price of about US$140 per cubic meter of log, only US$1.50 plus 75 cents for every cubic meter harvested went to government. These low fees tended to create excess demand for the exploitation of forests. Under Marcos, the number of concessionaires ballooned from 58 in 1969 to 230 in 1977, the highest recorded figure. Apart from these, Marcos issued short-term (meaning one to five years) 'special permits' to fell trees. Counting these, the number of licensees soared to 412 in 1969, 461 in 1970 and to 471 in 1976 (DENR 1992).

Marcos carved out parts of the country for his friends and family. Alfonso

Lim, a steadfast supporter of Marcos since his bid for the Senate in the early 1960s, operated in 533,880 hectares and gobbled up adjacent logging companies through corporate raids sanctioned by Marcos. In 1979, for example, Lim met with the boards of directors of companies operating in the area. He came for a 'showdown,' determined to push for control of the companies, one owned by retired veterans (Veterans Woodworks), through a management contract he imposed. 'The contract was approved by the President,' he tersely said in a tense meeting held at the Manila office (minutes of the meeting of the boards of directors of Veterans Woodworks, Tropical Philippines Wood Industries and Sierra Madre Wood Industries with Taggat Industries, 28 March 1979, from the records of the Presidential Commission on Good Government). After the take-over, Marcos personally looked into the operations of Veterans Woodworks and its affiliates. He approved, in marginal notes, Lim's request for privileges for his companies such as a lease-purchase agreement between Veterans Woodworks and a state bank.

Also in the north, another crony, Felipe Ysmael, Jr, president of Ysmael Steel Company, ran a logging operation. In 1965, the first Marcos bid for the presidency, he was said to have donated millions of pesos to the Marcos campaign chest. Ysmael was rewarded with forest concessions – close to 55,000 hectares in the northern Philippines and 100,000 hectares in Palawan. Aside from that, he was able to borrow US$13.5 million from foreign banks by using as collateral vast concessions he had received from Marcos that were guaranteed by the state-owned Development Bank of the Philippines. Marcos's sister, Fortuna Marcos, who was married to a military officer, also formed logging companies covering nearly 200,000 hectares of northern forests. One of their companies was granted a license through a presidential decree. Other relatives, including Marcos's uncles, mother and brother, were either members or chairpersons of various boards of logging companies.

AWASH WITH DOLLARS

Logging was the star performer among Philippine export industries. In the 1960s, logging concessionaires contributed as much as 29 per cent to total export earnings. From 1969 to 1972, logging firms raked in an annual average of $300 million. This reached its peak in 1973 with record export earnings of $472 million. Overall, the industry accounted for 5 per cent of the country's gross national product (*Philippine Lumberman*, various issues).

In 1965, the Philippines was supplying at least 30 per cent of the world's requirements, which made the country the biggest single log producer in the world. The industry created new millionaires who either entered politics themselves or became kingmakers. Those who entered politics directly include Democrito Plaza, former congressman and currently governor of Agusan del

Sur province; Lorenzo Sarmiento, Sr, of Davao, former congressman; Gaudencio Antonino, former senator; Alejandro Almendras, former senator and congressman. For their part, the kingmakers supported election campaigns of sympathetic candidates, particularly in the forest-rich provinces of Mindanao and northern Luzon. However, as the Philippine forests dwindled, Filipino loggers looked for greener options. Indonesia was their next haven. In the late 1960s, Filipino loggers trooped to Indonesia and taught their partners the business. Soon, Indonesia and Malaysia overtook the Philippines in log exports.

Eventually, log exports had to be regulated. Marcos predictably did not favor a total ban. Instead, he instituted a quota system tying allocations of export volumes to specified logging companies that fulfilled certain requirements. No less than the office of the President prepared the list of companies allowed to export logs. This practice was fraught with corruption. For every cubic meter of export allocation, some amount was charged by the Department of Environment and Natural Resources, which shared the largesse with the office of the President.

POLITICIAN LOGGERS

Loggers in politics became institutionalized in the Philippines. Some congressmen owned logging companies. Others, who were lawyers, had logging firms as clients. According to prominent academic, David Wurfel:

> Those who do not have great wealth themselves were found to have members of the economic elite among their legal clients. They tend to look after the client's interests in the legislative chamber . . . A common practice is for congressmen to be given a regular legal retainer's fee in return for aid and advice both in policy formulation and implementation affecting the interests of the firm.
>
> (quoted in Abueva and De Guzman 1969: 211)

To a great extent, the presence of loggers in Congress simply demonstrated the traditional ties between political power and access to the country's natural resources. Like other businessmen, they entered politics to protect and expand their financial interests.

Conflicts of interest were occasionally exposed. Senator Gaudencio Antonino was charged in 1960 with using his position as a member of the Monetary Board to expand his business holdings, primarily a logging company. Antonino was present during board meetings when dollar allocations were granted to his firm, Western Mindanao Lumber Company. Senator Pedro Sabido, chairman of the committee on banks, also owned a logging concession in the 1960s. Sabido's law office followed up dollar applications of the senator's firm, Lianga Bay Logging Company, with the Monetary Board. At that time, the financial system was not yet liberalized so that foreign exchange movements were still regulated by government.

Martial law exacerbated the interdependency of politics and timber. Timber licenses were suspended or revoked if those in power were displeased with the concessionaires, i.e. if they did not pay up or cooperate with the Marcos government. To insure the continuity of their licenses, logging companies would invite influential politicians to sit on their boards of directors. That move also sped up the renewal of licenses and avoided the high cost of delayed operations. 'The system created a need for politicians in logging,' Pat Dugan, a forester for more than 30 years, said in an interview. 'There was someone to holler for help, to expedite papers. It was influence peddling' (interview 1992). Bribery was, of course, a common resort.

Today, of the present crop of 196 congressmen, nine are engaged in the logging business. The dwindling of the forests and the cancellation of licenses has meant that the business is no longer as lucrative. Others have indirect interests in logging: they are not owners or shareholders but they lobby for the interests of the industry. In 1991–1992, when the bill to ban commercial logging was being hotly debated in Congress, no less than the Speaker of the House was closely identified with the industry. One of his major campaign supporters was a logging tycoon. In fact, wood for his vacation house in Palawan province was donated by his logger friend.

In the post-Marcos era, congressmen still use budget hearings – when the annual budget of the Department of Environment and Natural Resources is being deliberated – to seek favors, such as lifting a suspension of license belonging to them or their 'clients.' Others sought special permits to cut or haul trees. Some would attempt to corner funds for reforestation.

FORESTS AS BATTLEFIELD

In another arena, a battle for the forests was taking place and continues to do so. Logging companies operating in rebel lairs encounter the New People's Army, the military arm of the Communist Party of the Philippines. Usually, the NPA levies 'revolutionary taxes' from these companies. If they refuse to pay up, the guerrillas burn the concession's logging equipment.

The NPA tried to introduce environmental policies while continuing its taxation program. The denudation of the forests has become so severe that the need to protect and conserve them was not lost on the guerrillas, who need the money they collect from logging companies to survive. Ironically, they also need the forests – which offer protection and shelter – while fighting the war in the countryside. Bald forests mean open spaces which make them vulnerable targets. In 1990, the NPA tried a new tack by asking a few logging companies to reforest. They agitated for higher daily pay for workers assigned to reafforestation and threatened the companies with the burning of reafforestation sites if the workers were not given their increases.

To some extent, the presence of rebels in the mountains helped protect the forests but only in so far as this deterred loggers and settlers from penetrating the area. Once the logging companies were in, a relationship of convenience and coexistence evolved – logging companies cut the trees, paid up and let the rebels be. For the NPA, as long as the loggers did not hamper their operations, an unholy alliance prevailed.

With the decline of the communist insurgency throughout most parts of the country in recent years, forests are no longer a battlefield. Only those forests which were former guerrilla strongholds and where no roads had been built remain intact.

REFORMS UNDER AQUINO

After the demise of the Marcos regime, under the new government of President Corazon Aquino (1986–1992) significant reforms were introduced in forest management. It was a time of awakened environmental awareness in the country, partly influenced by the environmental movement in the West. Along with the flowering of democracy after two decades of authoritarian rule, non-governmental organizations (NGOs) advocating environmental issues appeared everywhere. They performed a watchdog function, as did the press, which was unshackled after 1986. At times, the NGOs played an adversarial role, as when lobbying for a complete ban on commercial logging; but in some cases – for example in community-based forestry and reafforestation programs – they cooperated with government. The debates in the Senate (1990–1991) on whether to ban commercial logging were important for the NGOs. The issue united some of the NGOs while dividing the environmental NGO movement as a whole. Some were for a selective ban on commercial logging while the more vocal ones were for a complete ban.

The issue tested the strength of the NGOs, their capacity to lobby Congress and to articulate their views in the media. A Task Force for a Total Commercial Log Ban was formed by groups like the Haribon Foundation, a former bird-watching club; Green Forum, a coalition of environmental NGOs; Green Coalition, led by Senator Orlando Mercado; Miriam Peace, a university-based NGO; Legal Rights and Natural Resources Center; Philippine Ecological Network; Philippine Environmental Action Network; and the Visayan Forum. Except for the Visayan Forum, the NGOs are Manila-based. Most are middle-class groups with no developed links to the grassroots. They stepped up their lobbying, attended Senate committee meetings, watched floor debates and aired their views in print as well as in broadcast media.

But for all their visibility in the media and their lobbying with the Senate, activist groups lost sight of the House of Representatives. 'We were not vigilant enough,' recalls Angelina Galang, Task Force member and an academic. 'We were focusing on the Senate while the House already went for a selective log ban. There is also a need to improve our strategic planning and get a critical mass of citizens to support us' (interview 1992). Having learned its lesson, the Task Force is monitoring both Houses of Congress. Other NGOs are pushing for the passage of the bill while monitoring the activities of timber concession holders and lobbying for their cancellation. The Cagayan Anti-

Logging Movement (CALM) adopted a strategy of presenting evidence of violations by TLA holders, potent grounds for cancellation of their licenses.

Many of the environmental NGOs have come a long way from being passive observers to becoming aggressive and outspoken advocates. Haribon, now one of the most active NGOs, evolved from a bird-watching club into a conservation foundation that focuses on scientific studies. It found its pollution studies sitting on the desks of politicians without effect. Says Maximo Kalaw, head of Haribon: 'Politicians told me at that time: "It is hard to listen to you. The trees don't vote and the fish don't vote. The farmers and fishermen have coalitions. But you don't have any. So why should I vote for the forest?"' (interview 1990).

Haribon then decided to build a constituency which would closely monitor environmental issues and support environment-friendly politicians. Green Forum later emerged with Haribon as the core force responding to the government's inadequate attention to environmental problems. A coalition of several NGOs, Green Forum stresses that the environment knows no political color.

An awakening to environmental problems was also occurring in various parts of the country. Communities organised to stop the logging operations of timber concessionaires. Environmental education was stepped up. The Catholic Church made an impact in 1988 when the influential Catholic Bishops' Conference of the Philippines (CBCP) wrote a pastoral letter warning of the perils of environmental destruction. The CBCP called on people to speak up and organize around ecological issues. The NGOs working in community development saw the degradation of the forests, the pollution of the rivers, and how this deprived people of their sources of livelihood. Environmental problems were so intrinsically linked to the social and economic milieu that it was difficult for NGOs not to speak up on green issues.

On another front, the Philippine Ecological Network and 43 children went to the Supreme Court on 20 March 1990 and asked that the highest court of the land stop the DENR from issuing and renewing timber license agreements. In a petition, they argued that government has violated their rights to environmental protection by granting more areas for logging than are actually available.

At the same time, the concept of 'sustainable development' was given international recognition in a report for the United Nations by the Brundtland Commission on Environment and Development (World Commission on Environment and Development 1987). Although there had been discussion of 'sustainable development' in the mid-1970s, this did not capture popular attention.

MAKING SUSTAINABLE DEVELOPMENT WORK

After the 'People Power' revolution in 1986 brought President Aquino to office, a strain of idealism ran through the DENR leadership, a belief that democracy could be made to work for public interest. There was also a very strong anti-Marcos sentiment in government which pressured against repeating previous malpractice. At the DENR, that meant several things.

First, the number of licensees was cut from 143 in 1987 to 32 in June 1992. A number of politicians' concessions were closed down. Even loggers close to politicians were affected. The allowed volume of harvest was reduced from 6.03 million cubic meters to 1 million cubic meters. Logging in virgin forests was banned. Reafforestation became a centerpiece program of the DENR. The deforestation rate was recorded at 80,000 to 88,000 hectares a year from 1988 to 1991 compared to 300,000 hectares a year in the late 1960s under Marcos (DENR).

But even reafforestation was colored by patron politics. A political decision was made by DENR Secretary Fulgencio Factoran to distribute reafforestation funds through congressional districts to make congressmen cooperate. Under the DENR's contract reafforestation program, private corporations, non-governmental organizations, communities and families were encouraged to enter into a contract with the DENR to regreen denuded forests. The majority of these were families residing in areas where reafforestation is a priority program. An NGO study found that family contracts were most beneficial in providing employment and enabling families to buy the work animals they need (Asian NGO Coalition for Agrarian Reform and Rural Development 1991).

POWER TO THE COMMUNITIES

Communities were also encouraged to manage the forests. Upland communities – where there is an estimated population of 10 to 18 million[3] – could manage and protect the forests and eventually reap their harvests. As organized communities, they could be awarded Community Forest Management Agreements (CFMAs) with the understanding that the community will have the privilege to harvest mature trees in the area. The CFMA is the key instrument of the program. Community organization and training are awarded to local NGOs.

The belief is that communities are in the best position to manage and protect the forests. However, before they can fully assume such a role, the problems of poverty and tenure must be addressed if these communities are to be convinced to assist government. It is one way of democratizing access to forest resources and alleviating poverty while, at the same time, protecting the remaining forests. 'It was a bold move,' says Ernesto Guiang, DENR consultant for community forestry during the Aquino administration. 'Financially, community forestry is viable. It is labor-intensive and geared for small-scale harvest' (interview 1992).

At the start of the program, communities were organized with the help of NGOs. Areas for community forestry projects should be able to offer adequate opportunities for livelihood, such as backyard farming and agro-forestry, so that cutting of trees is not their main source of income. These also give them sustenance while the trees are not yet ready for harvest.

Residents of upland communities usually do not have the operating capital to begin a forest products enterprise. The DENR therefore advances certain operating costs. The communities are required to deposit into a trust fund part of the revenues from timber sales. The fund is to be managed by the communities themselves.

The selection of which NGOs to work with is a sensitive process. The democratic space opened up after the demise of the Marcos administration resulted in an explosion in the number of NGOs. The Securities and Exchange Commission lists about 30,000 NGOs, including what are disparagingly called GRINGOs or government-initiated NGOs. The latter type of NGOs are backed by local politicians and have questionable non-profit credentials. 'The patronage system is strongly at work in the community level,' wrote Guiang and Bienvenido Dolom (then national coordinator of the Community Forestry Program, CFP) in an internal report. Many of the NGOs 'are hiding behind the cloak of community development when their main target is forest products extraction' (Guiang and Dolom 1991).

As for fees, the DENR set heftier forest charges: a reafforestation fee of P 12,500 (US$480) per hectare deposited with the Philippine Wood Products Association (PWPA), which is composed of all forest concessionaires; forest charges, from P 30 ($1.15) per square meter to 25 per cent of FOB (freight-on-board) value. Pending determination of FOB value, the forest charge was set at P 550 ($21.15) per cubic meter for common and construction hardwood and P 3,000 ($115.40) per cubic meter for premium species like narra and kamagong. The reafforestation fee is returned to the TLA holders if they comply with the DENR's reafforestation requirements. If not, the money is forefeited.

MAKING THE CHOICE

The first strategy the DENR chose to implement was the rehabilitation of degraded ecosystems, for obvious reasons. But the government's lack of resources forced the DENR to set its priorities. Competing for urgent attention were the problems of urban and industrial pollution; forest and upland ecosystems; and water resources conservation. Urban air quality is among the worst in the region and most of the urban rivers are biologically dead. Furthermore, city dwellers are the most politically influential and the most vocal. But the DENR chose the green environment over the brown. Recalls Factoran: 'It was a difficult decision to make. And we gambled on pouring our available resources heavily toward the rehabilitation of the forests' (interview 1992).

The decision was influenced by several major factors. The forests and uplands cover 15 million hectares of the total land area of 30 million. Of the 15 million hectares, 6.5 million are forest lands of which 1.8 million are virgin forests (DENR 1992). They are the 'primary regulators' of the Philippine environment, for to these ecosystems can be attributed the well-being of the soil cover and crop lands, freshwater supplies, air and even coastal areas.

Furthermore, the problem in the uplands was not only ecological; it was also social. Extreme poverty was driving the 18 million Filipinos in the uplands to cut timber. 'By putting government machinery to work for them, we had hoped that this would give them some of the political voice that would let them be heard in Manila,' says Factoran (interview 1992).

To implement its greening program, the DENR turned to foreign sources of funds. Soft loan packages from the Asian Development Bank (ADB) and the Overseas Economic Cooperation Fund of Japan (OECF), each donor providing US$120 million, went to a national forestry program which included reafforestation contracted to upland families, communities, and NGOs – and improved forest law enforcement. It was the largest assistance package for the forestry sector ever granted anywhere. In 1990, this was followed by a US$125 million grant-in-aid from the United States Agency for International Development (USAID); in 1991 by a US$369 million environment and natural resources sectoral loan from the World Bank, at that time the largest single assistance package ever developed by the World Bank for the environment.

However, field assessments made by the University of the Philippines in Los Banos showed that corporations and some non-governmental organizations, which covered two-thirds of the area funded by the program, had low survival rates and a number of them made profits much higher than was intended by the program (Severino 1994). The survival rate of newly planted trees after three years has been estimated at 65 per cent, well below the target of 80 per cent at the beginning of the first massive reafforestation program undertaken by government. It was resumed on a limited pilot project scale involving non-governmental and community organizations in 1995.

In 1995, community organizations whose reafforestation contracts had high survival rates entered into 25-year community forest management agreements, or CFMA, with the DENR to manage their forested areas. This means that they will have cutting rights to the forests. But the communities will have to present their development plans to be approved by the DENR and pay an annual license fee and application fee. Only then can they harvest trees. The use of heavy equipment such as bulldozers and yarders is not permitted. The CFMA holders are required to reforest open and denuded areas, usually at their own expense, using funds from the sale of forest products. They are also asked to organize forest protection teams that work closely with DENR.

THE PRESENT: WORKING WITH RAMOS

President Fidel Ramos is no stranger to logging. When he assumed the presidency in June 1992, he divested his shares in Greenbelt Wood Products, a logging company which was earlier found to have logged illegally. The President, his daughter and late father were among the seven stockholders. Its license was cancelled during the administration of President Corazon Aquino.

But Ramos claimed he was unaware of the operations of the company because he was not involved in the day-to-day running of the firm. In the 1992 presidential elections, the logging industry was said to have donated to the Ramos campaign. But Ramos wants to be known as the environmental president. He has put environmental protection on his list of top five priorities and has appointed an environment-friendly secretary of environment and natural resources.

Basically, forest management in the term of President Ramos operates as it did in the Aquino years.[4] The same political pressures exist but they have become attenuated because the number of logging concessions awarded has decreased to the present figure of 32. Records show that the logging companies increased to 38 during the early part of President Ramos's term. In some of the cases, DENR gave in to political pressure. For example, Woodland Domain, owned by Representative Renato Dragon, was no longer qualified for continued operations. Yet it returned to the active list of TLAs after June 1992. The same thing happened to Luzon Loggers, owned by Representative Junie Evangelista Cua. In other cases, politicians lobbied for the reinstatement of TLAs.

The lobbying from congressmen, governors and politicians on behalf of logging companies continues. For example, the license of Consolidated Logging and Lumber Mills Inc. (CLMI) was suspended for exceeding its allowed cut. DENR Undersecretary Ben Malayang admitted that political pressure from local officials to lift the suspension was intense,[5] but it remains closed. The prevailing problem for the DENR with regard to logging companies is still compliance with laws and the need for careful monitoring.

In the beginning of 1992, when President Ramos assumed office, he created an anti-crime commission led by Vice-President Joseph Estrada, a former movie actor. Estrada operates in a high-profile manner, and part of his program was to team up with the DENR in an anti-illegal logging crackdown. Thus, a number of arrests and confiscations were made and these became newspaper headlines. Though short-lived, it nevertheless sent signals to the industry of the risks of illegal activity.

Other than that, we see a continuity of policy today. Differences lie in the emphasis. Under DENR Secretary Angel Alcala,[6] the thrust is community-based forest protection, which was started during the Aquino administration. Multi-sectoral forest protection committees composed of Church, media, NGOs, and the military are being set up. Communities are organized by DENR to plant, and have access to forests. DENR provides money for seeds and a subsistence subsidy. This is done mainly in critical watersheds. The rate of deforestation has gone down marginally, from 80,000 to 88,000 hectares per year in 1991 to 75,000 to 80,000 hectares per year in 1993 (DENR 1994).

Overall, the NGO community is friendly to the DENR because Secretary Angel Alcala was formerly with an environmental NGO. In general, NGO cooperation with the government has been strong in the post-Marcos period. Following the Rio de Janeiro Earth Summit in 1992, a Philippine Council for Sustainable Development (PCSD), composed of representatives from government agencies and NGOs, including one representing the business sector (Philippine Business for the Environment Foundation), was formed with the blessing of President Ramos. This is a high-level partnership between government and NGOs which enables the latter to contribute to policy. The PCSD is a new layer in the bureaucracy but it represents a fresh initiative. The question is: will it really be effective? A lot will depend on the influence the Council will have on government agencies and the support given by President Ramos.

'Ramos has accepted a rather revolutionary concept, that of social movements as counterparts of the state, not just an extension. It is the whole idea of partnership,' points out Maximo Kalaw, PCSD member and head of Green Forum, an environment NGO (interview 1992). The PCSD also shows Ramos's sensitivity to what the NGOs have to say. He considers them politically important. So far, the best that the Council has achieved is the bringing together of government and private volunteer groups in a high-level body that could plan and experiment with this problematic concept of sustainable development.

There is some wariness among NGO representatives who sit in the PCSD that the President's overtures to this partnership are largely a cooption device. The large centralised NGOs believe that working within the parliamentary arena, rather than out of it, gives them a forum to help shape policy. They express awareness of the importance of keeping vigilant and remaining accountable to their constituents. The media also play a critical role as watchdog of government as well as NGOs. Since the end of the Marcos era, the Philippine media have been actively reporting on environmental issues. President Ramos is particularly attentive to what media have to say, prompting critics to describe his administration's agenda as media-influenced.

So far, a vacuum has been filled at the top, but there still remains a large one below – at the grassroots. To 1994, less than 2 per cent of the targeted area had been given over to community management agreements.[7] The space is wide for NGOs that are based in remote and rural areas, those that can assist upland communities in making the new alternative to the flawed TLA system work. Fox concludes that:

> [while] these programmes were only initiated after most forests were cut and degraded, the DENR should be credited for providing the means of empowering people to manage local forests. In addition, the Philippines should be acknowledged as the only South-East Asian country to have established procedures for recognizing the rights of indigenous peoples to their traditional homelands.
>
> (Fox 1993: 311)

NOTES

1 The term Timber License Agreement was introduced in the 1960s, but the system dates back to 1904 under the American colonial administration when the Philippine

Bureau of Forestry, then headed by an American, was given the power to issue timber concessions at discretionary scale and duration. From the outset, the system clearly favored commerce rather than forest protection.

2 Ferdinand Marcos officially lifted martial law in 1981 but it continued in practice. It came to an end in February 1986 when a popular revolt ousted Marcos, after he lost in an election, and swept his rival, Corazon Aquino, into power. Throughout the martial law period, free speech was stifled, Marcos's political opponents were jailed, and dissent came mostly from the underground communist insurgents.

3 The Philippines' fast-growing population puts pressure on the uplands and other natural resources. President Fidel Ramos is pushing for a family planning program that will slow down population growth, for which he has drawn the ire of the Catholic Church.

4 Under President Aquino the reafforestation program was credible, although by DENR calculations, about 17 per cent of the funds spent – P 390 million or US$15.5 million – may have gone to the pockets of some DENR officials, politicians, and parties contracted to reforest. The Commission on Audit found that some contractors abandoned their projects after collecting the initial 'mobilization fee,' the money given to help prepare the site for reafforestation.

5 Undersecretary Ben Malayang resigned from the DENR on 30 June 1995.

6 Secretary Alcala's term turned out to be a setback in terms of forest protection. He was weak and easily succumbed to political pressure. He approved the revivial of operations of a few timber concessions and did not run the community forestry program well. As part of a Cabinet revamp, President Fidel Ramos transferred Secretary Angel Alcala from the DENR to another Cabinet post on 30 June 1995. Under the new DENR secretary – Victor Ramos, former presidential assistant on energy and environment and DENR undersecretary – no canceled timber concessions are being revived and the community-based forestry program is taking off.

7 See Braganza 1996: 327 for an in-depth study of Community Based Forest Management in a Higaonan community.

BIBLIOGRAPHY

Abueva, J. and R. De Guzman (1969) *Foundations and Dynamics of Filipino Government and Politics*, Bookmark, Manila.

Asian NGO Coalition for Agrarian Reform and Rural Development (1991) 'Community Participation, NGO Involvement and Land Tenure Issues in the Philippine Reforestation Program', Makati.

Braganza, Gilbert C. (1997) 'Philippine Community-Based Forest Management: Options for Sustainable Development', in R. Bryant and M. Parnwell (eds), *Environmental Politics in Southeast Asia*, London: Routledge.

Broad, R. and I. Cavanagh (1993) 'From Plunder to Sustainability', in *Plundering Paradise: The Struggle for the Environment in the Philippines*, Berkeley, University of California.

Caufield, Catherine (1984) *In the Rainforest*, University of Chicago Press, Chicago.

CNN (1992) Documentary on the Philippine Forest, Network Earth.

Corpuz, O.D. (1989) *The Roots of the Filipino Nation*, vol. 1, Aklahi Foundation, Quezon City.

DENR, Department of Environment and Natural Resources.

Dugan, Pat, 1992 interview.

Factoran, Fulgencio, 1992 interview.

—— (1994) 'Reflections on the adoption of sustainable development as an approach to the environment', unpublished paper.

Fox, Jefferson (1993) 'The Tragedy of Open Access', in H. Brookfield and Y. Byron (eds), *Southeast Asia's Environmental Future: The Search for Sustainability*, Oxford University Press, Kuala Lumpur.

Galang, Angelina, 1992 interview.

Ganapin, Delfin (1986) 'Forest resources and timber trade in the Philippines', *Forest Resources Crisis in the Third World*, Sahabat Alam, Malaysia.

Garrity, D., D. Kummer and E. Guiang (1992) 'The upland ecosystem in the Philippines: approaches to sustainable farming and forestry', National Research Council, unpublished.

Guiang, Ernesto (1990) 'Lessons learned from the initial implementation of DENR's community forestry program', Department of Environment and Natural Resources (unpublished).

—— 1992 interview.

Guiang, E. and B. Dolom (1991) 'Internal report on the DENR community forestry program', Department of Environment and Natural Resources (unpublished).

Head, S. and R. Heinzman (eds) (1990) *Lessons of the Rainforest*, Sierra Club Books, San Francisco.

Hurst, Philip (1991) *Rainforest Politics*, Zed Books, London.

Kalaw, M. (ed.) (1989) 'A Haribon Reader on the Philippine Forest', unpublished MS.

—— 1990 and 1992 interviews.

Kummer, David (1992) *Deforestation in the Postwar Philippines*, Ateneo de Manila University Press, Quezon City.

Lim, T.G. and M. Valencia (eds) (1990) *Conflict over Natural Resources in Southeast Asia and the Pacific*, Ateneo de Manila University Press, Quezon City.

Lynch, Owen (1983) 'Withered roots and landgrabbers: a survey of research on upland tenure and displacement', National Conference on Research in the Uplands, Bureau of Forest Development, Quezon City.

Nectoux, F. and Y. Kuroda (1989) *Timber from the South Seas*, World Wildlife Fund International Publication.

PBS Documentary (1992) *Can tropical rainforests be saved?*

Philippine Lumberman, various issues.

Poffenberger, Mark (1990) *Keepers of the Forest*, Ateneo de Manila University Press, Quezon City.

Porter, G. and D. Ganapin (1988) *Resources, Population and the Philippines' Future*, World Resources Institute Paper no. 4.

Presidential Commission on Good Government (1979) Minutes of meeting of the boards of directors of Veterans Woodworks, Tropical Philippines Wood Industries and Sierra Madre Wood Industries with Taggat Industries, 28 March.

Roque, Celso R. (1990) *Earth, Water, Air, Fire: Essays on Environmentalism*, Kalikasan Press, Manila.

Schirmer, D. and S. Shalom (1987) *The Philippines Reader*, South End Press, Boston.

Severino, Howie (1994) 'Contractors wasting reafforestation funds', *Manila Standard*, 3 October 1994.

Turner, M., R.J. May and L. Turner (1992) *Mindanao: Land of Unfulfilled Promise*, New Day Publishers, Quezon City.

University of the Philippines Center for Integrative and Development Studies (1992) *Saving the Present for the Future*, UP Press, Quezon City.

Vitug, Marites Danguilan (1993) *Power from the Forest: The Politics of Logging*, Philippine Center for Investigative Journalism, Manila.

World Commission on Environment and Development (1987) *Our Common Future*, Oxford University Press.

Part III

Industrialisation and mining development

8 Mining, environmental impact and dependent communities

The view from below in East Kalimantan

Ramanie Kunanayagam and Ken Young

Large-scale resource projects in remote areas bring together small, politically vulnerable groups and modern industrial practices, as well as confronting highly evolved tropical environments with the massive application of technologically advanced extractive processes. It is a very one-sided encounter, further weighted in favour of the corporate side by the enthusiastic support of a national government eager to promote 'development' and the growth of export earnings from non-oil sources.

This chapter, like the authors' own research,[1] is largely concerned with the growth and internal dynamics of the fringe communities that invariably spring up around massive projects of this kind. We are not environmental specialists, nor, in our research, did we deliberately set out to investigate the environmental dimensions of our case. They were nevertheless present and intruded into the social, economic, cultural and political matters that were our main concern. Indeed, while clearly more pedestrian than some of the great issues that arise from the rapid exploitation of the rich biological storehouse of Kalimantan's forests, the issues we touch upon – principally those of the growth of settlements through in-migration and the local consequences for land use and the provision of urban water resources – need to be understood. The regional population of East Kalimantan, fuelled by sustained immigration from other parts of Indonesia, is expanding at a much faster rate than the national average, and the effects that small but numerous groups of spontaneous (as well as state-sponsored)[2] migrants can have on the environment can be every bit as significant as those of massive development projects.

Issues revolving around land use and water supply emerged from our investigation of the processes of the formation of a substantial fringe settlement, a village known as Teluk Lingga adjacent to a huge new coal mine in the regency (*kabupaten*)[3] of Kutai, East Kalimantan, and from our efforts to understand the motivations, needs, forms of self-identity and solidarity among the individuals and groups that made up the new community. We can understand the constraints within which the residents of Teluk Lingga seek to achieve the aims that drew them to this place in terms of a three-sided relationship: the residents, the coal mining company and the state. We will introduce our discussion with a brief history of the settlement and a sketch of the social composition of Teluk Lingga. From there we will discuss the company's role in the area, and explore the ways in which it has become enmeshed, often reluctantly, in the political as well as the economic life of local communities. We will then examine how the state acts to regulate the local communities and to manage relations with the company. This dual authority framework is the context for analysis of the community's orientation towards local resources, principally land and water, and the evident imperfections that exist in the institutional means available for negotiating the claims on resources of the interested parties, and complex problems with obvious environmental implications that these disputes create.

It will become clear that, in this frontier situation, the forms of collective consciousness and solidarity among these particular migrants are weak, be they those of community, of ethnic groups, of women, or of subaltern classes in an extremely asymmetric distribution of economic and political power. The discourses that are employed in the situation that exists in Teluk Lingga are rarely those that foster collective mobilisation around grievances shared by the residents – even though such grievances do exist – but rather express the preferred strategy of adaptation used by the individuals who live in this loosely knit settlement around the periphery of the mine, that of seeking the benefits of a patronage relationship. By contrast, the institutional means of solving collective problems – and environmental problems are typically collective – were deficient. This institutional weakness is a manifestation of the deliberate depoliticisation of the mass of the Indonesian population – the New Order government's 'floating mass' policy (Mackie and MacIntyre 1994: 9, 13). We want to argue that the failure to draw upon the knowledge of villagers through meaningful participation inhibits the development of sound policy formation, even where the elites concerned are well-intentioned. In ways that are less than obvious, democracy is important to development and to environmental protection, contrary to the assumptions of technocratic approaches.

THE GROWTH OF TELUK LINGGA

The company began exporting coal in large tonnages in 1992. The deposits of exceptionally high-quality coal were found in the mid-1980s, and preparation of the site for mining, coal preparation, transportation and export by sea from the company-owned terminal on the coast (13 km from the open-cut mine) was accomplished in the period from 1989 to 1992. The company, with exclusive rights to the site, in return for the provision of 13.5 per cent of its production to the Indonesian Department of Mines, is PT Kaltim Prima Coal, or KPC. KPC is jointly owned by British Petroleum (BP) of the UK and Rio Tinto Ltd (in 1991–1992 this was CRA Ltd of Australia).

The scale of investment in this mine is huge – over half a billion US\$ has been poured into the venture. It therefore dominates the immediate area. The only settlement of any size close at hand was the village of Sangatta, on the Sangatta River, about 7 km from the mine site. Pertamina has oil and gas exploration rights nearby and a small oilfield about 13 km from Sangatta. About 40 km south of Sangatta is the huge Bontang LNG facility, estimated to be worth around three billion dollars. (It is, for example, larger than the LNG facilities in Australia's northwest shelf.) Bontang, aside from being until recently the administrative capital (*kecamatan*) for the Sangatta area, is itself a major industrial centre, a gathering-point for gas drawn from sources all over East Kalimantan. In addition, it is the site for a major large urea factory, owned by the Indonesian government – PT Pupuk Kaltim. All this economic activity is only two to three hours' drive south from Sangatta. Other businesses have operated in the Sangatta area in the past, including a number of logging firms active in the forests adjoining the northern border of the mine site, in the Kutai wildlife park. The Kutai National Park, now the largest in Indonesia, was declared some seventy years ago by the Dutch colonial administration. However, since then it has been exploited commercially at various times, the government of the Republic of Indonesia electing only in the 1980s to revive its status and protect its natural values.

Before the development of the mine, Teluk Lingga was a sparse settlement of a few scattered houses populated by Banjarese farmers who migrated to the area from South Kalimantan in the past fifteen to twenty years to find cultivable land. A mining engineer who was part of the company's exploration team said that in 1985 he counted the number of houses and they did not exceed twenty-five. In July 1992, a survey conducted by us revealed a total population of 3,291 people.

The trigger for the explosive growth of Teluk Lingga was the construction of a road, 7 km long, linking the mine with Sangatta, and the most dependable means of access to the area at that time, the river. During its construction phase the mine created many jobs which attracted job-seekers from all over Indonesia.[4] Over 82 per cent of Teluk Lingga's 1992 residents came to the area between 1989 and 1992 to work for KPC directly or, more frequently, to work for one of the company's numerous contractors. The ethnic composition of Teluk Lingga is very mixed. Javanese, Buginese and Banjarese make up 77 per cent of its population, and the remainder is a blend of Torajans, Bataks, Timorese, Menadonese, Kutais, Dayaks, Ambonese, Balinese and Minangkabau. Practically all of these people came looking for work.

Teluk Lingga did not appear on any maps before the mine was created, nor was it given any official recognition by the government. The rise in population from nearly zero to a peak of several thousand at the height of construction and its subsequent decline are all directly related to variations in the company's labour requirements, either through direct employment, or through subcontracting firms. Figures kept by the Sangatta public hospital recorded a population in Teluk Lingga in 1990 and early 1991 of 4,826. Our survey in late 1991 revealed a population of 3,291. The sudden drop in population is attributable to the completion of the construction phase of the mine's development. This is clear from the figures for the overall numbers of contract workers, which declined between November 1990 and November

1991 by 45.6 per cent. Thus, from its beginnings as a recognisable settlement, Teluk Lingga was oriented overwhelmingly to KPC's operations. Its social fabric is composed of migrant workers from many different parts of Indonesia – government officials and technocrats of middle and lower rank, and a great medley of people looking for work in a variety of occupations ranging from skilled KPC employees to prostitutes and the small group of Banjarese farmers who remain in the area. While the community is, in most formal legal senses, quite separate and distinct from the mine and its internal organisation, it is in fact closely integrated with and highly dependent on the policies, practices and ongoing activities of KPC. While the hopes and expectations of the residents of Teluk Lingga are inextricably tied to the company, the company for its part has a benign, but distant and somewhat apprehensive, view of the inhabitants of Teluk Lingga.

THE COMPANY AS PATRON

KPC provides accommodation in its own concession area for most of its permanent employees, the large majority of whom are Indonesian. Not far beyond the point where the road that forms the spine of Teluk Lingga crosses the boundary of the mining lease, the company has built an orderly new township with housing, hospital, schools, market and other facilities for its employees. This unambiguous company town is named 'Sangatta Baru'. In addition, senior company staff have homes, schools, a golf course and other facilities near the port area of Tanjung Bara. The company airport is also located in the seaside Tanjung Bara area. To create access to Sangatta, the river and to the south, KPC built a road from the planned site of Sangatta Baru to Sangatta in 1989. What it got, unsolicited, in addition to the road, was a different sort of company town, Teluk Lingga, one that grew up rapidly and haphazardly along the length of the new road. While this new settlement was never part of KPC's plans, its people and services are integral to the mine's operations. There is a resident *camat* (district officer), a *kecamatan* office and a police presence, but, as we will see later, the local government authorities do not possess the credibility to match that of the company. Teluk Linggans have greater confidence in the capacity of KPC to solve their problems, and they value good relations with the company and company personnel more highly than they do their links with the local government authorities.

Almost without exception, the residents of Teluk Lingga look upon the company as the source of reliable facilities and welfare measures – and this is so in spite of considerable caution on the part of KPC management not to place themselves in an open-ended welfare role. In spite of the preference by the company to avoid this kind of social commitment, the settlement and the individuals in it are dependent to a very significant degree on the mine. This dependence creates a basis – again, not one that was deliberately sought, though one that is readily used when it is deemed strategic – for exercising a degree of control over the community. The contacts between KPC and its immediate neighbours are mediated by a web of complex patron–client relationships. In return for the provision of a number of essential services, the company is assured of a stable environment for its mining activities. That is merely the obvious side of the patronage relationship. In practice, the great majority of households have some kind of link to the company, ranging from direct and indirect employment, to the provision of services as local contractors, including 'contract wives' for expatriate KPC employees.

The extent to which KPC is perceived as a quasi-formal authority, and at times actually functions as one, came as a surprise to company personnel, but it is nevertheless clear that the company's influence over the life of this spontaneously developed fringe community extends well beyond the more obvious economic links.

The economic links are many. The most obvious are undoubtedly the wages and salaries that are either paid to employees or spent on services they provide. Even the road itself is a permanent reminder of KPC's economic importance. Villagers see the road as the company's responsibility, even though they are also aware that it is outside the company's concession area. They are grateful for the road and pleased that it is kept in good functioning order, as well as for the provision of water tankers to damp down the dust in the long dry season. The road is vital for local enterprises. As one person said: 'There is no point in owning a shop, restaurant or garage away from the road as no one will come to our business otherwise.'

To dwell on the many economic links would do little more than elaborate the massive and obvious disparity in resources between the villagers and the company. It is more interesting to examine how relations are difficult to contain within a fairly limited contractually based series of relations of mutual, if asymmetric, economic dependence. These patterns of dependence have a way of spilling over into other areas more within the domain of public welfare and even local politics. One of the most problematic of these relationships has developed around the issue of the provision of reliable drinking water to the village. Teluk Linggans continually say that their most pressing need is for a clean and reliable supply of water. The alternative sources to supply by the company are either shallow wells dug manually by the residents, or the river. Residents complain that both well water and river water supplies are dirty, contaminated, unhealthy and unreliable. In 1991 there was a five and a half month drought. Not only did all the wells dry up but the water level in the river dropped so much that residents complained that the water was *asin* (salinated) and therefore could not be used. The reduction in river flow caused by the drought had prevented the flushing of seawater intrusions from the mouth of the river, thereby raising salinity. The location of toilets in close proximity to wells and the use of the river for washing and bathing means that bacterial contamination of water sources is an ever-present danger. Two tanks were then installed by the company in Teluk Lingga. They were filled up twice a day by the company's tankers, although sometimes this schedule was not kept.

However, the only reliable long-term source of clean water for locals is the tank at the Sangatta Baru company township. The company employees living in Teluk Lingga, and those with their own transport who are both confident and familiar with the Sangatta Baru site, can get water from there. Although outsiders are not entitled to do this, many persons use their company connections to obtain water for friends and relatives. Some even sell water to those who do not have free access to Sangatta Baru. Over 30 per cent of Teluk Lingga residents obtain their supply of drinking water from Sangatta Baru in one way or another. The strong company connections one needs to have in order to obtain a clean supply of water contribute to the general perception among villagers that if one is working with the company or, failing that, has close associations with people affiliated with the company, life is much easier.

Medical facilities offer another important instance of company surrogacy. Although the government clinic (*puskesmas*) in Sangatta has a staff of twelve, including two doctors, a dentist, two midwives and four nurses, the villagers regard the government health services as markedly inferior to the medical services available from the company at Sangatta Baru.

Company employees and their dependants, as well as some contract workers, have unrestricted access to company health services. The rest of the population try to get access to the company medical services, either as private patients, or by using their contacts in the company. In emergency cases villagers have free access to the company hospital. Although infant immunisation is available from the local government clinic, the villagers are dissatisfied with it, and prefer to use the programme run by the KPC expatriate medical adviser. They complain that the *puskesmas* is expensive for other services too. Each visit to the government facility costs between Rp. 30,000 and Rp. 50,000. The government staff reject this charge, arguing that their prices compare favourably with those of the Sangatta Baru clinic. The locals have a different view of the relative worth of the two services, regarding the company facilities as clearly superior, and of no significant cost difference. Those who work for the company, or aspire to do so, cite access to the health clinic as one of the main reasons. Villagers who are not employees are, strictly speaking, not permitted to use the clinic. In emergencies this rule does not apply. Moreover, during the time of our fieldwork, we observed that significant numbers of villagers managed to obtain access to the company clinic. Even though they were expected to pay for treatment and medicines, they preferred to go there, rather than the *puskesmas*.

In fact, the government hospital staff will privately agree that the company facility is better for the villagers. People say that the hospital staff are indifferent and unconcerned about their patients; they go about their duties in a mechanical manner. When we discussed their policy for emergencies with the doctors in the *puskesmas* they were complacent and answered that they could always rely on the company clinic to come to their aid.

We see here in microcosm an instance of the ways in which the mine's presence distorts both local environmental conditions and local political dynamics, with consequences of serious significance for the settlers. The unregulated spontaneous growth of population along the road puts stress on sources of drinking water in good climatic conditions, and creates unresolved difficulties because of the unsatisfactory disposal of effluent. When the flow and volume of water diminish markedly, as they do in periodic droughts that affect East Kalimantan, then contamination spreads and water quality declines precipitously. The environmental conditions are set for serious health problems to develop, yet the political ambiguities about where responsibility rests to deal effectively with this situation contribute to a degree of inaction and lack of resolve among the local authorities. In formal legal terms the responsibility rests with local government. Yet in just such a situation, in September 1991, when the town was still in the throes of a diarrhoea epidemic, both of the government doctors left the district to go to Tenggarong, the *kabupaten* capital for a cultural festival (the annual *erau* festival).

Teluk Lingga residents are conscious of this relative neglect, and respond to it differently. Most view the company as a superior source of services of all kinds, and consequently their first response to all manner of difficulties was to turn not to the proper authorities, but, if at all possible, to the company. Those lowest down the economic scale – subsistence cultivators, those who have been perennially unemployed, or those who have escaped to the area from transmigration projects – have an almost fatalistic attitude towards health. Some of them said that there was little choice for them. They had to use whatever facilities were available, even though they had no illusions about their safety. As one person said, 'Life in Indonesia is like that.'

The elementary school in Teluk Lingga, which was opened in July 1991, was built by the company and is run by the state. In 1991 the school was staffed by eight teachers including the headmaster and had 372 pupils. Many Teluk Linggans are aware that the school was built by the company and feel that as the company is the 'largest' and 'wealthiest' organisation in the area, it is totally appropriate that it should have built a school. Company officials say that, while they cannot and have no need to build a school of the same standard as the one they erected in Sangatta Baru for their employees, they felt obliged to build a school in the 'village' to prevent feelings of 'social jealousy' arising among the locals. Nevertheless, KPC employees living in the village compare the standards of the two schools and believe the company school does produce better results. Company employees who live in Teluk Lingga feel superior and consider their children to be of higher status than those attending the village school. Some even go so far as to say that they do not want their children to mix with those attending the village school as it may affect their educational achievement.

Teluk Lingga has something of a pariah status in company circles. Some senior Indonesians working for the company refer to the settlement as *'kampong kotor'* (dirty village) and look upon the settlement as a place of crime, theft, iniquity and disease. Some expatriates refer to the place variously as a 'slum' and a 'den of vice', and others fear that its unregulated development might lead to the growth of a true slum. Those expatriates who frequent the settlement refer to it as 'the strip'.

There are many aspects of KPC's involvement with civic affairs in Teluk Lingga in which the company's presence does bring clear benefits. For example, in cases of fire, local emergency services are provided by the company. In 1992 a large fire broke out 500 m from the market in one of the most congested parts of the settlement. The fire spread with such rapidity that neighbours said they feared the whole village would be burnt down. Three fire trucks were sent by the company and the fire was extinguished by company fire-fighters. Again, the recurring shortage of water in the village meant that any local initiative was not feasible. Everyone interviewed about the fire agreed that their only hope lay with the company rescue operation. The company now has plans to install one of its older fire-trucks in the main market area, and to institute a training programme for some of the villagers to create an emergency fire brigade. When there was a flood in the settlement in 1992, those affected by the floodwaters were evacuated under a company contingency plan.

KPC has also assisted in establishing the local government infrastructure; it helped both the district office and the local police station by providing them with vehicles, desks, chairs, filing cabinets and so on, making it easier for them to operate in the area. Ironic in this regard and illustrative of the relative autonomy of the company and the lack of coordination among the separate levels of government is the long-running dispute between the company and the Provincial Department of Transport concerning vehicle registration. Much of the difficulty has to do with arrangements between Provincial authorities and the Central Government in Jakarta. Initially KPC paid its registration fees to local authorities and then attempted to invoice the State Coal company in accordance with an agreement with the central authorities. After experiencing long delays in payment, KPC then elected to deduct registration fees from revenues paid to the State Coal company in Jakarta. The central agency was unhappy about this practice, and instructed KPC to pay them in full, and to ask the Provincial government to seek payment of vehicle registration fees from the State Coal company. The Provincial authorities appear to have had difficulty getting paid. They requested fees from KPC. KPC refused, citing its instructions from Jakarta. New vehicles remained unregistered because of this impasse. This meant that the local police who were using company vehicles were themselves committing an offence whenever they drove outside the company lease area. They appeared to be untroubled about doing so, and were similarly disinclined to intercept other company vehicles found outside the mine concession. This case illustrates the complexity of the state–corporate nexus. The company needs to maintain a good working relationship with various state agencies at the central, provincial and local levels. However, each of these three levels may see their needs and responsibilities in ways that conflict with the demands of the other two.

An example of the company's quasi-civil authority can be seen in connection with the national park. KPC considers itself to be environmentally conscious and made sure that we knew of the praise it has received from the World Wide Fund for Nature for its work in the Kutai National Park. The company pledged funds and resources to maintain the park. Yet its concern to maintain its environmental credentials has led to difficulties with some local people. Company personnel have assisted park rangers in confiscating equipment used by poachers within the park. Incidents have occurred where company personnel have caught suspected illegal loggers within the mining lease and confiscated their chainsaws. In one case, a group of locals overpowered the guard in whose possession a chainsaw had been left and recovered their lost equipment. While the company sees this type of action as a measure to protect the environment, the locals see the company's behaviour as a threat to their livelihood. Moreover, they find it difficult to distinguish between the type of power exercised by the company in matters like this, and the power exercised by police. The locals tend to see the company's authority and capacity to impose its will as something that reaches into their local sphere, in spite of the fact that its regulations have effect only within the boundaries of the mine lease.

From the Teluk Linggans' perspective, the presence, power and affluence of KPC dominate most areas of public life. The company appears to be a source of patronage and a dominating locus of control whose influence overshadows even the powerful agencies of the state. We thus see that the company is involved in a wide range of activities that keep the village community viable. Certainly the local villagers are more dependent on the company than on the government for their general welfare.

For all this, there is still a radical mismatch between the way company personnel see their role in the community, and the privately expressed views of the villagers themselves. Company officials do not want to be responsible for local affairs, and still insist that the company is properly distanced, uninvolved and separate from the locals. That is not accurate, and the villagers certainly see the situation otherwise. To the locals, the company stands as a figure of authority and discipline, a source of wealth and jobs, and a relatively benevolent patron.

In reality, the influence of KPC on Teluk Lingga is tremendous. Names of KPC managers and other influential figures are familiar to most residents. In cases of private disputes – such as those which concern unpaid debts and financial obligations – it is to KPC that people threaten to go for a solution. Exposing the weaknesses of one's adversaries to senior KPC employers is considered far more effective a sanction than to attempt to obtain help and arbitration through official channels such as the local district office or the police.

THE RESIDENTS AND STATE AGENCIES

Whatever the villagers may think to the contrary, the company would prefer to extract itself from the degree of involvement in civil affairs that it has. Indeed, the company would be ill-advised to try to usurp the authority of Indonesian government authorities and does not want to do so. Senior government officials may appear to have a certain disdain for the villagers that they share with some senior company officials, but they would not forgo their authority on matters they deem important. Therefore, the villagers have no choice but to deal with a situation of dual authority, and are always subject to the agencies of the state.

In 1990, Sangatta was upgraded from the status of a *desa* (village) within *kecamatan* Bontang, to a separate *kecamatan*. Following this decision, the office of the newly appointed *camat* was opened in Teluk Lingga. The addition of a police post in April 1991 clearly signified that the settlement had become part of the recognised structure of civil administration within the new *kecamatan* of Sangatta.

Customarily, the *camat*, as the main representative of the government among a local population, oversees the smooth running of the district with the help of his officers, mobilising the people behind the government's policies and initiatives. But he also assists his wards in their dealings with other government departments by issuing various letters of identification, verification of data, licences, and so on. He may intervene in more personal ways, even, for example, finding someone a job. Within the paternalistic structure of local administration, he, too, acts very much as a patron. This, at least, is something approximating the model *camat*'s role.

The reality, certainly in the case of Teluk Lingga, is rather different. To begin with, the *camat* chose to build his office and those of his principal officers away from the main settlement, keeping their contact with the people at a minimum, and regulating contact through formal patterns of behaviour. One of the most blatant examples of this orientation of the *camat*'s office to the village was officers' behaviour on the occasion of the week-long *erau* festival held in the remote *kabupaten* capital, Tenggarong, in September 1991.[5] The entire staff of the *camat*'s office spent a whole month away from Teluk Lingga and many people had to delay urgent local business until their return.

The present *camat*, as well as some of his officers, are university educated. They are either Javanese or Buginese, and their culture is urban. Although they had worked in other parts of East Kalimantan prior to their arrival in Teluk Lingga, they see themselves as having little in common with their wards. They differ, to an important degree, from the residents of Teluk Lingga in dress, forms of speech, everyday behaviour and the conception of their work. They express these differences readily in front of expatriates from the company, outsiders like us, and others they consider their equal. As one of their officers once told us: 'I am only here because of my work. I would rather be elsewhere.' On the other hand, this overt reluctance of the *camat* and his staff to identify themselves as part of the local population has mitigated to a significant degree the sense of obligation among villagers to accept 'guidance and direction' from them.

The police station is located somewhat closer to the settlement than the *camat*'s office, but it too stands apart. The villagers did not have a high opinion of the *camat* and his officers, but their attitude towards them was rather passive, since only a few people had any unavoidable need to seek help from the office. By comparison, the people viewed the actions of the police with overt hostility. Accounts of police activities give some sense of why residents felt that way. Some Teluk Linggans told us how two local contractors went to considerable lengths to curry favour with the police. To take just one example: when the police chief married and brought his wife to live in Teluk Lingga, there was no accommodation available that was suitable for her. His problem was solved when one of the contractors (a builder) invited him to live indefinitely, and without rent, in one of his 'model' display homes. The reason for this generosity, according to the locals, was that the contractors were being supplied with illegally felled timber, and did not want to risk having their supplies interrupted. Some people also told us that the police used the contractors' vehicles whenever they needed them, and received frequent gifts from the proprietors. As one informant said: 'The contractors use their position and wealth to be on good terms with the police, but we are small people, we are helpless.'

Ibu Rosali, who runs a *warung* (small shop), told me:

Thieves stole my generator and the police later recovered it. The police want Rp. 100,000 from me in return for the generator. The generator cost me Rp. 500,000 second-hand. Recovering stolen goods from the police is often more costly than the value of the goods. The police allow the owner of Aires [a local contractor] to bring in illegal timber, but then he is a rich and powerful contractor, not like me a helpless shop-keeper.

Discussing greed and corruption in general, several other women running small shops commented: 'the police have no shame'; 'Always ask for money, cigarettes'; 'There are policemen who even ask for sugar and rice from shops' (fieldnotes).

Some of the worst examples of police harassment and corruption are found among the bars, and the bar girls and 'contract wives' are especially vulnerable. By October 1991, the owner of Bambawinda, one of the first and most profitable of bars, fed up with constant police raids, threats and having to make large financial handouts, went through the process of obtaining an *izin* (permit) at the price of Rp. 300,000 per quarter. By mid-1992, all four remaining bars operating in the area also obtained *izins* to protect themselves against police harassment. But they said that the police still constantly visited their bars for free alcohol and cigarettes and that they had to keep a certain amount of their profits aside as *'uang rokok untuk polisi'* (cigarette money for the police). The police were known to come periodically to their establishments and demand dry provisions such as sugar, coffee and tea. *'Itu tidak ada malu'* (They have no shame) is how the bar owners described the police force (fieldnotes).

The police ought to offer an alternative recourse for locals to deal with misdemeanours by company personnel, but their alienation from the police is so deep that it is generally unlikely that villagers would take this kind of action. For example, when an expatriate driving a company vehicle knocked down a woman, injuring her, although a number of villagers witnessed the accident and saw the driver of the vehicle, when the police arrived they refused to give evidence, claiming that they had not seen the accident. They later said that the police in Indonesia were 'bad' and were 'always trying to extort money from people' and 'were never helpful'. The company on the other hand had been good to them on a number of occasions and therefore they did not want to antagonise any person who might be considered prominent in the company by inadvertently putting him in trouble (fieldnotes).

KPC, for its part, while it has numerous links with the village, has also done a great deal to maintain as much social distance as possible from the local community. In matters of security, public order and access to its concession area, it can be extremely vigilant. In order to prevent unauthorised activity in its lease area the company has introduced stringent security measures to control the movement of people through its territory. The measures taken create confusion and contribute more than a little to the ambivalence that villagers show towards the company. While the company's presence and support are sources of great esteem among villagers, the company also has an authoritarian and, in the eyes of the villagers, a somewhat arbitrary face too. This is nowhere more obvious than in the attempts to seal out uninvited residents from Teluk Lingga from the company concession area. In such matters KPC can become nearly as assertive of its authority as the civil police.

When, from time to time, the company strictly enforced security regulations limiting access to vehicles for its own personnel going to Teluk Lingga, and denying many locals entry into the company area, this had far-reaching consequences for the economy of the village. A number of local business establishments, such as the bars and restaurants set up with a view to attracting a KPC clientele, were seriously affected by these regulations and their business revenues fell dramatically. The company is thus seen to be very much a political institution whose policies have direct bearings and consequences on the lives of local people. Although it may wish to maintain its distance from the village, the company finds itself drawn repeatedly into local affairs. Strict controls on the movement of people like this tend to slacken after a while, since there are people on both sides who need easier access across the boundary.

For their part, the residents prefer company involvement, even though the means of responding to the range of needs that arise are far from well-defined, and the outcomes of different initiatives can lead to disappointment and even anger. By contrast, their dealings with local government figures are formal and often indifferent from the residents' side, and distant, desultory and ritu-alised on the side of local government. What we see in the case of Teluk Lingga is that the settlement from its origins has been geared to the develop-ment of the mine, and its existence is inextricably bound up with the activi-ties of the mine. Even outside the more obvious avenues for benefit, such as employment and the procurement of contracts, the mine is central to the inter-ests of the overwhelming majority of residents. Although company officials do not wish this to be so, and say that this has never been part of company policy, Teluk Linggans are justified in believing that the company has a high degree of control over the village (though probably less than they imagine), and that it therefore has certain unavoidable responsibilities (certainly more than the *company* imagines it has). The clear pragmatic view of locals is that, if they want a problem resolved, they are better off to try to manipulate patronage and other relationships with the company, even in cases where this course of action appears to conflict with the rightful prerogatives of govern-ment authorities.

COMMUNITY ORIENTATIONS TO LOCAL RESOURCES

While KPC has been very willing to provide services, such as building a school, where it believed that there was a need and that its assistance would create goodwill, it has been slow to appreciate the need for reliable water sup-plies. An adequate sewerage system lay beyond that. Yet, particularly when drought affected the area, or when flooding swept into housing near the river, quite serious situations arose in terms of public health, contributing to grave illnesses among residents. The company's efforts to assist the community have been more easily attracted to projects that draw on its engineering skills. These often have the apparent merit of being highly visible (a school or mosque), and have the additional benefit of pleasing visiting officials from Jakarta as well as the local authorities. As we have seen, senior local officials are disinclined to mix closely with locals and are not especially good guides to local sentiment. On the other hand, more pressing needs for KPC's assis-tance may not be well promoted or received because they are less 'visible'.

Both the state and the company expressed, at different times, a strong, well-intentioned but paternalistic desire to bring good order to the Teluk Lingga settlement for the betterment of the residents. In many matters, the residents were quite prepared to look after their own affairs, indeed stubbornly insisted on doing so. Public supply of clean water, however, is beyond their capacities. Gradually, with some reluctance, the company has been persuaded to assist with water supplies. As outsiders, we found this dilatory response puzzling, since public health crises, when they occur, were not likely to remain con-fined to one side of the mine boundary. If a fraction of the concern expended on Teluk Lingga as a potential source of lawlessness was directed towards this and other public health problems, the company's esteem in the local commu-nity would rise to a degree that would leave its gloomier fears about local disaffection in the realm of fantasy. There are problems in the way communication occurs between the residents, the company and the state, and in the perceptions that each has of the others, that make such a welcome outcome much harder to achieve than one would reasonably expect.

From so many points of view, not least that of the environmental consequences of the growth of new towns, the need to secure potable water, and to control effluent waste from new or expanding settlements, seems obvious. In the present case, it is no doubt hindered by the company's unwillingness to negotiate its relationship with the fringe community. As we have seen, it is too simplistic to declare that Teluk Lingga is merely a place apart. The company showed some awareness of this in offering assistance in the orderly design and development of the new settlement. It argued that it could not afford to manage a number of fringe communities (where does one draw the line?), nor to provide facilities for a spread-out strip development such as Teluk Lingga soon became. It did some work with the local government to draw up a plan for a compact, regulated settlement. The authorities were consulted, but the settlers were not, and they chose to go their own way.

Planning efforts also raised sensitive issues related to land. Fortunately, the mine lease itself involves no serious disputes over land use. The occupation of the land on which Teluk Lingga stands took place in a quite orderly fashion, but it did so beyond the formal mechanism of legally constituted authority. While the outcomes here are relatively benign, the history of land issues illustrates the unreality of excessively legalistic perspectives one sometimes encounters in capital city bureaucracies and boardrooms.

In the months and years of Teluk Lingga's rapid growth, a regular system of land purchase and sale developed autonomously. On the other hand, practically none of the residents observed official procedures requiring the registration of purchase and the acquisition of letters of authority from various officers of the district. Interviews with a number of residents in the township show that most people are not even aware of this system for authenticating land ownership. They offer conflicting stories when they are asked what they think suffices as legal ownership of land. Locals insist that extra-legal charges are made in official transactions, and that the procedures covering land acquisition and sale can be expedited only by the payment of bribes. Furthermore, the prospective landowner must make at least two or three visits to the Department of Agriculture in the regional (*kabupaten*) capital before he or she is able to obtain a land deed. Most people in Teluk Lingga know this and therefore seldom go beyond obtaining a *surat pernyataan* (a 'declaration') from the village office. According to our survey (July 1992), of those owning vacant house-plots, 51.4 per cent had no land deed, and 64.7 per cent of those owning houses had no title deeds.

In the absence of any help from the *camat*'s office, the residents have devised their own system of regulating land and property ownership, one which bypasses the authority of the *camat*. Before KPC came to the area, occupation and active use of the land gave the occupier rights of possession, as is often the case in *adat* regulation of rural land throughout Indonesia. Asked about land ownership, several landowners said '*tanah itu negara punya, sekarang tanah saya*' (that was government land, now it has become mine).[6] However, since the late 1980s the rapid growth in the numbers of settlers has led to a fairly clear commodification of land. Newcomers to the area know they have to purchase land from the occupiers. A prospective house-builder makes enquiries as to ownership of the piece of land he is interested in, and then approaches the owner. The price of land varies widely from one transaction to another. The price of a plot is determined by factors such as kinship ties and the length and degree of friendship between the buyer and seller. Transactions take place only when an individual needs land.[7] District officials point out that they have arrived only quite recently, that they lack manpower, and that the villagers remain rather alienated from the authorities as reasons why they do not have effective control over the regular acquisition and disposal of land in the settlement.

By contrast, the company, with the support of local authorities, wanted to intervene – in the interests of residents as well as itself – in the planned development of Teluk Lingga. It had drawn up plans for a well-laid-out subdivision of land, with provision for proper drainage, access for emergency vehicles and so on. The residents showed no interest in these plans and continued to build, buy and sell and to locate themselves in accordance with their own informal processes. A subsequent proposal for a 'green belt' land acquisition scheme near the company boundary had the potential to create serious dissatisfaction and significant compensation claims. The company began investigating this plan believing it was dealing with vacant land. The locals knew otherwise. These misunderstandings were later addressed through negotiation, but the fact that the problem developed at all illustrates again the inadequacy of communication between the local community, the company and the state, and the lack of routine institutional processes that would allow such issues to be identified and resolved before conflict developed.

PARTICIPATION AND ADVOCACY

The case of Teluk Lingga is one in which there were no major disputes over land, or other difficult compensation claims that had the potential to interfere with the development of the mine. Yet the three main groups involved – the settlers, the state and the company – managed to reach a form of mutual accommodation that reflects local socio-economic and political realities. This is a pragmatic accommodation and not one that the settlers can influence in any direct way, their strategies being largely confined to passive resistance and other 'weapons of the weak' (Scott 1985). Their scope for initiative is narrow. If land and water resources in the province are to be used by the growing flow of migrants in an equitable, orderly and environmentally responsible way, then more effort has to be made to find procedures that work in the field, and not just on planners' desks. The issues are complex, but a major ingredient

would involve moves towards more meaningful and lasting forms of consultation with residents about the plans that are ostensibly made for their benefit.

Our case is not one that provides guidance on environmental issues for the
reasons that usually attract attention – flagrant abuse of the environment, dramatic political protest, or the growth of an articulate social movement
mobilised by discourses that deploy local cultural and environmental symbols. On the contrary, community solidarity in this recently formed frontier
settlement was low, adding further to the huge imbalance in power between
the villagers on the one hand, and the state and the company on the other. The
most serious environmental problem was the threat to public health posed by
an inadequate water and sewerage infrastructure. The speed and pattern of
settlement, along with periodic droughts, was largely responsible for the
recurring crises of water and effluent pollution. The company was not indifferent to this situation, and did provide some help with drinking water. However, it also argued that it had to set limits on the civic responsibilities it would
accept outside its lease area. Company executives also pointed out that they
had helped local authorities at an early stage to develop a plan for a compact
and orderly settlement in Teluk Lingga, which, if followed, would have made
possible the economic delivery of utilities and services. The residents showed
no interest in this plan (if they knew about it at all), and government authorities made no serious attempt to implement it. Further questions therefore
arise. Was the settlement plan well conceived? Why did the authorities
encourage its development, yet fail to ensure its implementation? What lay
behind the villagers' lack of interest in the plan?

The answers to these questions are not straightforward, and to the extent
that they are directed at apportioning blame among the protagonists, they are
misdirected. The fundamental problem, as we see it, is more systemic. Elsewhere in this volume (in the chapters by Yap, Warren and Aditjondro, for
example) one finds the identification of the means of access to the institutional bases of civil society as being vital to the production of adequate
responses to local needs, including local concerns about environmental conditions. Such institutions are necessary for the expression of local concerns
on environmental and social welfare issues, and to the building and maintenance of alliances that can bring about change. On the other hand, if the
principal institutions in the public domain are responsive largely to the state
and corporate interests, then the means of legitimate interest aggregation from
among the bulk of the people are significantly diminished. Local people may
find other ways of expressing their concerns, but they are largely excluded
from decision-making. Often in such circumstances, the most obvious means
of self-protection for members of subaltern classes, particularly in fragmented new settlements like Teluk Lingga, is for individuals to try to compensate
for their powerlessness by attaching themselves to a powerful patron. Thus,
in the situation we have described, patronage rather than class or ethnic solidarity became the most valued currency of personal and political interaction.

Clients are notoriously reticent about matters that might put continued patronage at risk. They also tend to try to solve problems for themselves or their families through their patronage networks. We have given many examples of this above.[8] It solves some problems for some individuals, but is totally unsuited to addressing collective problems, and environmental problems are almost invariably not individual but collective. Many such difficulties were shrugged off fatalistically with the phrase *'hidup di Indonesia begitu'* ('life in Indonesia is like that'). The institutional foundations of routine legitimate collective action were weak, and expressions of concern about communal issues were muted because of the pervasiveness of social relations dependent on patronage. In this context intermediaries of different kinds (NGOs, religious associations, welfare groups, consultants) could compensate for institutional weakness and failures in communication.

Our field experience gives us some guarded encouragement that this can be done, though a number of conditions are necessary, not least a willingness of powerholders to listen. Intermediaries can play a role in opening up opportunities for the voices and aspirations of ordinary villagers to be heard (see Burdge and Robertson 1990). It is too easy to indulge in self-congratulation, and difficult to judge how events might have developed had we not been involved. The mine will be active for decades and the management has taken a long-term view of its role in the area. The company had done a lot of work in designing and implementing a 'community development plan'. Some key individuals within KPC had done some exemplary work in contracting out a significant number of support functions to East Kalimantan firms, and in achieving valuable transfer of skills to local tradespeople. We would like to think that we made an important contribution here, by supporting initiatives already taken, and by successfully advocating the lasting benefits of distributing as many tasks as possible to local contractors. Advocacy contributed greatly to easing the water supply problem, which might otherwise have dragged on for some time, creating all kinds of resentments in its wake. Ramanie Kunanayagam, supported by Mr Alan Irving and others in KPC's environment department, tirelessly pursued contacts to make sure action was taken, and that it was effective. KPC eventually erected a water tank on its boundary with Teluk Lingga, which it keeps supplied with water from its own sources. A village cooperative has the franchise to sell drinking water within Teluk Lingga, with charges meant to cover distribution costs.

It is nevertheless difficult to be precise about the extent to which third-party involvement improved the situation. The problems we have discussed were serious. Even so, the context was relatively benign, and the company's management was willing to devote resources to selected projects of assistance to local communities. Yet even in these favourable circumstances, we believe that outside mediation was important to achieving satisfactory outcomes. That raises the question of why, beyond merely accidental factors of circumstance and personality, local institutional arrangements might not be able to cope satisfactorily with such massive external intrusion.

To be sure, there are important difficulties here of cross-cultural communication, including difficulties arising from the divergent discourses of different classes. Much of what we achieved was to communicate the unrestrained views of ordinary villagers and to tap their knowledge of local environmental conditions and their own problems.[9] Perhaps a major element in the tendency of local socio-political arrangements to fail is the pervasive disregard by the authorities for the views of ordinary villagers; and that is not so much the result of elite ill-will as of the social and cultural divide that prevails and the relative powerlessness of the settlers. There is a long legacy within state structures that discounts the knowledge of ordinary villagers. This orientation stretches back many decades from the paternalism of Dutch colonial authorities in the Ethical period to the '*rakyat masih bodoh*' ('the unenlightened masses') attitudes expressed by certain New Order officials.

One unsatisfactory aspect of our recommending a generalised role for NGOs, consultants, or other third parties is that this practice will always run the risk of simply adding one more layer of potentially paternalistic intervention. At a deeper level, the prevalent discourses of development, modernisation and nation-building (see Heryanto 1988, 1993) retain strong paternalistic orientations. Thus not only are critical decisions about large-scale projects and environmental assessment processes made in ways which discount or disregard the expert knowledge of local populations (see Aditjondro and Lucas in this volume), but the rectification of subsequent problems is also the prerogative of other elites (Pinches 1984). That is not to say that bureaucratic regulation and scientific knowledge have no place. It is rather to observe that the free expression of the knowledge, opinions and needs of members of communities affected by large development projects would lead to superior management of the processes of change. But for the subjugated knowledge of ordinary villagers to become a serious part of the mechanisms of policy-making, at either local or higher levels, there has to be a greater responsiveness in the Indonesian system than currently exists. In more abstract terms we refer here to notions of autonomy, accountability and participation. It is in areas like this that the fallacies of top-down developmentalism, the 'order for development' paradigm, become visible. This, however, is a broader, national problem, and while the distribution of power in New Order society remains as it is, there are few prospects for change in the environmental politics of dependent communities.

NOTES

1 This chapter is based on the research of the authors in East Kalimantan, Indonesia. The ethnographic material is drawn from the ten months of intensive fieldwork carried out by Ramanie Kunanayagam between July 1991 and December 1991, and October 1992 and December 1992. The research project was supervised by Joel Kahn and Ken Young, who both made a number of shorter visits to the site in the same period. While we tend to use the plural ('we', 'our') in the chapter, it is usually the case that, when we are reporting a conversation with

an informant, the reference is to fieldnotes recorded by Ramanie Kunanayagam alone.

2 Our reference is of course to settlements created under the long-standing transmigration programme of the Indonesian government. There is a large transmigration complex about one hour's drive from the mine site, communities mostly from Java, which we both visited. Any failure in the agricultural economy of this transmigration settlement would be likely to create a flow of job-seekers to the Sangatta/ Teluk Lingga area.

3 Below central government in Indonesia are several layers of government: Regency (*Kabupaten*), District (*Kecamatan*), Village (*Desa*), and village subdivisions (RK and RW).

4 Many of these jobs, especially the lesser-skilled occupations, were not with KPC directly. A high proportion of the projects that went into the overall development of the mine were subcontracted to other large firms, such as Theiss Industries and John Holland Constructions.

5 The *erau* festival celebrates the founding of Tenggarong. It was formerly an annual event, but the celebration now takes place at the discretion of the head of regional government, the *bupati*.

6 While clearly there was no settled body of 'custom' or customary understandings (*adat*) among the settlers of this frontier community that was distinctively theirs, we note that a shared acceptance of various local practices in their communities of origin prepared the settlers to abide by certain broad conventions about procedures, rights and customary practices with respect to land in Teluk Lingga. This was effective for two main reasons. Firstly, much of the land was originally settled by marginal Banjarese farmers (Young and Kahn were introduced in an earlier field trip in 1990 to one of the Banjarese known as the principal '*tuan tanah*'). Banjarese *adat* and practices thus set precedents that were mostly not challenged. Secondly, a number of crucial conventions, such as the right of cultivators who open up new land to claim ownership, are shared, with certain qualifications from place to place, by many *adat* systems.

7 In this type of situation pure market forces acting in accordance with neo-classical economic theory do not prevail. Prices fluctuate too, between each plot of land, rather than according to strictly impersonal determinations by factors such as location and time of purchase. It is thus difficult to express patterns of land ownership and exchange in readily understood Western or (official) Indonesian formal terms because of the complex make-up of each transaction and the complex, but regular, patterns of interaction among the settlers in Teluk Lingga that enter into the exchange relationship.

8 For a more extensive exploration of these issues, and the operation of patronage relationships in Teluk Lingga, see Kunanayagam 1995.

9 What Scott (1985) refers to as their 'off-stage' utterances, which contrast here with the more cautious 'on-stage' views that are channelled through local elites.

BIBLIOGRAPHY

Burdge, Robel J. and Robertson, Robert A. (1990) 'Social Impact Assessment and the Public Involvement Process', *Environmental Impact Assessment Review*, 10: 85–90.

Heryanto, Ariel (1988) 'The Development of "Development"', *Indonesia* 46: 1–24.

—— (1993) 'Discourse and State Terrorism: A Case Study of Political Trials in New Order Indonesia', PhD thesis, Monash University.

Kunanayagam, R. (1995) 'In the Shadow of the Company: Patronage and Status in a Mining Settlement in Indonesia', MA thesis, Monash University.

158   *Industrialisation and mining development*

Mackie, J. and A. MacIntyre (1994) 'Politics'. In H. Hill (ed.) *Indonesia's New Order: The Dynamics of Socio Economic Transformation*. Sydney: Allen and Unwin.

Pinches, M. (1984) 'Anak Pawis, Children of Sweat: Class and Community in a Manila Shanty Town', PhD thesis, Monash University.

Scott, James C. (1985) *Weapons of the Weak: Everyday Forms of Peasant Resistance*, New Haven: Yale University Press.

9 Environmental policy and conflicting interests

Coal mining, tourism and livelihoods in Quang Ninh Province, Vietnam[1]

Bach Tan Sinh

INTRODUCTION

Vietnam's environment has been undergoing rapid degradation. Its natural resource base is insufficient to fuel long-term economic growth. The present utilisation of an already constrained resource base tends to be unsustainable (SCS 1992). Environmental degradation and its management are closely related to changes in economic and administrative structures. This chapter shows how such changes highlight, and sometimes exacerbate, conflicts between actors and institutions concerned with resource use and management at various levels.

Examples of environmental degradation associated with resource exploitation are numerous. Forest resources have been depleted. The actual loss of forest is estimated to be about 200,000 ha annually, of which 55,000 ha is cleared for agricultural land, 50,000 ha is destroyed through forest fires and the remainder through exploitation for fuel-wood and timber. Mineral resources are used irrationally. It is estimated that loss in coal extraction is about 12 to 15 per cent in surface mining and 40 to 50 per cent in underground mining. The waste in apatite is 200 per cent of the utilised extracted minerals. Many extraction sites are creating serious problems of air and water pollution, and landscape deterioration. Estuarine and coastal biological resources are overexploited. Among 2,000 fish species found 30 years ago many have now disappeared, such as *Clupanodon thrissa*, *Dorosoma nasus* and *Megadops cyprinoides*. Many mangrove forests have been cleared for shrimp-breeding ponds. Loss of genetic resources is another concern, and about 500 species of plants and 200 species of animals require urgent protection (Le Thac Can 1992: 5–15).

Vietnam's environmental pollution in general and industrial pollution in particular is already in a critical situation, even though industrial development has not yet reached the level of industrialised countries. Industry's share of the gross domestic product (GDP) in 1992 was 22.6 per cent, while the agricultural share was 34.5 per cent. About 11 per cent of workers were employed in the industrial sector in 1992.

There has so far been very little effort to control and prevent industrial pollution (Ho Qui Dao and Do Thanh Bai 1992; see also Dang Duc Phu 1990;

Pham Ngoc Dang 1990; Le Minh Triet 1992; Phung Chi Si 1992). The total daily solid waste of Hanoi is estimated to be about 360 tons. The daily waste effluent from Ho Chi Minh City is 500,000 m^3. The emission of more than 50 toxic and hazardous gases has been recorded in Hanoi, Ho Chi Minh City, Viettri, Lamthao and other industrial areas (Le Thac Can 1992: 5–15).

In order to cope with this challenge accompanying industrial and economic growth, there is an increasing need to develop policy which takes into account the social and environmental consequences of development. On the one hand, the 'open door' policy, with the aim of attracting foreign investment, has created more opportunities to implement development projects than ever before. On the other hand, economic reform has raised issues concerning institutional arrangements, such as decentralisation of decision-making and state management responsibilities. Meanwhile, the role of government has changed from production towards regulation. In this context, a new institutional framework has to be created at various levels which is capable of assessing and dealing with impacts of development projects.

In this chapter, Quang Ninh province in general and Ha Long City in particular will be used as a case study to illustrate the dynamic interaction process between institutions with environmental responsibilities operating at local, national and international levels with their different interests and alliances. The increasingly complex and diversified economy of Vietnam, with disparate and decentralised economic actors and a plurality of social interests, implies conflicts and challenges. Environmental concern is important in the resources sector, especially in a resource-rich province such as Quang Ninh. The chapter concludes with discussion of implications for environmental policy in pursuit of a sustainable development path, taking into account the position of different institutions and interest groups. Key policy recommendations revolve around enhancing local participation and provision of opportunities for expression of local concerns.

SOCIO-ECONOMIC FEATURES OF QUANG NINH PROVINCE

Quang Ninh Province is located in the northeast of Vietnam (Map 9.1). Of a total area of about 600,000 ha, 280,000 ha is classified as forest land (though much less is actually forested) and 51,000 ha as agricultural land. Quang Ninh is divided into three main topographic areas: the mountains and islands consisting of six mountainous districts and one island district; the agricultural flat land covering two districts; and the industrial area, including the three towns of Cam Pha, Uong Bi and Hong Gai, which has recently been designated as Ha Long City.

The total population of Quang Ninh in 1992 was 865,000, with a density of about 140 persons per km^2. The population is not evenly distributed; most people are settled in coastal lowlands and towns. About 120,000 to 130,000 people live in each district or town in the lowlands, whereas only 20,000 to 60,000 live in each district of the mountainous and island areas. About 40 per

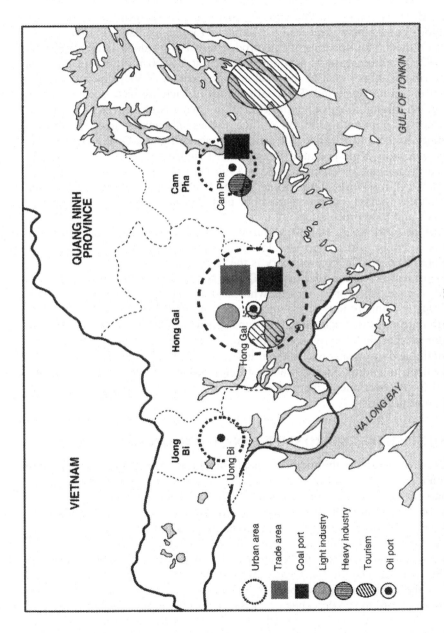

Map 9.1 Coal mining and popular tourist areas, Quang Ninh Province, Vietnam

cent of the total population is urban. Quang Ninh has quite a high proportion (about 12 per cent) of people employed in the industrial sector.

Quang Ninh province, especially the area of Ha Long Bay including Hong Gai-Bai Chay and Cam Pha, has considerable coal exporting potential. Coal exports contribute a great deal to Vietnam's foreign exchange earning capacity. Of the 5.6 million tons of coal produced in 1994, valued at approximately US$200 million, exports accounted for about US$60 million. Quang Ninh contributes 90 per cent of the total coal production of Vietnam and 100 per cent of volume exported. The coal reserves of Vietnam have been estimated at 2,345 million tonnes of anthracite, all in Quang Ninh Province, 78 million tonnes of semi-anthracite, 38 million tonnes of cooking coal, 96 million tonnes of thermal coal and 306 million tonnes of lignite. Quang Ninh is also an area with great potential in the tourist industry because of its natural scenery and unique environment. In 1994 Ha Long Bay was designated by UNESCO as a World Heritage site. Quang Ninh has potential in several other industries, notably ship construction, port transportation, construction materials and food processing.

As of 1994, some 60,000 people were employed by the coal industry in Quang Ninh, with others employed in subsidiary and service industries related to coal. The coal industry is the largest employer in the province. In the present economic structure of Quang Ninh, gross national product from industry accounts for 75 per cent whereas that from agriculture is 25 per cent.

Quang Ninh is thus a province where the conflicting interests between different industries and interest groups can be observed, as can conflicts of interest specific to particular institutions. The conflict raised between coal mining and tourism is due to the impacts of coal mining on the natural environment, including coastal waters, forests and agriculture. Between central and local government, there also exist different interests concerning development priorities.

POLITICS OF ENVIRONMENT IN QUANG NINH

Before we examine the social bases of competing interest groups existing in Quang Ninh, it is worthwhile to consider the meaning of the politics of environment in the context of Vietnam. The basis for environmental politics can be interpreted in three ways (see Hirsch in this volume). First, it can be seen as part of worldwide environmental concern, usually shaped by outside agendas. Second, environmental politics may be a reflection of the concern of middle classes over the quality of life. The first two approaches tend to be elite-focused. The third approach towards the politics of environment, which is at the centre of this chapter, is to look at the struggle for control over resources and the coalescence of social forces around this resource control.

In Vietnam, although not overtly regarded as politics, environmental issues are usually treated in terms of the first two approaches. Environmental problems have been identified early on by environmental scientists from universities and research institutes. The Natural Resources and Environmental Research Program was proposed by them and quickly accepted by the Ministry for Higher Education and State Committee for Science (now the Ministry of Science, Technology and Environment) in 1981. Since then, this Program has been in operation for three five-year periods (1981–1985, 1986–1990 and 1991–1995), during which it made a major contribution towards developing a comprehensive environmental policy. However, the Program is technocratically oriented, seeing its role as an objective task of identifying environmental problems and finding ways to solve them. Many environmental problems caused by disputes between competing social forces over resources at various levels are neglected.

As far as the globalisation of worldwide environmental problems is concerned, Vietnam has responded very quickly by joining a number of international conventions, such as the Ramsar Convention on Wetlands of International Importance in 1989, the 1985 Vienna Convention on the Protection of the Ozone Layer and the 1987 Montreal Protocol on Substances Depleting the Ozone Layer, and the Convention on International Trade in Endangered Species of Wild Fauna and Flora (CITES). In addition, a National Plan for Environment and Sustainable Development in the Period 1991–2000, which was formulated by the Ministry of Science, Technology and Environment (MOSTE) with the technical assistance of the United Nations Environment Programme (UNEP) and International Union for the Conservation of Nature (IUCN), has also revealed the awareness of Vietnam on global environmental issues.

The politics of environment arising from large-scale resource development projects, addressing social or spatial inequities in development and the struggle for control over resources, are increasingly relevant in the present context of Vietnam but still little discussed. The case of Quang Ninh thus provides a good example in which the politics of environment can be seen in such a light. In Quang Ninh there are six main economic activities under the management of five ministries. Coal mining – the most important industry in Quang Ninh – is under the management of the Ministry of Energy (MOE). Tourism, potentially a dynamic industry focused on Ha Long Bay, is attached to the General Department of Tourism (GDT). Transportation, mainly ports, is under the Ministry of Transport and Communications (MTC). Agriculture and forestry are under the Ministry of Agriculture and Food Industry (MOAF) and Ministry of Forestry (MOF). Last but not least is oil imported through Ha Long port – one of the most important ports for importing oil in the whole country – under the control of PETROLIMEX, which is attached to the Ministry of Trade (MOT).

Environmental conflicts and economic activity

Potential conflicts can be seen between sectoral ministries as well as between central and local governmental agencies. One can see the clear conflicting interests between coal mining and others such as tourism, agriculture and forestry. In the first place, coal mining has polluted the air and water (surface, underground and coastal) by discharging waste water, dust and overburden into the natural environment. In addition, open-cast coal mining is the main cause of deforestation and land destruction (Nguyen Dinh Uy *et al.* 1994: 30–31). In Hong Gai and Cam Pha, coal mining has affected an area of 5,497 ha accounting for 14.2 per cent of the total area of both towns, of which 1,008 ha is devoted to open-cast mines, 2,296 ha underground mines, 899 ha overburden disposal sites, and the rest to mechanical plants, service enterprises and residential areas. Coal mining in the three towns, Hong Gai, Cam Pha and Uong Bi, has destroyed 750 ha of forest. The percentage forest cover of Quang Ninh has declined from 42 per cent of the total area in 1969 to 18–20 per cent in 1985.

During the wet season the overburden is washed away, thereby destroying about 200 ha of agricultural land belonging to residents living in surrounding areas. As a result, several hundred families have had to resettle in other places. In addition, the runoff process has also destroyed roads and changed the flow direction of many small streams and rivers, such as Mong Duong and Dien Vong.

Coal mining affects the livelihood of people in Quang Ninh. Because of the deforestation caused by coal mining, Quang Ninh is potentially threatened by shortage of water for both agricultural and domestic use. Drinking water from the watershed forest serving Hong Gai and Cam Pha has been heavily polluted. The Dien Vong River, some 20 km in length, supplies Hong Gai with 360 million m^3 of water annually. In 1989 the water plant had to stop operating because the water was contaminated with particles, solid waste and coal dust. The polluted water has also affected the water quality at Bai Chay beach, a major tourist area. A number of water sources can no longer be used because of coal disposal, such as in Cao Son.

Deforestation also causes the ground water level to sink, which in turn leads to saline intrusion. For example, at one time six wells were in operation in Ha Long City with three daily working shifts supplying 7,200 m^3 per day, but now, owing to the intrusion of salt water, the number of shifts per day has been reduced to two and sometimes even one. However, the water is still contaminated by saline intrusion. Da Bac Dam previously supplied Ha Long City with 17,000 m^3 water per day but can now provide only 3,000 m^3. Ha Long City, with a population of 150,000, is experiencing water shortages.

Yen Lap Reservoir was constructed in 1980 with a capacity of 118 million m^3 of water supplying 10,050 ha of agricultural land. After 10 years the capacity decreased by 60 per cent and was only enough to irrigate 5,500 ha of agricultural land owing to the high rate of soil erosion and sedimentation. Another reservoir, Dien Vong, which supplies 25,000 m^3 of water per day for domestic use of both Ha Long City and Cam Pha Town, can now provide only 15,000 m^3 per day.

Central versus local interests

The conflicting interests between central and local government are reflected through disputes between MOE and the Quang Ninh People's Committee. These conflicts occur because of the different economic activities being pursued in the same place. On the one hand, at the national level, MOE is interested in developing the coal mining industry for domestic consumption and especially for export. On the other hand, the tourism industry is preferred over coal mining by Quang Ninh province for reasons discussed later in this chapter.

Besides conflicting interests between agencies, one can also find conflicts of interest within each agency, at both the central and the local level. In Quang Ninh, before Decisions Nos. 381[2] and 382 made by the Prime Minister in July 1994 to stop all small-scale coal mines licensed by relevant ministries and the Quang Ninh People's Committee, as well as all illegal private coal operations, there had been no control over licence-granting procedures. It was not only the Ministry of Heavy Industry (MOHI) which issued licences. The MOE, MOD and the Quang Ninh People's Committee were also involved. As a result, there were seven companies operating in Quang Ninh. Of the seven companies, five, along with 30 enterprises, belonged to the MOE, one company to the MOD, and the Quang Ninh Coal Company to the Provincial People's Committee with four enterprises. Five enterprises belonged to the District People's Committee and one to the Provincial Party. In addition, there were several thousand illegally operated individual mines. Granting licences and at the same time managing the operation of mines inevitably led to the problem of conflicts of interest within these governmental agencies.

The problem of conflicting interests and conflicts of interest can be summarised as attributable to three main causes. First, the legacy of the Government's institutional arrangement in the central planning system, according to which each ministry is in charge of its economic sector, has resulted in a fragmented system of policy-making between, for example, coal operation under the MOE and tourist activities under the GDT. It is often argued that part of the profit gained by tourism activities should be invested in upgrading technology in coal mining, thereby improving the environment for tourism. But in fact, there is no mechanism for cooperation between these two agencies at either national or provincial levels.

Second, besides the policy-making mandate, the line ministries are responsible for the operational aspects of their respective sectors, thereby raising issues of conflicts of interest. For example, the MOE is also involved in coal mining operation whereas the GDT is in the hotel business. Third, there is no clear-cut institutional demarcation among governmental agencies at the central and local levels regarding the administration of coal mining.

The MOHI, through the State Department of Management of Mineral Resources, was not the only ministry responsible at the central level for the granting of coal mining licences. State administration of mineral resources including coal is under the MOHI while state administration of the coal industry is under the MOE. The MOE repeatedly requests the transfer of licence-granting functions for coal from the MOHI. To pursue an objective of the state administration over mineral resources, the controlling agency should be attached neither to the MOHI nor the MOE. It should be directly attached to the Council of Ministers (now government) and independent from the branch ministries which administer industries related to production of mineral resources.

As far as inspection procedures for coal mining operations are concerned, there have been three governmental agencies involved. The MOHI, through its local office affiliated with the provincial Industry Department, conducts inspections solely to ensure that the conditions attached to coal licences (which it issues) are being met. The MOE sends its inspection teams from Hanoi to investigate whether operating standards are in accordance with the regulations issued by the MOE. MOSTE, through the provincial Department (DOSTE), has responsibility for carrying out inspections to ensure compliance with environmental standards. For DOSTE, this is a new responsibility. Because of the fact that the MOE does not have local affiliates, and the lack of capacity of DOSTE, inspections are not stringent, and hence enforcement and compliance are low.

Before the Ordinance of Mineral Resources was passed in 1991 there did not exist in Quang Ninh any governmental agency in charge of administration of coal mining. Sometimes the police took over the function of controlling mining operations of coal companies, and sometimes the companies had to control their coal mining operations themselves. Moreover, at the local level, it was often incorrectly assumed that if a coal company under the MOE is given a mining licence in one area, this company also had the right to provide the licence to any counterpart to mine in the defined area, thereby creating abuse of mining regulation by subcontractors.

INSTITUTIONAL BASIS OF ENVIRONMENTALISM

Organisational structure and responsibilities

The organisational structure of the coal mining industry shown in Figure 9.1 indicates the involvement of various governmental agencies in administration of the coal mining sector at central and provincial levels.

Because of the inefficiency of coal mining in Quang Ninh, the Quang Ninh People's Committee decided in 1992 to assign to the Provincial Industry Department the function of management of mineral resources and later to establish the Local Office for Management of Mineral Resources within the Industry Department. This Local Office is affiliated to its National Office – the State Department for Management of Mineral Resources under the MOHI. According to the Ordinance of Mineral Resources, the Office has a number of key monitoring and management functions.

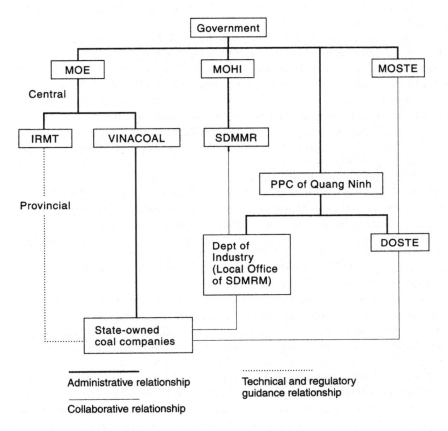

Figure 9.1 Organisational structure of coal mining

First, the Office is to propose measures for protection of unexploited mineral resources to the Provincial People's Committee and to the State Department for Management of Mineral Resources through the Director of the Provincial Industrial Department. It is also responsible for implementing those measures in coordination with other concerned agencies at the local and central level. Second, the Office is supposed to supervise organisations and individuals to ensure that they follow the Ordinance of Mineral Resources, state regulations on management and protection of mineral resources, for example through organisation and registration of exploration and mining areas, by monitoring practice licences, exploration licences and mining licences, and by enforcing laws and state regulations related to environment and mineral resources protection – including punishment of those violating state regulations on management and protection of mineral resources. Third, the Office is to liaise with the Chair of the Provincial People's Committee in documentation for approval of mining licences and in instances of their infringement, and in the drawing up of plans and economic or technical feasibility studies.

In addition to the Local Office for Mineral Resource Management, a Provincial Inter-sectoral Inspection Office within the Industrial Department consisting of members from the Industrial Department, army, police and courts was established to control coal mining. However, the situation has not been improved much, for the following reasons. First, there are three kinds of enterprises operating in coal mining in Quang Ninh: three big coal companies (Uong Bi, Hong Gai and Cam Pha) under MOE; Quang Ninh Coal Company under Quang Ninh People's Committee; and Dong Bac Coal Company under the Ministry of Defence. They are under the management of different state agencies, thus having no coordination among themselves. Second, there are several small coal mining workshops managed by the members of the Inspection Office as well as social organisations (e.g. the Youth Union, the Women's Union). Third, illegal mines have been supplying coal to some state-owned coal enterprises at low prices because of the low costs involved in production. They do not have to invest in other measures, such as reclamation or labour insurance for workers. For these reasons, it is inevitable that the Inspection Office fails to exercise its task as necessary.

With the Law on Environmental Protection, DOSTE (the Department of Science, Technology and Environment) was established as the new local agency in charge of environmental management, replacing the former Provincial Committee for Science and Technology. DOSTE's main functions are to formulate local regulations in environmental management, to develop the provincial programme including planning and budget allocation for environmental protection, to coordinate and supervise inter-sectoral environmental protection activities in the province, to investigate environmental impact assessment (EIA) for investment programmes and carry out environmental monitoring, and to inspect the implementation of environment-related legislation.

Although the awareness among officials working at the Department is high, little has been achieved concerning environmental management by this department owing to the lack of regulations to implement the Law on Environmental Protection, as well as limited expertise and equipment relating to environmental control and monitoring in the field. For example, there are only two provincial officials working in the environmental management field.

Meanwhile, DOSTE is in close cooperation with other local governmental agencies responsible for related environmental activities. These include the Health Prevention Centre where equipment for controlling, measuring and analysing samples of water is available; the Provincial Department of Quality Control, Standardisation and Metrology; the Provincial Office of Water Management; the Office of Mineral Resources Management under the Industry Department; the Provincial Department of Coastal Resources Protection; the Provincial Department of Forest Inspection; Quang Ninh Urban and Sanitation Department; and the Office of Culture under the Provincial Department of Culture and Communication.

Regulatory framework

At present there does not exist a mining law governing the granting of prospecting permits, mineral exploration or mining leases. As described above, conflicts occur between national and provincial government over the jurisdiction of mineral resources. While waiting for the mining law, both the central (council of ministers) and local government (Quang Ninh People's Committee) have promulgated several regulations concerning coal mining management.

The 1989 Ordinance on Mineral Resources remains the basic law on mining. Granting a mining licence is arranged as follows. The Prime Minister issues licences to foreign companies for exploration and exploitation of oil, gas and high-value mineral resources, for example gold and gems. The Minister of Heavy Industry issues licences to domestic and foreign companies for exploration and exploitation of mineral resources, except for foreign companies involved in oil and gas, and domestic and foreign companies involved in high-value mineral resources. The Chairman of the People's Committee of a Province issues licences for exploitation of mineral resources used for producing construction materials.

According to scale, mines with an investment value in excess of 2 billion Dong must be issued a licence by the authority of the Prime Minister. For those with an investment value of less than 2 billion Dong, the licence is granted by the Ministry of Heavy Industry. Mine operators conduct activities according to the Ordinance, its regulations, and the terms and conditions attached to their licence. The 1989 Ordinance has been supplemented by various sets of regulations. The Regulation on Principles and Procedures for Licensing 588 issued on 1 August 1992 as amended in September 1994 (after the Prime Minister's decision to curtail illegal mining and request to reconsider coal mining licensing procedures) provides that, for the approval of a mining licence, the applicant must undertake a socio-economic feasibility study approved by the responsible authority; must hold a business licence approved by the responsible authority; must furnish evidence of financial capacity to work the mine; and must furnish evidence of professional capability, including necessary engineering and other qualifications. This information is to be submitted to MOHI, together with an application form for obtaining a licence, a letter from VINACOAL stating that the mine will come under its supervision, and a letter from the People's Committee stating that a land-use licence has been issued. If the documentation is in order, MOHI must take a decision to approve or reject the application within 30 days of submission. If the application is approved, work must begin within six months of issue or the licence is cancelled automatically.

Meanwhile, Article 1.3 of the Technical Regulations on the Exploitation of Open-cast Mines (TCVN-5326-91) sets out the existing rules on environmental protection. Mine operators are instructed to carry out their operations in a way that minimises impact on land, forests and dwellings. They must limit the use of land for waste discharges. Waste from road and railway construction must be disposed of properly. Lake drainage must be prevented, or compensated for. Draining into rivers and lakes must be monitored, and dangerous discharges treated before disposal. Residential areas are to be protected from noise, dust and other hazards. Remedial measures must be taken, including planting on overburden dump sites. Reclamation is to be undertaken where possible, and abandoned sites left in the best possible condition.

A more general measure is the Law on Environmental Protection, which was passed by the National Assembly on 27 December 1993, and came into force in January 1994. The Law on Environmental Protection performs two functions. First, it sets forth broad environmental standards and directives for all of Vietnam, covering a wide variety of activities, industrial and otherwise. Second, it provides for the promulgation of a more detailed set of regulations, or other measures, which amplify the basic provisions.

The first set of such regulations, Government Decree on Guidance for the Implementation of the Law on Environmental Protection, was issued on 18 October 1994. The Implementation Decree provides a further level of detail on the protection of the environment in general. In this context, the most important provisions relate to the need to conduct an environmental impact assessment of projects such as coal mines as part of the approvals process. It should be noted that this Law and the Implementation Decree apply to all mines, regardless of which entity issued the licence, or whether the mine is licensed at all.

The Law on Environmental Protection and a 1994 Decree on Guidance for its implementation have added another level to the approval process by requiring the submission and acceptance of an environmental impact assessment report before work commences on the project. The 1994 Decree requires EIA reports for mines to cover the environmental status of the location of the mine, assessment of the environmental impacts resulting from the operation of the mine and recommended solutions to environmental problems identified in the report. MOSTE is responsible for reviewing EIA reports from large and medium-sized mines, and the provincial DOSTE for dealing with small mines (the terms 'large', 'medium' and 'small' are not defined).

The current state of the approval process has been complicated by the fact that other agencies, including the Ministry of Energy and local authorities, have granted mining licences in the past without reference to legal authority. In his decision of July 1994, Prime Minister Vo Van Kiet announced that only MOHI would be entitled to grant such licences. Mines operating under licences granted by other agencies remain in production, but are now required to obtain licences from MOHI, and their operations have been brought under VINACOAL.

A final regulatory development that is significant is the decision of VINA-COAL to establish an environmental fund as 1 per cent of the total revenues of annual coal production. The environmental fund is administered directly by VINACOAL for environmental protection activities of coal companies under VINACOAL, such as dust prevention, land reclamation and waste water treatment from coal preparation plants.

The description of the existing institutional framework of coal mining in Quang Ninh has shown that the unclear assignment of administrative responsibilities among the agencies involved and the inconsistency of relevant regulations have hindered policy implementation. In addition, a mechanism to incorporate environmental considerations into decision-making processes does not exist at every level, exacerbating conflicts between environmental protection and economic development. This problem is illustrated in this chapter by the case of Ha Long City Coal Preparation Plant.

On the other hand, the delay in implementation of the Law on Environmental Protection at the national level has affected the activities of Provincial Departments of Science, Technology and Environment generally and Quang Ninh DOSTE particularly in dealing with environmental problems caused by coal mining. A Guideline on Environmental Impact Assessment for Existing Enterprises issued by MOSTE in November 1994 (almost one year after the Law was passed) is not specific enough to provide directives to provincial DOSTE on how to evaluate the environmental situation of the coal mining industry. In addition, a lack of environmental standards in coal mining and a lack of pollution-measuring equipment do not permit the Department to conduct pollution control and monitoring. Under the supervision of the Department there are no local regulations dealing with environmental management in the province.

Local media

The local media, through newspapers and especially television programmes, has increased the environmental awareness of local people regarding coal mining operations. Some documentaries, for example, 'Where is coal mining in Quang Ninh going?' and 'Again the problem of coal mining', have been made by Quang Ninh Broadcasting and Television to publicise the coal mining situation in Quang Ninh and included coverage of environmental pollution caused by surface mining, underground mining, and transport and preparation of coal. These documentary films have been shown on the local television channel.

It is also interesting to note that a film named 'The Life of Mrs Luu' was recently shown on national television, addressing the issues of illegal coal mining operations and associated social problems. Vietnam Broadcasting also did some reports about environmental issues raised by coal mining in Quang Ninh. Writers and film-makers in Vietnam have responded to the issues of coal mining and its social and environmental problems and thereby created consciousness and awareness of these problems among people at various levels.

A CASE STUDY: HA LONG CITY COAL PREPARATION PLANT

Background of the project

The main function of coal preparation plants is to increase the quality of coal, especially for export purposes, by washing away dust and selecting the appropriate size of coal. In Hong Gai and Cam Pha there are two such plants. The first one was built during French colonial times and located right in the centre of Hong Gai Town (Ha Long City). Because of the location and backward technology used in this plant, there are a number of environmental problems related to air pollution. The second plant was constructed with the help of Poland during the 1970s and situated in Cam Pha, about 30 km from the centre of Ha Long City. Recently this plant was upgraded by the installation of a production line from Australia, with a designed capacity of three million tons per annum. However, with the present coal exploitation capacity this plant has not been fully operational.

Because of the technological backwardness of the first plant, a plan was formulated to replace it by building a new one located in the same place. The idea of obtaining a new plant from Australia was initiated by the former Vice-Minister of Coal and Mining (now MOE) when he paid a visit to Australia in 1990 and observed pollution-minimising coal-washing technology. This idea was then taken up by the Director General of Hong Gai Coal Company, one of the three companies under the MOE in Quang Ninh. The aim of the plant was to purify and upgrade the quality of coal before it is exported.

Institutions involved in the project

The project was formulated without consultation with the Research Institute of Coal Mining – an advisory institution to MOE in the field of coal mining. According to the agreement between Hong Gai Company and the technology-supplying company – Bulk Materials Coal Handling Pty. Ltd (BMCH) – Hong Gai Company would receive a loan from the Australian Export Finance and Insurance Corporation (EFIC) to build the plant. BMCH was responsible for design and for the provision of materials and equipment for the construction and erection of the main sorting facilities. Hong Gai has handled design, materials and equipment for other sub-projects, including railway lines, a coal yard, screening workshop, electricity, water supply and sewerage system. Hong Gai Company had to repay all the capital and annual interest of 8.13 per cent after five years, starting from the time when equipment for the plant arrived at Quang Ninh port. The total cost of the project was US$11.5 million, excluding the waste treatment facilities, which would cost around US$1 million.[3]

Because of its scope, as classified according to the total cost, the project had to be sent to MOSTE for investigation of its environmental impact as part of the approval procedure. The project could not be approved by MOE until MOSTE had been satisfied that its environmental impacts are acceptable according to environmental standards in the mining sector.

According to the EIA report carried out by a Vietnamese consultancy company, the new plant would not affect the surrounding environment or the life of local people. The environmental impact assessment, just five pages long, covers only the immediate area where the plant is located. In addition to this, the local authority in charge of environment in Quang Ninh – the Provincial Department of Science, Technology and Environment – was not informed about the results of this report. The EIA report was submitted only to MOSTE in Hanoi.

In 1992 the project was approved. However, it took almost two years before it could start to be implemented, owing to the strong opposition of local people, among whom coal workers account for more than 50 per cent. Construction of the project in the centre of Ha Long City had to be stopped after some months of construction. The reason was that the location of the project inevitably raised questions about the storage and transportation of coal from the mines to the coal-washing plant, and then from there to the port, causing air pollution. The workers themselves asserted that they did not want to spend the rest of their time in an unclean environment after working in the very polluted environment of surface and underground mining. About 14,000 signatures were collected and sent to the Quang Ninh People's Committee as well as to the Council of Ministers, asking for the project to be stopped. This created great pressure on the central government, resulting in a number of investigations led by high-ranking governmental officials. Ultimately, the Prime Minister paid a visit to Quang Ninh and later decided that the plant had to be moved about 8 km out of the city centre. By the time the Prime Minister made this decision, the project had already completed construction of the foundations of the plant in the city centre, which cost more than US$1 million. In addition, other related infrastructure, such as transportation (a railway line) and storage areas, had to be changed. This decision created a conflict between the MOE and Quang Ninh People's Committee.

It is interesting to note that the opposition was initiated by local people and supported by the Provincial People's Council. In this case, the interest of local people is in line with that of the local authority – that is, to protect the environment in Ha Long City. In addition to the opposition of local people, Quang Ninh People's Committee itself has also been very active in making requests to a number of different governmental agencies in Hanoi to reconsider the appropriateness of the project. Letters have been sent to the National Assembly and Council of Ministers. In response, besides a number of visits by the Vice-Prime Minister and Prime Minister, the National Assembly has sent a delegation led by the Chairman of the Committee of Science, Technology and Environment to Ha Long City.

Social and institutional basis for competing interests

Looking at the project, one can see different interests represented by different social actors or institutions involved (Figure 9.2). On the one hand, there is a

Economic sectors Administrative levels	Coal mining	Tourism	Transport	Agriculture	Forestry	Oil Import
Central (State)	MOE (VINACOAL)	GDT	MTC	MAFI	MOF	PETROLIMEX
Local (State)	Department of Industry	Department of Tourism	Department of Transport	Department of Agriculture and Forest	Department of Agriculture and Forest	

Figure 9.2   Competing interest groups and associated agencies in Quang Ninh

great interest at the national level in the coal industry, represented by the MOE. In the short term, there is considerable over-capacity in the coal sector. However, in the medium term, the domestic demand for coal is likely to increase sharply. With the completion of the 500 kV transmission line that transfers electricity from the North to the South, there will be a shortage of electricity in the North, leading to demand for rehabilitation of some coal-fired plants, such as Uong Bi and Ninh Binh, and full operation of Pha Lai plant. According to the Quang Ninh Master Plan, it is also planned to build another coal-fired plant in Mong Duong with electrical capacity of 1,200 MW. A major portion of this electricity will be sold to southern China through the 110 kV transmission line linking Uong Bi and Mong Duong plants. It is, therefore, anticipated that the coal sector will have to increase annual production capacity from 5.6 million tons in 1994 to 9 million tons in the year 2000.[4]

On the other hand, the local government wants to develop the tourism industry, which will play a very important role in the Quang Ninh economy. According to the Provincial Department of Tourism, it is planned to build 200 hotel rooms per annum at international standard and 1.5 million tourists are expected to visit Ha Long Bay each year, of whom 35 per cent will be foreigners. There are various reasons why the local authority favours tourism over the coal industry. In the first place, Quang Ninh coal mining, if it is not managed properly, will destroy the natural scenery and unique environment of Ha Long Bay, making this area impossible to attract tourists to visit. This was reflected in a statement by an official working in the Provincial Department of Construction, that under economic restructuring coal mining can be replaced by other industries by applying a number of new technologies available, but it will be impossible to have a beautiful Ha Long Bay again once it is polluted. Second, as already mentioned, coal mining has had major impacts on the livelihood of local people and forests, especially affecting the watershed areas. Last but not least is the structure of the revenue base of both industries. While the coal industry managed by MOE contributes direct revenue to the central government, the tourism industry has potential to raise direct revenue for the local government.

The different interests between the industries themselves can also be seen in this case, namely the coal industry represented by the Hong Gai Coal Company, and the tourism industry by the Provincial Department of Tourism. The reason the company excluded waste treatment facilities is economic, although it knows that without installation of these facilities the plant will pollute water. According to the chief engineer of the company, the coal revenue received from these facilities by the sedimentation method is much lower than the cost invested in the facilities. The environmental cost has not been taken into account. He argued that the environmental issue is not only an issue for the coal industry. It has to be solved on a cross-sectoral basis; part of the money earned by tourism should be invested in coal mining to improve the technology and environment. In addition, the loan used for environmental protection should be 'softer' than that for normal production purposes, otherwise nobody will be interested in investing in environmental protection activities.

Another issue concerning the agencies involved in EIA monitoring is also evident here. There is no interaction between the central governmental agency, MOSTE, and the Provincial Department of Science, Technology and Environment. According to the Guidelines on the EIA Procedure, the EIA report on the plant should be submitted to MOSTE for investigation. However, it is necessary to consult the local department before approval since this department has to deal with environmental impacts of the project in the long run.

The main lesson to be learned from this case is that the project could have avoided delay and wasted investment if from the outset those affected by the project had been able to participate in discussions on the project, especially local people. If they had done so, tensions would have been avoided between local (Quang Ninh People's Committee) and central authorities (MOE).

ENVIRONMENTAL POLICY IMPLICATIONS FOR SUSTAINABLE DEVELOPMENT OF QUANG NINH PROVINCE

Although regulations have been issued by central and local government, the environmental degradation caused by coal mining continues. Therefore, in July 1994 the Prime Minister promulgated a decision to stop temporarily all small-scale coal mining licensed by relevant ministries and Quang Ninh People's Committee, as well as all illegal private coal operations. Following this decision, the Vietnam National Coal Corporation (VINACOAL) was established in October 1994. VINACOAL, officially starting its operation from January 1995, consisted of 19 companies, among which 9 are involved in coal mining, including one under the Ministry of Defence (MOD) and one under Quang Ninh People's Committee. All other organisations previously involved in coal production and export but not belonging to VINACOAL have either to close down or to change their activities. The establishment of VINACOAL is an attempt by the government to coordinate all activities related to the coal industry, including mining, processing, domestic distribution and export. MOHI is now the only agency in charge of granting coal mining licences.

This institutional restructuring of the coal industry reflects the attempt of government to solve issues of control over resources (in this case coal) among different agencies involved. For the time being, this restructuring has created a number of impacts on the local community. Many local people have lost their jobs and main incomes from working in coal mining. The Quang Ninh People's Committee is concerned about the potential emergence of social problems, such as crime and prostitution, as a consequence of restructuring.

In Quang Ninh in general and Ha Long City in particular, one can see the true picture of conflicting interests between different institutions and interest groups and conflicts of interest within these institutions. Overcoming these conflicts requires an inter-sectoral rather than a fragmented sector approach. It requires change in the whole institutional arrangement among the agencies involved in Quang Ninh. It is important to ensure local participation in decision-making and to provide means for expression of local concerns. Moreover, there is a need for an agency that is in a position to coordinate the activities related to environmental protection in different sectors and to balance interests among institutions concerned, by implementing a number of policy instruments such as enforcement, economic incentives and, most importantly, environmental regulation and promotion of environmental awareness.

It is anticipated that an increasing number of investors will establish projects in Quang Ninh, covering various sectors such as coal mining, port transportation, processing industries, the construction materials industry, and hotel businesses. The conflicting interests among various economic actors may therefore become more serious. To cope with this challenge Quang Ninh needs to have a strong agency that is capable of ensuring that all projects meet environmental standards. Investigating EIA reports can be an efficient tool with which to monitor the development process. The most appropriate existing agency that could take on this role is the Provincial Department of Science, Technology and Environment.

However, the involvement of governmental agencies is not enough. The active participation of different social groups, as shown in this case of opposition to a large project by local people, has created substantial pressure on those who do not follow the laws and regulations on environmental protection.

NOTES

1 This chapter is written within the framework of a project entitled 'Institutional Reform in the Science and Technology System of Vietnam in the Transition to Market Economy' (1993–1995), sponsored by the Swedish Agency for Research Cooperation with Developing Countries (SAREC).
2 Decision No. 381/TTg of the Prime Minister on Institutional Restructuring in Coal Exploitation and Production, issued on 27 July 1994.

3 Interview with the director of the Technical Department of Hong Gai Coal Company in July 1994 and *Vietnam Investment Review*, Vol. 4, No. 143, p. 22.
4 Report on Master Plan of Coal Sector.

BIBLIOGRAPHY

Dang Duc Phu (1990) *The Situation of Environmental Pollution of Residential Areas from Industrial Discharges in the Big Cities of the North of Vietnam over the Last 10 Years*, Report at the National Workshop of Medical Sciences and Labour Environment, Hanoi.
Ho Qui Dao and Do Thanh Bai (1992) *Industrial Pollution in Vietnam*, Institute of Industrial Chemistry [Hanoi].
Le Minh Triet (1992) *The Pollution of Water and Environment in Ho Chi Minh City*, Report at the Workshop on Environment of Ho Chi Minh City, Ho Chi Minh City.
Le Thac Can (1992) *Current Environmemtal Issues in Vietnam*, National Research Programme on Environmental Protection.
Nguyen Dinh Uy, Tran Kim Phuong and Vu Ngoc Ky (1994) 'The Real Environmental Situation of Hong Gai–Cam Pha and the Project of Metrological Investigation for the Future Ha Long City', in the *Journal of Scientific Activities* No. 4, Ministry of Science, Technology and Environment, Hanoi [in Vietnamese].
Pham Ngoc Dang (1990) *Some Results of Research on Air Pollution in Hanoi*, Report at the International Workshop on Environment and Sustainable Development, Hanoi.
Phung Chi Si (1992) *The Situation of Air Pollution in Ho Chi Minh City and the Directions to Solve*, Report at the Workshop on Environment of Ho Chi Minh City, Ho Chi Minh City.
SCS [State Committee of Science] (1992) *Vietnam National Plan for Environment and Sustainable Development 1991–2000: Framework for Action*. Hanoi.

Part IV

Pollution and environmental health

10 River pollution and political action in Indonesia

Anton Lucas

In 1993, Sukatip, a primary school pupil who lives in a coastal village in Lombok, wrote a piece for a local magazine produced by fellow students. The journal was called *Geram*, an acronym for *Gerakan Anak Merdeka*, or the Children's Freedom Movement. This is what he wrote:

> The sea at the place where we kids used to catch fish was very clear, so we could see when the *nener* [small fish] were around. But the water is dirty now, because the people who live in the area where we go fishing often throw their rubbish into the sea. The sea has also become polluted because of the oil from the engines of the [motorised] fishing boats, which also kills the *nener*, and makes them disappear. The coral that is used by all the sea creatures for protection is destroyed now because it was taken to make lime [for cement].
>
> (Sukatip 1993: 8)

Air and water pollution (including pollution of rivers as a result of deforestation) are crucial environmental issues facing Indonesia today. For the inhabitants of Indonesia's major cities, air pollution from motor vehicle and factory emissions is now a major threat to health as well. City dwellers and workers on Indonesia's industrial estates are suffering increasingly from respiratory complaints. On Batam island, promoted as a showcase of New Order industrial development and, an hour by sea from Singapore, as a new gateway to Indonesia, hundreds of thousands of tons of waste from the Batam industrial estate are dumped untreated into the sea each year. According to a recent survey, workers at Batam are suffering from a high incidence of bowel infections, skin complaints and respiratory infections.[1]

Indonesia's most pressing pollution problem is the dumping of untreated liquid industrial waste (*limbah cair*) into its rivers. In a recent content analysis of reports on pollution in 16 national and regional daily newspapers in Indonesia, the environmental NGO Skephi found that 41 per cent of cases involved river pollution (Skephi 1994: 203).[2] The priority of river pollution in government policy is reflected in the establishment of the Clean Rivers Programme (Prokasih or *Program Kali Bersih*) to clean up 20 of the most polluted rivers in 8 of Indonesia's 27 provinces (SPES 1994: 200–203, 210).

The river pollution problem has a number of dimensions: technological (availability of effective waste treatment), economic (willingness of firms to invest in such technology), and legal (implementation of Indonesia's environmental laws). As well, there is a political dimension which, according to the Skephi study quoted above, includes the high priority given to industrialisation in Indonesian development plans, the absence of people's participation in decision-making, and 'collusion between businessmen, bureaucrats and the security apparatus' (Skephi 1994: 33).

In exploring aspects of industrial river pollution (Map 10.1), this chapter considers local causes and responses to pollution and the questions these raise about environmental protection in the context of Indonesia's political economy since the 1980s. With a particular focus on the milestone Tapak River case, the chapter traces political and legal action taken by environmental groups to date under Indonesian anti-pollution laws.

RIVER POLLUTION FROM INDUSTRIAL WASTE

Some cases of river pollution from several regions which have had press coverage in the leading Java-based daily newspapers during 1993 are set out in Tables 10.1–10.3. The list is by no means exhaustive and, because the newspaper sources are Java-based, is biased towards that region. Table 10.1 sets out five of Indonesia's biggest companies' involvement in some of the most publicised pollution cases, Tables 10.2 and 10.3 show river pollution in selected industrial regions in North Sumatra and Java, especially from industries in the Jakarta Bay region. Most of the investment in industrial development in Indonesia is occurring in Java (particularly West Java), the Medan region of North Sumatra and South Kalimantan, with only one pollution case, at the Freeport copper mine, in Eastern Indonesia receiving significant attention in the media (Table 10.1). Not included is the region of South Sumatra, where pollution by ammonia factories in Palembang is seriously threatening the river Musi (Cribb 1990a: 24; *Suara Karya* 28.7.94).

In the majority of cases it is the absence of industrial waste treatment units that causes river pollution. Occasionally malfunctioning waste storage facilities have caused toxic waste to be dumped into neighbouring rivers and rice fields. In many smaller cases (not included in Tables 10.2 and 10.3) inadequate design of waste treatment facilities has caused the malfunction. Under Indonesian environmental law companies are required to have prepared an environmental impact assessment (Amdal) by a private consultant. The effectiveness of the implementation of this requirement to date has been disappointing, however (World Bank 1994: 270–273).

At the local level, attempts to tackle river pollution in Indonesia are beset by implementation problems. While anti-pollution legislation has been enacted (see pp. 197–198), there is neither the political will for enforcement of the law, nor the trained human resources for effective monitoring of such large numbers of offending factories. In regions where large individual factories

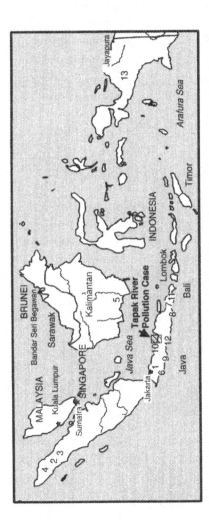

LEGEND

1   Fish contamination in Jakarta Bay
2   North Sumatra Pulp Mill (PT IIU), Porsea in Lake Toba ecoregion of Nth Sumatra, Asahan River
3   Various factories polluting Deli River in Medan, Nth Sumatra
4   PT Intri Indorayon Utama (PT IIU), Nth Sumatra
5   PT Barito Pacific Timber Mill Barito River, Sth Kalimantan
6   PT Indah Kiat Pulp and Paper in Bengkulu/Riau: Siak River and West Java: esp. Ciujung River, Tangerang
7   PT Ecco Indonesia factories and other factories in Sidoarjo district, East Java: Porong, Gedongan, Kedungguling
     regency
     Various companies in East Java along the Brantas River and also Kali Tapak, Semarang, Central Java
     and Bunting Rivers
8   Kali Tapak, Semarang, Central Java
9   Kali Tapak, Semarang, Central Java
10   Pekalongan region on nth coast of Central Java, rivers polluted include Pekalongang, Banger, Kupang, Bremi
     and Sampong
11   Shrimp farming destroyed around industrial areas of Gresik in East Java, and Tapak River
12   Textile mills in Surakarta, Central Java, polluted the Solo River
13   PT Freeport Indonesia Copper Mine, Ajikawa River, Amanapare, Irian Jaya

Map 10.1   Sites of well-publicised polluting industries in Indonesia

Table 10.1 Industrial river pollution in Indonesia: five largest polluters

Name of company	Region/Province and river	Products	Cause of pollution	Effect of pollution	Political action
PT IIU (Inti Indoyoran Utama) owned by Raja Garuda Mas Group chaired by Sukanto Tanato	Porsea in Lake Toba eco-region of North Sumatra. Asahan River	pulp and paper mill	rupture of waste lagoon (1988) pours 375,000 m³ of contaminated water into Asahan River; chlorine gas tank explosion (1993)	'terrible stench' of plant emissions; change in Asahan River colour and smell, pollution of Asahan hydro-electric power plant by gummy black waste in Asahan River; pollution of fish and drinking water	16 families on river bank successfully sued PT IIU in district court, and appeal to Medan high court failed; Walhi action against government in Supreme Court on basis that factory was licensed without proper environmental impact analysis (Amdal) failed. Environmental audit of company by American consultants in progress. (Skephi 1994: 77–83; M 7 and 8.10.93)
PT Pupuk Iskander Muda	Lhokseumawe (Aceh) region of North Sumatra	fertiliser factory (urea) produced from liquid natural gas	repeated poisonous ammonia gas leakages	500 ha of fishponds polluted; damaging to health of villagers; skin and eye irritations; 602 victims treated for gas poisoning in 1991	company blamed villagers for living 'too close' to factory, compensated each victim of chlorine gas poisoning with 'a tin of milk and one orange'; action in lower courts failed, YLBHI sued company in Supreme Court for Rp 1.3 million per victim, claims rejected (Hutapea 1993: 15–21)
PT Freeport Indonesia owned by an American joint venture company	Ajikawa River Amanapare, Irian Jaya (also Pika, Uamiua, Minayerwi, Aimua rivers)	copper mining	56,000 tons of tailings per day dumped into Wagawangon River, metallic pollution of other rivers	Ajikawa River silted up for 50 km	Indonesian parliamentary commission urges review of company's 'work contract' (Skephi 1994: 95–101; IO 23.9.93)
PT Barito Pacific Timber owned by Projo Pangestu	South Kalimantan: Barito River	plywood, particle board and related products	untreated waste	local fishing industry destroyed	activities targeted internationally by Greenpeace and 14 international NGOs; Skephi asks Jakarta Investor's Club members not to buy BPT shares (public issue vastly oversubscribed); products boy-cott discussed (Skephi 1994: 47–54)
PT Indah Kiat Pulp and Paper (IKPP) owned by Eka Tjipta Wijaya (Sinar Mas Group)	Bengkulu/Riau: Siak River, and West Java: Ciujung River, Tanggerang	pulp and paper mill	dangerous untreated chemical waste	loss of livelihood of local fishermen; skin diseases, villagers in Sentul, Serang, fainted and vomited from dumped poisonous waste	villagers protested to parliament, asking the gov-ernment to cancel production licence until waste treatment plant installed. (Company is fined Rp 300 million for illegal logging) (Skephi 1994: 87–92)

Table 10.3 Industrial river pollution in Indonesia: Central Java and Jakarta Bay

Region/Province and river	Name/number of companies	Products	Cause of pollution	Effect of pollution	Political action
Semarang Central Java: Kali Tapak	PT Semarang Diamond Chemicals (SDC), PT Kemas Teguh Indah Sakti, PT Bukti Perak, PT Agung Perdana Tegu Indah, PT Sukasari, PT Makara Dewa Wisesa, PT Apollo Jaya, PT Sanmaru	food processing, chemicals, soap, paper, textiles and garments	untreated waste, and inadequate waste treatment technology	Tapak stream polluted, loss of domestic water supply; 300 villagers lost livelihood from polluted shrimp and fish breeding ponds, and failed wet rice crops from polluted irrigation water; skin infections, diarrhoea and dysentery	campaign over 13 years by villagers, supported by local legal aid (YLBHI) and Ministry of Population and Environment; threatened consumer boycott of products produced by industrial estate and threatened court action finally produced a negotiated settlement (YLKI et al. 1991)
Pekalongan region, Central Java: Pekalongan, Banger, Kupang, Bremi and Sambong rivers	more than 30 factories, inc. PT Indonesian Miki, PT Naga Mas, PT Batang Alum, PT Sumbertex, plus 63 home industries	light industry (plastics rope), tapioca flour, food preservatives, textiles	untreated industrial waste	loss of livelihood, villagers no longer able to supplement diet with fish and shrimp catches	protest letters to officials (Bupati of Batang and Minister of Environment), resulting in visit by Bapedal; companies ordered to install waste treatment plants; Sambong and Kupang rivers included in Prokasih (SM 25.9.93)
Surakarta, Central Java: Solo River	PT Sari Warna Aseli	textile mill	untreated waste	unpleasant smell; polluted groundwater used for domestic purposes	NGO-initiated community action group (Team of 15) demanded immediate stop to pollution, compensation and rehabilitation of environment (ECO-Sounder 1992: 20–21)
Jakarta Bay	3 industrial estates including 308 joint foreign investment companies, 592 domestic (local) investment companies and 36,372 'other industries'	light manufacturing, food processing	17 rivers dumping untreated effluent into Jakarta Bay	suspected mercury poisoning from contaminated fish, marine life destroyed	companies considered to be worst offenders included in public disclosure to parliament by Minister for Environment Sarwono Kusumaatmadja, who announces administrative action (temporary closure) (T 23.12.89; JI 8–14 June 1991)

Abbreviations: IO: Indonesian Observer; JJ: Jakarta Jakarta; JP: Jawa Pos; K: Kompas; M: Merdeka; SM: Suara Merdeka; SP: Surabaya Pos; SPb: Suara Pembaruan; T: Tempo

Table 10.2 Industrial river pollution in Indonesia: regions of East and West Java and North Sumatra

Region/Province and river	Name/number of companies	Products	Cause of pollution	Effect of pollution	Political action
Sidoarjo district, East Java: Porong, Gedongan, Kedungguling and Bunting rivers	PT Ecco Indonesia, more than ten other factories	shoes, light industry	untreated industrial waste	failure of shrimp harvest in 605 ponds (9,000 ha), with est. value of Rp 13 billion	administrative action by government: 6 factories closed, 3 received 'strong warnings', one received 'notice'. PT Ecco Indonesia agreed to invest Rp 500 million on waste treatment plant (SP 23.3.94; T 16.4.94)
East Java: Brantas River	188 companies	pulp and paper, manufacturing	untreated industrial waste often dumped after heavy rain	dead fish; pollution of Surabaya municipal water supply	Assistant Governor of East Java (Drs H. Masdoekie) required companies to sign agreement to reduce pollution levels (SM 15.9.94: Koffel 1994)
Gresik region, East Java: Avur and Tengah rivers	Driyorejo industrial estate; PT Petrokimia Gresik; PT Semen Gresik, PT Nusantara Plywood, PT Miwon, PT AP and other factories	porcelain tiles, fertiliser, petrochemicals, cement, plywood, food preservatives, plastics	atmospheric pollution (dust from cement factory), untreated liquid waste	cadmium metal pollution in seas, shrimp industry destroyed, respiratory infections	print media publicity, relocation of two villages; according to subdistrict head (*camat*) 40 industries empty untreated waste into local rivers, and threaten to close off access (K 7.4.90; SP 3.3.92)
Bandung region West Java: Citarum River and main tributary, plus 20 other tributaries	textiles, leather goods, chemicals, timber, plastics, paper, rubber, electronics	30% of factories have no waste treatment plants	untreated industrial waste	rivers dangerous for domestic use	factories under investigation from Bapedal (Environmental Impact Management Agency) (R 8.10.93: SPb 10.3.93)
Deli River, Medan, North Sumatra	88 factories	plastics, soap, light industry	untreated industrial waste	pollution of domestic water supply	press publicity, 4 rivers now part of Clean Rivers Programme (Prokasih) (SPb 25.10.93)

Abbreviations: IO: *Indonesian Observer*; JJ: *Jakarta Jakarta*; JP: *Jawa Pos*; K: *Kompas*; M: *Merdeka*; R: *Republika*; SM: *Suara Merdeka*; SP: *Surabaya Pos*; SPb: *Suara Pembaruan*; T: *Tempo* are clearly identified as causing heavy pollution (Table 10.1), NGOs and the fledgling environmental bureaucracy have tried to implement a range of measures against the offending factories (three of these cases are discussed below). Unfortunately, it is these factories which are the most well-connected politically, and can extract concessions because of the size of project investment. The most serious problem in all regions where industrial development has taken place (notably West Java, parts of East Java and North Sumatra) is the large number of factories emptying untreated waste into rivers. It is in these areas that regulation is difficult because of the sheer number of polluting factories, which often empty waste into rivers only at night. The Deli River in Medan (provincial capital of North Sumatra, see Table 10.2) has 88 factories located along its banks, but only 20 were 'positively identified' as emptying untreated industrial waste into the river. Again monitoring must be an issue here. The main culprits are industries producing plastics, soap and other light manufacturing (*Suara Pembaruan* 25.10.93). In Pekalongan on Java's north coast (Table 10.3), a textile and batik cloth centre, 30 factories have been instructed under the government's Clean Rivers Programme to install waste treatment plants in their factories (*Suara Merdeka* 25.9.93). In West Java, which has felt the biggest impact of the government's industrialisation programme (Table 10.2), the Citarum River in Bandung regency (*kabupaten*) has 267 factories along its banks, 30 per cent of which have no waste treatment systems (*Republika* 8.10.93; *Suara Pembaruan* 10.3.94). Where waste treatment systems have been installed they are not always in operation because of the expense of running the equipment.

Effects of river pollution are wide-ranging on the health of villagers living by the rivers or near the industrial estates and factories. Pollution also affects productivity of adjacent industries and livelihoods. For example, shrimp farming around industrial regions such as Gresik (Table 10.2) and the Tapak River (Table 10.3) has been partially destroyed. Action taken against polluting industries is often initiated by villagers and landholders whose health and livelihood are directly affected by industrial pollution. The print media also has an impact in initiating action, particularly against large companies such as paper mills and oil refineries. Failure to improve waste treatment facilities when they could clearly afford the investment has prompted NGOs to bring legal action against the major companies (Table 10.1) and against the government for failing to enforce its environmental laws. None of these efforts has so far been successful. PT Barito Pacific Timber, responsible for emptying untreated waste from its plywood factories into the Barito River in South Kalimantan (Table 10.1), has been the target of international pressure regarding its illegal logging practices, but its polluting impacts have received much less attention.

The Environmental Impact Management Agency, Bapedal, has initiated action against companies in industrial regions under the Clean Rivers Programme, which has had much public support from the Deputy Governor of East Java, and (perhaps surprisingly) from the police force in that province. The previous Minister for Population and the Environment, Emil Salim, was publicly critical of companies which broke the law, and initiated legal action and out-of-court settlements in some cases (*Kompas* 3.6.91). NGOs involved in the Tapak River case, to be considered in depth below, sponsored a widely publicised proposal for a consumer boycott. The fact that the boycott had the qualified support of Emil Salim was no doubt an important political factor in securing an eventual settlement through mediation.

Both the PT Freeport Indonesia (Irian Jaya) and PT Inti Indorayon Utama (PT IIU, North Sumatra) pollution cases have been highly publicised in the Indonesian national press, as well as in the international media sympathetic to environmental issues. The national environmental non-government federation Walhi (Wahana Lingkungan Hidup Indonesia – Indonesian Forum on Environment) has initiated legal action against PT IIU, the company running the North Sumatran pulp mill, for gross environmental neglect. Both are huge projects in terms of levels of investment and impact on the local economy. While PT Freeport Indonesia is a North American joint venture company, the other four companies in Table 10.1 are all huge Indonesian–Chinese conglomerates with high-level political connections (the owner of PT Barito Pacific Timber is in business partnership with two of President Suharto's children). Foreign joint venture companies do not appear to be more environmentally conscious, at least in terms of installing waste treatment plants, than either state or privately owned Indonesian companies. PT Freeport Indonesia has a reputation for environmental irresponsibility in Irian Jaya, for dumping untreated tailings from its huge copper mine into local rivers, causing massive siltation. It also controls access to the region, so reporters find it difficult to visit the area (unlike North Sumatra).

The size of these projects, the scale of employment and taxation revenue, and the widely criticised collusion with the bureaucracy make these giant companies a kind of law unto themselves. Yet the PT IIU paper mill's actions in the North Sumatran case are well documented: breaking government regulations regarding waste treatment, damaging local roads, chopping down more trees for its pulp mill than the government quota permits, operating without a valid environmental impact assessment (*Merdeka* 7.10.93; *Republika* 21.3.94; Walhi and YLBHI 1993: 44–46).[3] While the question of expense for installing and operating waste treatment facilities is perceived by small industries to affect seriously their economic viability,[4] this is not the case for large industries with significant capital investment. In the case of PT IIU, the equipment installed eventually broke down causing further pollution (the reservoir containing untreated waste leaked, spilling waste into the river system), the mill was shut down by the government, but allowed to reopen before the waste treatment system was operating effectively. Recently the Indonesian Ministry of Population and the Environment has required PT IIU to hire American consultants to conduct an environmental audit under Bapedal's supervision (*Tempo* 14.5.94).[5]

The other pollution cases, while less dramatic than the North Sumatran paper mill or the Irian Jaya Freeport copper mine, are symptomatic of the dilemma which exists as a result of the government's commitment to a rapid industrialisation programme. Aimed at lessening dependence on exports of oil and agricultural products, government policy has meant facilitating private domestic and especially foreign investment to increase the country's industrial capacity. The resulting industrial growth has indeed been spectacular, but it has created competition for scarce resources, in particular land and water, resulting in an increasing number of compulsory land clearances since 1989 (Lucas 1992), as well as increasing rates of groundwater exploitation. It has also put pressure on the environment, and on the government to enact legislation to ensure that environmental protection occurs. In some cases, operating permits for development projects were issued before environmental impact assessments had been prepared. Companies such as PT SDC, the first chemical factory to establish itself near Tapak hamlet, and the North Sumatran pulp and paper mill, unwilling to make the expensive investment in waste treatment plants, argue that because they commenced operation before regulations were enacted, they are exempt from them.[6]

THE TAPAK RIVER POLLUTION CASE

The local impacts of pollution on people's lives as a result of industrialisation in Indonesia since the mid-1970s and the difficulties of their struggle to resolve the problem are illustrated by the case of Dukuh Tapak (Tapak hamlet), in Tugu subdistrict on the outskirts of Semarang in Central Java. The provincial city of Semarang was among the first designated as a site for industrial estates under a new government policy at that time; there are now chemical, food processing, soap, textile and paper industries located there (see Table 10.3).

The efforts of the 700 villagers of Dukuh Tapak to achieve social justice against the polluting factories is an important case study in terms of its dynamics, outcomes and implications (for residents, NGOs and polluting industries), as well as for what it reveals about the political economy of environment in Indonesia. Deserving note were the unprecedented coalition of village government, legal aid and NGO activists, the organisation of Indonesia's first consumer boycott, leading finally to an out-of-court compensation settlement for the villagers, and the inordinate length of time it took before landholders and residents finally obtained less than satisfactory compensation (14 years).

The Tapak[7] case first became an issue in the national press in 1991. This was 14 years after domestic wells, fishponds and rice fields became polluted from the original factory, PT Semarang Diamond Chemicals. Built by well-known Central Java businessman Budiarso (Bhe Hok Djwan) to make calcium citrate, a chemical preservative used in the manufacture of Coca Cola and Fanta soft drinks, it was a highly profitable investment decision closely linked to the establishment of a Coca Cola factory in a neighbouring region of the same province.

The early environmental degradation of the district was analysed at the time in a pioneering local case study by George Aditjondro (1979: 66–81), one of Indonesia's best-known environmentalists. PT SDC, the factory which commenced trial operations in September 1977, provided jobs for 228 workers, but 206 people (aquaculture farmers, wet rice field owners, agricultural labourers and fisherman) lost their livelihoods as 65 wells were polluted and hundreds of hectares of wet rice land were rendered uncultivatable over the next 14 years. The legal apparatus, still dependent on Dutch colonial regulations,[8] was ineffective against a company such as PT SDC which dumped its waste (ironically, the company's product, calcium citrate, was itself produced from agricultural waste products) untreated into the Tapak River. PT SDC installed temporary, later permanent, waste control measures, but other factories built after the district was declared an industrial estate in 1979 did not. By 1990 eight factories involved in food processing, chemicals, textiles, soap and paper had been named as polluters (Table 10.3; *Warta Konsumen* 1991: 14–15).[9] The factory owners' reply to the anti-pollution campaign was always that the government had designated the area for their factories, suggesting that the pollution of the water supply of three hundred villagers was a government rather than a company or industry responsibility.

Between February 1977 and November 1978, a special committee of Tugu subdistrict calculated that Dukuh Tapak landowners had lost Rp 119 million in agricultural production from the lucrative fish and shrimp ponds, as well as their rice fields (*Tempo* 24.3.79). This figure did not include any estimated value for the loss of the village water supply, which necessitates carting water from the spring several kilometres away for domestic needs, or for the decline in quality of the environment, including a noticeable increase in mosquitoes. The PT SDC factory management refused to pay the Rp 119 million compensation demanded, instead offering only Rp 5.4 million, but promising to install a new imported aerator at a cost of Rp 70 million (*Tempo* 6.6.81). Dukuh Tapak landholders refused the Rp 5.4 million compensation offer, although the BKPMD (Badan Koordinasi Penanaman Modal Daerah – Regional Investment Coordinating Board) considered it a fair offer at the time. BKPMD also considered that the coastal region, which included Tapak hamlet, was a good location for an industrial estate, because factories could dump their industrial waste almost straight into the sea. The head of BKPMD said this was a good reason for the residents of the areas which had been heavily polluted to be moved to other locations (Aditjondro 1979: 80), although local officials privately opposed any transmigration plan to resolve the issue, as did local villagers (*Tempo* 2.6.79) and the Muslim Development Unity Party (PPP) in the local Semarang municipal assembly.[10]

Aditjondro (1979: 76), in his study of the Dukuh Tapak pollution case, concluded that as a result of the pollution from PT SDC, 'the difficulties being faced by the Dukuh Tapak community were incalculable'. Workers employed by fishpond owners were forced to leave to find employment. The first to go sought employment in local quarries at a wage about one-tenth of what they were receiving previously. Landholders and other hamlet residents refused to be relocated, even after Semarang municipality unilaterally extended its boundary to incorporate Dukuh Tapak so as to re-zone 800 hectares as the Tapak industrial estate. It then issued permits for more factories to locate there over the next 14 years, increasing the already serious problem of pollution from industrial waste. The headman of Tapak hamlet put it this way: 'Since we were kids we have been used to living on the coast, working in rice fields and fishponds . . . We will have difficulties if we have to move to transmigration areas which are away from the sea.' Another long-time resident of Tapak said: 'Transmigration is for villagers who have experienced a natural disaster. But the pollution from SDC [Semarang Diamond Chemicals] is not a natural disaster, it's caused by human beings. So why should we move when this place is our home?' (Aditjondro 1979: 76). A feature of the campaign of the people of Kali Tapak was the unanimous agreement among all residents that they wanted to remain in the village despite the water pollution levels, at least until compensation claims were settled. The local government (both the hamlet head and the influential village headman) backed the villagers, the majority of whom refused to move before a negotiated compensation settlement was reached in September 1991.

Ten years after the people first reported that fish were poisoned, rice plants were dying, and their skin itched because of polluted water, the situation had not changed. If anything the pollution of the stream and fishponds was at higher levels. A 1986 report by Walhi and three affiliated NGOs estimated that the total untreated factory effluent being discharged was greater than the natural flow of the stream above the factories.[11] The report suggested that this was caused by the soap factory (PT Bukit Perak) and the cardboard factory (PT Kemas Tugu Indah Sakti) discharging their liquid waste into the river without treatment. While two of the original factories have installed water treatment systems, Walhi reported that 'the effluents are still strongly polluted [because] these treatment systems have been inadequately designed and are insufficiently maintained' (Walhi *et al.* 1986: 9). The well water in Tapak hamlet could only be used in toilets, as bathing with the water produced acute skin irritation. The report noted that:

> the incidence of diarrhoea and dysentery are believed to be related to the drinking of the well water. The well water can be characterised as follows: high turbidity, high concentration of suspended solids, low concentration of dissolved oxygen, a high total plate count of bacteria, the presence of chloroforms and a bad odour. A black sludge is found at the bottom of the wells.

The report goes on to point out that a family earning Rp 2,000 per day (US$1.76) will have to spend 15–25 per cent of their income on buying and transporting safe water from the spring 2.5 km away.[12]

During 1989 the media began reporting the Kali Tapak pollution case more frequently, after local Health Department laboratory tests showed that ammonia and sulphur levels in Tapak hamlet ponds were killing fish and shrimp

(*Mutiara* 18–24.7.89). Dutch government aid had built a water supply from the spring at the source of Tapak creek to provide a clean water supply to replace the polluted Tapak River water for domestic use. At this time (most likely through a lack of coordination of planning), Semarang municipality rubbish collection service opened a new two-hectare rubbish dump at Tapak hamlet, so waste started to pollute fishponds, and the smoke from smouldering rubbish polluted the atmosphere of the hamlet (*Suara Meredeka* 1.8.89). Throughout this period Walhi and the government threatened legal action. But it was the threat of a well-planned consumer boycott of industry products, rather than the possibility of an adverse ruling after a long-drawn-out case, which brought the factories and local government into serious negotiations.

While a series of earlier attempts by committees to mediate the dispute had failed,[13] a new Tapak River dispute settlement team, nicknamed the Team of Ten, succeeded partly where earlier attempts had failed because four of its ten members were NGO representatives.[14] This was the first time legal aid (representing Tapak hamlet residents) and other NGOs were formally included in the mediation process. They succeeded in negotiating a compensation settlement and environmental rehabilitation plan with factory owners, who were required to install waste treatment facilities which met government standards. Faced with a combined force of residents, NGOs, local and national government instrumentalities and parliament, factory owners cooperated in negotiations which produced the largest ever mediated pollution compensation agreement in Indonesia to date. On 19 September 1991 the Mayor of Semarang himself supervised the handing over of compensation totalling Rp 225 million to 247 residents at the Islamic primary school (*madrasah*) in Tapak hamlet (*Suara Merdeka* 20.9.91).

Even in the latter stages of the dispute, business interests used all the political and economic weapons at their disposal in a 'guerrilla campaign' to intimidate villagers. Factory henchmen had attempted to persuade villagers to revoke powers of attorney given to the Legal Aid Institute with a 'gift' of Rp 2.5 million; a Tapak hamlet youth group activist was accused of being a 'communist sympathiser'; kampung and hamlet heads were threatened with dismissal from Korpri (the government officials' functional group) if they did not convince people to accept the Rp 2.5 million; and it was feared that the Semarang Legal Aid Institute would be unable to protect villagers from intimidation. After six Tapak hamlet residents presented in person a letter signed by 85 residents to the Minister for Industry, who was visiting the province on 12 May 1990, municipal and subdistrict civilian and military security apparatus members visited Tapak hamlet, suspecting 'ulterior political motives' in the 'improper way' residents had acted by directly petitioning a government cabinet minister.[15]

Despite these countervailing pressures, which had the partial effect of consolidating resistance, a combination of factors finally led to the mid-1991 negotiated compensation agreement. These were:

1 The majority of residents refused offers to be relocated, and they were backed not only by the hamlet head but also by the village headman, a key figure in the local government bureaucracy.

2 The use of environmental laws (see pp. 197–198) under which offending companies could be prosecuted, and threats by Walhi (from 1989 to mid-1991) that they would proceed with legal action against the oldest polluting industry, PT SDC (*Kedaulatan Rakyat* 18.4.90), despite the acknowledged obstacles in bringing pollution cases to court.[16] In 1991 Bapedal again threatened legal action if the industries did not comply with their agreement with the Mayor of Semarang to install a central waste treatment plant within a stipulated time period (*Kedaulatan Rakyat* 24.4.91).

3 Scientific evidence collected by the local health department, the local state university and NGOs dating back to 1978, all of which showed extremely high pollution levels in both the stream and the fishponds.[17]

4 A threatened campaign initiated by 15 environmental NGOs,[18] supported by another 100, to boycott the products of the factories which were still emptying untreated waste into the Tapak River. The boycott campaign had effective publicity and, although drawing adverse comment from military authorities,[19] was supported by Emil Salim, the Minister for Population and the Environment, who visited Semarang and indicated that he expected the municipal government to find a negotiated settlement to the dispute. The NGO organisers of the boycott published a booklet, *Stop Pencemaran di Dukuh Tapak* ['Stop the pollution in Tapak hamlet'], which explained the background, legal issues, industries involved and their products, with press clippings showing how the case had developed. The booklet also explained various avenues of protest available to individuals and groups who wanted to support the boycott, including protest and persuasion, economic opposition and fundraising, and encouraged supporters to use both an example letter to the editor and a protest letter to managers of polluting companies (YLKI *et al.* 1991: 14–20). While the press reported there were 100 NGOs involved, the NGO campaign booklet claimed the support of 200 NGOs in Java, 61 in Sumatra, 18 in South Sulawesi, as well as others in Kalimantan, NTT and NTB. The boycott, which would have been Indonesia's first, was never fully implemented, however. Despite misgivings among some activists, it was agreed to cancel the boycott in order to take the dispute to mediation. According to Aditjondro (personal communication, 1995), some regarded this as a tactical error and accused Walhi of being too prepared to compromise. The threat of the boycott (as well as the strong NGO representation on the Team of Ten) was an important factor in reaching the negotiated settlement.

5 The assistance of the Semarang Legal Aid Institute (YLBHI) which led to the formation of the Team of Ten, representing local government, factory owners and NGOs, to negotiate the compensation agreement. As mentioned, a compensation fund of Rp 225 million was set up from

contributions from eight companies, which also agreed to install waste treatment equipment and stop emptying untreated effluent into Kali Tapak. However, no sanctions were specified if factories did not comply with this agreement. Because a negotiated settlement had been reached, Walhi and other NGOs (who were represented on the Team of Ten through LBH Semarang, YLBHI and YLKI) agreed to drop the boycott of products from the eight factories of the Tapak industrial estate. The Team of Ten agreement of August 1991 also announced that the issue of solid waste dumped in Tapak hamlet while Semarang local government had used the area as a municipal rubbish tip would be tackled (Santosa and Hutapea 1992: 73, 80).

6 The role of the print media was significant in raising local and national consciousness about the pollution at Tapak, and publicising broad support for the consumer boycott, also supported by two of Indonesia's most prominent environmental law experts (Professor Koesnadi Hardjosoemantri and Dr Daud Silahi), as well as Emil Salim. This helped considerably to mould public opinion; factory owners and the government feared that the boycott, if implemented, would be effective and spread widely throughout Indonesia (Santosa and Hutapea 1992: 31, n20). The boycott was never actually implemented because a mediated compensation settlement was reached.

The outcome of the mediation process, however, could hardly be seen to represent more than a symbolic victory. Comparing the final compensation settlement of Rp 225 million in 1991 with the Rp 119 million loss estimated for the 1977–8 period, and taking account of recurring damages and the impact of inflation in the intervening period, the amounts received by Tapak residents were insignificant and bore no relation to the damage to health and livelihood they had experienced. Moreover, there is no evidence to date of a significant reduction in pollution levels in the Tapak River.

Although the landholders won the compensation battle on 19 September 1991, Aditjondro (personal communication, 1995), who has followed the case since his original exposé 16 years ago, says the villagers are losing the wider struggle to preserve their community and livelihood. Already by 1989 the serious social impacts of the long struggle were becoming evident. A Protestant church report noted that people seemed apathetic about their future; that they no longer held *wayang* (shadow play) performances; and are described as preferring to drink and gamble instead (Tim Pra Seminar: n.d.). This is perhaps an indication of the level of community breakdown and alienation. The ongoing fight with the factories to stop pollution highlighted the deep social divisions within the Tapak community. According to Aditjondro, about one-third of the villagers (better-off landholders in their own right) have been 'geographically and sociologically able to resist' moving from the village. Either their wet rice fields and fishponds have not been so badly polluted (being located further from the worst-affected areas), or other resources enabled them to recover more quickly from the financial and environmental impact of pollution. The remaining 60 per cent have never recovered their lost livelihood. Half have sold their land, but still live in Tapak hamlet, because they have employment as horse cart drivers, aqua or agricultural labourers, or as workers in the factories which caused them to lose their livelihood as farmers in the first place. The last and probably the poorest third are landless villagers, who, being unable to find a livelihood locally, and having no financial or social resources to fall back on, have been forced to leave their homes to look for work in other villages or in the cities, or, as a last resort, have joined the government-sponsored transmigration programme. Throughout this period (1991 until the present), the factories have been actively seeking to persuade farmers to sell their land through *calo*, or middlemen. Farmers' acceptance of these offers may have been because factories have failed to install waste treatment plants according to the August 1991 agreement mediated by the Team of Ten (Santosa and Hutapea 1992: 73).[20]

The Tapak hamlet pollution case study reveals a number of issues related to the political economy of the environment in Indonesia. These include the pervasive problem of confronting powerful economic interests through a weak legal system; the difficulty of obtaining and the high cost of presenting admissible scientific evidence in court; the lack of coordination within and between levels of government; the obstacle of military authorities who tend to see environmental protest primarily in security terms (and therefore politically suspect). But the possibility of achieving a mediated settlement if NGOs and residents affected by pollution hold out long enough, campaign effectively, and are fairly represented in negotiations is also suggested.

The case shows the inability of the bureaucracy in Indonesia to deliver administrative solutions without pressure from NGOs, and the ambivalent attitude of members of local elected assemblies, who at the provincial and municipal levels were ineffective in their attempts to find a resolution of disputes such as Kali Tapak,[21] and tend to be reluctant to support popular protest. On the other hand the national parliament (the DPR) has been more critical of the government's handling of disputes, and supportive of popular protest such as that organised by the NGO coalition in the Tapak case.[22] The threatened loss of employment from NGO demands that local government close down factories if pollution does not stop adds an extra dilemma in protest actions: other sectors of the workforce may be hurt if campaigns are successful.

THE BUREAUCRACY AND POLLUTION CONTROL IN INDONESIA

Robert Cribb argues that the Indonesian government's growing concern with the pollution issue, indicated by legislation introduced since 1978 (see Warren and Elston 1994), is due to three factors: government receptiveness to outside pressure on environmental issues; concern over sea pollution (oil tanker spills) as damaging national interests; and the negative impact of pollution on the lifestyles of the influential Jakarta elite. Cribb also argues that one reason the government has used its 'formidable administrative powers' against pollution is that in an era of increasing deregulation, this is one area where continued intervention by the bureaucracy can be justified (Cribb 1990b: 1127). This raises a number of questions regarding the fragmented nature of bureaucratic power in Indonesia, with different instrumentalities often having incompatible agendas, and the effectiveness of pollution control implementation under existing legislation.

Bapedal, the Environmental Impact Management Agency, was set up by Presidential Decision No. 23 in June 1990. It is a 'non-departmental' government agency, reporting directly to the President, with the role of enforcing the government's environmental legislation, which the State Ministry of Population and the Environment, with its inadequate staffing and budget, and limited powers, has been unable to do. Although Bapedal has staffing shortages, and representation at the provincial level is limited, it does have substantial funding from external donors. Bapedal's priorities are surface water pollution control (the Prokasih programme), solid waste management (the Adipura programme), air pollution from mobile sources, sea and coastal pollution control, control of hazardous waste, cross-sectoral coordination and improvement of the environmental impact analysis (Amdal) processes. A main obstacle in the implementation of these priorities is the nature of the Indonesian bureaucracy, which 'is large and slow in its procedures and characterised by a marked tendency to favour compartmentalisation and fragmentation of responsibilities rather than coordination' (MacAndrews 1994: 99). At least eleven other established government departments and agencies have overlapping responsibilities with Bapedal. In addition, there was 'the Indonesian legal system's lack of experience in handling environmental cases, and the possibility that both the initial spurt of funding and the early support from all sides for Bapedal as an institution might diminish' (MacAndrews 1994: 99). Bapedal's lack of a provincial or regional presence appears to have been a deliberate move by former Population and Environment Minister Emil Salim, who did not want another top-down government bureaucracy to administer environmental protection and management. Rather, he wanted to raise the environmental consciousness of existing departments responsible for implementing government development programmes, through provincial offices of sectoral ministries (the kanwil), and through the regional planning boards (Bapeda). In addition, the Ministry realised that close cooperation with private institutes and universities where environmental research was being conducted was desirable, and set up a series of Environmental Study Centres (*Pusat Studi Lingkungan*) in the state universities.

A different kind of compliance strategy is the public disclosure of companies against which the government has taken action for violations of environmental regulations (see Table 10.3). In June 1991, the then State Minister for

Population and the Environment, Emil Salim, announced that 500 industries which were signatories to the Clean River Programme had not fulfilled their obligations and would be prosecuted (*Kompas* 3.6.1991), but refused to name the companies publicly. In July 1993 Sarwono Kusumaatmadja (the current minister) went further and announced to the parliamentary Commission on Population and Environmental Affairs that three factories had been charged with criminal activities, 26 had been temporarily closed, 5 were in civil courts with lawsuits lodged by members of the public, and seven were 'under investigation'.[23] While a couple of big-name firms with good political connections appear on the list (either involved in negotiations with local communities, with Bapedal as mediator, or being sued by communities in civil courts), the 26 factories listed as temporarily closed for pollution offences are all smaller or less well connected companies. This suggests that the extent of government action against polluters is inversely related to their size and political influence. The Kali Tapak case illustrates the ability of powerful companies to forestall government action through payoffs to local officials for political protection. But this is only part of the story. Both provincial and municipal governments were also trying to attract industries to locate their factories in the industrial estate and did not seem to want to do anything of a regulatory nature which would discourage investment.

REGULATION

On 19 September 1991 the Mayor of Semarang handed over compensation collected from the companies at a special ceremony at an Islamic school (*madrasah*) in Tapak hamlet. The 247 citizens of Kali Tapak received their compensation payment in the form of a special account set up by the government from polluting companies' contributions.[24] However, it is not clear to what extent the control measures agreed to by the polluting companies have since been implemented, or how effectively this situation has been monitored. Recently, some farmers of Tapak hamlet have begun selling their land. In a scenario common to recent compulsory land clearance cases all over Indonesia (Lucas 1992), a well-known middleman (*calo tanah*) working on behalf of existing factory owners (who presumably want to buy more land for plant expansion) has approached landholders via agents sent into the hamlet, offering them below market prices (Aditjondro, personal communication, 1994). So while landholders won the compensation battle, it seems some of them have lost the political struggle to keep their livelihood as farmers.

Former Environment Minister Emil Salim (replaced by President Suharto after the 1992 national elections) introduced a series of laws and implemented programmes intended to strengthen the role of the State in environmental management. Indonesia's Environmental Management Act (*Undang-Undang Lingkungan Hidup* No. 4 1982) provides broad statements of the basic principles of environmental management (Warren and Elston 1994: 18–19;

Fox 1994). Other legislation which followed this original law includes Government Regulation No. 29 1986, which established impact assessment procedures called Amdal (Analysis of Environmental Impact), implemented through Amdal commissions established in government departments and agencies at both national and provincial level.[25] Every company is obliged to present an assessment on any project proposal that is likely to have a significant social, cultural as well as environmental impact to the Regional Coordinating Investment Board (BKPMD) before permission to operate is given. Companies in operation before Amdal was set up are also in theory required to submit environmental impact statement reports but this has not been consistently implemented.

The implementation of these laws has been hampered by a number of issues. One is the availability of scientific evidence on sources of pollution, which is hard to prove and easy to contest, in court. Even obtaining the correct (or what villagers' local knowledge tells them is correct) scientific analysis is difficult. In a river pollution claim near Pekalongan to the west of Semarang, legal aid workers told villagers to record daily the condition of the river, its colour and its smell, although they were warned that this evidence might not be admissible in court. When villagers tried to obtain the required scientific proof by handing dead fish to local police for testing, the analysis from the provincial police criminal laboratories was that the fish died of an overdose of pesticide in the water, not from industrial effluent from factories along the river (Adjie 1993: 70).

Reference has already been made to Amdal or the environmental impact assessment process (including impact assessment report, management and monitoring plans) which companies are required by law to commission from private consultants before building permission or planning permits can be issued. The implementation and enforcement of Amdal again reflects a general problem of government regulation referred to earlier in this chapter. A recent press report suggests that bureaucrats regard the Amdal as just another permit procedure, for which they can ask companies for money, while businessmen consider that a bribe (*sogokan*) will give them environmental clearance (*Kompas* 25.10.93). Recently, as part of a government deregulation package (under a new regulation PP51/1993), companies are no longer required to give a Preliminary Impact Assessment (or PIL), the aim being to simplify and shorten the impact assessment process. Provision for evaluating an environmental impact assessment report is reduced from 90 to 45 days. Other environmental assessment and management procedures have also been streamlined. These include simplification of screening processes, clarification of permitting, reduced requirements for industrial estates, and time limits on the validity of environmental reports (World Bank 1994: 272–273; Warren and Elston 1994: 27–29). This, as the Director of the Indonesian Centre for Environmental Law commented, was avoiding the real issue, which was not the complexity of regulations but their lack of enforceability (*Republika* 26.10.93).

THE PRESS AND POLLUTION ISSUES

Representation of environmental pollution in both the print and electronic media has raised awareness of the health issues (such as contamination of fish in Jakarta Bay), and publicised, if not politicised, a number of other cases. The dynamics of recent cases such as the North Sumatran pulp mill (PT IIU), the American Freeport copper mine in Irian Jaya, Barito Pacific Timber in Kalimantan, Indah Kiat Pulp and Paper in Riau and West Java (see Table 10.1), Kali Tapak (Central Java), and pollution of Jakarta Bay have been reported by the print media in detail: reports cover the extent and nature of the pollution, attitudes of local government authorities and companies, and what the various outcomes of different cases have been, including government responses to compensation claims and legal action, and protest by landholders and NGOs. The now banned weekly magazine *Tempo* had an environmental column from the mid-1980s, publicising mainstream environmental issues, and familiarising readers with quantitative measurements of pollution such as BOD (biochemical oxygen demand) and COD (chemical oxygen demand), symbols for polluting heavy metals (such as lead, zinc, copper, etc.), and other technical or scientific terminology used in environmental discourse (*Tempo* 12.3.94). Detailed scientific measurement of air pollution in Jakarta is also appearing in the popular print media (*Jakarta Jakarta* 8–14.6.91).

In the context of the more open political atmosphere in Indonesian political life over the past several years (which came to an abrupt end with the banning of three news publications on 23 June 1994), comment on the environment from a popular perspective occasionally appears in the daily press. Reproduced here are two cartoons commenting on the impact of river pollution on daily domestic life (see Figures 10.1 and 10.2); a third shows a government official (possibly the chairman of Bapedal) threatening polluting factories with closure (Figure 10.3); and the final cartoon (Figure 10.4) depicts the plight of an angry villager whose fishponds are being polluted by a factory. Of course there is as much chance of the factory moving as there is of him moving his fishponds to the town square. So in despair he invokes the name of a well-known hero of the popular East Java *ludruk* theatre. Sarip Tambak Yoso (there is the play on words, as *tambak* also means fishpond) is one of a number of charismatic, rebellious characters who come to the aid of the oppressed poor in traditional East Java popular theatre. Most cartoons on environmental issues, however, remain on politically safe territory; for example, criticising the dumping of poisonous industrial waste sent to Indonesia in containers addressed to local companies.[26]

Nevertheless, these cartoons heighten awareness of political or social issues which may be too sensitive for editorial or 'corner column' comment in the local or national press. As such, these cartoons are often the only way of expressing grassroots community opinion about environmental issues in an oppressive political environment.

Figure 10.1 'The pollution level is still below the limit, really!' (*Kompas*, 5 June 1993)

Figure 10.2 'You're right Mat, we're itching from the dirty water, blotches on our skin, all sorts of things. If you don't believe us, come and have a bath together . . . ha! ha!'(*Sura Karya*, 12 August 1993)

NON-GOVERNMENT ORGANISATIONS AND REPRESSED LOCAL KNOWLEDGE

Robert Cribb has pointed out the role of NGOs in supporting people affected by industrial pollution (Cribb 1990: 1132–1134). As we have seen, the planned consumer boycott of products produced in Kali Tapak factories, initiated by 15 NGOs, was the first of its kind in Indonesia, drawing NGO representatives to Semarang from provinces as distant as NTB (Lombok and Sumbawa) to support the boycott. The NGOs produced a booklet as part of the campaign and were involved in establishing the Team of Ten which

Figure 10.3 'Factories causing air pollution are threatened with strong action by the government' (*Surabaya Pos*, 4 November 1993)

Figure 10.4 'If they won't move the factory, then I'll move my fishponds to the town square' (*Surabaya Pos*, 4 November 1993)

eventually negotiated the compensation agreement for the villagers of Kali Tapak.

In mid-1991, when Walhi threatened legal action against the Tapak companies that were breaking the law, it was revealed that some 'experts' (i.e. scientists who are also government officials working in university chemical laboratories) who had conducted tests of polluted water over the years would not give evidence in court for fear of 'political repercussions' or recriminations. Throughout the debate on legal action, the admissibility and strength of evidence based on scientific tests became an issue. There was doubt that the court would admit evidence from farmers themselves, passed on through direct observation and experience. Farmers had seen and smelt the pollution, they had seen their fish die and their rice crops wilt, but this was not admissible in court as proof based on scientific evidence. In fact, the Semarang municipal government's TKP2LH (see note 13) produced evidence from scientific tests which they claimed showed that pollution levels had actually declined, while villagers maintained from their experience that they had not. As the Kali Tapak case never got to court, the issue of recognising farmers' local knowledge was not resolved. Aditjondro refers specifically to the Tapak River case as an example of 'repressed local knowledge', the non-recognition (or discounting) of people's own experiences by the State. Because it is outside official control, local knowledge about pollution is denied recognition, especially when it challenges hegemonic State power (Aditjondro 1994: 59–64). But local knowledge could play a more important role in both political and legal spheres through media and NGO channels.

The potential for mobilising repressed local knowledge brings us back to Sukatip's perceptive observations of sea pollution in Lombok, with which we began this chapter. Two further examples indicate the degree of uninstitutionalised local knowledge and suggest the potential for institutional linkages. Lastri is a ten-year-old student in 4th grade of a primary school near the Sari Warna Asli (SWA) textile mill, located in the densely populated poorer urban neighbourhood of Puncangsawit in Solo, Central Java. A local NGO journal notes that hundreds of families live close to the factory, some houses almost touching the factory's walls, and 'the most immediate, discernible and offensive form of pollution is the bad smell coming from the factory. The extent of the odour varies quite a bit, but some odour is almost always present, and it is often quite unpleasant' (*ECO-Sounder* 1992: 20). Lastri has written and illustrated a story about the horrible smell and about how this air pollution affects herself and her friend Aziz (see Figure 10.5). She clearly identifies the source of the pollution problem in her illustrations, the offending company's initials 'SWA' labelling the factory roof at the top of her drawing. The story is simply called 'Limbah' ('Effluent'):

> One evening I was studying. After I had finished, and I was playing with Azis, suddenly there was this unpleasant smell around the kampung [urban neighbourhood]. We were amazed, how could such a smell come into the kampung? We went looking for the [cause of the] smell; we thought it was coming from a dead rat, but we couldn't find it. So we went to bed. The next morning I got up, had a bath, got dressed, had breakfast and left. After arriving at school the smell was there again. I think that the smell comes

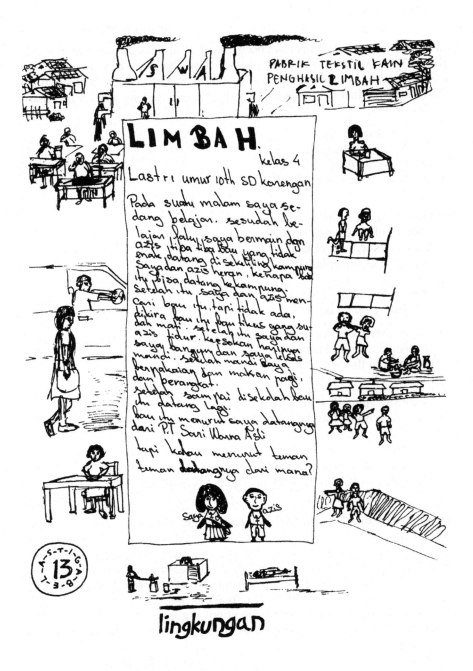

Figure 10.5   'Limbah' ('Effluent')

from [the textile mill] PT Sari Warna Aseli. But my friends are still asking where is it coming from?

(Suara Kampung 1994: 13)

In Solo, where textile mills have been emptying untreated waste into the Solo River (Table 10.3), a local NGO, Gita Pertiwi, has been encouraging river-bank residents to express their views. Lutyo Sunarto wrote 'A River Bank Poem' which alludes to the political and economic reasons why Lastri's question is ignored:

Mother always said
Don't take a bath in the river
Or the spirits there will get you
When the river swirls and floods its banks

Now I say
Don't take a bath in the river any more
Your whole body will start to itch
Your sores will never heal
They'll start to get infected
The water is filthy
Polluted by modern industry
Created by foreigners

Maybe there are people from the kampung
Or people nobody knows
Drowned in the murky water
Buried in the mud

Tomorrow you will say
Don't keep doing this
It's breaking the law
(Be aware . . .
Employers are using fine words
While they whittle away workers' rights to complain)

(Girli 1994: 17)

These examples of recorded local knowledge (doubtless there are many others) are important sources for understanding the impact of industrial pollution and other forms of environmental degradation in Indonesia. Until now such local experience remains just that, inaccessible to outsiders, written down perhaps, or published in print media which do not normally circulate beyond the local school or village. Despite this, publicity for efforts to verify local knowledge of environmental conditions is a sanction which can be exercised independently of the new environment bureaucracy, the courts or the parliament.

Apart from wider publicity, another means of validating local knowledge of environmental degradation in Indonesia would be to link the high school curriculum with NGOs and university-based Environmental Studies Centres (PSL). The State University of Airlangga already offers one-month environmental impact (Amdal) courses for NGOs, after which an additional course in water pollution measurement is available. With training in scientific procedures for measuring water pollution, the kind of evidence needed to validate NGO statements can be collected. This needs to be broadened to include the senior secondary school system. Senior high schools could run water monitoring projects as part of their basic biology or chemistry practical work, for example. As a way of demystifying the environmental bureaucracy, some of the simpler and less expensive water quality testing procedures (which are now taught to NGOs) could also be put in local hands (most obviously through the school system), an attractive funding project for international agencies with links to NGOs on both environmental and educational fronts. This would be another way of recognising that local knowledge of the environment exists, and can be recruited to the management of common resources in a new political economy of environmentalism.

NOTES

1 According to the consultants' survey of hospital and polyclinic records on Batam, produced for the Amdal report in 1990, out of a total population of 110,000, 3,000 people were treated for respiratory infections, 925 for skin diseases and 2,300 for diarrhoea, while a further 800 had respiratory problems (*Tempo* 7.5.94).
2 The remaining cases concerned air (23.5 per cent), groundwater (18.0 per cent), landscape (8.5 per cent), sea (6.5 per cent), soil (2.5 per cent) and noise (1.7 per cent) pollution.
3 PT IIU was also underpaying compensation to farmers for land compulsorily acquired and violating traditional systems of land transfer, all of which caused disruption of livelihood and breakdown of local communities (Walhi and YLBHI 1992: 42–43).
4 A recent World Bank report argues that even for small firms such waste treatment technology can in fact decrease operating costs, enabling them to recoup the initial investment outlay in about five years (World Bank 1994: 161).
5 The environmental audit contract was won by the North American company Labat Anderson, assisted by the Bandung Institute of Technology and a former Director General of the Department of Food and Drugs Control. Labat Anderson was reported to have been assisting Bapedal with the problem of industrial pollution in seven Indonesian cities over the past three years (*Tempo* 14.5.94).
6 Under the original 1986 environmental impact assessment regulations (PP29/1986), existing industries were in fact required to undergo environmental impact assessment (SEMDAL). However, by the 1992 designated deadline for compliance, it was estimated that 85% of liable industries had not done so, and reference to the SEMDAL requirement was omitted from the 1993 revised regulations (PP 51/1993). See Warren and Elston (1994: 24, 27–28).
7 Tapak village is named after Kali Tapak, a stream that runs from low foothills north through several villages, supplying fresh water to shrimp and fish breeding ponds on the coast.
8 Until 1978, Indonesia's legal apparatus for dealing with pollution was largely limited to the 1926 Nuisance Ordinance, which provided for sanctions against businesses (or individuals) that created a public nuisance (Cribb 1990b: 1125).

9 Minister for Population and the Environment Emil Salim also named the eight companies in a letter from Bapedal to the Ministers of Industry and Labour on 15 April 1991 supporting the consumer boycott of products produced by these eight companies (Santosa and Hutapea 1992: 57–59).

10 Of the three options open to the government – namely, to pay compensation, relocate the community or temporarily close down the factory – the last option was favoured by the Muslim PPP group. Their leader thought it unlikely that the large compensation would be paid by PT SDC, but that a factory shut-down was feasible, allowing it to reopen after the necessary waste treatment plant had been installed (*Kompas* 17.5.79).

11 Based on data supplied by factory management, the Walhi report calculated that total industrial waste water discharge was 245 m^3/day while the estimated flow of the Tapak stream in its upper course was 200 m^3/day. The Walhi report notes, however, that after all the branches of the stream have joined, the average dry season flow is about 1,250 m^3/day. This low flow probably explains another startling finding, namely that the chemical oxygen demand (COD) was 1,490 gm^3, while the average biological oxygen demand (BOD) was 375 gm^3; 'such a waste water discharge equals that of a town of more than 6,000 inhabitants' (Walhi *et al.* 1986: 9).

12 From a sample of 32 villagers covering nine different occupations, including rice and aquaculture farmers and labourers, factory workers, peddlers and horse cart drivers, the average per capita income in Tapak hamlet in 1985 varied enormously from Rp 500 to Rp 3000 per day (Walhi *et al.* 1986: 7).

13 These committees were the TKP2LH (*Tim Kordinasi Penangulangan Pencemaran Lingkungan Hidup*, Coordinating Team for Tackling Environmental Pollution), formed by the Semarang municipal administration in October 1989 to investigate the extent of water pollution (*Wawasan* 25.10.89); a *Tim Tripartite* consisting of NGOs, Departments of Fisheries and Industry, TKP2LH, representatives of five factory owners, Bapedal, and an independent mediator.

14 The NGOs were the local Semarang Legal Aid Institute (LBH), the Jakarta Legal Aid Institute (YLBHI), the Indonesian Institute for Consumer Affairs (YLKI – Yayasan Lembaga Konsumen Indonesia) and Walhi (Santosa and Hutapea 1992: 34, n22, 81). Other members comprised representatives of factory owners, Bapedal, and local government.

15 The 'proper' way, following correct bureaucratic procedures, was to take their protest to the Mayor of Semarang, or at least the provincial Governor of Central Java. The local security apparatus described residents as being *kelancangan* (brazen), acting on their own behalf before instructions were given. As poor or dispossessed people are incapable of acting on their own behalf in the eyes of the Indonesian security apparatus, political interests which are a threat to security are always presumed to lie behind such actions (Santosa and Hutapea 1992: 24, n12).

16 These difficulties included obtaining laboratory evidence acceptable to the courts, the high cost of mounting a case (including the cost of research and laboratory tests of polluted water), and the fact that the Tapak residents were faced with *orang berpotensi*, 'potentially powerful people', able to influence the court to get a decision favouring factory owners in a judicial system notably lacking independence.

17 The boycott campaign pamphlet lists seven different laboratory testings of Tapak River water conducted between 1977 and 1990, all of which showed that extremely high water pollution levels from untreated factory effluent were killing fish and shrimp, making domestic wells unusable, reducing yields from rice fields and fishponds and causing health problems (YLKI *et al.* 1991: 4–5).

18 The NGOs that initiated the consumer boycott plan were YKSB (Yayasan Kaha Setya Bhuana); LP2K (Lembaga Pembinaan dan Perlindungan Konsumen,

Semarang); YLKI (Yayasan Bakti Kesejahteraan Semarang); Bintari Semarang; ESP (Ecological Studies Project Solo); DASA (Yayasan Darma Shanti, Semarang); Sansayama, Semarang; LBH (Lembaga Bantuan Hukum) Semarang; YLBHI (Yayasan Lembaga Bantuan Hukum Indonesia Jakarta); YK3 (Yayasan Kelompok Kerja Kemanusiaan Semarang); YSS (Yayasan Sosial Soegiyopranto Semarang); Presidium Walhi Jawa Tengah; (Santosa and Hutapea 1992: 28, n15). A slightly different list (including the Muslim student group HMI) with full titles of NGOs appears in *Warta Konsumen* 1991: 18.

19 The provincial military commander described the boycott action as an example of NGOs being involved in 'practical politics (*politik praktis*)', which could be misused by those wanting to 'destabilise the nation' (Aditjondro 1991: 22).

20 In December 1991, three months after compensation was paid out, residents took polluted water to the village headman, and gave power of attorney to LBH Semarang to take eight industries to court, but the matter was apparently never pursued for reasons that are unclear. Santosa points out that the mediated Team of Ten agreement made no mention of sanctions if companies did not install proper waste treatment facilities (Santosa and Hutapea 1992: 43).

21 As a result, the DPR Kodya Semarang (Semarang municipal assembly) was not represented on any of the mediation committees formed to settle the dispute. Their one attempt at mediation failed because the companies refused to admit any liability for the pollution (Santosa and Hutapea 1992: 50–51).

22 Drs Markus Waraun, chairperson of the DPR's *Komisi X*, in a statement supporting the Kali Tapak consumer boycott, said he was amazed that local government had been trying to settle the dispute for ten years without success, and urged that recalcitrant companies be taken to court to teach them a lesson (*Kedaulatan Rakyat* 24.4.91).

23 The factories temporarily closed were in Jakarta (11), Lampung (10) and East Java (5). Five companies being sued by local communities in the civil courts are Mobil Oil in Aceh; PT Sari Murni (cooking oil) and PT Sarana Surya Sakti (metals) in Surabaya; Banyumas Washing Center (textiles) in Bandung; and PT IIU (pulp and paper) in North Sumatra. For a complete list of the names and locations of the companies see *Jakarta Post* 12.7.93.

24 The compensation payment was made in the form of a City Residents Account (*Simpanan Masyarakat Kota*, called Simaskot), but it is not clear from the report how each of the 247 people entitled to compensation had their own access to this fund (*Suara Merdeka* 20.9.91).

25 This regulation has undergone major revisions under Government Regulation 51 (PP51/1993) whereby Amdal commissions with broader membership (including members of investment and land use agencies and NGOs) have to prepare technical guidelines for environmental impact assessment and to assist in decision-making (Warren and Elston 1994: 22–24).

26 This is part of a highly profitable international waste recycling business of major environmental consequence (Skephi 1994; *Suara Karya* 19.3.93; *Tempo* 9.4.94).

BIBLIOGRAPHY

Aditjondro, G.J. (1979) 'Industriawan dan Petani Tambak: Kisah Polusi di Dukuh Tapak', *Prisma* 7: 66–81.
—— (1991) 'Aksi boikot, etis?', *Tanah Air* 4: 21–23.
—— (1994) 'Pengetahuan-pengetahuan lokal yang tertindas: Meneropong gerakan lingkungan di Indonesia Melalui Konsep "Kuasa/Pengetahuan' Foucault', *Kalam: Jurnal Kebudayaan* 1: 59–64.
Adjie, Puspo (1993) 'Pencemaran Kali Sambong', in Hutapea, Anthony L.P. (ed.), *Beberapa Penanganan Kasus Lingkungan Hidup*, Jakarta: Walhi.

Andal (1990) 'Air cemar; masyarakat Dukuh Tapak protest' (Report by the Editors), No. 9. Jakarta, SKREPP (Sekretariat Kerjasama Relawan Pengendalian Pence-maran).

Cribb, Robert (1990a) 'Cleaning up Indonesia's air and water', *Inside Indonesia* 23: 24–25.

—— (1990b) 'The politics of pollution control in Indonesia', *Asian Survey* 30 (12): 1123–35.

Fox, James J. (1994) 'The legal framework for managing the environment in Indo-nesia', Paper to the Asian Studies Association of Australia [ASAA] Biennial Con-ference, Murdoch University, Perth.

Hutapea, Anthony L.P. (ed.) (1993) *Beberapa Penanganan Kasus Lingkungan Hidup*, Jakarta, Walhi.

Koffel, Peter (1994) 'Riparian politics: the case of the Brantas River clean-up in East Java', Paper to ASAA Biennial Conference, Murdoch University, Perth.

Lucas, Anton (1992) 'Land disputes in Indonesia: some current perspectives', *Indo-nesia*, 52: 95–103.

MacAndrews, Colin (1994) 'The Indonesian Environmental Impact Management Agency (Bapedal): Its role, development and future', *Bulletin of Indonesian Eco-nomic Studies* 30(1): 85–103.

Mulyadi, M. Hari (1991) 'Tragedi Dukuh Tapak', *Andal*, No. 11, published by SKREPP (Sekretariat Kerjasama Relawan Pengendalian Pencemaran).

Nicholson, David (1994) 'Environmental public interest litigation in Indonesia', Paper to the ASAA Biennial Conference, Murdoch University, Perth.

Santosa, Mas Achmad and Hutapea, Anthony, L.P. (1992) *Sebuah Pengalaman Men-dayagunakan Mekanisme Alternatif Penyelesaian Sengketa (MAPS) di Indonesia*, Jakarta, Walhi & USAID.

Skephi (1994) *Delapan Perusahaan Perusak Lingkungan dan Anatomi Masalah Lingkungan Hidup Indonesia* [Eight Companies Which Damage the Environment and an Anatomy of Indonesian Environmental Issues], Jakarta, Biro Penerbitan Seri Lingkungan Hidup Skephi.

SPES (Society for Political and Economic Studies) (1994) *Economy and Ecology in Sustainable Development*, Jakarta, Gramedia Pustaka Utama.

Sukatip (1993) 'Nener semakin berkurang pengangguran meningkat', *Geram*, vol. 4, No. 15.

Tim Pra Seminar (n.d.) 'Laporan Hasil Kunjungan ke Kali Tapak', Semarang.

Walhi [Indonesian Environmental Forum], Tool [Dutch Technical Development with Developing Countries], KSB [Kaha Setya Bhuana Foundation], and Sawa [Consul-tancy for Sanitation, Water and Agriculture] (1986) 'Dukuh Tapak: Impact of indus-trialisation policy and development in West Semarang Industrial Area (survey report and proposal for small ponds rehabilitation project and integrated commu-nity development programme).

Walhi and YLBHI (1992) *Mistaking Plantations for Indonesia's Tropical Forest*, Jakarta.

Warren, Carol (1994) *Bali sing ken-ken!?: Tourism, Culture and the Environment in Bali* [catalogue to the exhibition of cartoons from the *Bali Post*], ASAA Biennial Conference, Murdoch University, Perth.

Warren, Carol and Elston, Kylie (1994) *Environmental Regulation in Indonesia*, Perth, University of Western Australia Press.

World Bank (1994) *Indonesia: Environment and Development Challenges for the Future*, Washington DC, Environmental Unit Report No. 12083-IND.

YLKI [Yayasan Lembaga Konsumen Indonesia], YLBHI [Yayasan Lembaga Bantuan Hukum Indonesia] and Walhi [Wahana Lingkungan Hidup Indonesia] (1991) *Stop Pencemaran di Dukuh Tapak*, Jakarta.

Periodicals

Eco-Sounder (Gita Pertiwi Environmental Quarterly)
Girli: Warta dari Kali
Indonesian Observer
Jakarta Jakarta
Jakarta Post
Kedaulatan Rakyat
Kompas
Merdeka
Republika
Suara Karya
Suara Merdeka
Suara Pembaruan
Surabaya Pos
Tempo
Warta Konsumen
Waspada
Wawasan

11 The politics of environmental health
Industrialization and suspected poisoning in Thailand

Timothy Forsyth[1]

INTRODUCTION

Thailand's rapid industrialization not only has introduced new environmental hazards of pollution and poisoning, but also has revised the political balance of Thai society. Previously powerless groups such as women workers or professional experts outside the government have grown in importance with industrialization as their labour and expertise form the basis of economic change. In Thailand, where environmental concern has always been closely linked with the trend towards democracy, a new alliance of women workers, specialist medical staff, media and activist groups has helped bring attention to the neglect of environmental health issues in government policy.

With rapid industrialization, workers' health is emerging as a major concern throughout Southeast Asia. While much research has pointed to the rising problem of industrial pollution as an environmental hazard, the hazards of poisoning within the industrial workplace have largely been unobserved. Unfortunately for many Southeast Asian factory workers, it is often their illness or death that starts the investigation of the problem instead of an adequate pre-emptive approach (Duffus, 1980; Karan *et al.*, 1986; Lin, 1986).

Past research on industrialization has concerned the nature and impact of foreign direct investment in the rapidly developing industrial powers of Asia (e.g. Amirahmadi and Wu, 1994). Since the rise of Japan as a world economic power, other East and Southeast Asian countries including South Korea, Taiwan, Hong Kong, Singapore, Malaysia and Thailand have attracted investment because of cheap land and labour costs, and the absence of well-developed trade union networks (e.g. Brown, 1991; Hewison and Brown, 1994).

Supporters of industrialization have pointed to the positive impacts of development resulting from the attraction of manufacturing industry. Increasing trade and employment from industry have brought prosperity to the so-called newly industrialized countries (NICs), a chance to reduce their dependency on the outside world for imports, plus the opportunity for many people to have an alternative source of income to traditional agriculture (Parnwell, 1994).

Yet critics of industrialization have claimed that it has made NICs dependent on the demands and successes of First World economies, and on the transnational corporations that initiate much of the industrialization. A new global division of labour has developed, making previously less developed nations, and especially their female workers, the production force for developed nations (Lim, 1990). Some have accused northern countries of deliberately locating hazardous production systems in the south with the agreement of governments to avoid environmental hazards or political opposition from within their own countries (e.g. Tuntawiroon, 1982; Sharma, 1984; Ives, 1985; Rasiah, 1988; Koomsup, 1993).

Accordingly, environmental policy in developing countries is often an attempt to maximize the benefits of industrialization while also limiting its potentially damaging impacts. However, while effective legislation may maximize development, increased costs resulting from regulation may encourage industry to locate elsewhere and therefore lead to interrupted or uncompetitive industrialization. The impacts of international competition are greater for countries favouring export-oriented industrialization (EOI) than for those adopting import-substituting industrialization (ISI) policies (Utrecht, 1986; Cooper, 1987; ESCAP/UNTC, 1988; Rigg, 1991: 202).

The recent history of industrial environmental and occupational health in Thailand illustrates these points. A government office formed to tackle new forms of industrial poisoning in 1990 was effectively closed a year later when it accused a major foreign investor of causing lead poisoning. Since then, further suspected poisonings have occurred elsewhere in Thailand, but there has been no specialist office to investigate.

Environmental protests have been intimately connected with political change in Thailand. Since the early 1970s, the kingdom has moved shakily from military rule to democracy, often through street demonstrations and violent confrontation with the military. Commonly, street protesters have demanded greater government commitment to environmental protection. In 1988, a long-running series of demonstrations secured the cancellation of a major dam project at Nam Choan, and in 1989 logging was banned in Thailand largely as a result of public outcry (Hirsch and Lohmann, 1989). In 1992, the government passed a number of acts to create agencies for monitoring and controlling pollution from industry.

In this chapter, case studies illustrate conflict between the mainstream power base of industry and government on the one hand, and the hitherto powerless groups of factory workers and sectors of government empowered with environmental protection on the other. Such groups, often including women, have traditionally been powerless within the institutional bureaucracy of Thailand, but have achieved gains through alliances with media and concerned elite groups. The cases presented below illustrate a chilling avoidance of health care responsibilities by government. They nevertheless also indicate the extent to which political conflicts over environment in Thailand are associated with a wider process of democratization, and with the emergence of a civil society able to challenge both state and new industrial interests.

INDUSTRY, LABOUR AND ENVIRONMENT IN THAILAND

In Southeast Asia, Thailand is a relative newcomer to industrialization when compared with the so-called 'tigers' of Hong Kong, Singapore, Taiwan or even Malaysia. Yet Thailand may have greater potential as an industrial power because of its own large market and access to the still undeveloped economies of Burma, Indochina and southern China. From the perspective of foreign investors, Thailand also has natural resources, is less burdened by debt and has a relatively poorly developed labour movement (Mabry, 1977; Lok King Choi, 1986; Brown, 1991; Hewison and Brown, 1994). There is considerable debate within the Thai press concerning whether Thailand is an NIC already (Sander, 1990).

Industrialization in Thailand may be dated to 1961, when the first five-year national economic and social development plan began. Since then there has been a steady progression from import-substitution to export-oriented industrialization (Akrasanee *et al.*, 1991). Thailand has benefited most recently from a wave of Japanese and Taiwanese investment after labour costs rose to uncompetitive levels in Hong Kong and Taiwan, and a number of new factories producing high-technology goods have located in Thailand. In the late 1980s, for example, a Taiwanese worker was paid six times as much as a Thai worker, but productivity was only four times as high (*The Economist*, October 1987: 6, cited in Sander, 1990: 304). Thai governments have generally encouraged industry to locate in Thailand, where it is seen to be an important part of the development process. The main government agency attracting industry is the Board of Investment (BOI). The Industrial Estate Authority of Thailand (IEAT) coordinates Thailand's 24 industrial estates (BOI, 1993; IEAT, n.d.). Between 1985 and 1992, merchandise exports from Thailand rose 450 per cent, more than for any other Asian country during that period. The second highest rise in exports, of 310 per cent, came from Hong Kong (EIU, 1993: 52; Thingsabadh, 1994).

While it must be stressed that virtually any manufacturing process can, under certain circumstances, be hazardous to workers, industrialization in Thailand is increasingly featuring new high-technology products that are commonly associated with workplace hazards. Electronics in particular have grown rapidly in Thailand since the mid-1980s (e.g. *Bangkok Post*, 10 Feb. 1993) (see Table 11.1).

Potential risks in electronics factories include lead poisoning from the inhalation or consumption of lead used for soldering. There is also a risk from solvent liquids used for cleaning or gluing (Gassert, 1985; Lin, 1988). Factories may protect employees through training, protective clothing and the provision of equipment that reduces fumes (e.g. Nicholas and Wangel, 1991). However, accidents occur where these practices are not carried out, or if train-

Table 11.1 Numbers of BOI-promoted electronics producers or assemblers

Numbers of factories, BOI industry category 4.6

Year	1985–6	1988	1990	1992–3
Factories	20	50	176	280

Source: Directories of companies promoted by the BOI, several editions

ing fails to convince workers of potential hazards. Acute lead poisoning may be fatal if large quantities are consumed in a short time period, causing abdominal pain and nausea. Chronic (long-term) poisoning is more common and generally not fatal (Barltrop, 1981).

Solvent poisoning can be very sudden and fatal if large quantities are inhaled or spilt onto the body (Browning, 1953, 1965; Kalliokoski, 1986; Riihimäki and Ulfvarson, 1986). Poisoning commonly causes brain haemorrhage or liver damage but is difficult to identify as poisoning after death because solvents evaporate quickly or become absorbed by fat cells inside the body. Post mortems may therefore only identify solvent poisoning as a likely, rather than certain, cause of death. In cases where companies may be liable for costly damages for the deaths or illness of workers, such an indefinite conclusion may be insufficient legal evidence to prove liability. Doctors may prefer to leave the cause of death unspecified rather than risk legal action from the company.

With such risks, there is strong public concern about the potentially damaging effects of industrialization. In recent decades, calls to protect the environment have been made alongside the pro-democracy movement by students and the educated elite (Hirsch and Lohmann, 1989; Stott, 1991). Protesters, NGOs and activists claim that recent economic change involving industrialization, rural development or tourism actively encourages environmental damage, while favouring foreign interests over local and national interests (e.g. Tuntawiroon, 1982; Phantumvanit and Panayatou, 1991; Hussey, 1993; Brummitt and Flatters, 1993; Mekvichai, 1993).

In the early 1990s, the Thai government began to develop responses to demands to control the health and safety impacts of industrialization. In 1990, the National Institute of Occupational and Environmental Health was set up at the Rajawithi Hospital in central Bangkok as a specialist unit researching and treating cases of industrial poisoning. Under the Seventh National Economic and Social Development Plan, this institute was allocated US$17.2 million to establish a national network and a staff of 200, including 70 doctors. In addition, in 1992, a series of new laws aimed to enhance the political infrastructure controlling industrialization in the lead-up to the United Nations Conference on Environment and Development (UNCED) (Thai Government, 1992; Taylor and Gordon, 1992; England, 1994). Under the 'Environment Act' (the Enhancement and Conservation of National Environmental Quality Act), the old Office of the National Environment Board (ONEB) was absorbed into the Ministry of Technology, Science and Environment (MOSTE).

A new Pollution Control Department (PCD) was established under MOSTE, with the brief to investigate and, if necessary, fine or close factories causing pollution. A new National Environmental Committee was also established, chaired by the Prime Minister and allowing a platform for both industry and NGOs. Two new funds for environmental projects and energy conservation schemes were also set up to assist industry. 'Pollution control zones' were established in the tourist resorts of Phuket and Pattaya, and at the industrial centre of Samut Prakan south of Bangkok. Government policy aimed to locate polluting industry in industrial estates as a way to concentrate and therefore control pollution.

In 1991, a major industrial dispute erupted in Samut Prakan, and became the first major test of the new regulatory framework.

SEAGATE AND THE NIOEM, 1991[2]

The potential hazards of industrial poisoning were acknowledged by the Thai government in 1990 with the establishment of the National Institute for Occupational and Environmental Medicine (NIOEM). NIOEM's first major test of power came in 1991 when the Ministry of Public Health sent it to investigate the possible causes of workers' deaths at a major foreign investor's factory.

The factory was owned by the US company Seagate Technology Inc., the world's largest independent producer of computer disk-drives. The computer disk-drive industry is a fast-moving, highly competitive industry where manufacturing margins are generally low. Although a major player in the industry, Seagate is vulnerable to smaller, more flexible companies that can compete by developing products for specific demands within a short time period. Seagate, however, has traditionally competed on the basis of mass production, in which production costs, including labour, are critical in governing profits.

Attracted by cheap labour, Seagate first located in Southeast Asia when it opened a hard-disk assembly plant in Singapore in 1982. It next came to Thailand, where it opened two new plants in 1988 and 1989, in the provinces of Pathum Thani and Samut Prakan to the north and south of Bangkok. Seagate now produces about 40 per cent of its total disk-drive production in Thailand. With 16,000 employees, it also claims to be Thailand's largest industrial employer.

In the early 1990s, Seagate experienced financial hardship as a result of competition within the disk-drive industry. Under such circumstances, Seagate was particularly sensitive to increasing costs, such as the threat of unionization among its cheap workforce in Asia. The company embarked on a change of strategy which was intended to increase the industrial giant's responsiveness to market changes rather than simply competing on costs alone. However, it was at this time that a major industrial dispute developed at its Samut Prakan factory.

The origin of the dispute is controversial. Seagate maintained that workers were simply asking for more money. Workers, however, said they wanted an explanation for the deaths of four workers between 1990 and 1991, which they claimed may have resulted from poisoning. Workers later claimed that Seagate was also using the dispute as an opportunity to dismiss staff who were involved in organizing a trade union.

The Ministry of Public Health ordered NIOEM to investigate. The institute, under its 36-year-old female director, Dr Orapun Methadillokul, investigated lead poisoning among Seagate workers by using existing blood test data from 1,175 factory workers collected by factory health workers during annual inspections.

Orapun used the level of 20 micrograms of lead per 100 millilitres of blood to indicate chronic lead poisoning. She found that 36 per cent of all 1,175 workers tested at Seagate had blood-lead levels above this level. This compared with similar studies at the same time showing just 2 per cent of all Bangkok residents and 8 per cent of Bangkok traffic police at or above this level, the latter being significant because Bangkok traffic police are constantly exposed to lead from traffic fumes. Such comparisons indicated that there was an unusually high proportion of workers contaminated with low levels of lead. Furthermore, the proportion of affected Seagate workers rose even higher in those sections of the factory conducting soldering work.

The official NIOEM report was supposed to be confidential, but its findings were leaked to the press and to the demonstrating workforce. Orapun denied responsibility for the leak. As a consequence of the report, demonstrations suddenly grew in size, and almost overnight it became Thailand's most serious industrial dispute, with workers marching on parliament and even petitioning the then US President George Bush for intervention against the US-based company. Worryingly for the Thai government, Thai trade unions threatened sympathy industrial action, and immediately tainted Thailand's image among investors as a country without a strong labour movement.

The report and strike had serious implications for Seagate, which responded aggressively against Orapun. Seagate claimed firstly that the blood-lead level of 20 micrograms per 100 millilitres was far below the levels of 70 to 100 micrograms which are normally considered life-threatening. The company also stated that its soldering equipment did not produce lead fumes because it only heated to 700 degrees Celsius, compared with the 1,000 degrees necessary to produce fumes. An independent expert on lead poisoning[3] later supported Seagate's claim about blood-lead levels, but pointed out that lead fumes can be generated at a temperature of 621.5 degrees Celsius.

Orapun countered Seagate's claims by pointing out that the comparatively high incidence of blood lead among workers in the factory suggested that a few may have had significantly higher levels. She also suggested that Seagate was controlling test results by moving employees around the factory floor, so that workers with high blood-lead levels were effectively removed from the survey. Belatedly, she also questioned the use of solvents at Seagate. One common cleaning agent called TP-35 was shown by laboratory tests to contain derivatives of the carcinogen benzene. Seagate now no longer uses TP-35 because it damages the ozone layer, but claimed that the solvent in question was a product of the DuPont company called Freon, and harmless to humans. However, other research has claimed that Freon may induce heart failure and breathing difficulties among workers (Gassert, 1985). Such symptoms were shown by some of the workers who died at Seagate.

Seagate denies industrial poisoning occurred at its plant, and today there is still a lack of clear-cut proof. However, the dispute led to a conflict within government agencies which radically changed the status of NIOEM. In August 1991, Orapun was called to the boardroom of Seagate when she was conducting her investigations. Inside, she was handed the telephone and spoke to Staporn Kavitanon, the Director General of the Board of Investment (BOI) and secretary to then Prime Minister Anand Panyarachun. She claims he threatened her with dismissal if she continued her criticism of Seagate. Staporn confirms he made the telephone call, but denies threatening Orapun in any way.

Shortly after this, NIOEM was removed from the Seagate case, and new studies were carried out by industrial hygienists at the National Institute for the Improvement of Working Conditions and Environment (NIWCE) under the Ministry of Industry. These tests investigated workplace conditions rather than workers' health, and showed that Seagate was not breaking any law. The industrial dispute faded.

The case has certain similarities with one in 1973 when environmentalists accused the Japanese Asahi company of discharging mercury from its caustic soda plant in Thailand. The Ministry of Health measured a discharge of 2.718 ppm in surrounding water, while the Ministry of Industry measured just 0.003 ppm. It was later revealed that the Ministry of Health collected samples by boat at night without warning, but the Ministry of Industry announced its arrival well in advance and arrived punctually at the front gate of the factory (Tuntawiroon, 1982: 371).

NIOEM was effectively closed down after the Seagate dispute. NIOEM employees were told to find work elsewhere, and the official nameboard for the institute was removed. Orapun remained at the Rajawithi Hospital, where she treated some 200 Seagate workers suffering from chronic lead poisoning. NIOEM never received the funding or staff allocated under the Seventh Five-Year Plan. The Ministry of Public Health claimed its duties have been absorbed by other divisions within the ministry, a claim said by Orapun to be false.

THE NORTHERN REGION INDUSTRIAL ESTATE, LAMPHUN, 1993–4

Critics claim that events at the Northern Region Industrial Estate (NRIE), in the provincial town of Lamphun some three years after the Seagate incident, proved the folly of closing NIOEM. In March 1993, workers at NRIE began to die suddenly from unexplained causes. Victims all experienced symptoms including headaches and sometimes inflamed stomachs and nausea. According to different estimates (*Bangkok Post*, 27 May 1994), between 11 and 23 people associated with the estate died from these causes over eighteen months.

NRIE was established in 1985 to attract industrial development to the largely rural northern Thailand. Most factories in the estate are Japanese electronics companies. The BOI also has attempted to concentrate electronics manufacturing in the north as a way to develop a specialized workforce (Phantumvanit and Panayotou, 1991; EBG, 1993b). Lamphun is 30 km from the regional capital of Chiang Mai, and is an old town of just 15,000 inhabitants. The estate attracts many migrant factory workers from the northeast of Thailand, which is typically poorer than the north.

The workers' deaths at the estate caused a storm of controversy. Local workers suspect that the causes of the deaths were lead or solvent poisoning. At least eight deaths involved workers at Japanese companies making circuitry, electroceramic circuit boards or lenses using soldering or solvents. At least one victim's job involved burning chemical waste in the factory grounds. Two well-known companies where there have been fatalities are Hoya Optical Co. and facsimile machine manufacturer Murata Co., although all companies deny any industrial poisoning or dangerous work practices. The fatalities include two children, who may have had lead poisoning passed on to them via breast feeding, or through physical contact with people covered with dust (see Theobald, 1995, for a gender-related analysis of the estate's problems).

Meanwhile in November 1993, the Industrial Estate Authority of Thailand (IEAT) called a press conference to dispel rumours about safety. The governor, Dr Somchet Thinapong, angrily condemned the press and other critics for trying to make political capital out of the problem. He and the local Lamphun Health Authority blamed the deaths on AIDS.

While AIDS is indeed particularly common in Lamphun, its symptoms are very different from those recorded for the deaths of the workers at the estate. AIDS is associated with gradual weight loss and opportunistic infections causing diarrhoea and pneumonia, for example. The estate deaths were almost always sudden, and came with headaches. For this reason, the deaths at the estate also do not match the so-called Sudden Unexplained (Nocturnal) Death Syndrome noted among Thai workers overseas during the early 1990s, from which workers died in their sleep with no apparent illness beforehand. The estate-workers' symptoms in fact match descriptions of lead or solvent poisoning, and are similar to the deaths at Seagate in 1991.

A further complicating factor is that many of the workers who died were also those who worked the longest hours in the factories. Workers can win financial bonuses by working extra hours, and therefore exposing themselves to factory conditions longer. At least one dead worker had run up large debts buying consumer goods for his family and so had to work long hours.

In addition to this official denial of any industrial health problem, one worker received a more personal rebuff. In late 1993, a female worker at Murata complained of constant headaches and body pains. The factory doctor only prescribed painkillers, so the worker went for an independent checkup at the McCormick Hospital in Chiang Mai. The McCormick is well known to be one of the best hospitals in Chiang Mai, and it had the contract to undertake annual health tests for the Lamphun estate until this was awarded to the local health authority. The McCormick doctor suggested the worker was suffering from aluminium poisoning. However, when the worker approached Murata with this diagnosis, the hospital withdrew its statement. When questioned about this in 1994, the hospital medical director denied the patient had ever been to the hospital, despite there being a signed receipt from the hospital for her visit.

This incident revealed the absence of an adequate testing system for industrial poisoning. Although the worker assembled aluminium–ceramic plates in the factory, independent doctors agree that aluminium poisoning was unlikely to have caused her symptoms. However, no hospital in the region has the equipment required for identifying this kind of industrial poisoning. The problem recurred in December 1993 when a 21-year-old woman died at the Murata factory and samples were taken from her body and kept at the Suan Dok hospital in Chiang Mai. By September 1994, these samples had still to be analysed either there or in Bangkok. According to the original plans made at the formation of NIOEM, such equipment would have been available in northern Thailand, or the tests could have been done at the NIOEM headquarters in Bangkok.

Environmental health quickly became an issue of national importance, reflecting the pros and cons of industrialization. Local inhabitants of Lamphun used the Lamphun Action Group, a local NGO, to voice concern. This group organized demonstrations outside the governor's office in 1993 about suspected contamination of water flowing through the industrial estate. It also raised attention by contributing features to national newspapers (e.g. Yangderm, 1994), and by contacting academics at Bangkok universities.

The Lamphun Action Group is composed of local residents concerned about the impact of industrialization upon Lamphun. Its strength lies in the persistence of its members in pursuing its causes. It also has some key members in Bangkok who are natives of Lamphun. One of these, a lecturer at Chulalongkorn University, also helped form the 'Toxic Watch Network', an organization seeking to publicize and monitor industrial pollution. The group includes members in Lamphun who experiment with organic farming, and who write regularly to newspapers about developments in Lamphun that they consider to be damaging to the environment or the rights of local people. In 1994, such local interest by the Lamphun Action Group led to the discovery of untreated toxic waste in woods near the Northern Region Industrial Estate, and an invitation to national journalists to investigate the discovery (Jitravi, 1994).

The discovery of untreated waste near the industrial estate was a major embarrassment for the IEAT, and forced the Authority to act. Previously, the IEAT had claimed that a central waste treatment plant was unnecessary at Lamphun because none of the factories produced hazardous waste. The disclosure forced the Pollution Control Department (PCD) under the Ministry of Science, Technology and Environment (MOSTE) firstly to investigate the disposal of waste at the NRIE in March 1994, and then to announce in April 1994 that it would investigate all industrial estates throughout the country for management of hazardous waste. The move further indicated the growing struggle between the new, anti-pollution departments of government, and the older, pro-industry bodies.

There were also calls for investigations into the deaths. Three investigations by the Ministry of Public Health, the House Committee on the Environment, and a full panel involving government, NGO and specialist advice, have concluded that industrial poisoning cannot be proven. Yet the evidence continues to suggest that it may have been implicated. Any suggestion of industrial poisoning is, of course, furiously denied by the industrialists, who have been pursuing their own publicity campaign in the national press by writing letters, and by issuing press releases denying charges and alleging inaccuracies in reporting (Boller *et al.*, 1994; McCarty, 1994).

Although workers at Lamphun were writing to Dr Orapun at the Rajawithi Hospital from late 1993, she was prevented from becoming involved by her employers at the Ministry of Public Health because of the impacts of the Seagate case three years earlier. However, after continued references to her in the press as a specialist on industrial poisoning, her expertise was finally acknowledged when she was included in the final panel investigating the deaths. Nonetheless, while this was seen to be a positive move, the appointment coincided with (unpublicized) disciplinary action against her by the Ministry of Public Health on account of her public criticism of her employers in the press. It is therefore probable that her comments to the panel were tempered by this disciplinary action, and the fear of losing her job.

Public concern, however, remained strong among the Lamphun Action Group, newspapers and concerned elite. In 1994, environmental activists in Lamphun published their own 'Haripunchai Declaration', named after the oldest temple in the town, and symbol of the age and distinctiveness of Lamphun. This declaration, written in the form of an open letter to the government, drew attention to the deaths of workers and to local water pollution, calling for greater attention from the government to these issues (Lamphun Action Group, 1994). In 1995, the Thai pop group Carabou, popular among the urban middle classes of Thailand, released a new compact disc, including a song about Lamphun and the problem of factory poisoning. It signified the growing awareness of environmental issues among the urban elite of Thailand. A problem in a remote industrial estate had entered mainstream debate and led some openly to challenge authority.

DISCUSSION: POLITICS OF INDUSTRIALIZATION AND ENVIRONMENTAL HEALTH

The two case studies presented above indicate how local groups and factory workers may ally with urban elites and media against traditional power bases in business and state. In this particular case, the role of women workers and a woman specialist suggests that new environmental movements are also linked to the rising power of previously unrepresented groups.

As stated in the introduction, environmentalism in Thailand has long been associated with the pro-democracy movement (Hirsch and Lohmann, 1989). While some of these pressures may be attributable to the activities of the new business elite who wish to challenge the old hegemony of the military in Thailand, environmental politics are often directed at both the state and the new business elite. Indeed, the problem of pollution and poisoning in Lamphun has also led residents to support the formation of trade unions in the Northern Region Industrial Estate as a general protection of workers' rights (*Bangkok Post*, 16 September 1994).

In both the Seagate and Lamphun conflicts women were the main protagonists: the victims, the demonstrators and the medical specialist (Theobald, 1995). Orapun is known internationally as a Thai expert on occupational and environmental health, yet within the Thai Ministry of Public Health she is largely alone as a specialist in this area, and also as a woman doctor of high rank. Other doctors and government officials clearly see her as something of a troublemaker. Orapun claims her employers have called her a 'troublesome woman', while the deputy director of the Department of Public Health said she was deprived of power at NIOEM because she was 'too young' (Forsyth, 1994: 33).

Virtually all factory workers at Seagate and Lamphun were women, as were most of those who died suspicious deaths. In December 1992, one 22-year-old woman Seagate employee sent a long, hand-written letter to Prime Minister Chuan Leekpai to ask for support in her claim against the company for chronic lead poisoning. She and some 200 other employees had been diagnosed by Orapun, and had been receiving treatment for headaches and loss of balance. In Lamphun, the woman who had been diagnosed as suffering from aluminium poisoning by the McCormick Hospital later went to the press with her story, and contacted Orapun on the advice of a local lawyer's office. Such assertive action by young women workers indicates a growing sense of power among groups who have been traditionally marginalized in politics. (The woman eventually lost her case in 1996.)

The alliance of women workers with a woman professional is only part of a newly formed alliance that includes the press, academics and NGOs. The Lamphun Action Group liaises with the press, Dr Orapun and with academics in Bangkok, some of whom come from Lamphun. In 1994, a group of concerned individuals created the Toxic Watch Network, a regular forum and newsletter to monitor the hazardous impacts of industrialization (Toxic Watch Network, 1992). The Lamphun Action Group does not have the same publicity or status as, for example, Project for Ecological Recovery, a Bangkok-based NGO which has campaigned successfully against logging and dam construction. However, the Lamphun group's links with the press mean it has access to a powerful political force which is run by the wealthy educated elite of Thailand and is also a key agent in the pro-democracy movement.

Industry and state in Thailand are allied together in an effort to move industry to previously agricultural areas where the workforce and land are cheaper. The Sixth and Seventh National Economic and Social Development Plans emphasized diversification of the rural economy. Decentralizing industry is a top priority. In Thailand, the government has traditionally been linked with the military, and many important companies feature important army figures on their boards of directors. The director of the BOI, Staporn Kavitanon, has military connections after studying at a military college in 1987 with some of the most important political military figures (the Class 5 graduates of the Chulachomklao Royal Military Academy), although he denies this had any influence on his appointment (Khongnirandsuk, 1992).

The rise of the environment as a political issue has also been reflected in conflict between government agencies. Although founded as recently as 1992, the Pollution Control Department (PCD) moved quickly to display its power after the alleged failure of the Industrial Estate Authority of Thailand (IEAT) to ensure adequate waste disposal in industrial estates. Similarly, the BOI has been criticized in the press for allegedly encouraging hazardous industrialization, and for being slow to admit there may be a problem of industrial poisoning.

However, the power of agencies varies considerably. NIOEM was effectively closed probably because it was run by a young woman and because it was only part of the Ministry of Public Health. The PCD, on the other hand, is a new, high-profile agency created in Thailand's review of environmental policy before the 1992 UNCED conference (England, 1994). It is also possible that the comparative weakness of NIOEM reflects the poor perception of environmental health as a risk of industrialization or its low priority as a political factor. There are other environmental health agencies within the Ministry of Public Health, although these do not focus on industrial problems and research, as had been the intention for NIOEM.

Part of the difficulty is the poor perception of industrial poisoning as a threat to the workforce. As a problem, it is new and also difficult to measure, particularly in the case of solvent poisoning, which seems the more likely cause of adult death than lead poisoning. However, much debate still focuses on lead poisoning as a possible cause of death, possibly because the government and industrialists know that it is easier to disprove than solvent poisoning. Debate about lead poisoning may therefore be an attempt to draw attention away from solvents – as perhaps is shown by the continued remonstrations from IEAT which deny lead poisoning, while failing to mention solvents at all in discussion of the case (Thinaphong, 1994). Such difficulties in proving the existence of solvent poisoning make its regulation difficult. Although solvents are controlled in workplace conditions by law, the lack of clear evidence linking them to human deaths will make it easier for industry to oppose further restriction of their use.

However, the public concern shown about the workers' deaths in Lamphun, and the resentment that the government had closed NIOEM to protect business interests rather than Thai citizens, has already forced some response by government. In 1995, the Public Health Ministry announced it would support new proposals to establish councils to protect workers' health, particularly in industrial estates. This was a response to the controversy in Lamphun, although the effectiveness of such measures has yet to be seen.

CONCLUSIONS

This chapter has reviewed responses in Thailand's emerging civil society to the unexplained deaths of workers in new electronics factories, and the apparent decision of government to close an environmental health agency because it encouraged such activism. Although still technically unproven, evidence suggests that industrialisation is leading concomitantly to new forms of industrial poisoning. However, the conflicts resulting from the deaths also illustrate wider changes occurring in the eco-political landscape of Thailand.

The case studies show that Thailand's Environmental Law and associated legislation of the early 1990s was not sufficient to produce effective environmental protection in factories. While industrial poisoning is still unproven at Seagate or the Northern Region Industrial Estate at Lamphun, the main concern has been the apparent slowness of the Thai government to investigate whether poisoning did cause the deaths. Much research is still awaited into the nature and extent of poisoning.

Equally important, however, is critical analysis of the institutional and power structures that facilitate or hinder openness. It is clear that changes must occur in the political infrastructure of environmental protection in order to challenge the existing power base of industry and the Board of Investment. This must be associated with a greater platform for traditionally powerless groups, such as women workers or specialists. There must also be a greater overall perception of the problem of poisoning. This conclusion is likely to be the same for other countries in Southeast Asia and elsewhere that passed environmental legislation at the time of UNCED (England, 1994). Such environmental concern by workers is also apparently increasing the support for unionisation.

Attempts to control pollution by concentrating industry into industrial estates have evidently done little to restrict hazards within the estates as originally envisaged. The problem appears worse when the factories associated with poisoning and pollution are 100 per cent foreign-owned and produce only goods to be sold outside Thailand. While export-oriented industrialization has a greater potential for profits than import-substitution, it appears that these profits are being won at the price of poisoning and pollution. This is politically as well as clinically dangerous in Thailand, where the environment is a contentious political issue, and many members of the educated elite accuse the government of favouring outsiders' interests above Thai interests for the sake of rapid wealth.

As Vietnam and southern China open to foreign direct investment, the status of Thailand as a cheap source of labour will decline (Samudavanija, 1994). It therefore seems time for the Thai government to invest in its workforce to improve specialization and quality. Between the start of the poisoning debate in Lamphun in 1993 and September 1994, 40 per cent of the industrial estate workforce resigned because of fears over health. The places were quickly filled by poor migrants from the northeast of Thailand who were either unaware of the hazards or prepared to risk them (*Bangkok Post*, 1 August 1994).

Such rapid turnover of staff does not produce a stable or specialized workforce. Also, the international publicity about suspected poisoning does not reassure foreign investors about Thailand's commitment to building a quality workforce. Thus the final irony could be that the BOI and IEAT concern for image has ultimately hindered rather than helped in achieving their strategic industrial objectives.

ACKNOWLEDGMENTS

I would like to thank Dara O'Rourke (ex-UNEP, Thailand); Kamol Sukin of *The Nation* (and previously *Manager* newspaper); and Veerasap and Ooy Yodrabam of the Lamphun Action Group. The Project for Ecological Recovery provided assistance with newspaper archives. Research was partly financed by the Chaiyong Limthongkul Foundation of Thailand and *Asia, Inc.* magazine.

NOTES

1 This chapter was researched with the help of the Chaiyong Limthongkul Foundation of Thailand and *Asia, Inc.* magazine, Hong Kong.
2 These case studies are based on research for an article in *Asia, Inc.* magazine (Forsyth, 1994) and information collected from newspapers and other sources since.
3 Dr Yvette Lolin, Department of Chemical Pathology, Chinese University of Hong Kong.

BIBLIOGRAPHY

Akrasanee, Narongchai, Dapice, David and Flatters, Frank (1991) *Thailand's export-led growth: retrospect and prospects*, TDRI (Thailand Development Research Institute) Policy study no. 3, TDRI, Bangkok.
Amirahmadi, Hooshang and Wu, Weiping (1994) 'Foreign direct investment in developing countries', *Journal of Developing Areas* 28: 1, 167–190.
Barltrop, D. (1981) 'Lead poisoning', in Vale, J.A. and Meredith, T.J. (eds) *Poisoning: diagnosis and treatment*, Update Books, London, pp. 178–185.
BOI (Board of Investment) (various years) *Thailand investment: a directory of companies promoted by the Board of Investment*, BOI, Bangkok.
—— (1993) *A guide to investing in Thailand*, BOI, Bangkok, September 1993.
Boller, Hans; D'hont, Danny; Teratani, Keisuke; Decroix, Jean-Jacques; Branston, Chris; Hungerbuehler, Werner; Brotschi, Beat; Hirota, Shozo; Matsuki, Yoshio;

Schneiter, Jean-Jacques; Benraheem, Hassan; Thepper, Ulf; Ang, Kim; McCarty, Daniel, and Teriyapirom, Boonsong (1994) 'Reports unfair to industrial estate', Letter to *Bangkok Post*, with reply from the editor, 19 July, p. 5.

Brown, Andrew (1991) 'Thai unions since the overthrow of the Chartchai government', *Thai-Yunnan Project Newsletter*, 14, September 1991, pp. 1–2; 15, December 1991, pp. 2–6: Australian National University, Canberra.

Browning, Ethel (1953) *Toxic solvents*, Edward Arnold and Co., London.

—— (1965) *Toxicity and metabolism of industrial solvents*, Elsevier Publishing Co., Amsterdam, London, New York.

Brummitt, William E. and Flatters, Frank (1993) *Exports, industrial change and Thailand's rapid growth*, TDRI (Thailand Development Research Institute) 1992 year-end conference: *Thailand's economic structure – towards balanced development?*, Background report, TDRI, Bangkok.

Cooper, Steve (1987) 'Review of: Utrecht, Ernest (1986) (ed) "Transnational corporations and export-oriented industrialisation", TNC Research Project, University of Sydney', *Journal of Contempory Asia* 17: 2, 249–251.

Duffus, John H. (1980) *Environmental toxicology*, Edward Arnold Resource and Environmental Science Series, London.

EBG (Environmental Business Group Co. Ltd) (1993a) *Study: industrial pollution control in Thailand*, submitted to United Nations Industrial Development Organization, Vienna, by Paul Clements-Hunt and Peter Brimble, EBG April 1993, Bangkok.

—— (1993b), *Project report: Environmental issues and sustainable development in Thailand: the role of the Board of Investment*, prepared for the Office of the Board of Investment and the ASEAN Promotion Center on Trade, Investment and Tourism, by Paul Clements-Hunt and Sonia Berry, EBG May 1993, Bangkok.

EIU (Economist Intelligence Unit) (1993) *Asia's investment flows*, EIU Report Q157, January 1993, EIU, London.

England, Philippa (1994) 'National agendas in Malaysia and Thailand before and after the adoption of the authoritative statement of forest principles at Rio', unpublished monograph, Department of Law, Griffith University, Brisbane.

Environment and Urbanization (1992) 'Will UNCED sustain development?', *Environment and Urbanization*, editorial comment 4: 1, 3–7.

ESCAP/UNTC (1988) *TNCs and environmental management in selected Asian and Pacific developing countries*, ESCAP/UNTC Publication series B, no. 13, Bangkok.

Forsyth, Tim (1994) 'Shut up or shut down: how a Thai medical agency was closed after it questioned worker safety at a factory owned by Thailand's largest employer', *Asia, Inc.* (Hong Kong-based monthly business magazine), April, pp. 30–37.

Gassert, Thomas (1985) *Health hazards in electronics: a handbook*, Asia Monitor Resource Centre, Hong Kong.

Hewison, Kevin and Brown, Andrew (1994) 'Labour and unions in an industrialising Thailand', *Journal of Contemporary Asia* 24: 4, 483–514.

Hirsch, Philip and Lohmann, Larry (1989) 'Contemporary politics of environment in Thailand', *Asian Survey* 89: 4, 439–453.

Hussey, Antonia (1993) 'Rapid industrialisation in Thailand 1986–1991', *Geographical Review* 83: 1, 14–28.

IEAT (Industrial Estate Authority of Thailand) (n.d.) *Industrial Estate Authority of Thailand*, information booklet, IEAT, Bangkok.

Ives, Jane H. (ed.) (1985) *The export of hazard: transnational corporations and environmental control issues*, Routledge and Kegan Paul, Boston.

Jitravi, Nirarub (1994) 'Down in the dumps: uncontrolled waste-dumping by factories at an industrial estate in Lamphun has left villagers fearing for their health', *The Nation*, 8 April, pp. C7–8.

Kalliokoski, Pentti (1986) 'Solvent containing processes and work practices: environmental observations', in Riihimäki, Vesa and Ulfvarson, Ulf (eds) *Safety and health aspects of organic solvents*, Progress in clinical and biological research, vol. 220, Alan R. Liss Inc., New York, pp. 21–30.

Karan, P.P., Bladen, Wilford A. and Wilson, James R. (1986) 'Technological hazards in the Third World', *Geographical Review* 76: 2, 195–208.

Khongnirandsuk, Supranee (1992) 'Sweeping the board: the BOI's new secretary general vows to do no less than bring perestroika to the country's bewildering bureaucracy', *Manager* (Bangkok-based monthly business magazine), No. 40, April, pp. 20–7.

Koomsup, Praipol (ed.) (1993) *Economic development and the environment in ASEAN countries: Proc. of the sixteenth conference of the Federation of ASEAN Economic Association*, Economic Society of Thailand, Bangkok.

Kuratsune, Masanori and Shapiro, Raymond E. (eds) (1984) *PCB poisoning in Japan and Taiwan*, Progress in clinical and biological research, vol. 137, Alan R. Liss Inc., New York.

Lamphun Action Group (1994) *The line of pollution and death: the facts in the case of Lamphun*, Lamphun Action Group booklet, Lamphun (in Thai with some English articles).

Leightner, Jonathan (1992) 'On the periphery of phenomenal growth: Lampang, Thailand in 1981, 1991 and the future', *Journal of Southeast Asia Business* 8: 1, 47–58.

Lim, Linda Y.C. (1990) 'Labour organisation among women workers in multinational factories in Asia', *Journal of Southeast Asia Business* 6: 4, 1–8.

Lin, Vivian (1986) 'Health and welfare and the labour process: reproduction and compliance in the electronics industry in Southeast Asia', *Journal of Contemporary Asia* 16: 4, 456–474.

—— (1988) 'Review of: Gassert, Thomas (1985) "Health hazards in electronics: a handbook", Asia Monitor Resource Centre, Hong Kong', *Journal of Contemporary Asia* 18: 4, 505–506.

Lok King Choi (1986) 'Thailand', in DAGA (Documentation for Action Group in Asia) (ed.) *Evolution of labour legislation in Asia*, DAGA, Kowloon, Hong Kong, pp. 61–72.

Mabry, Bevars D. (1977) 'The Thai labour movement', *Asian Survey* 17: 10, 931–951.

McCarty, Daniel (1994) 'Mysterious deaths in Lamphun', Letter to *Bangkok Post*, 2 March.

Mekvichai, Banasopit (1993) 'Is there hope for "Green Urbanization" in Thailand?', in Koomsup, Praipol (ed.) *Economic development and the environment in ASEAN countries: Proc. of the sixteenth conference of the Federation of ASEAN Economic Association*, Economic Society of Thailand, Bangkok, pp. 195–220.

Neville, Warwick (1986) 'Economic development and the labour force in Thailand', *Contemporary Southeast Asia* 8: 2, 131–150.

Nicholas, Colin and Wangel, Arne (eds) (1991) *Safety at work in Malaysia: an anthology of current research*, Institut Pengajian Tinggi/Institute of Advanced Studies, University of Malaya, Kuala Lumpur.

Parnwell, Michael J.G. (1994) 'Rural industrialization and sustainable development in Thailand', *TEI Quarterly Environment Journal* 2: 1, 24–39, Thailand Environment Institute, Bangkok.

Phantumvanit, Dhira and Panayotou, Theodore (1991) *Industrialization and environmental quality: paying the price*, TDRI (Thailand Development Research Institute) year-end conference: *Industrializing Thailand and its impact on the environment*, Synthesis paper no. 3, TDRI, Bangkok.

Rasiah, Rajah (1988) 'The semiconductor industry in Penang: implications for the new international division of labour theories', *Journal of Contemporary Asia* 18: 1, 24–46.

Rigg, Jonathan (1991) *Southeast Asia: a region in transition*, Unwin Hyman, London.
Riihimäki, Vesa and Ulfvarson, Ulf (eds) (1986) *Safety and health aspects of organic solvents*, Progress in clinical and biological research, vol. 220, Alan R. Liss Inc., New York.
Samudavanija, Chai-anan (1994) 'Capturing opportunities and managing constraints in the new growth circles', *Proceedings of the conference on Asia's new growth circles*, 3–6 March 1994, Chiang Mai, The Chaiyong Limthongkul Foundation, Bangkok, and Asia, Inc., Hong Kong.
Sander, Ingvar (1990) 'Industrial pollution in Thailand', *Internationales Asienforum* 21: 3–4, 301–318.
Sharma, Basu (1984) 'Multinational corporations and industrialization in Southeast and East Asia', *Contemporary Southeast Asia* 6: 2, 159–171.
Stott, P. (1991) 'Mu and Pa: elite views of nature in a changing Thailand', in Chitakasem, M. and Turton, A. (eds) *Thai Constructions of Knowledge*, School of Oriental and African Studies, London.
Taylor, Annie and Gordon, John (eds) (1992) *Trade and environment policies after UNCED: reconciling the irreconcilable*, REFER.
Thai Government (1992) *Thailand national report to the United Nations Conference on Environment and Development (UNCED), June 1992*, various government agencies, Bangkok.
Theobald, Sally (1995) 'Pressure points and industrialisation: a gender analysis framework of the Northern Region Industrial Estate, Thailand', unpublished MA thesis, MA Gender Analysis and Development, School of Development Studies, University of East Anglia.
Thinaphong, Somchet (1994) 'What killed the workers?' Letter to the editors, plus reply by Tim Forsyth, *Asia, Inc.* 3: 9, October, p. 6.
Thingsabadh, Charit (1994) 'Economic development and environmental management issues in Thailand: a review of recent trends', in Rigg, J. (ed.) *Counting the costs: economic growth and environmental change in Thailand*, ISEAS, Singapore.
Toxic Watch Network (1992) Toxic Chemical Watch Newsletter, *Jodmaay khaow phaisaanphit*, no. 1, May 1992 (in Thai).
Tuntawiroon, Nart (1982) 'Environmental impact of industrialization in Thailand', *Contemporary Southeast Asia* 4: 3, 369–380.
Ulfvarson, Ulf (1986) 'Organic solvents: concept, utilization in industry and occupational exposure', in Riihimäki, Vesa and Ulfvarson, Ulf (eds) *Safety and health aspects of organic solvents*, Progress in clinical and biological research, vol. 220, Alan R. Liss Inc., New York.
Utrecht, Ernest (ed.) (1986) *Transnational corporations and export-oriented industrialisation*, TNC Research Project, University of Sydney.
Watanabe, Seisuke (1993) 'Who benefits from the urbanisation of Thailand in late 1980s?', *Proceedings of the 5th International Conference on Thai Studies*, School of Oriental and African Studies, London, July 1993.
Yangderm, Kheun (1994) 'Grain to greed: Lanna is dying', *The Nation*, 18 February, pp. C7–8.

Newspapers and Magazines

Electronic Business Asia
Bangkok Post
Far Eastern Economic Review
The Nation
Asia, Inc.
Manager (Bangkok-based monthly business magazine)

Part V
Tourism development

12 Tanah Lot

The cultural and environmental politics of resort development in Bali

Carol Warren

This essay explores the environmental politics of resort development in Bali in the 1990s. It will focus especially on the political and economic context and cultural discourses in which environmental issues have become embedded. The controversy surrounding the luxury resort development at Tanah Lot provides a watershed case study for exploring the social and ideological ground of emergent environmentalism and for tracing alignments between formal institutions, activist groups and the general public. The case reveals the changing relationship of peripheral provinces to the centre as Jakarta comes to exercise more pervasive political and economic influence, and the importance of the regional press in articulating resistance to the appropriation of local resources.

ENVIRONMENTAL POLITICS IN LATE NEW ORDER INDONESIA

Throughout Indonesia, environmental activism has been evolving alongside broadly based dissenting positions on the direction of development policy more generally. Aside from the international prominence of the issue, mounting evidence of the economic and social costs of environmental degradation, the changing class structure in Indonesia and the connection between environmental questions and other hotly contested political issues (land tenure, the rights of workers, farmers and indigenous minorities, the demand for democratisation and greater press freedom) all played a part in moving the environment to centre stage. In Indonesia, environmental issues have become highly politicised, not only because the environment became for a time a surrogate for the expression of dissent on broader issues, but also because they are ultimately connected with questions of cultural identity and social security. Official and contesting constructions of the nation-state and of the relationship between local, metropolitan and transnational interests within it have become part of the sub-text of environmental discourse.

The recognised difficulty of disarticulating the 'environment' from social and cultural contexts is particularly problematic in Indonesia. In fact, the Indonesian term for environment, *lingkungan*, has always had a primarily social connotation in the Indonesian language (Cribb 1990: 1126–27).[1] This conceptual conflation has been compounded by the practical exigencies of contemporary Indonesian politics, where opposition movements of any kind face dual processes of cooptation and repression. Aditjondro (1994) argues that the prominence of environmentalism in Indonesia reflected a marriage of convenience between non-governmental organisations and student activists hoping to gain political space for the expression of dissent, and a regime seeking to use the environment bandwagon to secure international credibility and restore some legitimacy in the eyes of its critics. Environmental protection also offered the state, under pressure to liberalise and deregulate, an interventionist role and a rationale for bureaucratic expansion. The consequence has been an ambiguous response by government to environmentalism, at times using environmental rhetoric to recruit public support against business and at others to serve bureaucratic or well-connected investors' interests against the public (Cribb 1988).

The environment has been from the outset, then, a highly ambiguous site of political contestation in Indonesia. Neither the state, business, nor the non-governmental organisations or institutions claiming to represent 'the people' are homogeneous entities and the processes of alliance formation on environmental questions reflect this complexity. In exploring the coalescence of social forces around competing constructions of the environment, therefore, attention must be paid to the broader political tensions inevitably implicated in the content and framing of these issues.

THE MEGA-PROJECTS OF THE TOURISM SECTOR AND LOCAL INTERESTS

The period of the late 1980s and early 1990s has proved a watershed in the direction of development in Bali and in the relationship between central government and this previously peripheral province. Regional economic development, which had earlier been based on agricultural intensification, small-scale tourism and handicraft export, began to assume a very different character after 1987 when deregulation of the banking system fed an unprecedented investment boom. Official figures show a ten-fold increase in foreign and domestic investment in major projects on Bali between 1987 and 1988 from US$17 million to $170 million, almost doubling again in 1989–90 (Statistics Office, Bali 1991). As of 1991, approval had been granted for over 1.5 billion US dollars worth of new investments in star hotels for the already overbuilt Badung area alone (UNDP 1992, Appendix 3: 21). The heavy skewing of investment policy towards the development of tourism and the infrastructure to support it is indicated by the dominance of the Communication and Tourism sectors in the breakdown of investment approvals for the island. For the 422 foreign and domestic project approvals recorded by the Regional Investment Board (BKPMD) over the 25-year period to 1994, 88 per cent of the Rp 10 trillion[2] worth of realised investments went into Communication and Tourism (BKPMD 1996). In the wake of this investment boom, popular reaction to the effects of the increasingly visible Jakarta conglomerates began to shake the sacred cow status of the tourist industry and government development policy itself. These reactions initially found their way into the public domain as part of an emerging discourse of environmentalism.

By 1990 a number of acute environmental problems connected with these developments were receiving intense coverage in the regional press. The unregulated mining of limestone and coral for hotel construction and extensions to the airport; the incursion of high-class hotels into the remotest parts of the island against the provisions of the 1971 Master Plan for tourism; the erosion of beaches; increasing levels of plastic, sewage and air pollution; salination of underground aquifers; the diversion of water from farms to hotels and golf courses; the conversion of productive land – often forcibly expropriated – to these tourist facilities; and the complicity of the army and government officials in facilitating projects in breach of regional planning regulations became subjects of front-page news, political cartoons and letters to the editor in the local Indonesian-language newspaper, the *Bali Post*.

Already by the end of 1990, disquiet over uneven and uncontrolled development was sufficient to lead the Minister of Tourism to announce a one-year moratorium on major tourism projects until a UNDP-funded consultancy, commissioned by the Indonesian government to review the industry's development on the island, could provide the basis for future planning. It soon became apparent, however, that the expansion of the industry was a foregone conclusion. Even before the UNDP study had been completed, the moratorium on investment approvals was lifted. The study was carried out in a context in which control of tourism development was never on the agenda, given the power of vested interests in its expansion. The UNDP study itself notes, 'The planning scenario which had no new classified hotel rooms after 1995 has disappeared in the face of investment pressure' (UNDP 1992, Annex 9: 28).

Despite a continuous flow of rhetoric espousing earlier commitments to 'Cultural Tourism' and 'Tourism for Bali, not Bali for Tourism', development policy had become almost entirely geared towards gross maximisation of the number of tourists visiting the island and the income they might generate. From under 5,000 rooms available in star-classified hotels in 1987, Bali registered 13,000 operating and another 20,000 under construction or approved by 1992 (Statistical Office Bali 1991; UNDP 1992, Annex 3: 20–21). Planning authorities were projecting expansion to accommodate 5 million foreign and domestic visitors by 1998 (*Tourism Statistics Bali* 1993). The UNDP report in effect rationalised up-market investment outside the three enclaves specified in the original 1971 Master Plan, concluding that 'Quality Tourism' focused on high-spending visitors would 'foster economic growth, protect the environment and maximise cultural expression' (UNDP, vol. I 1992: 1). Little more than the concept made its way into the government planning agenda, where it has mainly been used to legitimate the rapid expansion of capital-intensive resort-oriented tourism projects.

Provincial and regional government authorities for their part demonstrated an insatiable appetite for tourism growth. Eager to increase their revenue base – not to mention the opportunities for graft – they played midwife to enormous quantities of outside capital seeking a literal and figurative 'home'.[3] The three established tourist zones identified by the original Master Plan in 1971 to contain the impacts of mass tourism were expanded to 15 in 1988 and to 21 in 1993 by decree of the Governor (see Map 12.1), legally opening one quarter of the land mass and one in five Balinese villages to commercial exploitation for the tourist industry.[4] Furthermore, agreements between the Ministries of Forestry, Agriculture and Tourism opened even the supposedly protected areas zoned for these purposes to 'agro' and 'eco' tourism development.[5]

After decades of controls on visa entry and a gateway policy which had the effect of restricting the rate of growth of the tourism industry, national deregulation policies aimed at raising the proportion of foreign exchange coming from the non-oil sector turned tourism into one of Indonesia's cinderella industries (Booth 1990). According to government figures, almost half of the US$8.8 billion in foreign investment in Indonesia in 1990 was for hotel development, with tourism already the fourth largest foreign exchange earner after oil, gas, textiles and processed wood (*Far Eastern Economic Review* 22 April 1993).

Economic arguments, however, are insufficient to explain the scale of this investment boom or its concentration at the elite end of the market. Mass tourism, although continuing to expand significantly in this period, was not keeping pace with the amount of capital seeking a place to invest in the island. Hotel occupancy rates declined in the early 1990s, with price-cutting star-hotels threatening the mostly locally owned middle-range accommodation in an effort to fill their vacant rooms. The sudden attractiveness of the industry to domestic capital,[6] especially at the luxury end of the market, also reflected changing national class structures within Indonesia and the desires and self-image of a new wealthy elite (see Robison and Goodman 1996). In search of new clients to fill the gap, luxury resort and residential markets joined the down-market version of leisure tourism pitched to the sun and surf set in shifting 'cultural tourism' further from its proclaimed status as Bali's unique model of development. The controversial new developments in the industry aim to lure well-to-do visitors by catering to leisure lifestyles – now for the select few on a full-time basis in residential apartments and condominiums they can purchase.

The modern lifestyle desires and capital accumulation interests of the Jakarta elite fused to produce a scramble for property in Bali in the 1990s. Luxury residences with resort facilities are intended to service the New Rich (*Orang Kaya Baru*) among the Indonesian elite, who seek to escape the traffic and pollution of Jakarta in this 'last paradise'. Compounding the effects of the new combination of real estate marketing and resort tourism were new investment regulation reforms which undermine prohibitions on foreign ownership of land, a once sacrosanct pillar of Indonesian nationalism.

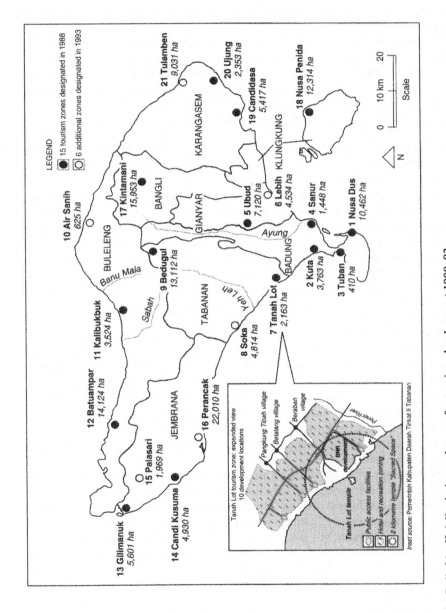

Map 12.1 Bali: 21 officially designated zones for tourism development 1988–93
Source: Kaputusan Gubernur Kepala Daerah Tingkat I Bali: No. 528 (1993)

Both the quantitative acceleration and the qualitative shift in the nature of tourism developments set in train complex and ominous conflicts over Bali's natural and cultural resources between local and 'foreign' capital and labour ('foreign' often now extended in local perception to include non-Balinese Indonesians).

The new direction in tourism industry development reflects what might be called a 'mega-complex' driving economic expansion and intensifying environmental impacts in the late New Order. This orientation is closely associated with the controversial high technology and large-scale investment strategy of Research and Technology Minister Habibie,[7] who has gained increasing prominence in Indonesian policy-making over the last decade. But it also reflects the dominant cultural orientation of Indonesia's New Rich seeking status and economic power in an international arena, and projecting the extravagances often associated with *nouveau riche* lifestyles onto the nation's policy agenda.

Two projects came to epitomise the new direction in tourism development, bringing together previously diffuse concerns over the direction of environmental, cultural and social change in Bali – the Golden Garuda Monument and the luxury resort complex at Tanah Lot. The discourses surrounding these controversial examples of the mega-complex at the same time reveal growing tensions between centre and periphery across Indonesia, a polarisation that must be understood in both geographical and class senses. The mega-projects are large-scale, highly capitalised and in most cases owned by outside interests with close connections to Indonesia's ruling elite.[8]

The plan to build an enormous golden statue as a tourist attraction on a 100 hectare site near the three original centres of mass tourism (Kuta, Sanur and Nusa Dua) is a particularly expressive manifestation of this mega-complex.[9] Intended to rival the Statue of Liberty in New York as the largest of its kind in the world, the Garuda Wisnu Kencana (GWK) monument will accommodate 20,000 visitors daily and cost an estimated 80 billion rupiah (US$40 million). Its design includes a museum, theatres, exhibition space, an amusement centre, souvenir shops, restaurants and other attractions and recreational facilities.

In the same way that the size and scale of monuments and public works have always been used to signify the power and authority of the state,[10] hi-tech monumentalism is meant to display the sophistication and cosmopolitan status of contemporary Indonesia and its urban elite. Lifts and escalators in the GWK monument will take visitors to gaze at the landscape from the top of this 'mega-proyek', as it is appropriately described by its sponsors, while laser beams from the Garuda cast illuminated images over the surrounding waters by night. A 3-D theatre, offering animated versions of folk tales and special-effects experiences of *leyak* (witch-demons), has been planned to re-create the atmosphere of Bali 'in bygone days'.

The statements of project proponents, the Nuarta Studio of Bandung, are revealing indications of the value complex which dominates policy in contemporary Indonesia. 'This task truly forms a *mega-proyek* on a world scale' (Nyoman Nuarta Studio 1993: 1). References to grandiosity – *mega, ekstra besar, spectakuler* – pepper the proposal document, whose cover sketch contrasts the height of the Garuda statue with those of other great monuments of the world. In tandem with the prevailing hi-tech line in late New Order policy espoused by the influential Minister Habibie, Nuarta asserts that the GWK will demonstrate that Indonesians are no longer victims of a cultural and technological inferiority complex. 'We are capable of building any kind of statue; however big, we can do it' (*Bali Post* 16/6/93). 'The GWK project is offered to the Indonesian people to raise the status and prestige of our nation in the international forum' (Nyoman Nuarta Studio 1993: 5).

The instrumental appropriation of Indonesian nationalism to legitimate large private developments is typical of late New Order political style. The gilded monument was originally intended for completion on 17 August 1995 as a 'gift' to celebrate Indonesia's 50th anniversary of independence. '[I]t is appropriate that we build a new feeling of nationalism in keeping with the momentum of the rate of growth and development that we have reached' (Nyoman Nuarta Studio 1993: 3). In fact, the debate generated by the GWK proposal feeds into two very different versions of nationalist discourse, which in turn closely parallel competing conceptions of the environment. 'Mega'-discourses play on one strand of the old 'national meta-narrative' (Tickell 1994: 8), combining pride in technical achievement with appeals to national unity in the 'common' interest. Here the similarity with Aditjondro's case of large dam development in the national psyche deserves note. But this strand strikes only some of the chords associated with the Indonesian nationalist and revolutionary movements of the mid-twentieth century. Also central to the revolutionary ethos were conceptions of equality and participation in a common effort. The latter strand is associated with a different kind of development in the popular view, one that had more to do with social process than competitive acquisition or display[11] and one deeply suspicious of unbridled capitalism.[12]

Popular criticism in Bali, which had been seething beneath the surface for several years, became focused initially on the debate over the Garuda monument and reached boiling point when another, still more sensitive project was announced. Construction had already begun on the Bali Nirwana Resort (BNR) before the general public became aware of the project in December 1993. Facing the ancient and beautiful temple of Tanah Lot, a religious shrine of great significance to Hindu Balinese, the BNR was the first of a new-style integrated resort development to be approved for the island. The project involved a 401-room five-star Meridien hotel, 450 residential units (the most expensive of these each with its own pool), an 18-hole international golf course and a range of other recreational facilities. Valued at US$200 million, the BNR project absorbed 120 hectares of rice-land in the fertile agricultural region of Tabanan, known as the rice storehouse (*lumbung beras*) of Bali. While luxury hotels had for several years been mushrooming outside the limited enclave originally established for them at Nusa Dua, the inclusion of permanent residential dwellings and full-scale resort facilities in the BNR development posed impacts of a new order.

ENVIRONMENTAL AND SOCIAL IMPACTS

Tourism is widely promoted as a culturally and environmentally soft development option, and Bali has often been held up as a successful example of the accommodation of this modern industry to local material needs and traditional cultural ends (McKean 1978; Booth 1990: 71–2). The problem for the industry is that economic expansion tends to overtake planning (Francillon 1990; Parnwell 1993). With the rapid growth of tourism, new environmental problems were added to the accelerating impacts of old ones. Beach erosion as a consequence of coral extraction and widespread violation of the 100 metre set-back regulations for hotel construction, green strip incursions and the prevalence of plastic waste are among the more visible environmental impacts, both commented upon and contributed to by Bali's nearly one million annual foreign visitors. All have been subjects of little-heeded and selectively enforced government regulation as well as a considerable amount of publicity in the budding environmental journalism fostered by the local press.

Most important from the point of view of Balinese livelihood and identity are the direct and indirect impacts of tourism development on land and water and on the cultural basis of Balinese community life, with which they are intimately connected. In all three respects, the new-style resort developments pose problems of a quantitatively and qualitatively different order. The diversion of productive land and water resources is among the most serious of the physical impacts wrought by expansion of the tourist economy in general and resort facilities in particular. Resort developments demand disproportionately more of these resources than smaller-scale facilities (UNDP 1992, Annex 3: 22, Annex 9: 21–30).[13] At the staggering rate of more than 1,000 hectares a year, land is being diverted from agriculture for large-scale resort and residential developments along with infrastructure projects required to serve them. The effect of diversion of land and water in Bali will mean rice shortage and high prices in one of the world's most fertile and productive traditional agricultural regions (*Bali Post* 5/9/94).

Golf courses are a notoriously land and water hungry aspect of this kind of development. At Tanah Lot, two-thirds of the land expropriated for the Bali Nirwana Resort project will be taken up by the golf course. In the first of a series of articles responding to the announcement of the BNR project, Professor Manuaba, head of the Department of Physiology at the state university in Bali and a respected commentator on environmental issues, levels a broadside at 'The Golf Course – Maniac Consumer of Water and Purveyor of Environmental Disaster' (*Bali Post* 4/12/93). Citing chemical inputs of 7–10 times those used in agriculture and up to 400,000 litres of water per day required to maintain greens to support this 'manufactured environment', alongside the social effects of farmers becoming labourers on what was once their own land, he urges serious reconsideration of golf development in Indonesia through the stringent application of the impact assessment process.

Water shortages have already been reported for downstream agricultural areas in Bali; and the salinisation of aquifers as a result of over-exploitation of ground-water supplies in the Sanur, Kuta and Nusa Dua areas was noted in the UNDP study (UNDP 1992, Annex 9: 8–14). Five-star hotels require an average of 2,300 litres of water per room per day, compared with 400 litres in non-star accommodation and an average of 77 litres per person per day in Balinese households (UNDP 1992, Annex 3: 20–21, Annex 9: 22–23; Martopo and Suyono n.d.: 11). The UNDP projects that on current rates of use and existing policies for the expansion of tourist facilities, water supply for Bali would be in deficit within a decade, and demand would reach four times potential supply by the middle of the next century (UNDP 1992, vol. I: 207–13). It specifically flags conflicts of interest between farmers and the developments at Tanah Lot (still then officially at proposal stage) because of the impact of decreased water supplies for irrigation (UNDP 1992, vol. II: 14).

Land and water have cultural significance as well as practical importance in Bali. The earth is mediator of life and death and a basis of local citizenship in Balinese villages. Certain classes of village land in many parts of Bali are regarded as ancestral heritance which cannot be alienated under local customary (*adat*) law (Warren 1993). Water is the life-blood of the complex wet-rice agricultural system and the spectacular 'engineered landscape' of Bali. It is also at the centre of Bali-Hindu religion, sometimes referred to as '*agama tirtha*' (the religion of holy water), cleansing and renewing the earth and its human dependants (Lansing 1991). Water sources and land near or associated with temples, graveyards or other ritually significant spaces must be protected from spiritual as well as physical pollution. Hence, while physical environmental impacts on land and water might be more or less localised, the effect of spiritual pollution at Tanah Lot, one of the ancient sea temples which protect the island, had Bali-wide dimensions.

From the point of view of local social and economic welfare, the rationality of resort developments has also to be questioned. Erawan's economic research (1994, 1995) shows that local multiplier effects are significantly greater at the non-classified hotel end of the tourism market than for four- and five-star accommodation. The multiplier effects for the local economy from semi-permanent residents of condominiums and apartments who shop in supermarkets and have no reason to purchase souvenirs or patronise tourist performances are likely to be much lower still.

Luxury tourism developments were already in the early 1990s beginning to squeeze small local hotels and to displace land and labour in Bali.[14] As of 1991, 76 per cent of four- and five-star hotels were owned by non-Balinese Indonesians either outright or as joint ventures with overseas partners, and they account for an undoubtedly underestimated 17 per cent of the workforce in the hotel industry (UNDP 1992, Annex 3, 27–33). Immigration from other parts of Indonesia, initially attracted by employment in the booming construction industry, has reached annual levels of 60–80,000 in the 1990s, and is beginning to generate serious ethnic and religious tensions (*Editor* 11/9/93: 73; Couteau 1994: 43).[15] Local reaction to these developments reflects a growing unease over the consuming power of Jakarta-centred interests to appropriate the physical and cultural landscape of this previously economically peripheral region. Indeed, the term 'Jakartan' (*Orang Jakarta*) has become synonymous with the transformation Bali is currently experiencing – and 'environmental protection' (*kelestarian lingkungan*) a legitimating defence of local identity and interests.

THE PRESS IN THE CONSTRUCTION OF ENVIRONMENTAL DISCOURSE

Debates about the environment featured prominently in the regional paper at a time when editors were still uncertain of the limits of the government-proclaimed 'openness' (*keterbukaan*) policy in the Indonesian media,[16] when suggestions of political reform during the 1992 election had been aborted, and even as official rhetoric was turning away from previous claims of common cause, towards fixing an image of environment and human rights activists as the 'new traitors' threatening Indonesian national interests (*Editor* 11/9/93). In the period between 1990 and 1994, the local Indonesian-language newspaper, the *Bali Post*,[17] came to play a critical role in promoting consciousness of environmental issues and defining the relationship between these and broader questions of politics and culture.

The first sweeping public criticism of the environmental impacts of large-scale development projects occurred during a weekend seminar in 1990 on 'Culturally and Environmentally Sensitive Development' organised by Udayana University's Technical Faculty at the Bali Beach Hotel.[18] The presence of Emil Salim, then Minister for the Environment, precipitated the first muted volley between centre and periphery in a debate that to that point had largely revolved around the failure of regional government planning and law enforcement.

Over the three days of the seminar, the initially academic presentations of planning problems became increasingly confrontational, and reporting shifted from a news item on the bottom of the front page to the headlines. The *Bali Post* reports that Salim appeared 'stunned' by the opinions expressed at the conference and stated that he intended to engage in a 'dialogue' with the Governor over contravention of regional planning regulations, urging the public to 'report to the Centre if projects do not comply with the law'. But an academic participant reminded him that major developments were in fact approved and facilitated by central government.

It was apparent in the staging and coverage of the seminar that environmental issues had become a vehicle for the expression of disaffection on broader social and political questions. Corruption, press freedom, the power of global capital to override local interests, and increasing social inequalities were raised by participants in only mildly modulated tones, and remained a feature of press coverage of environmental issues thereafter. The significance of the press increased during the early 1990s and played a pivotal role in mobilising response to the Garuda Wisnu Kencana monument and Bali Nirwana Resort projects. In both cases, public controversies erupted following front-page announcements of the developments in the *Bali Post*, soon followed by colour photographs, editorials, by-line articles, cartoons and letters to the editor.

Several innovations in media presentation of these issues were deployed to arouse and engage the public. The 'seminar', unlikely as it may seem, developed into a vehicle for focusing attention on controversial local issues, with a popular style of reportage that took a long-standing relationship between bureaucracy, academia and the local media in new directions. Seminars are frequently organised by the *Bali Post* itself, usually in a contentious atmosphere in which invited academics, government officials and prominent (sometimes notoriously outspoken) public figures felt prompted to make informative, even provocative, statements. Another novel feature which functioned to mobilise public opinion and maintain momentum was the special comment column, 'Your Turn' ('*Giliran Anda*'). The column, inviting public response on topical themes of serious import, typically ran for a month and gave as many as a hundred contributors space to express their opinions.

Not only did the regional newspaper play a key role in bringing these tourism projects under public scrutiny, but it self-consciously set out the terms of discourse. Excerpts from the introductory invitations to contribute to the '*Giliran Anda*' column on both subjects are indicative:

'*Giliran Anda: "Landmark" Bali GWK*' (26 June–28 July 1993)
The plan to build a Golden Garuda Wisnu monument has brought responses from a number of supporters, including the Governor of Bali . . . Many explanations, comments and questions on the origins of the concept, its financing, location, form, and benefits in the context of the Hindu religion have been raised in the *Bali Post*. Now, it is your turn, readers, who have not yet had the opportunity to give comment, criticism, advice or praise concerning this idea to build the GWK monument. Please send the editors no more than one double-spaced page with photo by July 10th.
(*Bali Post* 26/6/93)

'*Giliran Anda: Kawasan Tanah Lot*' (9 December 1993–5 January 1994)
As our readers know, Pura Tanah Lot is a unique, great and holy temple. Its sacredness is protected by a sanctified area known as the Hutama Mandala. Now with the arrival of development the sacred site of Tanah Lot will also function (let us hope this does not mean to 'shift' function) and become a tourist area, with the construction of very large hotel facilities

including apartments and a golf course that is now starting. At this junc-
ture, we offer the opportunity for you to comment on two questions: first,
how should the Tanah Lot area be developed if the intent is for it to become
a comprehensive Tourist Zone? Second, is apartment development for private use and purpose, which is likely to have very limited impact on work
opportunities and income creation for the Balinese public, the kind of
development appropriate to the island of Bali whose environment has a
limited carrying capacity?

(Bali Post 9/12/93)

From the outset, the connection between environmental and cultural integrity
framed these debates. This is the link that captured the public imagination and
that has contributed to a significant shift in attitude among Balinese towards
the large-scale tourism development that was entering a new phase in the
1990s. The linkage of other discourses of a socio-economic nature should not
be overlooked either. Local impacts of conglomerate capital and aspects of
private consumer culture, regularly criticised in the editorial columns, cartoons and feature articles of the paper, are directly addressed in the invitations
to readers to take their turn.

The emerging discourse of environmentalism sets centre against periphery,
big capital against the little person, and growth-driven development against
cultural and environmental balance and preservation. This discourse, while
certainly a rhetorical construction that over-simplifies the situation (and partly
because it does), has strong resonance across the spectrum of Balinese society. And indeed general awareness of environmental problems has become
widespread and sophisticated among the Balinese public.

It is indicative of growing awareness of the importance of environmental
issues that the term '*lingkungan*' appears in so many of the numerous commentaries on the subject of the GWK monument published in the *Bali Post*
over several months in 1993. Objections were raised to further concentration
of tourism in the Badung region of South Bali and consequent socio-
economic distortions and environmental strains. The increase in traffic would
burden an already overloaded road system and add to rising levels of air
pollution. The waste problem had become 'an epidemic'. The huge new
tourist facility, like the high-class hotels in the Nusa Dua area, would place
further demands on water reserves in other parts of the island already showing signs of crisis. The displacement of farmers as a result of land expropriation was another issue that prompted disaffection with a pattern of
capital-intensive development on a grand scale that has caused social unrest
throughout Indonesia. The extravagant costs of the project, amounting to two-
thirds of the annual budget of the province, could be better put towards reducing poverty and dealing with Bali's waste, pollution, land degradation and
water problems.[19]

The perceived integrity of culture and the environment is at the same time
a striking feature of comment on the project. Reaction centred on the inap-

propriateness of the monument in both respects, arguing in particular that it was not in keeping with basic Hindu philosophy, requiring the maintenance of balance between divine, human and natural orders: 'The arrival of the grand (*megah*) and super-expensive GWK monument will only bring into being a heap of meaningless concrete, whose significance cannot be compared with the small monuments . . . for the guardian spirits in every household in Bali . . . So what is its meaning for Bali . . . except as an indictment of devastation and environmental rape?' (letter to editor, *Bali Post* 16/6/93). 'We have no reason to be shy about the efforts of our ancestors who have bequeathed us their brilliant work . . . Our enthusiasm for development is not shackled by our resistance to arrogant attitudes and thinking. As heirs to the ancestors' legacy our primary duty is to protect and preserve' ('Your Turn' column, *Bali Post* 6/7/93).[20] Not least cause of offence was the name of the monument, which appropriated the Hindu Deity, Wisnu, the protector of life and source of well-being, to a purpose that threatened both environmental and cultural integrity.[21]

But resistance to the Garuda monument proposal never developed beyond the stage of public debate. First of all, since the 1965 massacre of those accused of Communist party affiliations, Bali appeared in most matters beyond local affairs thoroughly depoliticised. Secondly, there were some differences of opinion among Balinese, reflected in press coverage, on the relative evaluation of costs against benefits of the monument project.[22] Finally, ambiguous signals from proponents suggested that the monument might remain in limbo – as had other previous controversial proposals. Statements such as Nuarta's that it was 'only an idea that might eventuate or not' depending on 'the acceptance of the people and government of Bali' (11/7/93) and the Governor's insistence that he would support the project only 'if it is the will of the Balinese people' (15/7/93) defused some of the urgency in the public debate.

In hindsight, ambiguity and disengagement appear part of a systematic official tactic for minimising reaction to sensitive projects. The orchestration of public information on potentially controversial developments of this sort appears to follow a pattern: little or no information of substance is released during the planning stages; once the project is sufficiently advanced, a media event unveiling it is organised in Jakarta, involving a select group of coopted officials and private sector notables including several Jakarta-based Balinese. In the GWK case, Nyoman Nuarta, a Balinese artist residing since his youth in Bandung, Ida Bagus Sujana, the Minister of Energy, and the Governor of Bali served the purpose. Having connected the project to prominent figures with whom the public supposedly identified, the proponents issued a few press releases and interviews (typically again from Jakarta) and then absented themselves from the media stage.

Without further official comment, reaction to the GWK monument proposal abated towards the latter part of 1993. Many of the active participants in the debate suspected the project would proceed if capital could be raised, with or without the unambiguous consent from the 'people' by and for whom it was supposed to be built (see Nyoman Nuarta Studio 1993: 5). The *Bali Post* editorial summarising public reaction to the monument proposal appeals to Nuarta not 'to sacrifice the feelings of the Balinese people' in making this 'donation'. 'He himself ought to be aware the people of Bali have been forced to sit quiet and say nothing for so long . . . about several tourist projects that suddenly appeared in Bali' (15/7/93). No organised resistance accompanied the intense media discussion the GWK monument proposal had precipitated in the press. But growing environmental consciousness and cultural sensitivity did contribute to active resistance several months later, when the next of the mega-projects set about 'developing' Tanah Lot, a religious site and symbol of island-wide significance.

TANAH LOT: CULTURAL SYMBOLS AND SOCIAL ACTION

Opposition to the BNR development went further than it had in the case of the Garuda Monument, partly because activists were able to build on the experience gained in the earlier case. But Tanah Lot also presented opponents with symbolic capital of a higher order. The Temple, perched on a tiny rock outcrop off the coast, epitomises the integrity between culture and environment of Balinese aesthetic and religious sensibilities. The terms *tanah* and *lot* mean land and sea, and indicate the temple's physical character as well as its importance in the complex of mountain and sea temples which protect the spiritual balance and natural fertility of the island. It is also undoubtedly the most photographed of the island's temples – the silhouette of Tanah Lot at sunset, an immediately recognisable representation of Bali and its culture in the iconography of the international travel industry.

The cultural link is a crucial dimension of emerging environmentalism in Bali and the metaphoric associations which connect the two are essential to understanding the unfolding of environmental politics there. A common fate for culture and environment is explicit in the rhetorical allusions of the opponents of the mega-projects, and a deeply felt unease with the political economy and cultural politics of late New Order Indonesia is the barely veiled subtext of local response. The threat of environmental and cultural 'erosion' is expressed in many of the feature articles, editorials and letters to the editor published in the *Bali Post*. As one writer expressed it:

> At the moment Bali is still 'walking in place', accepting everything that comes from outside as if it were of benefit. In this condition, Bali could erode in both a literal and a figurative sense. All the more, when Balinese have repeatedly witnessed, and with 'forced consent' (*paksa rela*) had to accept, so much deception.
>
> (*Bali Post* 12/7/93)

The strong cultural–religious symbolism evoked by these projects was critical in galvanising island-wide opposition. Religious symbols seem to have

been able to represent Balinese collective interest in a less ambiguous or fragmented way than the apparently more complex and localised environmental
aspects alone. In the case of the Garuda monument the latter lent themselves
to ambivalent interpretation around which political action proved more difficult to mount.

Proponents of both mega-projects in fact proved adept at wielding environmental images and arguments in their own interests. As part of their 'idealistic
mission' (*Bali Post* 16/6/93), the group supporting construction of the Garuda
Monument claimed the project would rehabilitate the barren and eroded land
of the Bukit site. With the land made productive by conversion to an alternative use, local people who had only been able to scrape a meagre existence from
dry farming would now be able to find employment in the more lucrative tourist
sector (Nyoman Nuarta Studio 1993: 1; *Bali Post* 17/7/93). Espousing a technocratic version of environmentalism (Pepper 1986), proponents display a
keen faith in the scientific and technical expertise which these mega-projects
can afford to deploy. They point to the large budget and range of professional
consultants employed in field studies. In a token gesture to environmental considerations, the Minister of Mining and Energy promised to contribute recycled
copper from waste cabling to cast the statue (*Bali Post* 16/6/93).

Similarly the literature on the Tanah Lot project promotes it as 'Preserving
Bali's Natural Beauty . . . The master planners of Bali Nirwana Resort have
exercised great care in preserving the natural contours of the land and the varied richness of local vegetation. The entire complex blends harmoniously into
the landscape' (BNR brochure 1993). Existing rice terraces were to be incorporated into part of the fairway (although these had already been levelled by
bulldozers by the time the project was temporarily halted in February).
Responding to concerned letters to the editor about the future demands of the
project on local water supply, the landscape manager points to plans for establishing a three-stage waste water treatment and recycling facility, 'the first of
its kind in Indonesia', for garden and golf course maintenance (*Bali Post*
3/12/93).

Such claims of employment potential and environmental enhancement
complicate public perceptions of major development projects everywhere, the
more so where the 'development' concept is invested with the mantra-like status (Van Langenberg 1986) it has in Indonesian national ideology. It was only
when environmental exploitation became tied to the appropriation of important cultural symbols in the Balinese case that an unequivocally shared public stance could be achieved. In the repressive political climate which still
prevails in Indonesia, that culturally based solidarity was essential to mounting an activist campaign. The fusion of cultural and environmental metaphors
proved explosive. The arrival of the bulldozers was met by an outcry – was
this important temple now 'to be eaten by the times' and were 'Balinese to
become foreigners in their own land?' asked one of the contributors to the
'Your Turn' column (*Bali Post* 28/12/93). A Balinese living in Sulawesi wrote
to the paper:

I keep asking why the conglomerates find it so easy to get permits to scoop up the area around Tanah Lot which is so sacred to us ... To the power-holders in Bali, don't be taken in by the dollar or rupiah that has made you so easily give permits to the conglomerates to take over our religious sites. From one angle the government is asking the people of Bali to transmigrate with the excuse of reducing the population, while from another you open the door as wide as possible for the conglomerates. Haven't you ever measured how small this island of Bali that we cherish really is?

(*Bali Post* 21/12/ 93)

Anxiety that local people were losing control over both environmental and cultural resources comes through very strongly in *Bali Post* reporting as well as in readers' comments in letters to the editor and in the 'Your Turn' column. Representations of the underlying cultural politics and opposed economic interests between centre and periphery in the regional newspaper were becoming increasingly polarised by the 1990s. Public opinion fuelled as much as it was incited by press coverage. Powerful front-page colour images of earth-moving equipment moving across the flattened landscape, maps indicating the layout of the Bali Nirwana Resort complex and the adjacent location of nine others to follow suit in the Tanah Lot tourism zone, and the BNR's own sketch of golfers playing at hole 12 in view of Tanah Lot Temple reinforced the conflated sense of physical dispossession and cultural displacement.

It was, in fact, an act of desecration which finally brought former land-holders into open opposition. A few days after approval was granted to resume construction in September 1994, a shrine on rice-land already appropriated for the project was bulldozed despite guarantees of protection by the project managers.[23] The farmers' relative silence throughout the public protests of 1993–4 had been a weak link in the opposition movement and allowed the BNR to claim that local people had been consulted and that the majority had sold out willingly for reasonable compensation and job assurances. Several days after the incident, 96 former landholders presented a petition to the head of the regional parliament asserting that they had been deceived and forced into selling their land. They demanded cancellation of the project so that the land could 'be managed with care and ceremonial treatment as before ... and so that we and our families are not faulted for the wrong and improper use of these ancestral lands' (petition 20/10/95).[24] They asserted they had been led to believe the land was being resumed for development 'in the national interest', only to find it appropriated to a private project. Their irrigation water had been cut off, and those who resisted selling had their lives threatened and their land impounded by the court.

The power of religious symbols in the debate was such that questions of environmental protection were ultimately subordinated to those of cultural preservation, so intimately bound up with social and economic tensions between centre and periphery. It is notable that most of the groups allied in the struggle bore religious or cultural names. These included the Society for

Balinese Studies, the Forum of Concerned Hindu Dharma Community of Indonesia, Forum of Hindu Students, Balinese Youth and Student Alliance, Young Artists Group, and other Hindu, Muslim and Christian student groups from outside Bali. Environment groups remained actively involved but were less visible as environmental discourses became subsumed by those of cultural and religious idioms, and the metaphor of erosion was overtaken by images of invasion.

In the case of the Bali Nirwana Resort, not only were religious and cultural symbols appropriated to outside interests, but the development was physically located at one of the most important sacred sites on Bali. Condensing so much of significance to Balinese, the site and symbol of Tanah Lot mobilised a more powerful and unambiguous reaction to the BNR development. Public outcry culminated in the first major political demonstrations on the island, and swelling opposition brought about an unprecedented eight-month suspension of construction on the project.

SOCIAL FORCES AND FORMAL INSTITUTIONS

A key question raised in this chapter is how formal institutions (in this case, the press, religious and state authorities) interact with social movements and interest groups (student organisations, environmental and cultural associations) and broader political processes in influencing the outcome of concrete cases in the political economy of Indonesia's environment. Despite highly organised social structures at local level,[25] Bali has to date developed surprisingly little in the way of organised social movements around the environment or any other contemporary social issue. The generally apolitical orientation of Balinese society in the recent period has to be understood in the context of the traumatic effects of the 1965–6 massacres which brought the New Order government to power. That period, in which tens of thousands of Balinese associated with the then legal Communist Party lost their lives, has been a powerful reminder of the dangers of political factionalism.

It was apparent from the ambiguous stalemate in the debate over the Golden Garuda Monument that the expression of adverse public opinion in the local newspaper alone had been unable to provoke a definitive rejection of major projects so closely tied to the interests of state and capital. With the earlier experience of the limits of press power, but with heightened public awareness of the issues at stake created by media coverage, the stage was set for a new phase of resistance. When news of the Tanah Lot project broke, a hastily constituted coalition of students and intellectuals formed to attempt to stop the project. The only organisational base they had was an entirely apolitical association of scholars, the Society for Balinese Studies, and an *ad hoc* network of student groups and small NGOs, organised around a few unfurnished rooms and postbox addresses.

In a preliminary attempt to trace the possibilities and limits of roles played by key agents (the media, business, parliament, bureaucracy, army, students, religious and cultural organisations) in the unfolding environmental politics of Bali, a brief chronology of events surrounding the Tanah Lot case will serve to introduce the formal institutions and informal social groups engaged in the controversy:

- 31 December 1991. The Indonesian Investment Coordination Board issued approval for investment in the PT Bali Nirwana Resort (BNR) to include a 250-room hotel, 266 cottages, an 18-hole golf course as well as 'cultural villages'.
- November–December 1993. A small, unpresupposing article in the *Bali Post*[26] announced land clearance for the Bakrie conglomerate's Bali Nirwana Resort project at Tanah Lot (17/11/93). Bulldozers had already begun to level the land before all landholders had agreed to sell, and before the required building permit was issued or the environmental impact assessment (AMDAL) process completed. A series of critical feature articles by a prominent Balinese academic and commentator on environmental issues appeared over the next several weeks: 'Bali Hit by Disturbing News' (23/11/93); 'The Golf Course – Maniac Consumer of Water and Purveyor of Environmental Disaster' (4/12/93); 'Cultural Tourism Requires Desire, Ability and Courage' (6/1/94). These articles in turn precipitated emotional letters to the editor objecting to the development (29/11/93); asking readers to reconsider whether 'any further expansion of tourism, not dismissing its economic benefits to date, was worth the ruin of Bali's environment' (4/12/93); and urging the preservation of the island's natural beauty and 'most importantly the sacredness of its temples' (20/12/93).
- December 1993–January 1994. The 'Your Turn' column published comments from the general public on the Tanah Lot project (*Bali Post* 9/12/93–5/1/94). These were almost unanimously opposed to the development, unlike comment on the GWK monument, where a substantial minority among the contributors had expressed qualified support. During this period, a series of headline articles implied that the Governor had been bribed to approve the project, questioned environmental impact assessment procedures, and challenged the Hindu Organisation (Parisada Hindu Dharma) and the Regional Parliament to take a stand. These were accompanied by large colour illustrations graphically depicting physical and cultural impacts:
  Photo: earthmoving equipment levelling ricefields. **Headline**: 'BNR Construction Continues at Tanah Lot' (29/12/94).
  Photo: map of the Tanah Lot tourism zone showing the BNR and nine other hotel-resort developments yet to proceed at the site. **Headlines**: 'Governor Rejects Claims He Received Land in the BNR Complex', 'Hindu Students Go to the Regional Parliament (DPRD)' (30/12/94).
  Photo: Tanah Lot Temple on a ritual occasion surrounded by pilgrims and worshippers in ceremonial dress. **Headline**: 'The Hindu Organisation (Parisada) of Tabanan Asked to Explain its Stand on BNR' (2/1/94).

Photo: map of BNR complex. **Headlines**: 'BNR Environmental Impact Assessment (AMDAL) Handed Over'; 'Supply of Clean Water Critical' (5/1/94).

Photo: sketch of golfers playing at hole 12 in view of Tanah Lot Temple taken from the BNR promotional brochure. **Headline**: 'Presentation of BNR Environmental Impact Assessment (AMDAL) Closed [to the press]' (9/1/94).

Photos: student demonstrations; **Headlines**: 'Hindu Students of Malang Call for Rejection of BNR',' Hindu Students and Youth Demonstrate at the Governor's Office' (14/1/94; 20/1/94).

- January–February 1994. Student groups, allied with a number of scholars and respected cultural commentators, organised a campaign of protest demonstrations and marches, as well as poetry readings, traditional shadow puppet performances and prayer-sessions. They sent a delegation to the national parliament, met with opposition party leaders and the head of the national Legal Aid Foundation (YLBHI), and networked behind the scenes to link sympathetic individuals and groups. Demonstrations grew steadily larger, reaching an estimated 5,000 people at the 21 January rally.
- 21 January 1994. Following mass demonstrations, the Regional Parliament (DPRD) called a temporary suspension of construction on the BNR until the religious, cultural and social issues surrounding the project could be sorted out.
- 25 January 1994. Parisada Hindu Dharma, the national Hindu organisa-tion, issued a 'Bhisama' (religious pronouncement) on the sacred space of temples.[27] Although weakly framed, its explicit provision of a two-kilometre radius within which developments potentially polluting a sacred site should not take place provided an authoritative statement around which public support could be rallied. This was seen as a decisive event in bringing the government-sponsored religious organisation directly into the debate on the protestors' side and delineating a specific issue as the focus of opposition.
- 12 February 1994. Following an abrupt change of military command (9/2/94), the army cracked down on a student demonstration at Jagatnatha Temple near the Governor's residence in the capital. Several students were hospitalised, ending this form of active resistance.
- 21 June 1994. Three national weeklies – *Tempo*, *Editor* and *DeTIK* – had their licences to publish removed for political criticism of Minister of Technology Habibie, indicating how vulnerable the media still was to the arbitrary exercise of central government power.
- 9 August 1994. It was announced that the Garuda Wisnu Kencana monu-ment proposal had been approved.
- 12 September 1994. The long-awaited review of the BNR environmental impact assessment by the provincial AMDAL Commission was presented, recommending formalisation of job guarantees to former landholders, restrictions on water use, design revisions reducing and shifting dwellings,

and planting a green belt to screen the development from view of the temple to uphold the 'essence' of the Bhisama; the Governor immediately approved resumption of construction on the BNR project.

- 20 October 1994. Farmers whose lands had been expropriated for the Tanah Lot project came forward to declare their opposition and call for cancellation of BNR and the return of their land. The general unpopularity of the project throughout the rest of Bali and their direct experiences dealing with the project proponents turned early ambivalence among landholders to outright opposition by the end of 1994. Ninety-six landholders signed a petition declaring that they had been deceived into giving up their land and threatened by the regional government head (a military officer).
- 25 February 1995. Twenty-four landholders and members of the local irrigation association (*subak*) built a fence across a *subak* road being used by BNR construction vehicles. The fence was removed by authorities and one *subak* member sued in court. The court found the villager not guilty (17 July 1995).
- 29 December 1995. Three Balinese farmers lost their legal suit against the owners of the Bali Nirwana Resort in the Tabanan court, and were ordered by the judge to pay Rp 75 million (US$35,000) to cover legal costs as well as damages 'to restore the company's good reputation' (*Bali Post*, 30 December 1995).
- 1996. Construction of equally controversial projects of the same type as the BNR near the ancient temples of Sakenan and Ulu Watu is also scheduled, again without public consultation. Suharto family members are closely associated with these developments.

The interaction between institutional forces and more informal social groupings is one of the interesting facets of the development of activist resistance in the Tanah Lot case, and is an issue of considerable importance to the environment movement generally. Unquestionably the synergism between the press and the student groups spearheading the campaign to stop the Tanah Lot project was catalytic.[28] Without sustained pressure from students and the press, construction of the resort would doubtless have rolled on without impediment. Protesters depended upon the press for information dissemination and for the vital expressions of public opinion which legitimated their actions. At the same time, the *Bali Post* could not have maintained focus on the issue without a series of attention-drawing events which gave a sense of direction, momentum and possibility to opposition demands.

The atmosphere of broadly based common cause was probably the most important effect of the tacit alliance built slowly between press and activists between December 1993 and February 1994. Strongly worded headlines levelled at the Provincial Parliament and Hindu Organisation put each of these formal institutions under intense public scrutiny, forcing them to adopt public positions they would certainly have preferred to avoid. Even the editors of the *Bali Post*, adventurous as they had become over the previous few years on environmental issues, were reluctant to go beyond brief informational accounts without clear indications of mass support for their stand (interview 1994). More than a month had elapsed between the initial announcement of the project and the concerted media attention the *Bali Post* devoted to the issue from December until the forceful stop the army put to public demonstrations in mid-February. In this respect the 'Your Turn' column had the double effect of testing public opinion and building conditions for local action.

The style of press publicity for the activist campaign contrasted sharply with the standard presentation of bland official pronouncements and placed the Regional Parliament (DPRD) and the Hindu religious organisation of Indonesia, historically constrained by official sponsorship, in a position where they were obliged to respond. Unlike the press, these other established institutions were drawn more or less unwillingly into the fray. Only after the January demonstrations and relentless media attention did they finally act.

When the Provincial Parliament suspended the BNR project, it passed the burden of responsibility on to the Environmental Impact Assessment (AMDAL) Commission, which was explicitly given the directive to take account of unaddressed cultural and social issues in its review of the Bakrie project's EIA report. In what many hoped would prove the critical turning point, the Parisada Hindu Dharma issued its Bhisama religious pronouncement interpreting traditional religious texts on the sacred space at temple sites. Hedged with formulaic acquiescence to 'development' and 'progress' in the spirit of the national ideology, Pancasila, the Bhisama effectively prohibits any development that might pollute the 'zone of sanctity', a two-kilometre radius around Tanah Lot Temple. From that point the controversy came to revolve almost entirely around this question, since the Bhisama interpretation of Hindu principles, upon which religious figures were adamant, would preclude use of any of the land bought by the Bakrie group for the BNR development.

Institutional action was critical to the prosecution of resistance. The suspension provided legitimacy and space for contestation and the Bhisama a focal point for opposition that was apparently simple and politically incontrovertible.[29] Religious tolerance had been a central principle of national ideology (Pancasila) and one of the most sensitive underpinnings of the Indonesian state – so sensitive, the President himself felt obliged to issue a statement indicating that the decree should be the basis for resolution of the conflict. Although heavily compromised by their positions in the Indonesian political system, the Provincial Parliament, the national Hindu organisation and the Environmental Impact Commission had been forced by public pressure and by their own charters to produce statements which at least offered a handle upon which further resistance could be mounted. Still, public institutions are only as powerful as the civil society which supports them and in Indonesia are still subordinated to political processes of patronage. Agents of formal institutions, precisely because of their relative stability and security, tend to be disproportionately both more influential and more sensitive to subtle pressures and self-censorship than independents.

As it turned out, other institutions closer to the centres of power in Indonesia proved compliant agents of the interests of corporate capital and its rent-seeking political counterparts. Two interventions altered the possibilities for continued expression of those critical voices of emerging civil society that had ground the project to a halt. The first was replacement of the military commander who had permitted demonstrations to continue unimpeded to that point and who was regarded as too sympathetic to the dissidents' position (Suasta and Pujastana 1994). Soon after taking up his post, the new commander forcibly ended the series of demonstrations which had been growing steadily larger and attracting mass support. The second event was the revocation of the publishing licences of three national weeklies – *Tempo, Editor* and *DeTIK* – for fuelling controversy surrounding Minister Habibie's defence purchases. Already muted by informal pressures since February, critical coverage of local affairs in the *Bali Post* virtually ceased after the national bannings.

The press release announcing resumption of the Tanah Lot project some months later makes it appear that a compromise had been struck and significant concessions made. According to it, the Environmental Impact Assessment Commission requires that the 'essence' of the Bhisama ruling be observed, and that the project be redesigned, eliminating condominiums, relocating buildings away from the temple, and planting a green strip to screen the project from view. But gaps in the newpaper coverage and the dead silence which followed the announcement invited reverse readings. The statement that the 'essence' of the Bhisama ruling would be respected suggested that its literal proscription would not (*Bali Post* 12/9/94). Unreported documents, in fact, reveal that the central government's Department of Development Coordination had been involved in a manipulative revision of the interpretation of the Bhisama to alter the two kilometre ruling. It claims to 'adapt' the Bhisama by a perverse use of the *adat* concept of '*Desa, Kala, Patra*' ('according to place, time and circumstance'), which is in fact supposed to legitimate local autonomy and variation in customary law.[30] Critics also questioned whether the claimed elimination of 'condominiums' from the project was simply a play on words, since advance sale of residential accommodation was subsidising construction costs. Throughout the suspension, full-page advertisements for investment in BNR luxury villas continued to appear in the national press and airline magazines. As it turned out, the final 'compromise' only succeeded in bringing the number of hotel and residential units back to the total originally determined by its 1991 National Investment Board permit (see ANDAL BNR 1993, to which this document is appended).

The central importance of the media in the prosecution of the case became especially evident after military intervention in the demonstrations and the banning of three national publications. The *Bali Post* article covering the September announcement is in the bland and uncritical old style of reporting on government activities, classically accompanied by a picture of the governor shaking hands with the BNR's Chief Manager (13/9/94). There were no editorials or follow-up commentaries this time on the irregularities or obscurities in the official announcement (for example, the fact that the impact assessment document was not available to the public for scrutiny, and that some members of the Commission reviewing the EIA had conflicts of interest), nor did any of the flood of letters to the editor received by the paper appear in subsequent editions. Only some time later did the paper again begin to cover the subject, in a circumspect and deflective way.

The whole process of organising resistance became extremely difficult without the source of information and stimulus to mobilise presented by the media. The alternative press blossomed in this period, with more than a dozen new publications, mainly by student groups, reporting subsequent events. But these, of course, had limited circulation and relied upon volunteers to gather information and produce and disseminate them. As the potential for use of formal channels was closing off, the fragmented resistance groups had difficulty maintaining coordinated action as well as their earlier sense of solidarity.[31] Often some of the key actors were unaware of the current course of events because activist resources and networks were spread too thin. Distrust among activist groups compounded the effects of their loss of formal sources of information.

As government strategies of cooption and repression took their toll, the solidarity and momentum of the resistance movement began to unravel. Some previously outspoken objectors fell silent; tensions emerged between student groups and NGOs, and between dissidents and journalists over ulterior motives and susceptibility to the pressures and enticements brought to bear. Academics and other public servants feared refusal of promotion or research funding,[32] editors and journalists, the loss of their jobs or publishing permits. Funding grants to scholars and student groups, overseas trips to public servants and parliamentary members, and outright bribes to speak or write favourably about the project, or simply to be silent, were real and rumoured sources of friction. Such practices have become so pervasive a phenomenon in Indonesian politics that local people say it has become 'national culture', and one in no way confused with the subtleties of traditional patronage or reciprocity.

Throughout the Tanah Lot conflict, institutions wittingly and otherwise provided important sites for contest. Explicit charters became points of engagement, critical in mobilisation of political resources. But the extent to which institutions depend upon expressed and effective public pressure to perform their duty brings us full circle to the question of political context. The dilemmas posed by the political economy of environment in Indonesia cannot be separated from questions of constructing civil society generally.

Analysis of environmental disputes often neglects to confront the fundamental advantage held by established institutions over the more loosely structured instruments of civil society drawn upon by social movements. The former have the weight of established authority and vested resources to prosecute their interests, while the latter must draw on moral authority and voluntarily contributed materials and labour to make their case. That originary imbalance can be mitigated in political contexts where democratic processes enable resistant social forces to direct institutional resources to their purposes (though rarely to the extent of completely redressing the imbalance). Asymmetries may also be redressed to some extent when competing interests within sectors of the state or business ally themselves with activist demands, but such support tends to be strategic and provides an insecure base for sustained prosecution of environmental causes.

It is as yet unclear whether in the longer term anything more than symbolic concessions will have been won from the concerted opposition mounted to the Tanah Lot development, or how the unanticipated ferment it has generated will impact on expansive plans for further developments of this type. Certainly, the constraints on the *Bali Post* that were already being felt before the June media bans made it clear that the press would be unable in the immediate future to provide the exposure that galvanised public sentiment initially. It is indicative of media importance in the case that Abu Bakrie, the head of the conglomerate investing in Tanah Lot, was involved in resurrecting a rival regional newspaper, *Nusa Tenggara*, which began publication a month following resumption of the BNR project.[33]

It might have been unrealistic to expect that public opinion could stop the Tanah Lot development with instruments of civil society so weakened by decades of military-backed executive domination of Indonesian politics. Certainly some activists were sceptical from the outset about the possibilities of halting a development for which ground was already broken and when a long string of similar projects waiting in train (many directly involving the Suharto family) would be jeopardised. The resumption of construction activity in this watershed case was certain to be taken as a green light for investors. Indeed, by 1995, the Indonesian Investment Board (BKBM) had approved 20 golf courses/resorts in addition to the three already operating in Bali. The most extravagant of these, involving a 335 hectare, 45-hole course at Ulu Watu, has sparked the newest phase of local opposition.[34] Meanwhile the Governor, flanked by the Indonesian Investment Board agents, was calling on regional authorities to do everything they could to attract the US$850 million in the coming budget year claimed necessary to maintain Bali's 7.8 per cent growth rate (Antara News Agency 19/12/95 indonesianet@indonesianet.com).

But resistance in the Tanah Lot case has also to be assessed in terms of the shifts in public opinion and the reworking of meanings which this experience brought about. It was a surprise to me that two years after the violent end of the demonstrations, the press bans and resumption of construction, activists, landholders, religious leaders and ordinary people on the street were still so open in their expressions of antagonism to the project and the political system that had left them ultimately powerless to prevent it.

Towards the end of 1995, a new coordinating group had been established to try to overcome rifts in the earlier struggles, this time with suggestions of more active involvement from affected farmers and community groups, thanks to the quiet and persistent liaison work of several small NGOs and the Legal Aid Institute. The open meeting establishing the liaison group was attended by lawyers, students, academics, NGO activists and a few representatives from the community at Ulu Watu, now embroiled in the latest controversy over the new mega-development there. Their aim was to link general opposition to the kind of development represented by the Tanah Lot resort and equally controversial projects at Serangan Island and Uluwatu to an attempt to revoke and revise the entire planning document which facilitates these new forms of tourism development. The December 1995 damages award to the BNR was a salutary reminder of the heavy price of popular resistance in late New Order Indonesia; but legal action on this and other fronts was still being pursued by legal aid groups.

The general public remains quietly angry and cynical, both of government objectives and of opposition effectiveness. Nevertheless, the emergence of open and organised resistance to the Tanah Lot development was in many respects itself a watershed in Bali's history under the New Order. It had after all succeeded in halting the construction of the Bali Nirwana Resort for eight months at considerable cost to the Bakrie group, and in forcing some redesign of the project. More importantly perhaps, it signalled a significantly changed attitude among the general public to the new mega-developments and a more reflective phase in local political and cultural consciousness.

THE TOURISM SECTOR: ENVIRONMENT, CULTURE AND POLITICS

Culture and environment form separate but convergent battlegrounds in the contest over the direction of development in Bali. They are interdependent 'resources' that for Balinese are the basis of local livelihoods, social relations and spiritual meanings. At the same time, they offer prime assets upon which the tourism industry seeks to capitalise. Sacred sites such as Tanah Lot magnify the contest of interests and meanings ascribed to tourist potential and other values. The aesthetic (natural and humanly constructed) and historic heritage values which make cultural and environmental icons so important to local identity are the drawcard which multiplies their commodity value to the tourism industry.

Exploitation of these resources in the unique context of the tourism sector has complex and paradoxical effects for conservation. Hotels and golf courses consume water and land at the expense of alternative uses by the local population, but, proponents argue, may provide more jobs or better incomes than agricultural options, and less natural destruction and pollution than industrial alternatives. Opponents insist that the mega-developments are short-term and less secure or sustainable options than agriculture combined with smaller-scale, locally owned forms of tourism and handicraft industries.

On the cultural side, income brought by visitors may subsidise artistic endeavour which might otherwise wither under the pressures of modernity and globalisation. But, although the kind of 'consumption' affected by the tourist gaze upon culture does not directly 'use up' a limited natural resource as it does in extractive industries such as timber or mining, it may be part of a cultural colonising process with analogously transforming effects. Certainly the character of the tourist gaze (see Urry 1992) affects and is affected by the political economy of the industry. This is one of the reasons why site, scale, ownership and the inclusion of residential units made the new kind of leisure industry developments in Bali so explosive. The BNR project offers investors the opportunity to consume a piece of this 'last paradise'. Like the GWK monument, its preservationist claims of environmental and cultural protection are about synthesising their forms while displacing their content.

Tourism *per se* was not the real bone of contention in the debates surrounding the Tanah Lot resort. There had long been a general consensus among Balinese that tourism within certain limits offered a form of development complementary to local interests. For Balinese critics the fundamental issues raised by the Garuda monument and Bali Nirvana Resort projects revolve around questions of balance and control in the use of cultural and environmental resources. As a letter to the editor in the *Bali Post* concerning the Garuda monument proposal expressed it,

> We have to be conscious of the threat this poses . . . It exceeds the dimensions of our Balineseness. Bali is small and small can be very beautiful. The era of bigness is past. Faced with the interdependence among fellow human beings, and the fragility of our dependence on the environment which is under continuous threat, the concepts of *Tri Hita Karena* [balanced relations between the divine, human and natural domains] and *Desa, Kala, Patra* [appropriateness to place, time and circumstance] are more suitable. The problem of the future is the problem of balance between people and environment.
>
> (*Bali Post* 16/6/93)

The Tanah Lot dispute has made it clear to Balinese that environmental and cultural integrity cannot be taken for granted; that the struggle over meaning is a central aspect of the politics of environment; and that cultural and environmental protection cannot be separated from broader political and societal processes.

NOTES

1 Although Cribb does not indicate the historical roots of this usage, my impression is that it is connected with the strong socialist grounding which Anderson 1990: 139ff points out played a formative role in the evolution of Indonesian as a language of revolutionary nationalism in the early twentieth century. The

notion of 'environment' in this social sense has long been a key concept in discourses of social change and reform in the Western Marxist and social democratic traditions, which strongly influenced the Indonesian nationalist movement.

2 Almost US$5 billion at 1994 exchange rates.

3 Propelling the current drive to approve new projects is the desire of other regencies to gain access to the tax and rent-seeking opportunities which Kabupaten Badung, the region in which the original three tourist centres are located, has long enjoyed. The processes of selecting the heads of regional and provincial government in any case ensure compliance with central government policy.

4 Kep Gub Bali 15/1988 and 528/1993. The areas identified in the appendix to the 1993 Governor's decree cover 140,000 hectares within the boundaries of 121 villages.

5 SK Menteri Parpostel, Kehutanan dan Pertanian No. 1/UM.29/MPPT.89; No. 24/KPTS-II/89 and SK Menteri Pertanian tentang Agrowisata 1989 (cited in Gelebet 1995: 2). A Balinese academic with some experience of environmental impact assessment mentioned seeing two environmental impact assessment reports currently under review by the provincial Commission under the aegis of agro-tourism which were proposals for the development of golf-courses (personal comm. 12/10/95).

6 In 1994–95 and 1995–96 budget years, domestic investment in Bali outstripped foreign investment by 3 to 1 and 7 to 1 respectively (BKPMD 1996).

7 B.J. Habibie was specifically invited back to Indonesia from his position with the Messerschmitt aeronautics company in Germany, where he had studied engineering, to steer Indonesia's technological development. The Habibie high-technology strategy has gained increasing prominence in Indonesian policy-making over the last decade. See 'Indonesia: From Big to Great', *Asiaweek*, 6/10/93. Habibie was also at the centre of controversies which culminated in closure of three major Indonesian magazines for coverage of allegations concerning defence purchases and of a court case which the Indonesian Legal Aid Foundation pursued against President Suharto for diverting reafforestation funds to Habibie's pet aeronautics project.

8 See Aditjondro 1995, who details major hotel and golf course project investments by Jakarta conglomerates. Prominent among these are companies associated with members of President Suharto's family, the Minister of Tourism, and the Governor of Bali.

9 This project, however 'monstrous' it seemed to Balinese critics, pales in comparison with the magnitude of the Bintan Beach International Resort currently being developed by a consortium of Indonesian and Singaporean companies. It will occupy 23,000 hectares and will absorb estimated investments of $3.5 billion. According to the general manager this 'master planned environmentally aware . . . mega complex . . . will feature everything from exclusive resort hotels and holiday homes, marinas, a golf academy, retail, commercial and entertainment centres, independent food and beverage outlets to tourist attractions such as art and cultural villages; theme parks, wildlife and nature parks and, of course, world class golf courses - as many as ten, each with the signature of a Big Man of the game' (*Australian Golf Digest*, October 1995: 119–20). The imperial rhetoric of the mega-complex (the term itself is part of the lexicon) is clearly global. Other examples of efforts to maximise grandiosity and profit in the leisure industry include multi-storey apartment blocks studding the fairways of golf-villes around Surabaya.

10 See Anderson 1990, Lindsey 1993 and Pemberton 1994 for earlier examples of monumental representation as state-building exercises under the Old and New Order.

11 Taxi drivers, as usual, were particularly informed commentators on the national scene, and scathing of Indonesia's digression from the egalitarian goals of the revolution. One driver discussing with considerable sophistication the economic advances of the last decade of growth and weighing them against what he regarded as serious social and environmental counter-indicators, said to me that he did not regard these transformations as genuine 'development', which he believed was a fundamentally 'mental' process (interview with K.S. 22/10/95).

12 A member of the provincial parliament (DPRD) from the government party Golkar was reported in fiery language comparing greedy investors and blindly consenting government officials to 'traitors' in the revolution who were selling out their homeland (*Bali Post* 15/9/90). He accused all parties of talking glibly about the environment, while sitting quiet and even facilitating its destruction.

13 The UNDP study notes a disturbing trend towards increasing ratios of land to unit of accommodation associated with the new leisure styles promoted in these developments. Densities were dropping from an average of 53 rooms per hectare for established hotels to 27 for those under construction and 19 for new approvals (UNDP 1992: Annex 3:22).

14 The threat posed by the sudden inflow of investment and labour from outside Bali was a source of friction which gave common ground to sections of the old middle class and Balinese workers. This alliance plays an important part in the development of environmentalism in Bali and is reflected in a more and more clearly articulated stance in the *Bali Post* on labour, human rights and environment issues.

15 For discussions of in-migration to Bali see *Editor* 11/9/93: 73 and Couteau 1994: 43. The continued 'flood of workers to Bali from Java while Balinese are being asked to transmigrate' was the subject of investigation by a national parliamentary commission at the end of 1995 ('DPR RI Gugat Oka Soal Jawanisasi di Bali', *Nusa Tenggara* 22/12/95).

16 The 'openness' policy relaxed to some extent the tight control over the press characteristic of much of the New Order (post-1965) period. The policy was tarnished almost immediately after it was announced in 1990 with the closure of *Monitor* for alleged breach of the so-called SARA rules prohibiting treatment of sensitive issues which might enflame ethnic–religious tensions. The 1994 banning of three of the most important national weeklies in June of that year on purely political grounds indicates the limits of the government's tolerance of a free press. Nevertheless, a significant space for critical discussion had opened up during the previous four years, much of this revolving around environmental and human rights issues.

17 The *Bali Post* is among the oldest of Indonesia's existing newspapers and one of a minority of regional papers still independent of the media conglomerates. For a more thorough treatment of the recent history of this interesting newspaper and its editorial policy on matters of the environment, human rights and the direction of Indonesian development in general, see Warren 1994. Translations from this and other Indonesian-language publications in the text are mine.

18 The irony of holding the conference at the high-rise hotel whose construction in the 1960s marked the beginnings of mass tourism in Bali was not lost on participants. Originally built with Japanese war reparations funds, reaction to its impact on the landscape resulted in the one regional planning regulation which *has* been observed since, limiting the height of hotels to 15 metres (Perda (1989) §15). When the Bali Beach Hotel burned down in 1992, the opportunity to rectify this glaring exception was ignored. Regional authorities permitted reconstruction to its original height. Now called the 'Grand' Bali Beach Hotel, it is, if anything, less in keeping with Balinese aesthetics than the original. Several academics pointed to it as an example of the Javanisation of Balinese architecture.

19 See, for particularly strongly worded examples, Letters to the Editor (*Surat Pembaca*) and Your Turn (*Giliran Anda*) columns in the *Bali Post* (29/5/93; 3/6/93; 5/6/93; 14/6/93; 7/7/93; 13/7/93).

20 Most contributors to the debate in the press were evidently middle-class intellectuals, students, artists and small-business people who were at pains, however, to express their views as representing those of the public at large (see, for example, letters to the editor, *Bali Post* 16/6/93; 19/6/93). The editorial which followed protracted public input concluded that the majority of the Balinese people opposed the concept and called upon those responsible to make the decision 'on behalf of the Balinese people, not entrepreneurs, no matter who or from where' (*Bali Post* 15/7/93).

21 Wisnu is also associated with water and through his consort Sri with rice, reproduction and balance. The first explicitly environmental non-governmental organisation in Bali took the name Wisnu Foundation. 'Imagine expecting the God Wisnu to guard the tourist district and all its glitz' (*Bali Post* 7/6/93), remarked Nyoman Gelebet, outspoken architect and lecturer at the Technical Faculty of Bali's Udayana University.

22 Some examples of the minority positions favouring the development from the Your Turn column include: 'Why must it be rejected?' (30/6/93) 'The GWK isn't AIDS, why be horrified?' (16/7/93), 'Let it become a Jewel in the Island of the Gods' (17/7/93). See also 'Pro–contra positions colour presentation of GWK', *Bali Post* 11/7/93).

23 The incident seems to have been intentional, and was certainly interpreted as such. The person whose shrine was demolished had been among a number of former landholders who had begun expressing discontent some time earlier.

24 These excerpts are translated from the original petition, also published in full in the student newspaper *Suara Bali*, October 1994. Its main points were reiterated in a signed letter to the editor of the *Bali Post* by one of the former landholders (1/11/94), and marked the resumption of coverage by that paper. Its subsequent treatment is in conspicuously modulated terms except when, as in this instance, strongly worded accusations were clearly attributed to an outside source.

25 For in-depth studies of *subak* (irrigation) and *banjar* (hamlet) associations, noted in the ethnographic literature for their organisational sophistication, see Lansing 1991 and Warren 1993. It is also worthy of note that these local institutions are strongly dependent on the religious and ritual basis of community life for their institutional strength.

26 The Tanah Lot project is a joint venture between the Bakrie Group, the largest indigenous conglomerate in Indonesia, and UK-based Timeswitch Investments Ltd. Although independent, the Bakrie brothers have close business ties with the Suharto family (see *Far Eastern Economic Review* 9/11/95). Aburizal Bakri, chairman of the group, was chosen to head the Indonesian Chamber of Commerce (Kadin) at the height of the Tanah Lot demonstrations (*Bali Post* 14/1/94). Achmad Baramuli, also an executive of the Association, led the Human Rights Commission delegation investigation of the Tanah Lot case, which concluded that the only violation of rights that could be argued was the loss of work to labourers caused by suspension of construction on the project; but its findings were discredited by later developments (*Bali Post* 23/2/94).

27 See the *Bali Post* (2/3/94), which reproduces the full text of the Parisada document on the front page. The Bhisama was greeted favourably by students and the media, who accorded it the status of religious law. And indeed the President of Indonesia issued a statement through the National Secretariat asserting that it should provide the basis for resolution of the issue.

28 The success of the Muslim student protests against the national lottery (SDSB) a month before demonstrations against the BNR began in Bali inspired the first

serious stirrings of the student movement in Bali. The *Bali Post* reported the abolition of the lottery under the headline 'Revocation of SDSB Permit, Proof of Invulnerability of People's Power' (26/11/93).

29 In fact, the issue was not so clear-cut. The existence of a substantial cluster of kiosks, restaurants and small hotels already located on the cliff facing the temple presented something of an Achilles' heel to a strict interpretation of the Bhisama. Among Balinese there were serious differences of opinion on whether these represented a qualitatively different and compatible kind of development or needed to be cleared in a consistent application of proscriptions. Evidently, the mushrooming of permanent establishments amidst what had earlier been only itinerant vendors was facilitated by regional government to help make the large-scale projects already in the planning stage by the late 1980s more palatable.

30 This interpretation was neither discussed nor agreed to by the head of Parisadha (interviews 1994, 1995). Government interventions seem to have caused serious rifts within Parisadha itself and have certainly affected its public reputation. Critics accused it of being a rubber stamp of bureaucracy, too much influenced by economic issues and political pressures, and of failing to anticipate the problems facing the Hindu community or to act on its behalf before conflicts are exposed in the press; and questioned the religious credentials of some of its leaders and Parisadha's tendency to preserve 'feudal' and conservative attitudes (*Bali Post* 1, 3, 4/11/95).

31 In many respects the resistance coalition had appeared more united than it was. The appearance of common purpose rallied around the symbol of Tanah Lot disguised varied underlying objections and degrees of political commitment and risk protestors were prepared to take. Significant differences emerged, for example, between those for whom the primary issue was religious and those whose agenda was more focused on socio-economic, political or environmental issues raised by this new direction of development. Even from the apparently more straightforward religious perspective, varying stances reflected differences of interpretation between those who adopted modernist versions of Hinduism and those whose religious commitments were oriented to the principle of maintaining ancestral traditions (*adat*).

32 The Society for Balinese Studies includes among its membership a large number of foreign scholars who responded to the situation in relatively muted terms out of similar concerns that they would be blacklisted, or because they doubted that much could be done to alter the course of development that should have been foreseen long before.

33 *Nusa Tenggara*, originally owned by the armed forces, was bought by Nirwan Bakri, the brother and business associate of Abu Bakri, and began publication in October 1994. To the end of 1994 no news related to the Tanah Lot development was reported in the paper, including news of the protest of farmers whose land had been appropriated for the project, which was reported in the *Bali Post* (1/11/94; 1/12/94)

34 Located near another important ancient temple, some of the land to be expropriated is Laba Pura, tied to local community obligations and devoted to temple support. Projects previously shelved because of their incompatibility with Balinese religious sensibilities – an expressway around Denpasar and a geo-thermal plant at Bali's Mount Batur – are also resurfacing (Gelebet 1995).

BIBLIOGRAPHY

Aditjondro, G. (1994) 'The Environment as a Battleground of Conflicting Interests in Indonesia', keynote address, Asian Studies Association Conference, July 1994, Murdoch University, Perth.

—— (1995) *Bali, Jakarta's Colony: Social and Ecological Impacts of Jakarta-based Conglomerates in Bali's Tourism Industry*, Perth: Murdoch University Asia Research Centre Working Paper No. 58.

ANDAL BNR (1993) *Analisis Dampak Lingkungan Pembangunan Bakrie Nirwana Resort Tanah Lot, Laporan Utama Bali*, Pusat Studi Lingkungan Universitas Udayana, Denpasar.

—— (1994) *'Ringkasan' Analisis Dampak Lingkungan Pembangunan Bakrie Nirwana Resort Tanah Lot, Bali Nirwana Resort*, Jakarta.

Anderson, B. (1990) *Language and Power: Exploring Political Cultures in Indonesia*, Ithaca: Cornell University Press.

—— (1991) *Imagined Communities*, New York: Verso.

—— (1992) 'Long-Distance Nationalism: World Capitalism and the Rise of Identity Politics', The Wertheim Lecture Centre for Asian Studies, Amsterdam: University of Amsterdam and The Free University of Amsterdam.

BKPMD (1996) *Perkembangan Penanaman Modal PMA/PMDN di Bali dlm Pelita VI (1994/1995 and 1995/1996)*, Denpasar: Badan Koordinasi Penanaman Modal Daerah, Pemerintah Propinsi Daerah Tingkat I Bali.

Booth, A. (1990) 'The Tourism Boom in Indonesia', *Bulletin of Indonesian Economic Studies*, 26(3): 45–73.

Bourdieu, P. (1977) *Outline of a Theory of Practice*, Cambridge: Cambridge University Press.

Budiman, A. (1982) 'The Pancasila Economic System, Capitalism and Socialism', *Prisma*, 26: 3–16.

Couteau, J. (1994) 'Transformasi Struktural Masyarakat Bali', in U. Wiryatmaya and J. Couteau, eds, *Bali di Persimpangan Jalan: Sebuah Bunga Rampai II*, Denpasar: NusaData IndoBudaya.

Cribb, R. (1988) 'The Politics of Environmental Protection in Indonesia', Monash University Centre of Southeast Asian Studies Working Paper No. 48.

—— (1990) 'The Politics of Pollution Control in Indonesia', *Asian Survey*, 30(12): 1123–35.

Dwipayana, G.N. (1994) 'Membangun dari Pinggiran: Suatu Penalaran tentang Desentralisasi dan Otonomi Daerah', *Balairung* (Edisi Khusus) 8: 86–92.

Erawan, I. Nyoman (1994) *Pariwisata dan Pembangunan Ekonomi (Bali sebagai kasus)*, Denpasar: Upada Sastra.

—— (1995) 'Dampak Pariwisata terhadap perekonomian daerah Bali (1984–1994)', *Majalah Ilmiah Unud*, XXII(44): 24–32.

Francillon, G. (1990) 'The Dilemma of Tourism in Bali', in W. Beller, P. d'Alayala and P. Hein, eds, *Sustainable Development and Environmental Management of Small Islands*, Man and the Biosphere Series, vol. 5, Paris: UNESCO.

GBHN (1993) *Garis-Garis Besar Haluan Negara*, Semarang: Penerbit Beringin Jaya.

Gelebet (1995) 'Strategi Pengendalian Kawasan dan Persinggahan Wisata', unpublished paper presented to a meeting of the Society for Balinese Studies, 22 October 1995, Denpasar, Bali.

Hansen, Anders (1991) 'The Media and the Social Construction of the Environment', *Media, Culture and Society*, 13(4): 443–59.

Helmi, Rio, Made Suarnatha and Putu Suasta (1993) *Tanggapan mengenai Garuda Wisnu Kencana* (mimeo), 9 July 1993 (a condensed version appears in *Tempo* 11 August 1993).

Hill, D. (1991) 'The Press in "New Order" Indonesia Entering the 1990s', Working Paper No. 1, Murdoch University, Perth, Asia Research Centre.

Hirsch, P. (1993) *Political Economy of Environment in Thailand*, Manila: Journal of Contemporary Asia Publishers.

Keputusan Gubernur (1993) *Keputusan Gubernur* No. 528, Tahun 1993 tentang Kawasan Pariwisata.

Lane, Max (1982) 'Voices of Dissent in Indonesia', *Arena*, 61: 110–28.

Lansing, J.S. (1991) *Priests and Programmers: Technologies of Power in the Engineered Landscape of Bali*, Princeton, NJ: Princeton University Press.

Liddle, R.W. (1982) 'The Politics of Ekonomi Pancasila', *Bulletin of Indonesian Economic Studies*, 18(1): 96–101.

Lindsey, T. (1993) 'Concrete Ideology: Taste, Tradition, and the Javanese Past in New Order Public Space', in V. Hooker, ed., *Culture and Society in New Order Indonesia*, Kuala Lumpur: Oxford University Press.

McKean, P. (1978) 'Towards a Theoretical Analysis of Tourism: Economic Dualism and Cultural Involution in Bali,' in V. Smith, ed., *Hosts and Guests: The Anthropology of Tourism*, Oxford: Basil Blackwell.

Mardani, N.K. (1993) 'Peranan Lingkungan Hidup dalam Pembangunan Kebudayaan dan Kepribadian Bangsa', *Kebudayaan dan Kepribadian Bangsa*, Denpasar: Upada Sastra.

Martopo, S. and Suyono (n.d.) 'The Potentials of Provision and Usage of Water in the Island of Bali', Center for Environmental Studies, Gadjah Mada University (unpublished report).

Nyoman Nuarta Studio (1993) 'Paparan: Pusat Kebudayaan Garuda Wisnu Kencana', Bandung, Team Pengolah Proyek, 7 July 1993.

Papadakis, Elim (1993) *Politics and the Environment: The Australian Experience*, Sydney: Allen and Unwin.

Parnwell, M. (1993) 'Environmental Issues and Tourism in Thailand', in M. Hitchcock, V. King and M. Parnwell, eds, *Tourism in Southeast Asia*, London: Routledge.

Pemberton, John (1994) 'Reflections from "Beautiful Indonesia" (Somewhere beyond the Postmodern)', *Public Culture* 6: 241–62.

Pepper, D. (1986) *The Roots of Modern Environmentalism*, London: Routledge.

Perda (1989) Peraturan Daerah No. 6, 1989 tentang Tata Ruang Bali (Regional Zoning Law, Bali).

Picard, M. (1996) *Bali: Cultural Tourism and Touristic Culture*, Singapore: Archipelago Press.

Robison, R. and D. Goodman (eds) (1996) *The New Rich in Asia*, London: Routledge.

Sachs, W. (1992) 'Environment', in W. Sachs, ed., *The Development Dictionary: A Guide to Knowledge as Power*, London: Zed Books.

Statistical Office Bali (1991) *Bali Dalam Angka*, Denpasar: Statistical Office Bali.

Suasta, P. and Pujastana (1994) 'Dominasi Politik dan Politik Kebudayaan: Telaah mengenai kelas menengah di Bali', unpublished paper presented to the Third International Bali Studies Workshop, University of Sydney.

Randall, V. (1993) 'The Media and Democratisation in the Third World', *Third World Quarterly*, 14(3): 625–46.

Tickell, P. (ed.) (1987) *The Indonesian Press: Its Past, Its People, Its Problems*, Monash University Centre for Asian Studies, Clayton, Victoria: Monash University.

—— (1994) 'Free from What? Responsible to Whom? The Problem of Democracy and the Indonesian Press', in J. Legge and D. Bourchier, eds, *Indonesian Democracy 1950s–1990s*, Clayton, Victoria: Monash University Centre of Southeast Asian Studies.

Touraine, A. (1992) 'Beyond Social Movements?', *Theory, Culture and Society* 9: 125–45.

Tourism Statistics Bali (1993) Denpasar: Bali Government Tourist Office.

Turner, V. (1967) *The Forest of Symbols*, Ithaca: Cornell University Press.

UNDP (United Nations Development Programme) (1992) *Comprehensive Tourism Development Plan for Bali*, vols I and II; Annexes 1–12 (Report by Hassall and Associates).

Urry, J. (1992) 'The Tourist Gaze and the "Environment"', *Theory, Culture and Society*, 9(3): 1–26.

Van Langenberg, M. (1986) 'Analysing Indonesia's New Order State: A Keywords Approach', *Review of Indonesian and Malaysian Affairs* (RIMA), 20: 1–47.

Wallerstein, I. (1991) 'Culture as the Ideological Battleground of the Modern World-System', in M. Featherstone, ed., *Global Culture: Nationalism, Globalisation and Modernity*, London: Sage.

Warren, C. (1993) *Adat and Dinas: Balinese Communities in the Indonesian State*, Kuala Lumpur: Oxford University Press.

—— (1994) 'Centre and Periphery in Late New Order Indonesia: Environment, Politics and Human Rights in the Regional Press (Bali)', Perth: Murdoch University Asia Research Centre Working Paper No. 42.

Newspapers and periodicals

Asia Week
Bali Post
Far Eastern Economic Review
Nusa Tenggara

13 The Chiang Mai cable-car project

Local controversy over cultural and eco-tourism

Chayant Pholpoke[1]

Tourism has become a highly promoted development strategy throughout the world because of its potential for rapid growth and for contributing foreign exchange to national economies. It also has the image of being a 'soft' form of development with lesser environmental and social impacts than other types of natural resource exploitation. The expansion of tourism in Thailand, however, is increasingly perceived as posing a serious threat to the cultural and environmental resources of host communities. In fact, the sustainable exploitation of cultural resources in the tourism industry is proving as problematic as the protection of natural values. This chapter contends that, while tourism is uncritically promoted at national and international levels for its economic potential as a foreign exchange earner, in the local sphere a more complex set of 'values' is at stake.

The development of travel and tourism in Thailand is examined in this study with a specific focus on the Chiang Mai region of northern Thailand. It suggests that many projects purporting to operate under the label of 'cultural' or 'eco-' tourism reproduce the same contradictions as other forms of capital-intensive development in Thai society, exacerbating economic and social disparities, diverting resources, and alienating the majority of people from their resource base. Indeed, it is argued, they typically facilitate the degradation of the very cultural and natural resources which attract visitors to the Chiang Mai region.[2]

This case study of the cable-car project in Chiang Mai explores the cultural and environmental issues at stake in such projects and the competing social interests and values represented in public debate. These are far broader and more complex than mainstream, discreetly pro-establishment tourism critics would wish us to believe. For this reason, another objective of this review is to contribute to a broader information base and a critical perspective on the environmental and cultural politics of tourism development.

TOURISM DEVELOPMENT TRENDS IN THAILAND

In both developed and rapidly growing economies, the demand for the tourist experience continues to expand. Projections of the World Tourism Organisation are for a steady growth in world tourism of 3–4 per cent through the first decade of the twenty-first century. Tourism growth in East Asia and the Pacific, expanding at an even faster rate than the global figure, is expected to account for nearly a quarter of the 1 billion annual international arrivals predicted for the year 2010 (WTO 1996). Rising incomes and more diversified demands for leisure experiences will continue to drive the dynamic growth of the tourist market, regardless of its impact. Although people's choice of travel destination will be guided by changing political, social and economic factors, and the structure of the industry will be affected by changes in technology and resources, we can reasonably assume that the basic desire to travel will remain. At the same time, the competitive world-wide expansion of the industry means that destinations will be put under additional pressure to provide the kind of experience that middle-class travellers will demand for their 'dollar'. It is likely that this structure will grow in complexity as the industry attempts to provide a variety of travel experiences in an increasingly competitive atmosphere.[3]

By any international standard, the magnitude of tourism growth in Thailand is stunning. In 1995, Thailand registered almost 7 million international arrivals,[4] an increase of 12.7 per cent over the previous year. Government economic targets project annual increases of 6 per cent in the number of foreign tourist arrivals, and of 14 per cent in foreign exchange earnings for the coming five-year plan.[5] Political problems over the last decade in Thailand did not affect this sector of the economy significantly. If the government and trade industry predictions are correct, Thailand could become one of the most sought-after destinations in the world. In addition to its substantial share of the holiday tourist market, Thailand is also fast emerging as a convention centre and business hub in Asia. Thus, the demand for facilities is increasing rapidly, and business is eager to respond with new products to create and accommodate new demand.

The corporate sector in tourism as in all industries seeks investments that yield the best opportunities for expansion and profit maximization. This inclines the industry towards promotion of luxury consumption for the cash-rich and privileged, or a mass market of middle-class tourists who are encouraged by the industry to develop similar tastes that can be satisfied through a standardized 'package'. The result is a capital-intensive pattern of tourism development, which has the same tendency as extractive industries to expand to the limit the use of all available 'resources' in its search for profits.

Driven by the need to maximize profits, growth in the tourism industry has been characterized by a tendency towards more and larger accommodation centres and transport facilities, and an ever-increasing demand for new attractions. Nature and culture are vulnerable commodities in the search for unique sources of comparative advantage. 'Nature' and 'culture' are marketed as new products for tourist consumption without regard for intrinsic worth or value context. Habitats of hill tribes such as settlements of the

Akka and Karen are converted to tourist centres, and people 'exhibited' as attractive showpieces.[6] Wildlife too becomes victim to the price tag on its rarity.[7]

In such a policy context, local people face a wide range of threats, including diversion or destruction of the resources upon which they depend, loss of cultural identity and consequent economic and cultural dependence. The constant uprooting and relocation of communities by tourism sector interests and associated corporate projects exacerbate rural indebtedness and landlessness. Skilled labour and custom-produced luxury foods are imported, marginalizing local products and leaving local people unemployed. The economic and social problems that result from this distorted development model remain unresolved, while eroding Thailand's capacity and potential for self-reliance. Such strategies induce structural dependence on technology, finance and marketing through transnational corporate control of the local industry, with negative impacts on the very cultural integrity and natural resource base upon which the comparative advantage of the region in the tourism industry depends.[8]

ECO-TOURISM[9]

The 1970s and 1980s witnessed the rapid growth of tourism in Thailand, especially sex-tourism, which attracted severe criticism for its impacts on Thai society. Coinciding with opposition to certain aspects of tourism development and the entry of environmental issues into mainstream politics, has been the emergence of interest in 'eco-tourism' or 'sustainable tourism'. The idea of 'nature' tourism is not new. Natural history tours attracted Western tourists in the 1950s; later, 'discovery tours' were marketed as products for travellers. Eco-tourism is described as 'purposeful travel to natural areas to understand the cultural and natural history of these habitats while maintaining the integrity of the ecosystems and providing economic opportunities that make conservation of natural resources financially beneficial to the inhabitants of the host region' (Whelan 1991: 201).

It is argued that eco-tourism offers the advantage of supporting local communities while protecting forests and other habitats since it provides more income than other forms of exploitation, generating employment for the local people while earning foreign exchange. But critics challenge these assertions. Investments are made by outside financiers who have no concern for local people or resources; residents simply cannot compete with or control the demands of the tourism industry, and find their way of life increasingly dominated by external forces. Both wilderness and cultivable land are fast disappearing in eco-tourist areas, and families are forced to seek wage labour to survive. Tourism creates external dependence rather than appropriate development predicated on local autonomy. Cultural and eco-tourism, like other models of the industry, change the socio-cultural as well as the environmental landscape, despite claims of protection. Indeed, 'eco-tourism' in Thailand is increasingly seen as a device for appropriating the country's national parks, wildlife sanctuaries and other protected areas.

National governments and international institutions such as the World Bank, the US Agency for International Development (USAID), the International Union for the Conservation of Nature and Natural Resources (IUCN), the World Wide Fund for Nature (WWF), the Eco-tourism Society, the Domestic Technology Institute, the European Union (EU), the Business Council for Sustainable Development and the United Nations Environment Programme (UNEP) are among the agencies which advocate wise-use, market-driven, integrated, sustainable development principles and programmes, and have begun to celebrate the 'greening of development practices' within the industrial tourism sector (Fernandes, 1994).[10] They claim that cultural and eco-tourism approaches which adopt a sustainable development model are capable of empowering marginalized communities and practically influencing global and local development strategies to meet the needs of the present without compromising the ability of future generations to do the same. But as Worster concludes,

> [S]ustainable development ... like most popular slogans ... begins to wear thin after a while. Although it seems to have gained a wide acceptance, it has done so by sacrificing real substance. Worse yet, the slogan may turn out to be irredeemable for environmentalist use because it may inescapably compel us to adopt a narrow economic language, standard of judgement, and world view in approaching and utilising the earth.
>
> (quoted in Fernandes 1994: 4–5)

THE CABLE-CAR PROJECT: BACKGROUND ISSUES

Chiang Mai is an important tourist destination in northern Thailand. Over the years, investors with government support have created several attractions within Chiang Mai to draw more visitors and bring substantial profits. To maintain momentum in the tourism sector, in 1980–81 the Tourism Authority of Thailand (TAT) hired a number of consultants to carry out feasibility studies to identify and promote new tourist locations in Chiang Mai and neighbouring areas. Four Aces Consultants, a private Bangkok-based architectural firm, was hired to prepare a master plan for Chiang Mai with a specific focus on the development of tourism. Completed in 1984, this master plan proposed Doi Suthep as a potential location for tourism development as 'it offers a unique combination of natural, historic and cultural places that could be supplied in an attractive package to visitors' (Four Aces Co. Ltd 1984).

Doi Suthep is a mountain lying at the outskirts of the town of Chiang Mai, named for a seventh-century Lawa chieftain who converted to Buddhism, became a monk, and retreated from the world to the mountain which now bears his name. It is the location of an important Buddhist monastery, Wat

Pra That, which houses a relic of the Buddha. Local people revere the mountain temple as a destination of spiritual significance for Buddhists. Since the construction of the temple in the fourteenth century, Doi Suthep has been an important pilgrimage site. The temple as well as a royal palace are enclaved within the national park reserve, Doi Suthep-Pui, created in 1981 and covering 261 square kilometres of mountainous terrain (Elliott 1994). Visitors to the temple are mostly local people, although in recent years increasing numbers of foreign tourists also visit the site.

In 1985, Four Aces, the consultants who had produced the Master Plan for Chiang Mai, submitted a proposal to the local government to erect a cable-car system between the foot of the Doi Suthep hills and the temple, covering a distance of about 3 km and requiring an investment of around 115 million baht (US$4.6 million at 1985 rates). It was to be a joint venture involving two Bangkok-based companies, the Four Aces Consultants Company itself, and Phaibun Sombat Co. Ltd, proprietors of several real estate properties in Bangkok. Financial support was offered by Phatra Thanakit, a finance company in the Thai Farmers' Bank Group.

The proposal argued that the number of local tourists to the temple was growing, and the present roadway was subject to constant congestion and increasing numbers of accidents. Consequently, an efficient and accident-free communication system was necessary. They proposed to erect a cable-car route that would be more convenient and safe. The other alternative, to expand the presently available road, was considered to be unsuitable as that would involve clearing a larger proportion of the forest area and might cause permanent damage to the ecology of the mountain and neighbourhood. The project proposal overall considered only narrowly defined environmental costs and benefits of the cable-car system, and only casually looked into the cultural aspects and carrying capacity of Doi Suthep.

Initial opposition emerged from the corridors of the Chiang Mai University campus as academics began to study the impacts of the cable-car proposal on the precincts of the university and on Doi Suthep reserve, which served as the 'natural science laboratory' for its students. Biological surveys showed the park to hold exceptionally high levels of plant diversity (Elliott *et al.* 1989).[11] Academics also challenged some of the claims of the project proponents concerning the technical feasibility of a cable-car system on the hills and the need for any further expansion of the existing road facility.

From an aesthetic point of view, the slopes demarcated for the cable-car route were visible from the town of Chiang Mai. Such an obvious alteration to the landscape and the closed process of approving the project came to be seen as an offence to the religious sentiments of the devotees of the Doi Suthep temple and the people of Chiang Mai. Slowly, local people and monks also joined the protest because they believed that the cable-car system would intrude on the natural ambience of the area, invading the quiet Buddhist temple and devaluing their way of life. This dissent received support from several people's organizations, social action groups, the local press and the general public of Chiang Mai who regard their town and surroundings as a heritage to be preserved for the coming generations.

Criticism steadily developed into broadly based opposition against certain characteristics of tourism development in the area. In their struggle, issues concerning preservation and local use of natural resources came to assume importance alongside the cultural position put by monks and scholars. Environmental activists considered Doi Suthep a common property resource and heritage site, and opposed any plan that would make it private property or destroy the local ecological balance. This multi-faceted nature of popular protest led to the temporary withdrawal of the project in 1987, the year officially designated as 'Visit Thailand Year'. However, the project was not shelved entirely, and revival is periodically mooted.

CONTENDING POSITIONS

Local government, consultants and investors asserted that environmental, cultural and economic objectives would be jointly served by the cable-car development. It would reduce traffic congestion on the mountain and make travel more convenient and safe for devotees. Brochures published by the project proponents claimed that the attraction of Doi Suthep and the consequent deterioration of the site as tourist numbers increased might lead to the decline of tourism, an industry of great economic importance to the Chiang Mai region. They argued that the cable-car project could boost the image of Doi Suthep, while protecting the environment and enabling the expansion of tourist numbers (Skyline Projects 1986). With easier access, the number of visitors to the temple would rise, in turn facilitating forward and backward linkage effects, and increasing employment opportunities. They insisted that the design of the cable-car route would maintain the aesthetics and architectural values of Doi Suthep.

For the growing number of opponents, the cable-car project proposal was a threat to the natural and cultural values of the area. A place beloved and revered by all Buddhists, Doi Suthep is a unique synthesis of nature and culture, where sanctity is enshrined in the purity of the natural environment. Doi Suthep popularly refers to the famous temple complex as well as the mountain and the forest reserve area in which it stands. It contains an unusually rich community of plants and animals,[12] much of it still unstudied, which local conservationists argue is of inestimable value to Thailand and the world.

At first the Abbot of Wat Phra That of Doi Suthep had welcomed the move to build the cable-car, publicly stating that the proposed facility would bring in more funds to support the temple. Phra Khru Anusorn Silakhan, Abbot of Wat Muen Lan, however, argued that the temple was 'deliberately located in the mountain to make access difficult so that the pilgrimage emerges as a task of devotion. Making access too easy will encourage people to be less concerned about religion and sacredness' (*The Nation*, 24 September 1987). There was already an adequate road, laid by the devotees through voluntary work. The intention to build a cable-car appeared like proposing a 'Magic Land' amusement park style for the site. He contended that the proposal was a profanation of the hermit's lofty ideals, and a lack of respect for those who believe in Buddhism.

From the point of view of the environment, Doi Suthep's unique mountain features would be eroded with every new activity in the area. Some of the rare animals and plants which are localized in very small areas would be exterminated. And most of these still await recognition of their importance as genetic reserve or as medicinal plants. Dr Hanz Banzinger, a well-known botanist and naturalist, argued, 'I am open-minded to all new, imaginative and appropriate projects. But such a baffling and utterly misleading statement about the lack of wildlife in a place so rich in flora and fauna as Doi Suthep National Park by a private firm which intends to build a cable-car way [makes one question] their credibility and understanding' (*Bangkok Post*, 24 March 1986). He also pointed out that the area to be developed had been designated as a 'B-1' watershed, which means that only the cabinet can authorize any construction, and for essential economic or security reasons. No such rationale was indicated in the cable-car project proposal.

Some critics noted the conflict of interest involving consultants who served as planners, later as investors and businessmen, and the fact that the master plan had been silent on socio-economic issues. There are about 2,500 *song thaew* (pick-up vans) plying the city, providing a livelihood to about 5,000 families. With the introduction of the cable-car and more sophisticated modes of transportation, these families were threatened with job losses. Although the company assured the public that it would employ the *song thaew* drivers in the project, it was an insufficient guarantee in the view of many commentators. To such objections, the company responded: 'There are already answers . . . to questions over the project's impact on social and economic conditions such as minibuses operating up and down Doi Suthep . . . If the answers were not reasonable enough, the project would not have been approved' (M.L. Chainimit Navarat, Project Manager of the Four Aces Consultants, quoted in the *Bangkok Post*, 20 January 1986). Opponents also suggested that the substantial investments needed would not pay in the long run unless associated with further development. On the basis of the experience of the 'Chiang Mai Night Bazaar', the critics pointed out that the investors would, over a period of time, demand more and more space to install more tourist-related activities on the mountain in order to recover their investment.[13] Otherwise, the project would go bankrupt, leaving permanent scars on the landscape, and none of the promised economic benefits.

For the social activists, concern went beyond the destruction of Doi Suthep. This was seen as a test case reflecting a more widespread dilemma that arises when culture comes into conflict with economic development. They viewed the scheme for Doi Suthep as the forerunner of a new phase of expansion in the tourism industry which would cover other parts of Thailand with more such harmful 'development' projects.[14] In 1986, peaceful demonstrations were held in Chiang Mai against the project and a petition with 30,000 signatures was submitted to the government.

The Tourism Authority of Thailand and the National Environment Board, however, discreetly sided with the investors. Officials from these two organizations engaged in lengthy, cumbersome technical debates that totally ignored cultural questions. Four Aces organized a press conference in Chiang Mai to highlight the project benefits and 'present the facts'. On that occasion, TAT and NEB official statements implied that the cable-car project was part of official tourism policy, and that failure to proceed might doom the industry in Thailand. The suggestion that opposition to the cable-car project challenged the tourism industry as a whole legitimated participation of the government agencies in the debate. For the press conference and public relations campaign, journalists were flown in from Bangkok and treated to one of the most extravagant parties ever held in Chiang Mai.

As television and radio are controlled by the government, these channels delivered cooperative 'news' in support of the project. However, such efforts failed to constrain popular opposition to the project, and the print media played an important role in providing alternative information. An article in *The Nation* quoted Gerald Roscoe, formerly with an advertising agency which handled TAT's work in the United States and now a resident of Chiang Mai, who argued that the cable-car would not attract more tourists. His American survey data indicated that a significant number of tourists were 'offended by the commercialisation of sacred places they had visited in other countries including Thailand' (*The Nation*, 21 August 1987).

Continued protests led to some tension between various social groups, with proponents accused of profiteering and opponents labelled 'communists'. At this time, anonymous leaflets were distributed as part of a smear campaign against opponents. In an unsigned article, *Phalang Thurakit*, a local business fortnightly, described opponents as 'old lobbyists who have never done anything in their lives for society', and described dissident monks as following anti-Buddhist precepts. Some opinion surveys attempted to influence the 'silent majority' who did not directly participate in the controversy. There were actually two surveys, one by 'Indra', owned by a public relations representative of Four Aces, and the second by the Social Research Institute of Chulalongkorn University in Bangkok. The then director of the institute, Dr Warin Wonghanchao, was also known to be a close associate of the Four Aces Co. Thus the kinds of questions framed in the surveys, and the selection of generally sympathetic participants (for example no monks were interviewed in the surveys) allowed the proponents to declare that 80 per cent of Chiang Mai's citizens were in favour of the project. Thus, at this stage, it appeared that the project might commence.

Nevertheless, in the face of growing community division over the issue which many feared might lead to social unrest, in 1986 the Governor of Chiang Mai suspended the cable-car project. In December of that year the new Governor, Phairat Decharin, announced that investors had withdrawn their financial support under pressure from the Buddhist clergy, community leaders and academics. The action taken by provincial officials left the impression that the project was frozen. But in 1989 and again in 1994, efforts were made to revive the project by its original promoters, and the central government pressed local authorities in Chiang Mai to reconsider its viability.

THE STATE AND PROFESSIONALS

During the last decade a substantial body of critical literature has been published on the problems of the mass, commercial and sex tourism industries in Thailand and elsewhere. With growing public awareness and mounting criticism, the tourism industry and its government backers could no longer assume *carte blanche* in its expansion. They sought the support of professional consultants to plan, manage and project tourism as a renewable enterprise based on local capacities and community decision-making. Eco-tourism then emerged as a new sphere for tourism promotion in Thailand.

The government's promotion of ecotourism has to be understood in the context of its role as 'tourism marketer'. In Thailand, the government agency, the TAT, undertakes responsibility to promote tourism development. It and local authorities compete with other sectors within the government for allocation of resources, facilities and services (e.g. housing, transport, water or finance). To be successful within the government planning framework, it has to project a positive, revenue-making impression of 'tourism' while simultaneously presenting 'social' concerns as the rationale for new developments. The government and tourist industry enrolled the support of professional, pro-establishment conservationists, and seized some of the mainstream jargon like ecology, sustainability and local participation. This new approach, adopting more publicly acceptable labels and obtaining the certification of professionals, was evident in the strategy adopted to promote the cable-car project of Chiang Mai, and raises serious questions about the assumed independence of professional advisers and decision-makers.

The Four Aces consultants supported their assessment with the rhetoric of environmentalism and local religious sensibilities as well as professional claims to technical expertise:

> With conscience, we fully understand the sanctity of *Doi Suthep* where the Royal Palace and the Phra That are situated. The people of Chiang Mai are proud to see that all Thais from various regions feel it is a must to visit this temple . . . But there are no adequate public facilities for these tourists (70 per cent of whom are Thais), especially traffic accommodation and car parks. Police statistics of accidents emphasise the need for a change in the communication system – to establish one which provides more convenience and safety. There were then two choices: to expand the road or to find another mass transit system. We chose to build an electric cable-car system because we knew that it will not only provide convenience and

safety but also will give the locality higher tourism value. More importantly, it will have less negative effects on the ecological system than road expansion.

(*Bangkok Post*, 20 January 1986)

Theoretically, local government officials are in an independent position to act as arbiters between public and private profit interests. But opportunities for graft and insider investments mean that the government's role in promoting tourism frequently conflicts with its social responsibility functions. Professional consultants therefore help to legitimate its planning and approval processes. Local government tourism marketers may defer to the 'specialist' who proposes and executes plans for 'national development' projects. Thus, the tourism marketers, whether state officials or private professionals, want to be identified as possessing an established body of systematic knowledge, a commitment to client-centred service, and the right to control their own work. In predominantly tourist-centred regions, local government officials perceive themselves as tourism professionals first, and only secondarily as state officials with public service obligations. On the theory that tourism development is always in the public interest, the government official as marketer can ultimately be made accountable only to the policy-makers and investors as opposed to the local community. The overlapping interests of consultants, planners, promoters and investors prevent any possibility of presenting an 'independent view' in 'master plans' presented to the government.

SOCIAL ACTION INITIATIVES

In the case of the cable-car project proposed for Chiang Mai, a number of social groups and community organizations took part in popular protest against the aggressive development plans of government and business interests. The initial participants in the protests were largely concerned citizens and academics, later joined by other social interest groups. The For Chiang Mai Group, a broad coalition of social activists, concerned citizens, academics and farmers living in the surrounding area, was formed in 1987. The participating groups in this social action could be classified into three broad categories.

Crusading Buddhists. A large number of Buddhist monks, who regularly participate in social and community development efforts, were supported by religious sympathizers in their opposition to the project. This group relied heavily on religious idioms in its rejection of the modern way of life. It upholds the pre-capitalist and pre-World War II village community as the exemplar of ecological and social harmony. The methods of action favoured by this group revolve largely around Buddhist traditions – offerings to monks, ceremonies and poojas (homage to ancestors) – in which a traditional cultural idiom is used to further the cause of environmentalism. Crusading Buddhists are not social revolutionaries, nor can they be classified as 'progressive' activists; they are concerned with the stranglehold of modernist philosophies on the Thai people; through their work they propagate an alternative philosophy whose roots lie in Thai culture. They are totally opposed to tourism as promoted by commercial forces, and view proposals like the cable-car project as anti-people and anti-nature.[15]

Appropriate technologists, moderates. Members of this category are less confrontational and less strident in their opposition to the formation of an industrial society. They strive for a working synthesis of agriculture and industry, big and small units, Western and Eastern techno-traditions. They are mainly drawn from the technocratic professions, yet they are socially conscious and strive for the well-being of the masses within that framework of appropriate technology. Their emphasis is not so much on challenging the structure or system, as in demonstrating the practicability of a set of technological and social alternatives to the present model of urban-industrial development, of which eco-tourism is a part. They argue for more appropriate technology to alleviate problems presented by the current model of development (e.g. more water treatment plants). This group generally adheres to the 'development for conservation' approach.

Progressive solidarity group. This category includes a variety of social activists who seek a just and equitable society and genuine development for the poor; it is mainly composed of academics, professionals, social action groups and concerned citizens. Their activities largely revolved around the People's Science Movement, which attempts to 'take science to the people' and includes environmental and resource-base protection in its agenda. They differ from other groups in two important ways: they work towards social justice and emphasize building solidarity as part of a broad social movement. They view fundamental changes in the economic system as essential to bring about distributive justice and as a logical prerequisite to ecological stability. Political action towards social justice and people's participation has become their overriding priority. They offer a rounded critique of the present state of tourism and strive to provide proposals for alternative forms of development. Protests against the cable-car project originally emerged from this group. Members collected data and evidence, and presented it to the general public. They also presented their evidence in a broader framework linked to societal concerns. Their organized and documented efforts gave momentum to the resistance and increased their credibility in the debate.

Public protest involving all three groups broadened the terms of reference in public debate about the relationship between tourism and the environment. This has proved a doubled-edged sword, however. While there have been a number of initiatives pursued by the tourism industry (including the Tourism Authority of Thailand) in the name of environmental and cultural preservation, in fact, a large segment of what presently passes for eco-tourism among officials and professionals is the commercial face of the tourism industry draped in the cloth of environmentalism. During the debate, it became apparent that for grass-roots groups these conflicts were not about 'productive' versus 'protective' uses of the environment and resources, but about alternative productive uses. To them, for example, wilderness tours and projects like the cable-car represent intensive and profit-oriented modes of resource use that threaten the ecological and social viability of their own traditional uses of those very resources.

COMMON PROPERTY RESOURCES AND TOURISM

An important factor completely disregarded by tourism development policies and programmes in Thailand is the capacity of common property resources (CPRs)[16] to take care of some of the needs of the local population. This was obvious in the cable-car project debate. Despite their significant contribution to the local economy, common property resources, like Doi Suthep, have seldom received enough attention by policy-makers and planners. This neglect arises partly because the contributions of CPRs are often a matter of local routine and remain unnoticed by central planners. Development planning has systematically emphasized private property resource (PPR)-centred activities, be it the promotion of high-yielding crop varieties, infrastructure development for tourist centres, or supply of credit. Certainly there is inadequate understanding of the survival mechanisms used by the poor as well as the complementarities between CPRs and PPR-based activities.

Since the beginning of the 'tourism boom' in 1970s, the decline of common property resources has taken the following three forms in Thailand: the physical loss of resources, such as the area of CPR that could be covered by roads and buildings; deterioration of the natural productivity of resources, as revealed by degradation of pastures or forest lands; and reassignment of usage and property rights through transfer of common property lands to private ownership or privately initiated activities (e.g. tourist guest-houses and entertainment places in the national parks). It is obvious that the complete privatization of CPRs 'disentitled' local people, especially the poor. The proposed cable-car project in Chiang Mai was viewed as one more encroachment into common property resources, and reassignment of use and property rights to enable private investors to make profits.

EMERGING TRENDS

In the last decade and a half, resource conflicts have given rise to a number of local initiatives in defence of traditional rights, which can be read as an indictment of the resource illiteracy of development planning. Underlining the close links between impoverishment of the resource base and impoverishment of large sections of the population, the NGO movement has called for a complete overhaul of the present tourism development strategy, with its narrow economic focus, and its replacement by a socially and environmentally responsible path of development. Local NGOs are allied with a number of umbrella groups funded by international non-governmental organizations such as TERRA (Towards Ecological Recovery and Regional Alliance) and the Ecumenical Coalition on Third World Tourism, both based in Bangkok. The bulletins of the two organizations – *New Frontiers* and *Contours* respectively – regularly publish articles covering the contradictions between developmentalist claims and critical impacts of cultural and eco-tourism.

At one level, the need for redefining development through genuine efforts at cultural and environmental sustainability and social justice is obscured by the introduction of a false alliance between 'development' and 'ecology' which covers up real contradictions between ecological protection and unsustainable economic growth. The impact of mass tourism in Thailand on the local people, their culture, natural resources and built environment has been substantial. Two striking effects of over-zealous profit-oriented tourism development efforts have been: (1) the disproportionate shift of capital to mass tourism-related construction and real estate developments at the expense of other sectors such as agriculture and tourism and small industry which are locally oriented, and (2) the promotion of over-consumption and excessive exploitation of local resources with attendant new social and economic pressures on local people and environments. The cable-car project in Chiang Mai came to be understood in the context of the broader capital-shift to quick-profit areas like tourism.

CONCLUSION

Over the years the tourism industry (that is, government tourist promotion departments, tour operators and businessmen engaged in tourism) has been strongly criticized for the character of the tourism market pursued. To shed this past image, the tourism industry has responded by coopting popular slogans like 'cultural' and 'eco-tourism'. In these developments, it is evident that the government plays an ambiguous role in promoting tourism in Thailand, seeking the support of professionals and businessmen to justify actions which run contrary to cultural and ecological sensitivities.

In the cable-car project controversy, an eco-local perspective on these resources developed from outside professional and official circles. Among the locals, the experience of the cable-car project has led to a close monitoring of the efforts by the state to promote tourism and eco-tourism in the Chiang Mai region. For example, the For Chiang Mai Group now functions as a watchdog on ecology and tourism issues in Chiang Mai. Its experience has developed into a formidable social tool and fostered a community sense that offers a potential source of empowerment to local people. Such a consciousness could enable cultivation of broader social–ecological perspectives, and contribute to building a forceful environmental solidarity movement in the region.

Experiences with the cable-car project in Chiang Mai and the growth of capital-intensive tourism more generally have convinced local people that unconstrained expansion of the industry should be resisted. There is growing recognition of the common roots of culture and environment and of a common cause between the social and environmental movements, despite variations in philosophy and outlook. Finally, there is awareness of the need to re-evaluate the attributes of 'eco-tourism', which is now offered as a sustainable development alternative.

EDITORS' EPILOGUE

While the concerted action of opposition groups in Chiang Mai has prevented construction of the cable-car on the slopes of Doi Suthep to date, their resistance to the development of Doi Suthep has not been an unqualified success. The road up Doi Suthep mountain is currently being widened, in the view of local environmentalists unnecessarily, and causing serious environmental damage. Beyond a letter to the Highways Department and a meeting with the road construction company after widening operations had begun, the For Chiang Mai Group did not manage to organize high-profile protests on the scale it had mounted against the cable-car project. Although its sophisticated campaign against the cable-car development provides a model for future resistance strategies and an indication to planners and investors that 'tourism development' can no longer be assured of unchallenged acceptance, its limited ability to respond to the road-widening is indicative of limitations facing NGOs generally. Their *ad hoc* organizational basis and dependence on voluntary work and donations place them at a distinct disadvantage in long-term resistance against state or commercial interests with vast public and private resources at their disposal.[17]

NOTES

1 Chayant Pholpoke works in the alternative tourism industry and is a member of the 'For Chiang Mai Group' and the Ecumenical Council for Third World Tourism. Materials presented in this review were mostly derived from his active involvement in the cable-car issue and thus rely primarily on participant observation. The author is grateful to Dr Stephen Elliot from the Faculty of Science, Department of Biology, Chiang Mai University, who contributed important information on the environmental aspects of the case and on recent developments. The assistance of John McCarthy in obtaining statistics is also gratefully acknowledged.
2 See for example 'Tourism Destroys Tourism', *The Nation*, 8 September 1996 (reprinted in *Contours* 1996: 26–27).
3 Recently, the WTO Chief of Market Research warned that if governments did not want to be left behind in the travel market stakes they would have to, among other things, increase niche marketing, open up new areas of their countries, and focus on sustainable tourism with fast growth (WTO 1996). This chapter suggests that there is a fundamental contradiction between 'sustainability' and the other policy directives promoted by the WTO.
4 International visitor arrival statistics include business travellers and treat multiple entries separately.
5 Tourism has been Thailand's largest source of foreign exchange since 1982 (*Far East and Australasia 1995*).

6 See *Bangkok Post* and *The Nation* (29 September 1996) for reports on conflict between tour agents over threats to the established 'attractions' of 'long necked' ethnic minority women from new operators drawing on the influx of Kayan (Padaung) refugees from Burma into the Chiang Mai region (*New Frontiers* 2(10): 6–7).

7 In a recent statement, Thai government officials have expressed concern that the killing of protected species to grace the tables of wealthy tourists could deal a blow to Thailand's reputation, already damaged by its highly publicized role in the exotic species trade. Officials agree that some tourists specifically demand exotic game meat dishes (*Bangkok Post*, 4 December 1994).

8 The Tourism Authority of Thailand, recognizing the damage caused by unplanned development, is reported as 'appealing for help to the Thai people, seeking to educate them about the economic value of tourism and the need to preserve their land and culture' (*Bangkok Post*, 2 July 1996).

9 For a broader review of the debate on 'eco-tourism' and 'sustainable tourism', see Fernandes (1994), Cater (1993), May (1991), Lindberg (1991), Boo (1990).

10 See, for example, articles in the *Bangkok Post* (12 and 27 September 1996) on efforts to 'green' the industry through staff education programmes and tourism awards.

11 Elliott *et al.* (1989) found the highest tree species richness of any dry tropical forest yet surveyed in the forest through which the cable-car would have passed, and the Chiang Mai University Herbarium Database holds records for 2,139 vascular plant species for the park, a figure more than 50 per cent higher than the entire recorded flora of Great Britain (Stephen Elliott, personal communication).

12 Dr S. Elliot, a researcher working at Chiang Mai University, has carried out a number of studies on Doi Suthep's biodiversity, and has concluded that the region has several unique species. He also suggests that the natural seed dispersal system which sustains the mountain region's diverse flora and fauna cannot be replaced by human seed dispersal techniques (personal communication 1994).

13 Four Aces Consultants Co. Ltd were advisers and executors for the now famous Night Bazaar in Chiang Mai, renting space out to traders. This scheme was unable to achieve projected targets, and the firm later opened many 'night entertainment' centres in the area to enable renters to gain some returns from investments.

14 These apprehensions appear to be justified as more and more 'development' projects are planned in cultural areas. For example, Nakhon Pahtom (about 50 km southwest of Bangkok) is an ancient cultural site where Hinayana Buddhism is believed to have been born centuries ago. It has a famous and much revered Chedi. Currently, a 250 million baht project for the construction of a road leading to Nakhon Pathom's Phra Pathom Chedi was proposed. It has drawn a great deal of criticism from preservationist groups, which claim that it will destroy the natural beauty of the Chedi's surroundings (*Bangkok Post*, 5 December 1994).

15 For a discussion of the deployment of Buddhist philosophy and the role of Buddhist monks in the environment movement see Taylor (1997).

16 CPRs, broadly speaking, are the resources accessible to the whole of a particular community and to which no individual has exclusive property rights. In Thailand, these typically include village pastures, community forests, waste lands, common places meant for religious purposes, watershed drainage, village ponds, tanks, rivers/rivulets, and river beds.

17 See also Aditjondro and Yap in this volume for other cases illustrating the difficulties faced by NGOs in sustaining resistance strategies over the long term.

BIBLIOGRAPHY

Bangkok Post: 20 January 1986; 24 March 1986; 4 December 1994; 5 December 1994.

Boo, E. (1990) *Ecotourism: The Potentials and Pitfalls,* Washington, DC: WWF.

Cater, E. (1993) 'Ecotourism in the Third World: Problems for Sustainable Tourism Development', *Tourism Management,* 14 (2): 85–91.

Elliott, Stephen (1994) 'The Effects of Urbanization on Soi Suthep-Pui National Park', in *Urbanization and Forests,* Chiang Mai University: Proceedings of the International Symposium on Urbanization and Forests.

Elliott, S.D., J.F. Maxwell and O.P. Beaver (1989) 'A Transect Survey of Monsoon Forest in Doi Suthep-Pui National Park', *Natural History Bulletin Siam Society* 37(2): 137–171.

Far Eastern Economic Review, various issues.

Fernandes, Desmond (1994) 'The Shaky Grounds of Sustainable Tourism', *TEI Quarterly Environment Journal,* vol. 2, no. 4.

Four Aces Co. Ltd and Sumej Jumsai and Associates (1984) *Tourism Master Plan,* submitted to the Tourism Authority of Thailand: Bangkok.

Lindberg, K. (1991) *Policies for Maximising Nature Tourism's Ecological and Economic Benefits,* Washington, DC: World Resources Institute.

May, V. (1991) 'Tourism Environment and Development: Values, Sustainability and Stewardship', *Tourism Management* 12 (3): 112–124.

Michaud, Jean (1993) 'The Social Anchoring of the Trekking Tourist Business in a Hmong Community of Northern Thailand', paper presented at the 5th International Conference on Thai Studies, 5–10 July, at the School of Oriental and African Studies (SOAS), London.

The Nation, 21 August 1987; 24 September 1987, Nation Publishing Group Co., Ltd: Bangkok.

NESDB (National Economic and Social Development Board (1992) *Seventh Five Year Economic and Social Development Plan 1997–2001,* Bangkok: NESDB, Office of the Prime Minister.

Skyline Projects (1986) *Doi Inthanon Company Brochures,* Skyline Projects: Bangkok.

Taylor, J. (1997) '"Thamma-chaat": Activist Monks and Competing Discourses of Nature and Nation in Northeastern Thailand', in P. Hirsch, ed., *Environment and Environmentalism in Thailand,* Chiang Mai: Silkworm Books.

Whelan, T. (1991) *Nature Tourism,* Island Press: Washington, DC and California.

Worster, D. (1993) 'The Shaky Ground of Sustainability', in W. Sachs (ed.), *Global Ecology: A New Arena of Political Conflict,* Zed: London and New Jersey.

WTO (1996) World Tourism Organisation, Homepage, 19 February 1996.

Part VI
The politics of response

14 The environment and local initiatives in southern Negros

Emmanuel Yap

INTRODUCTION

The emerging environmental movement in southern Negros in the Philippines, which has active participation and leadership from peasants and other poor communities, is the latest in a series of struggles by marginalised people against dominant forces. To understand the formation of local activist initiatives therefore requires consideration of the area's social history. This entails situating these initiatives within the people's larger struggle for survival and empowerment, involving various key actors, processes and resources, and interpreting environmentalism as part of the politics of response to threats on local livelihoods.

The first section of this case study surveys the historical development of the migrant populace in southern Negros and that of its degraded environment. This is followed by a deeper discussion of the various key social, economic and political actors, their role and dynamics, and wider interactions within the Philippine political economy. Then, within these broad contexts and dynamics, the emerging environmental movement is discussed and analysed. Finally, in the concluding section, a brief interpretation of the role of environment and environmentalism in legitimising marginalised peoples' claims over resources is presented.

HISTORICAL DEVELOPMENT

The area discussed in this chapter is the southern mountainous district of Negros Occidental province, in Negros island of the Philippines (see Map 14.1). A majority of the largely migrant populace in the area has had a long history of land dispossession, exploitation and repression. The same is true of the indigenous tribal people, who have practically lost their cultural identity and have now been fully integrated, with a few exceptions, into this migrant population. The history of local people is thus marked by a series of individual and collective struggles for survival and empowerment as they have used various strategies, from accommodation and migration to hidden and more open and violent resistance, by themselves or in alliance with varied social actors.

Map 14.1   Map of Negros Occidental

Six generations ago, many of the migrants' ancestors were new settlers in
Negros from the neighbouring islands of Panay, Cebu and Bohol. When
sugar production expanded in the mid-nineteenth century, peasants were dispossessed of their lowland farms and forced either to become labourers or
to resettle hinterlands. In sugar plantations, work was hard and harsh, and
with minimal compensation. They were placed in constant debt. Indebtedness was used by planters as a means to achieve the secure and disciplined

workforce needed for sugar production (Larkin, 1993: 60–82; McCoy, 1984: 80–86).

Two events signify the extent and degree of this early land dispossession, exploitation and repression. The first is the mass killing in 1856 in Carol-an Mountain, in the south, of some 15,000 tribal people who put up their last and strongest recorded resistance (McCoy, 1984: 81–82; Bauzon, 1991: 48–50). The second is the messianic peasant uprising, which ended in class warfare between workers and planters at the turn of the century. This uprising, led by charismatic peasant leader 'Papa Isio' (Dionisio Sigobela), had a 10,000-strong following but was crushed by the combined force of the sugar elites and the newly arrived American colonisers (McCoy, 1984: 89–96; Larkin, 1993: 136–138). These events also indicate the readiness of these oppressed groups to struggle for self-determination (Bauzon, 1991: 46).

During the American colonial period, many more powerless small farmers were displaced. Among them were those who had earlier moved inland. This resulted from the rapid expansion of sugar production as the Americans introduced modernised milling and provided privileged access for Philippine sugar to their market. Both raised the profitability and security of the sugar enterprise (McCoy, 1984: 96–97). The complicated, Australian-based, Torrens land-titling process introduced by the Americans, and monopolised by the sugar barons, did little to help the illiterate small farmers strengthen their claims to land (Bauzon, 1975: 11–13).

It was this continuing displacement, together with the upland settlement programmes to arrest and prevent agrarian conflict under the newly independent Philippine government, that pushed many small farmers and embittered workers into the mountains of southern Negros. Without bothering to get legal claims, because of constraints similar to those under the American period, farmers migrated into the uplands, following the tracks opened by uncontrolled logging of a big US company (Insular Lumber Company or ILCO) and by other local logging enterprises owned by wealthy planter-capitalists. Lumber for export had become another lucrative source of income and power for the elite (for a more comprehensive account of the political economy of logging in the Philippines, see Vitug in this volume).

Unrestrained logging, exploitation in sugar plantations, continuing land dispossession of lowland farmers, and sidestepping of the agrarian problem by the landlord-controlled government marked the beginning of environmental degradation in southern Negros. Essential tree cover of the fragile upland soil was removed and watersheds destroyed, causing erosion and negative downstream impact on river systems, mangroves and corals. In addition, the wave of induced migration to the uplands imported inappropriate lowland farming practices, putting additional stress on the embattled ecosystem.

From the 1960s onward, there was an even more rapid process of land alienation and exploitation of peasants and workers who had established subsistence farms in the uplands. This process began when sugar production crept into the uplands as the US sugar quota increased following the Cuban revolution. Aside from large and medium-sized planters (McCoy, 1984: 196), local professionals from the growing public and private service sector also ventured into sugar production for extra income and for prestige. In addition to sugar expansion, a number of very wealthy sugar barons began leasing vast tracts of upland areas for pasture (O'Brien, 1987: 73). As these powerful claimants emerged, many peasants who did not have legal claims on their lands became tenants or outright workers again. Others moved even further inland and farmed on steeper slopes. A number of those who retained control of their land tried sugar production. However, owing to lack of capital and indebtedness, many lost their land to planter-capitalists or to the growing class of local capitalist entrepreneurs in the increasingly cash-oriented economy.

In this period of capitalist expansion, more pressure was placed upon the fragile upland ecosystem, leading to severe degradation. First, conversion into sugar production had destroyed the relative diversity that characterised most subsistence farms of early migrant settlers. Second, displacement and land-lessness led to over-exploitation of land and remaining forest resources as people began to engage in charcoal and fuel wood production and started farming on highly erosive slopes. Third, small-scale logging by local capitalists using the landless labourers was intensified. And fourth, areas previously managed as commons of various sorts in remote villages were made open-access because of increasing encroachment by outsiders and more powerful claimants.

A number of those dispossessed of their lands filed formal complaints but few were heard. Even those who were assisted by an increasingly sympathetic Catholic Church rarely won their cases in court (O'Brien, 1987: 70–72). The local government, the local police and the judicial system remained under effective control of the economically powerful planters. Peasants who used force to fight back were thus easily repulsed and became even more vulnerable. Many had to express their resistance in hidden ways: tenants would report less than actual yields to their new landlords, who mainly stayed in town centres; and disgruntled labourers in sugar plantations slowed down their work in order to increase their working hours. A few, however, decided to join the communist-inspired rebels, who at the time had begun organising peasants in more remote areas.

Land dispossession, labour exploitation and repression worsened and were pervasive throughout the whole province in the next decade. First, Marcos had declared martial law, which banned strikes on the labour front and militarised the countryside. This enabled planters to have significant control over their workers. It also enabled the military, who had then become more abusive, to exercise control over the local populace. Second, starting in 1974 when the US sugar quota expired, planters coped with the plummeting price of sugar and escalating production costs by introducing farm mechanisation and by withdrawing from paternalist relations (McCoy, 1984: 50–73). In the process, thousands of hand-tied and 'orphaned' labourers were displaced. Third, particularly for southern Negros, dispossession of small farmers increased as planters cushioned their losses by further expansion of their plantations in the uplands (McCoy, 1984: 106). Land dispossession also increased as traders and local capitalists increasingly took control and ownership of rice and corn lands of small farmers. The latter were victims of the indebtedness associated with green revolution technology and the commercialisation of subsistence agriculture.

Under extreme exploitation, repression and military abuse, and with hardly any place to seek refuge, embattled peasants and workers were forced to confront their continuing marginalisation. They sought support and established alliances with sympathetic groups and institutions. Thousands joined the Basic Christian Communities (BCCs) organised by the Catholic Church. But the state, with planters' prodding and support, used more force and violence to contain the peasantry and harass even Church leaders. This included the frame-up and 14 months' imprisonment of three priests and six lay workers who were actively involved in organising BCCs (McCoy, 1984; O'Brien, 1987). As a result, many joined or sought refuge with the rebels, who had by then grown significantly in number.

Marcos' downfall and Cory Aquino's populist ascendancy to power initially raised positive expectations among many Negros workers and peasants. Anticipating a more favourable and sympathetic response from government, a number of peasants and workers took over and tilled idle lands (de los Reyes, 1989), since very little work was available in the crippled sugar industry. But their success was short-lived. Soon after government and rebel peace negotiations collapsed, militarisation resumed with even more vigour. In addition, Aquino reserved her power to legislate an agrarian reform programme by decree to the newly installed landlord-dominated congress, diminishing farmers' hopes of a swift and general reform (Putzel and Cunnington, 1989: 63–74; Fegan, 1987: 49–56).

The new dispensation has brought with it a more complex and tricky playing-field for oppressed groups, particularly for those more politicised and committed to collective action. Various social actors (allies and antagonists) have changed their postures and agenda and have shifted alliances. New actors have also come onto the scene in the form of developmental NGOs and their international donors. Thus peasants and other rural poor communities have to devise new ways of dealing with ongoing and unfolding problems, consciously building on their gains and taking advantage of new opportunities.

In adjusting their responses and coping mechanisms within this new social and political setting, marginalised but significantly more empowered rural poor communities have been increasingly drawn into livelihood and environmental programmes. The new buzz-words of various social actors and resource holders, including the government, are environment and sustainable development. These objectives have become arenas for resource access claims and for some democratic space to continue articulating basic and historic livelihood concerns and aspirations on the part of marginalised social groups in southern Negros.

KEY ACTORS AND THE SOCIAL AND POLITICAL CONTEXT

To understand the contemporary relevance of these historical developments, it is helpful to look in more depth at their socio-political context. This involves consideration of the roles, dynamics and recent shift of alliances among various key actors involved, as well as at the increasing politicisation of peasants and labourers. While few of the 'wars of position' and struggles over resources among these actors were expressed in terms of environmentalism until quite recently, the discourse of environment is built on the socio-political foundations described below (see Table 14.1).

Peasants were at the centre of this socio-political drama. There were two main types of peasant communities. In very remote upland areas, peasant communities were generally homogeneous and naturally cohesive. They were highly responsive to Church and rebel organising. Almost all peasants tilled at least a small piece of land for subsistence, growing various food and cash crops (rice, corn, banana, vegetables, rootcrops and livestock). These lands (public and private) they either owned, rented or claimed by usufruct. Those who could not fully meet their minimum subsistence needs from their farms augmented their income by working for others with larger farms. Everyone in a village was often related to each other by blood or by intermarriage. Mutual help in the form of labour exchange (*dagyaw*) was commonly practised. Their relative economic and political independence, their strong social bond, and their collective experience of living in isolated and frontier settlements provided the foundation for peasants' unity and strength in opposing dominant groups.

In less remote and more accessible upland, lowland and coastal areas, which have been significantly affected by the expansion of sugar plantations and the increasing commercialisation of subsistence agriculture, villages were generally more heterogeneous and stratified. To survive, many of the poorer villagers engaged in various sorts of livelihood: as labourers in lowland rice farms and sugar plantations, as hook and line fisherfolk, as vendors, as carpenters, and so on. Because of significant social and economic gaps among villagers, their varied livelihood concerns, and the tendency among poor villagers to compete with each other for limited work opportunities, these villages were less united. However, their common experience of militarisation, together with the organising and education programme of the Church, cause-oriented groups and rebels, provided the poor villagers, and to some extent those from higher-income groups, with opportunities to collaborate in responding to common threats to their livelihood.

Initially, as a major pillar of Spanish colonisation, the local Catholic Church, through the Spanish friars, had been a key player in pacifying indigenous people and in indoctrinating subservience among sugar workers. As a

Table 14.1 Key actors in different time periods (southern Negros)

	Post-Independence	Marcos	Aquino	Ramos
Local politicians	Wielded significant control over local people	Politicians' power clipped by martial law, the creation of Marcos' oligarchies, and the increasing New People's Army rebel activity	Began to regain some of their pre-martial law power	Continuing
Landlords	Wielded significant influence over the government and the church	Established pasture lands and expanded sugar farms in the uplands with sugar boom; coped with plummeting price of sugar by farm mechanisation, cutting back on their paternalism; expanded sugar farms in the uplands to cushion their losses; later abandoned their farms owing to peace and order problems	Initiated moves to regain their control over abandoned lands; resisted implementation of agrarian reform	Continuous resistance to agrarian reform
NPA rebels	Not present	Increased dramatically in membership and local support as they introduced revolutionary land reform and controlled usurers' and traders' abusive practices	Received lesser support from various sectors with collapse of Marcos dictatorship	Weakened presence in villages as a result of internal split
Institutional Church	Shift in orientation after Vatican II in 1960	Became an active advocate of oppressed and marginalised communities, organising them into Basic Christian Communities	Became less militant with the break-up of the Diocese of Bacolod and the appointment of conservative bishops	Beginning to involve itself in environmental advocacy
NGOs	Not present	Emergence of cause-oriented groups from middle-class professionals and students	NGO sector mainstreamed as politicians, business people, planters, etc. formed their own NGOs stimulated by increased funding	NGOs being drawn into environmental programmes
People's organisations (POs)/communities	Growth of independent-minded villagers in frontier areas	Established open and covert alliances with Church, cause-oriented groups and rebels to confront exploitation and repression	Enhanced formation of POs with increase in NGO funding and with promulgation of the Cooperative Code and the New Local Government Code	Politicised poor communities giving token support for or actively participating in environmental programmes for resource access and legitimacy
Military	Limited presence in the area	Active presence in the area; often as willing tool of big landlords and politicians	Gained legitimacy with change in government; launched 'Operation Thunderbolt'	Consolidating their power by, among other things, involvement in the environmental crusade

former big landholder, the institutional Church's economic interest aligned with that of the sugar barons. Inspired, however, by Vatican II in the mid-1960s, the local Church (which had by then divested itself of much of its land-holdings) began breaking its historic alliance with sugar elites at a time when plantation workers and peasants were in great need of an ally. During Marcos' repressive regime, the Church thus provided poor and exploited people with financial, legal and organisational resource support and legitimacy (moral backing) as it actively pushed for social reform. This the Church did by organising farmers' and workers' unions and later by organising BCCs which became prominent in southern Negros (McCoy, 1984: 1–49, 106–158).

The BCCs, farmers' and workers' unions provided the social space for the poor and oppressed to organise and articulate their marginalised interests under Marcos' repressive rule. Progressive interpretation of Christianity through the theology of liberation has provided a legitimate language and more coherent ideology for poor and oppressed groups to express their aspirations and ideas. After three centuries of Christianity, the life and passion of Christ have been deeply embedded in the ethos of the Filipinos and have in fact continuously provided the basis for a number of millenarian peasant rebellions (Ileto, 1979; McCoy, 1984). It was thus not altogether surprising that the BCC movement quickly became popular with the poor and exploited.

Through the BCCs and labour unions, frontier settlers in the south, who had substantial experience in self-governance, were able to improve their individual and collective social and political skills. These skills they exercised during religious rituals that placed them and the local elites on more or less equal footing, during negotiations with landlords and plantation management, during court litigation, and also in the parliament of the streets (O'Brien, 1987).

The New People's Army (NPA) rebels served as the alternative group which provided opportunity for the people to express their dissent, this time in a more clandestine manner. The NPAs quickly grew in strength, particularly in southern Negros, where the people had experienced historic marginalisation. By demonstrating their capacity to establish just governance, maintain peace and order, and increase material gains of the poor through revolutionary land reform and control of traders' and usurers' exploitative activities, they easily gained the sympathy of the poor majority (Porter, 1987: 15–31; McCoy, 1984: 175–176). Until then, governance had generally been perceived by the poor to be against their interest.

Under the leadership of the NPA, a number of remote villagers learned further how to govern themselves in more formal ways. They established cooperatives, people's courts and local security forces. Mothers were organised and provided with education in preventive health care and natural medicine. Men had also their own education programme and organisation, as did the youth. After reaching a certain level of organisational development, villages were left to the management of their local collectives in coordination with higher rebel organs, as the NPA organisers moved on to organise other villages.

During Marcos' repressive regime, many oppressed people straddled between the Church and the rebels. The former gave them an opportunity to express their demands openly, while the latter provided them with the opportunity to strike back in hidden ways. Though there was a thin line that divided the BCCs' and the NPA's local mass organisations, the two actually coexisted, respecting each other, except in a few areas (McCoy, 1984: 159–205; O'Brien, 1987). In a sense the Church and the rebels provided avenues for the people to articulate two sides of themselves; one peacefully demanding justice and the other forcefully taking it.

Another set of socio-political actors was the range of cause-oriented groups formed by concerned middle-class professionals and students. These groups played a critical role in providing practical support to peasants and workers, which the Church alone could not provide. Their support in legal and para-legal work, in running campaigns and mass actions, in education and organisation-building, helped convince many poor people of the viability of opposition against the status quo. Together with the organising efforts of the Church and the NPA rebels, these non-governmental organisations' (NGOs') initiatives later contributed to the emergence of more autonomous people's organisations (POs) in southern Negros.

All of the above social actors had been on one side of an increasingly polarised social fabric of Negros before the collapse of Marcos' despotic rule. On the opposing side had been the sugar barons, the military and other government instrumentalities at the local level. The sugar barons (big planters and millers) were at the helm of the block that resisted social reform and feared the empowerment of the poor. Generally, they have relied on their own tremendous power and influence to maintain a submissive, disciplined and underpaid workforce in order to maintain large profits and accumulate wealth.

With the growing militance of their workers and the peasantry, as a result of Church and middle-class backing, many of the barons drew on the state and local government apparatus for support. This was not new to those who had long monopolised local elected positions and wielded significant influence on the national government because of sugar's importance as an export crop and revenue earner. Thus, when the insurgents' activities became more visible, the barons felt justified in using increasing military force to quell the growing mass advocacy for change.

The military proved a willing tool to control and coerce the growing militance of the labour force and the peasantry. In exchange, the soldiers received planters' largesse and local government's tolerance of their illegal and abusive activities to enrich and satisfy some of their caprices. A number of military units for anti-insurgency were thus used instead to protect haciendas, to harass or sometimes even kill 'subversive' BCC or union organisers, labourers and peasants. They were also used to break up 'communist-inspired' protest actions, which were demanding compliance with what were only government-legislated minimum wages or peacefully advocating agrarian reform.

As antagonism between the two opposing alliances during the latter years of Marcos' rule worsened because of increasing violence, unity within each alliance strengthened. However, upon Marcos' downfall, this broad unity almost immediately collapsed as the inherent divergence of interests and inclinations among allied groups and within each institution resurfaced (Krinks, 1987: 1–7; McCoy, 1984: 9–33). In addition, various social actors changed strategies, learning from the past and taking advantage of new opportunities, including the massive inflow of international donor assistance.

Within the Catholic Church, for example, a division reappeared between the traditionally more conservative Church hierarchy and the more progressive clergy and a few bishops (Krinks, 1987: 4), exemplified by the local Negros church. This division, accompanied by the break-up of the progressive Diocese of Bacolod and appointment of conservative bishops, significantly tempered many local priests' militance. A number of them began to waver in their support of harassed communities when militarisation resumed, assessing first the community's rebel links and determining how pro-Church each was before assisting.

In addition, among cause-oriented groups, a split likewise emerged between those who believed that reform was possible and those who did not. When politicians, planters, business people, ex-government employees and other concerned middle-class players established new NGOs as overseas aid increased, the non-government development arena became even more diverse and complex. Meanwhile, planters and their associations began to engage in or facilitate relief and livelihood assistance programmes, allowing their militant workers access to farm lots (Gonzaga, 1989: 111), to appease and to regain control over them.

Attention accorded to people's organisations (POs) by these various interest groups and donor agencies provided opportunities for the emergence of POs as key players in the development arena. This was significantly facilitated by the passage of the Cooperative Code and the new Local Government Code, which provided the institutional framework and basis for greater grass-roots participation in local governance. A number of BCC communities that could no longer get solid support from the Church groups linked up with government agencies and NGOs for resource access and assistance in acquiring legal status. Strong BCC groups and more independent informal village organisations also took advantage of these opportunities to gain greater legitimacy and better access to resources with the help of their NGO and Church allies.

Among the many POs in southern Negros which became very active were PUMOLUYO ('Nest of Progressive People's Organisations') federation, AMACAN ('Association of Small Farmers in Candoni'), BUGANA ('Living Guide for Nature Conservation and Sustainable Agriculture') federation, PMMK ('Federation of Small Farmers in Kabankalan'), and a few other cooperative organisations.

The tendency of government agencies and of planter, politician or big business-led NGOs to operate under a traditional patron–client framework, and channel their funding assistance through local (village) elites, inhibited active participation of politicised poor villagers in these areas. In these instances, PO formation and resources intended for POs became a source of inter-village conflict, particularly in the more heterogeneous and differentiated villages. This local conflict was often compounded as the diverse set of external social and political actors competed for influence in these villages and community groups.

In the provincial government, young and liberal-minded business people and planters associated with the Negros Business Forum (big stake-holders of the province), who realised that Aquino might be the last chance for peaceful reform, assumed provincial leadership. Their image as non-traditional politicians attracted significantly increased assistance for stop-gap, relief and rehabilitation programmes from international donors such as UNICEF, International Labour Organisation, World Food Program, CIDA, USAID, CARE Philippines, and others. While this opened new opportunities and political spaces, it also shifted further the political balance in favour of the planters (and the status quo), who had more access to and influence over these resources.

Capitalising on this more favourable political climate, the increasingly politicised military (Selochan, 1989) launched its most massive campaign to date on the island, this time targeting not only the armed rebels but also the local populace (from the military's point of view, the rebel mass base). In one major military campaign in 1989, dubbed 'Operation Thunderbolt', at least 10,000 people in the south were forced to evacuate their homes and farmland. This was the largest single displacement in the island since World War II, as several upland villages were declared 'no man's land'. When people returned to their villages, they were hamletted and forced to form civilian defence forces against the rebels. It is in this socio-political context that the environmental movement in southern Negros has emerged.

THE EMERGING ENVIRONMENTAL MOVEMENT

Amidst the above break-ups, realignments, power shifts, and renewed but more intense militarisation, many villagers and politicised rural poor communities scrambled for assistance and support. Depending on their particular circumstance and assessment of their reality, they either expanded and diversified their 'partnerships' or worked to strengthen existing ties, adopting if necessary new bases for collaboration with their allies within the transformed socio-political setting.

It was thus not uncommon for the people, who could not get any viable support from their former allies, to join supposed anti-rebel civilian defence forces (called Civilian Volunteers Organisations or CVOs) organised by the military, while maintaining some contact individually or as a group with the rebels (depending on how much they trusted each other) to keep their balance. Even if not immediately useful to them, they would also continue to keep in touch with their former allies (the Church, etc.). And, if the opportunity arose, they would join in government or new NGOs' livelihood and environmental programmes, where they could access resources to rehabilitate their disrupted livelihoods and acquire legitimacy and protection from further harassment.

On the other hand, a number of those who were more politicised, and could still get viable support from their former allies, stood their ground. They saw the resources and political spaces in the NGO and development arena, which was now accepted and encouraged by government (under the Cooperative Code and New Local Government Code), as an opportunity at least to protect, if not alleviate, their threatened livelihoods and legitimise their rights to organisation. With active assistance or intervention from their partners (depending on personalities and orientation), they thus worked out new strategies to consolidate their ranks. They also set out to prevent, overcome or reduce the negative impact of militarisation, as well as the political resurgence of planters, traders and village elites.

A number of small farmers joined or organised alternative credit and marketing programmes to counter usurers' and traders' power. Others got involved in farm diversification to reduce dependence on traders who could monopolise trade terms if they did not have alternative produce to sell. They also tried organic farming, for example vermi-composting, intercropping and use of herbal plants to reduce the use of commercial fertilisers and pesticides and therefore lessen dependence on multinational companies. Many others were drawn into reforestation and agro-forestry projects.

For many of those living in the uplands, who were often branded by the military as 'communist' fronts or 'communist' infiltrated, these various 'experiments' in alternative livelihood and in environmental conservation and rehabilitation, regardless of viability and practicability, were critical in overcoming 'red scare' tactics. It enabled them to win political points against the military and local elite groups. What was often most useful to them in these involvements, apart from access to funding, was the opportunity to gain legitimacy; to be in close contact with international or national donor agencies that had established field offices in Negros and were credible to the establishment.

By acquiring legal personality and status as government-registered people's organisations, BCC federations and informal village organisations were also able to gain more legitimacy. They were able to negotiate with their NGO and Church partners greater control (ownership) of project resources. Their bargaining power was enhanced, to a certain extent, by increasing competition among varied NGO actors and Church groups for 'influence' in their villages.

It is from among these various tactical initiatives and broader strategic goals and partnerships of such politicised peasants that environmentalism began to take root. Environmentalism to politicised communities was an arena where they could effectively respond to external threats to their villages and their livelihood. It provided them with a means to forge or sustain partnerships and alliances with resource agencies (government and private) as well as with former allies (Church, cause-oriented groups, and others) who have themselves been increasingly drawn into the environmental arena.

While it would seem that peasants' environmentalism was largely driven by a need to respond to militarisation and economic dislocation, a closer look at the farm level reveals long-standing concern and action by many farmers about the degraded environment and depleted resource base. It is on these resources, after all, that their livelihood and their lives have generally depended.

For example, in a number of upland villages, particularly where drinking water has become a problem, many have been consciously protecting their few remaining springs. Villagers have agreed to disallow cutting of trees in areas close to these water sources and have independently initiated tree planting in these areas. Others, as in *sitio* (hamlet) Tumpok of *barangay* (village) Balicotoc, Ilog municipality, have successfully agreed among themselves to prohibit unsustainable methods of fish capture such as the use of toxic chemicals and electrocution, which have significantly reduced yield from their river. To control outsiders, they have formalised their agreement into a village ordinance, which they have vigilantly imposed and enforced. Villagers have also petitioned through their *barangay* council urging upstream villagers to do the same.

In many villages of the very hilly mountains (public lands) of Carol-an and Camingawan in Kabankalan (the site of tribal peoples' mass slaughter referred to above), people have long established rock retaining walls to prevent further soil erosion in their *ba-ol* or *uma* (farm in Cebuano and Hiligaynon). Many have also successfully incorporated in their farming system fuel wood and charcoal production by establishing small-scale tree plantations using fast-growing indigenous forest trees and fast-growing species of ipil-ipil (*Leucaena leucocephala*) and G-melina (*G-melina arborea*).

Despite these real concerns about their degraded resource base, it was, however, common for peasants, particularly those who had tactical partnerships, to give only token participation in the application of so-called environment-friendly packaged technologies or in the implementation of environmental projects such as reforestation. Apart from insecure land tenure, there were several other reasons for such hesitation.

First, peasants often found the so-called 'appropriate' technologies and projects for environmental rehabilitation not viable, requiring labour investments which on their own could not be sustained. For example, complex types of contour farming technologies which required establishment and maintenance of hedgerows, check dams, soil traps, contour and drainage canals were very difficult for peasants to maintain. In addition, production of some herbal pesticides and vermi-composting were highly labour-consuming tasks. These activities became a burden particularly when rice and corn crops placed heavy demands on farmers' labour time.

Second, many of those who were in a tactical partnership were afraid that a successful rehabilitation project, for example reforestation, with significant external assistance (paying people to plant trees, rice subsidies under food-for-work programmes, and so on) would enable a distrusted partner (a new NGO) or supporter (government agency) to exert more control over them or lay greater claim to their land. In a number of government-sponsored reforestation projects in southern Negros, 'accidental fire' was common. Government reforestation was thus declared a general failure in Negros, with very low survival rates of seedlings planted.

Third, leadership in a number of these tactical partnerships was controlled by local elites whom poorer villagers distrusted. This was particularly true for many livelihood and environmental projects of government agencies and non-government organisations controlled by politicians and planters' groups. These projects were extensions of traditional patronage politics.

Fourth, peace and order problems and recent evacuations and economic dislocation have placed many of the people at or below the margin of survival, temporarily paralysing a number of their initiatives. In some instances, it has destroyed their sense of trust in their community and its future. In the midst of economic instability and an uncertain future, many concentrated on meeting their day-to-day food and safety needs, unable to engage in long-term endeavours like reforestation.

While funding was available to subsidise adoption or implementation, however, peasants generally obliged, but when funding was terminated or when they already had access to and control of the funds or resource they wanted, they reverted to token participation. Token participation coated with articulate environmental rhetoric was necessary to maintain their legitimacy and protection from military harassment as well as their contact with local elite leaders and resource agencies for possible additional or future support.

It was mainly among those who had strategic partnerships with trusted allies, those who felt more secure, that environmentalism became not only a means to access resources for livelihood rehabilitation and to acquire legitimacy for protection against military harassment, but also a means to sustain and build on their local initiatives in addressing environmental degradation. Because of open and established feedback systems with their partners, inappropriate introduced technologies were immediately identified and scrapped, or modified. It was also often easy for farmers' own approaches in environmental rehabilitation to be incorporated into 'official' environmental projects because of the generally participatory nature of their partnership, built over the years of trust and collaboration.

MASIPAG AND MAPISAN

The ability of the environment/sustainable development arena to provide mechanisms and space for politicised peasant groups to deal with forces of domination was boosted in 1991. At this time, an informal network among southern Negros-based POs, cause-oriented NGOs and Church groups, which had naturally formed as a support group amidst continuing military harassment and the vacuum created by the break-ups and realignments within institutions and allied groups, was able to link up with a national sustainable agriculture network called MASIPAG ('Farmer–Scientist Partnership for the Advancement of Science and Agriculture').

MASIPAG is composed of various NGOs, peasant organisations and concerned scientists from the University of the Philippines at Los Banos. Organised in 1985 after a series of peasant (regional and national) consultations, the network has been involved in participatory research and advocacy of sustainable farming systems (Masipag Secretariat, 1992). MASIPAG advocates the use of indigenous seeds and farming practices, emphasising the need for biodiversity and the importance for farmers to regain control of farming (of their land, their farming system and their lives) (Patayan, 1990: 15–17; Mendoza, 1990: 3–8). In particular, for rice farming, MASIPAG has been collecting traditional rice varieties from all over the country and has been involved in breeding improved cultivars (high yielding even without the use of inorganic fertiliser and pesticide, with good eating quality, and having other farmer-based characteristics) in partnership with farmers, using simple techniques which the latter are taught. Appropriate soil fertility and pest management practices are also encouraged, emphasising the use of local resources and knowledge systems (Mendoza *et al.*, 1989).

From MASIPAG, local peasant groups were not only able to gain more legitimacy in their programmes, being connected with scientists from the premier agricultural institution of the country (University of the Philippines at Los Banos) and respected and established national NGOs and peasant organisations. They also acquired, or regained, a more sustainable farming system which enabled them to deal squarely with the many short- and long-term problems confronting rice farming; problems which started with the commercialisation of rice and the introduction of high-yielding varieties with its capital-intensive technology (Shiva, 1989; Mendoza, 1990: 3–8). Several features of the MASIPAG approach have facilitated this.

First, the MASIPAG farming system has enabled peasants to increase their net income from rice farming by reducing costs of production (no pesticides, fertiliser or certified seeds) without significantly reducing production yields. Income has also increased with the re-emergence of fish and other edible aquatic life (shellfish, etc.) in rice paddies in the absence of pesticides. Furthermore, farm income potential has been enhanced by integrating livestock such as ducks in the rice paddies, which has become more viable without toxic chemicals.

Second, lower costs of production have reduced the expected loss and risk of becoming indebted to local moneylenders, from whom farmers usually borrowed capital for production inputs. Over the last decade, meanwhile, crop failures have recurred with increasing frequency owing to natural calamities such as droughts and flash floods, often leading to indebtedness that puts farmers in financial trouble and sometimes causes them to lose control and ownership of their land. The ability to produce rice without high production inputs has also provided the opportunity for farmers to be less vulnerable to price controls of traders, who usually take advantage of the fact that farmers, after harvest, immediately have to sell a large proportion of their produce to settle their debts, mainly from using inorganic fertiliser and pesticides, and to be able to buy the necessary inputs for the next production cycle.

Third, rice technologies associated with MASIPAG have provided farmers with a viable means of rehabilitating their soil. Southern Negros soils have become very acidic owing to repeated use of inorganic chemicals, or have become in worse cases 'dead', with few of the micro-organisms or earthworms that are necessary for decomposition of organic matter and farm residue into basic nutrient elements of plants.

Fourth, health problems associated with intensive spraying of pesticides, often done without adequate protective masks, have been prevented. Farmers have often taken as given the fact that after intense spraying, their eyes and skin usually become irritated. Also, many experience respiratory disorders after successive spraying. Health problems actually eat up a significant portion of farmers' meagre income and in serious cases can be devastating and trigger long-term debt.

Fifth, the MASIPAG farming system has enabled peasants to regain confidence within themselves and in their farming, enabling them to deal with their problems without having to rely on funding support from donor agencies or on technical support from even their NGO partners. And, as farmers shared their experiences in testing various cultivars and cultural management practices during on-site training conducted by farmer-trainers or as they planned ways to control and monitor the dissemination of the seeds to prevent potential sabotage from traders or chemical companies, they also found increasing opportunities and space to discuss and take common stands on issues like military harassment and agrarian reform. This has enabled many villagers to overcome the paralysis which had engulfed them.

As a matter of policy and strategy in the MASIPAG network, replication of this rice-based farming system including the dissemination of improved cultivars has been cautiously undertaken. The objectives are to benefit foremost the poor peasants and help empower their ranks to push for agrarian change. Land redistribution is recognised as an essential component for sustainable development. In Negros, replication of the MASIPAG farming system has been mainly undertaken within allied farmer groups of this informal network in southern Negros.

The successful self-help replication of the MASIPAG farming system within this informal network has encouraged the four federations of BCCs and peasant groups (PUMOLUYO, BUGANA, AMACAN, SONEDCO), their NGO partner (Paghida-et sa Kauswagan Development Group or PDG), and Church supporters (Cabacungan and St Francis Borgia Parishes and the Diocesan Commission on Livelihood) to formalise their alliance in what they now call MAPISAN ('Progressive Alliance of Sustainable Agriculture Initiatives in Negros'). They felt a need to establish a strong network to act as a support group against possible intimidation from traders or chemical companies, who might use red scare tactics or military harassment to stop their initiatives.

Aside from becoming a coordinating body for MASIPAG replication and promotion, they also anticipate that the network will act as a lobby group to push
for agrarian reform, which has remained elusive to many of their members.

The success of MASIPAG replication in Negros can actually be gauged
from the fact that only a total of 3 kilograms of 108 various rice cultivars was
given by the MASIPAG network for farm trials in 1991 and 1992. From these
initial seeds there is now a total of at least one thousand farmers who are
growing these various cultivars of rice completely without commercial pesticides, herbicides or fertilisers. In addition, about 2,000 other farmers are now
in the process of freeing their rice farms from inorganic chemicals. Without
any external funding support, 63 day, on-site, sustainable agriculture training
sessions with a total of 1,500 participants have been conducted to date by the
four people's organisations involved. Furthermore, requests for training and
for demonstration or trial farms have now come not only from within Negros
but from the neighbouring islands of Panay and Leyte.

Through their success in chemical-free rice farming and their active leadership in the conduct of sustainable agriculture orientation and training, peasant groups and farmer-trainers in MAPISAN have gained more credibility
and stature. They have been invited to speak in sustainable development
forums in the University of Saint La Salle in Bacolod and in Kabankalan
Catholic College in Kabankalan. They have also recently been tapped by the
Social Research Center of the University of Saint La Salle Bacolod to act
as the local partner in a DENR (Department of Environment and Natural
Resources) funded pilot programme called Mass Environmental Education
and Information Program (MEEIP). More importantly, they have also
recently been tapped by the Provincial Agrarian Reform Office through the
MAPISAN network to provide training on sustainable agriculture to priority
agrarian reform communities. Keen to gain more legitimacy and to establish
strategic connections with the Agrarian Reform Office because of their own
agrarian problems, these people's organisations in MAPISAN have cautiously accepted the offer.

In short, through these various resources and tie-ups which politicised
peasants have accessed and established, they have now become local resource
institutions, servicing not only their members but other communities as well.

ENVIRONMENT AND ENVIRONMENTALISM IN PERSPECTIVE

On the basis of the case presented, it is clear that concern for the environment
and sustainable development in southern Negros has become the latest arena
for marginalised but politicised peasant groups to articulate their historic concerns and aspirations. The overriding objective remains to gain access and
control of some livelihood that could sustain the peasantry and give them dignity and respect as human beings.

The export-oriented, elite-centred, and recently more capital-intensive
nature of Negros development, which dates from the island's early integration

into the world market economy under Spanish colonial rule, has spawned a large mass of poor, exploited and disgruntled labourers and displaced peasants living on an over-exploited and depleted resource base and environment. There has thus been a long history of resistance and struggle for empowerment among these oppressed and subordinate groups. Depending on opportunities and political circumstances, their resistance has been manifested openly or in more hidden ways, by themselves or in alliance with other social forces – the most powerful being their active involvement in both legal and armed opposition against the Marcos dictatorship. Caught up, upon Marcos' downfall, by a sudden realignment of political forces which ironically tilted the balance in favour of the military and elite groups, the increasingly politicised peasants, who were in the midst of a political catharsis, have sought refuge in the environment and development arena.

The collapse of orthodoxies and the crisis of ideologies and development paradigms, both capitalist and socialist, amidst major global threats and uncertainties, have recently placed the environment, among others, at the centre of global development concerns (Taylor and Johnston, 1989). Urgent calls for greater cooperation and commitment in carrying out a global agenda for change have been made by many world leaders (WCED, 1987), the most recent and prominent of which was the 'Earth Summit' in Rio de Janeiro. Various international institutions, particularly multilateral development banks, have been asked to increase financing for environmentally oriented projects.

In response, multi-lateral lending agencies such as the World Bank and Asian Development Bank have opened favourable windows for environmental loans, hoping to combine their environmental commitment and their loan restructuring objectives (Korten, 1993: 4–9, 12–17). On the other hand, many western NGOs and donor agencies have made environmental action a condition for their grant assistance. For the Philippines government, which desperately needs fresh loans to cover up its dollar deficits and service its debts, the environment, at least in this respect, has become a very important state agenda. Likewise, for a number of Philippine NGOs, whose operations are largely dependent on their ability to secure grant assistance, the environment has also become an imperative concern.

In addition, a series of catastrophic human-induced and natural calamities such as flash floods, droughts, earthquakes and volcanic eruptions have swept various parts of the Philippines, destroying millions of properties and killing thousands of people. These catastrophes have made the environment and its rehabilitation an even more important and urgent national concern.

As a common concern of government, of other powerful resource holders, and the general populace at large, the environment and sustainable development arena has thus readily provided legitimacy and some democratic space for politicised peasant groups in Negros. It has enabled them to access resources and gain concessions from dominant forces, which they have used to protect their threatened marginal livelihoods.

Using James Scott's concept of everyday resistance by subordinate groups, the environment has become to peasant and other marginalised groups an arena for 'infrapolitics'. Scott defines infrapolitics as an 'unobtrusive political struggle' providing 'cultural and structural underpinning of the more visible political action' (Scott, 1990: 183–201). He argues that 'each realm of open resistance to domination is shadowed by an infrapolitical twin sister who aims at the same strategic goals but whose low profile is better adopted to resisting an opponent who could probably win any open confrontation' (Scott, 1990: 184). For example, 'piecemeal squatting is the infrapolitical equivalent of an open land invasion: both are aimed at resisting the appropriation of land' (Scott, 1990: 199).

Subordinate groups ordinarily disguise their ideological insubordination and their attempts to prevent or reduce material appropriation of their labour, their production and their property, through, for example, 'poaching, foot-dragging, pilfering, dissimulation, [and] flight' (Scott, 1990: xiii). Both disguised ideological and material struggle, which continuously 'test and probe' the limits of what is 'permissible', form the building blocks for the more 'elaborate institutionalised political action' (Scott, 1990: 200–201).

In the same vein, token and more active participation in environmental and rural development programmes were and are thus part of peasant and subordinate groups' circumspect strategies to get concessions, access resources, gain political points, or even strike back at dominant forces. More substantive environmental concern is concentrated in livelihood-focused initiatives based on local knowledge and threats to the resource base.

Similarly, adoption of MASIPAG farming systems and active participation in the MAPISAN network are part of peasants' infrapolitical struggle to cope and deal with dominant forces. This enables peasants simultaneously to gain more legitimacy as environmental advocates, meet their concerns of raising income, rehabilitate their depleted resource base, as well as enable them to deal with traders' monopoly and usurers' exploitation.

What underlies all these struggles is access to resources and control of livelihoods which have been threatened by hamletting, forced evacuation, military harassment, as well as by indebtedness to usurers and traders. It is also a struggle for dignity and respect. This is best captured by what one peasant leader said during the federation council meeting to decide on possible partnership with the Department of Agrarian Reform:

> Kon ginahatagan kabilinggan ang kahoy, ngaa indi man mahatagan pagtamod ang tawo? Ang kinahanglanon naton gamay lang nga duta nga puede mapangabuhi-an, makasagod sa aton pamilya, makasabat sa mga matagadlaw nga kinahanglanon para mabuhi bilang tawo, indi lang na parang tawo-tawo o sapat.

> [If trees are valued why can't people be valued too? What we need is only a small piece of land that can support our family and our daily needs so that we can live as real human beings, not live like animals.]

For many of those who are landless or have experienced land dispossession, their struggle is clearly directed towards gaining some land for livelihood, a yearning that made many of them join or support the NPA rebels under Marcos' dictatorship.

As in any political arena, peasants' environmentalism is, however, being contested by competing interpretations and challenged by concrete actions of dominant forces. For example, an 'environment-friendly' congressman from Negros has recently publicly proposed that 10 to 20 per cent of planters' sugar lands be exempted from current implementation of agrarian reform to encourage and enable planters to establish commercial tree farms to meet lumber shortage and environmental concerns (*Today*, 9 August 1993).

In its most recent decision, the Provincial Environment Concerns Commission of Negros Occidental has mandated the deployment of at least 400 military and paramilitary men to protect the remaining forest reserve in northern Negros (Mounts Kanlaon and Mandalagan) from *kaingeros* and illegal logging (*Panay News*, 25 November 1993). This action is interpreted by cause-oriented groups as a mere ploy to legitimise militarisation of the area. Many people are aware that the majority of illegal carabao-logging (using carabao, water buffalo, to drag lumber from the forest) in this area and in many other areas in Negros is perpetrated by powerful people, including the military and paramilitary groups.

In March 1994, at a national conference organised by the Upland NGO Assistance Committee (UNAC) held in Bacolod city in Negros, the provincial governor suggested that business establishments, industrial corporations, planters' associations and sugar milling corporations might be in a better position to undertake reforestation and rehabilitation of the environment. He implicitly hinted his reservations about rural poor and community-based approaches to resource management.

Finally, the Visayas Regional Command of the military (to which Negros Island Command belongs) has started piloting the implementation of the government's Contract Reforestation Project in the neighbouring island of Panay. This is an action perceived by many cause-oriented NGOs as part of the military's attempt to maintain their power by taking on civilian roles.

As the term infrapolitical implies, it would not be far-fetched to imagine that conflicting interpretations of environmentalism and competing claims of who has rights to the uplands may lead to another escalation of conflict in Negros. After all, the historic aspiration of land access and control over a livelihood base that could sustain them underlies the environmentalism of the poor.

BIBLIOGRAPHY

Bauzon, Leslie (1975) *Philippine Agrarian Reform 1880–1965: The Revolution that Never Was*. Singapore: Institute of Southeast Asian Studies.

—— (1991) 'Social Movements in Negros, 1857–1907', pp. 46–62 in L. Bauzon (ed.) *A Comparative Study of Peasant Unrest in Southeast Asia*. Pasir Panjang, Singapore: Southeast Asian Studies Program, Institute of Southeast Asian Studies.

de los Reyes, Romana (1989) *Claims to Land: Lessons from Haciendas in Negros Occidental*. Quezon City: Institute of Philippine Culture, Ateneo de Manila University.

Fegan, Brian (1986) 'Tenants' Non-Violent Resistance to Landowner Claims in a Central Luzon Village', pp. 87–106 in J. Scott and B. Kerkvliet (eds), *Everyday Forms of Peasant Resistance in South-East Asia*. London: Frank Cass and Company Ltd.

—— (1987) 'The Rural Areas', pp. 49–70 in P. Krinks (ed.), *The Philippines under Aquino*. Fyshwick, ACT: Australian Development Studies Network.

Gonzaga, Violeta (1989) *The Socio-politics of Sugar: Wealth, Power Formation and Change in Negros (1899–1985)*. Bacolod City: The Social Research Center, University of St La Salle.

Ileto, Reynaldo Clemena (1979) *Pasyon and Revolution: Popular Movement in the Philippines, 1840–1910*. Quezon City: Ateneo de Manila University Press.

Kerkvliet, Benedict (1986) 'Everyday Resistance to Injustice in a Philippine Village', pp. 107–123 in J. Scott and B. Kerkvliet (eds), *Everyday Forms of Peasant Resistance in South-East Asia*, London: Frank Cass and Company Ltd.

Korten, Frances (1993) 'Environmental Loans: More Harm Than Good', *Philippine Uplands Resource Center News and Views*, 7(1): 4–9, 12–17.

Krinks, Peter (1987) 'Introduction', pp.1–8 in P. Krinks (ed.), *The Philippines under Aquino*. Fyshwick, ACT: Australian Development Studies Network.

Larkin, John A. (1993) *Sugar and the Origin of Modern Philippine Society*. Berkeley: University of California Press.

McCoy, Alfred (1984) *Priests on Trial*. Ringwood, Victoria: Penguin Books Australia Ltd.

Masipag Secretariat (1992) 'MASIPAG Operations Manual'. Unpublished manuscript.

Mendoza, Ted (1990) 'Nature Farming Systems in the Philippines', pp. 3–8 in Sibol ng Agham at Teknolohiya (SIBAT). *Sibol*. Quezon City, Philippines: Sibat Publications.

Mendoza, Ted, A.A. Briones and A.M. Briones (1989) 'Green Revolution and its Impact on Ecosystem and Traditional Culture'. Paper presented in a seminar on *The Environmental, Social, and Cultural Impacts of Development Projects of Italian NGOs* held at Cortona, Italy, 20–24 November 1989.

O'Brien, Niall (1987) *Revolution from the Heart*. New York: Oxford University Press, Inc.

Panay News (1993) 'Military Detachments against Illegal Loggers', 25 November 1993, p. 1.

Patayan, Felicisimo (1990) 'Empowering the Peasantry through Sustainable Agriculture', pp. 15–17 in Sibol ng Agham at Teknolohiya. *Sibol*. Quezon City, Philippines: Sibat Publications.

Porter, Gareth (1987) *The Politics of Counter-insurgency in the Philippines: Military and Political Options*. Honolulu: Center for Philippine Studies, University of Hawaii.

Putzel, James and J. Cunnington (1989) *Gaining Ground: Agrarian Reform in the Philippines*. London: WOW Campaigns Ltd.

Scott, James (1990) *Domination and the Art of Resistance: Hidden Transcripts*. New Haven: Yale University Press.

Selochan, Viberto (1989) *Could the Military Govern the Philippines?* Quezon City: New Day Publishers.

Shiva, Vandana (1989) *The Violence of Green Revolution*. Dehra Dun: Research Foundation for Science and Technology.

Taylor, Peter J. and R.J. Johnston (1989) *A World in Crisis? Geographical Perspectives*. Oxford: Basil Blackwell Ltd.

Today (1993) '2 Solons Oppose Plan to Set Up Detachments for Forest Drive', 9 August 1993, p. 1.

Vitug, Marites D. (1993) *The Politics of Logging: Power from the Forest*. Quezon City: Philippine Center for Investigative Journalism.

WCED (World Commission on Environment and Development) (1987) *Our Common Future*. Oxford: Oxford University Press.

15 Epilogue
Analysis and action

Philip Hirsch and Carol Warren

The chapters of this book take an analytical approach to the politics of resource-based disputes in Southeast Asia. They reveal that an important set of roots underlying the region's new environmentalism lies in the soil of material struggles over means of livelihood. The studies also indicate the extent to which appropriation of resources by the powerful and wealthy at the expense of the poor and marginalised has led to active responses by and on behalf of such groups. The overriding narrative is thus not merely a story or exposé of injustice heaped upon injustice in an unequal world, but also one of active and positive responses. An important part of the collective response is a complex set of fluid coalitions, emerging social forces built on alliances across classes and nation-states around environment and community resource rights. Both the material and discursive bases for such coalitions form an important part of the case studies presented in the preceding pages.

What is the value of such analysis? Our intent is to contribute to a broader, deeper understanding of the resource disputes hitherto described, and to give voice to the efforts of resistance and reclamation by the ordinary people involved in such movements, who normally receive little public attention. Their struggles are often quiet, manifest in the everyday 'infrapolitics' described in Chapter 14.

The headline-making environmentalism of the urban, educated middle classes inevitably receives greater exposure than the many and widespread instances of resistance to resource appropriation represented by the case studies in this book. The effect of this biased exposure is at best misrepresentation, and at worst a more pernicious portrayal of environmentalism as a kind of enlightenment that is dependent on achieving a certain level of income, prosperity or 'development'. This is so clearly at odds with the livelihood-based environmentalism represented by the struggles to defend and reclaim land, forests, water, minerals and healthy working environments by less educated and poorly resourced peasants and workers, as to represent an effective appropriation of environmentalism on the part of those with access to the media and other public means of expression.

Another strategic purpose for the approach we have adopted is to reveal the commonality of experience and range of responses across the spectrum of political–economic and ecological circumstances described in the case studies brought together in this book. As indicated in the introduction to this volume, the nation-state as an environmental actor can be as much a limiting as a facilitating construct, given the range of interests within nation-states as well as between them. Thus, to construe the Mekong River Commission, for example, as a body that exists primarily to articulate and resolve environmental and resource-based disputes between the constituent riparian member states deals with only a part of the resource politics engendered by accelerated Mekong development. Diverse interests within each of the nation-states and common interests of resource users (e.g. fishers) that transcend national boundaries are equally if not more important.

Environmental internationalism is thus a significant imperative. However, the real challenge is to move beyond the networking of largely North American-, Australian- and European-based groups towards regional alliances within Southeast Asia. To an extent, this has been achieved through initiatives such as the new Bangkok-based non-governmental organisation, TERRA (Towards Ecological Recovery and Regional Alliance), whose aim is to facilitate regional alliances among local community-based groups, NGOs and some governmental players concerned with the livelihood and ecological implications of mainstream development in mainland Southeast Asia, or Focus on the Global South, an alternative think-tank established to examine and provide strategic input on linkages between macro-level changes and micro-level impacts and responses. While both these groups receive most of their funding from 'northern' NGOs, they maintain a distinct Southeast Asian focus and identity. Nevertheless, even these groups have made only very limited progress in facilitating a genuine grass-roots-based environmental internationalism within the region.

It is also important to read into the dynamic political–economic contexts described in the studies in this book, the limiting as well as facilitating role of environmentalism. We have seen that environmentalism can be a political space for voices with limited alternative means of asserting claims over resources. Environmentalism as a legitimising discourse thus has an important role to play in enabling those affected by dams, logging, mining concessions, industrial development or tourism to develop strategic alliances within mainstream discourses. Yet environmentalism has also been applied in a cooptive and regressive way. National park encroachment on villagers' lands, resettlement of shifting cultivators from inaccessible uplands, and 'afforestation' with fast-growing exotic species have all occurred in the name of environmental protection or rehabilitation, at the expense of local livelihoods; and even large dams are back on the international agenda in part because of their purportedly beneficial potential in providing an alternative to greenhouse-gas-emitting energy production based on fossil fuel combustion.

Moreover, success of environmental action at one level can sometimes merely displace rather than eliminate the pernicious aspects of the development activity in question: the cancellation of the Doi Suthep cable-car proposal (see Chapter 13) was the pretext for a potentially even more destructive road-widening project; cancellation of Thailand's logging concessions in response to environmental protest was quickly followed by the granting of logging concessions to Thai companies in Burma and Laos; and similarly, protests over dam construction in Thailand have encouraged the Electricity Generating Authority of Thailand to seek new sites in neighbouring countries where protest is less likely, rather than within Thailand's borders.

Still more displacing are the multiplier effects of failed resistance to the appropriation of local resources for large-scale development projects, so often justified in the name of national interest. The diversion of land and water for dams, industrial plants, resort and residential developments across Indonesia – precipitating local struggles over land, culture and environment described in the chapters by Aditjondro, Lucas and Warren, for example – has led to a national shortage of good agricultural land. In response to declining rice production before the 1997 election, the Soeharto government introduced a programme to clear one million hectares of peat swamp forest in Central Kalimantan for rice cultivation by transmigrants (*Far Eastern Economic Review* 7 September 1995). Reafforestation funds have been diverted to provide seed money to facilitate forest clearing (logs will be used to satisfy the shortfall at local pulp mills) and subsidise the establishment of the new scheme. The relocation of transmigrants from highly fertile agricultural areas in Java and Bali to peat swamp soils generally regarded as unsuitable for rice production represents a multiple displacement of people and resources, which in turn impacts on the viability of other communities and environments in chain reaction.

Finally, it is worth re-emphasising the distinction between environmental politics and politics of environment. Environmental politics, as conventionally conceived, typically involves disputes, confrontation and negotiation between organised environmental groups with mobilised public support, on the one hand, and state or corporate interests engaged in an activity seen as environmentally destructive, on the other – the Greenpeace action to stop the sinking of the Shell oil platform is a typical international example, while the Nam Choan Dam in Thailand provides an outstanding Southeast Asian case in point. The politics of environment has a somewhat different purview. It refers to a range of everyday actions, responses and trade-offs that arise from less focused, hence more dispersed but also more generalised, competition over the resource base, or resistance to one-sided imposition of unacceptable externalities by a more powerful set of social actors onto less powerful or influential groups. Like environmental politics, the politics of environment have material as well as discursive underpinnings and forms of expression. Like environmental politics also, the nature of the politics of environment is governed in considerable part by political–economic as well as ecological contexts. However, the more generalised nature of the politics of environment reflected in the case studies presented in this volume may reveal a good deal more about the specifics of emerging social forces and less ephemeral coalitions than the higher-profile environmental politics that are the more common object of public attention.

POSTSCRIPT

As this book goes to press, the Asian monetary crisis has jolted the economic and political fortunes of the region to a largely unanticipated and unpredictable extent. The environmental consequences of the dramatic economic fallout are equally uncertain. It is possible that new regimes with greater transparency and more sober planning could bring about better regulation than the growth-at-all-cost approaches of the preceding era. Certainly it will lead, in the short term, to postponement or cancellation of some of the costly infrastructure projects which have had severely displacing environmental and social impacts across Southeast Asia.

At the same time governments in the region may try to compensate for heavy debts, declining growth and shortages of foreign exchange through even more rapacious resource extraction policies. They may also be tempted to cancel environmental programmes and to short-circuit normal assessment procedures on the grounds of economic expediency. Meanwhile, the jobless and landless may respond to their own crisis of subsistence with survival strategies that intensify pressures on the local environment. Ultimately, the environmental future of the region will depend upon the ability of various actors to acknowledge that, as the Indonesian forest fires of 1997 demonstrated so dramatically, the costs of unsustainable and inequitous resource expropriation are real, and that the strains they impose on ecological, social, political and economic well-being exacerbate – rather than ameliorate – these problems.

Index

Lightning Source UK Ltd.
Milton Keynes UK
UKOW05f1811270217
295459UK00016B/406/P

9 780415 172998